Portugal's three wars in Africa in Angola, Mozambique and Portuguese Guinea (Guiné-Bissau today) lasted almost 13 years - longer than the United States Army fought in Vietnam. Yet they are among the most underreported conflicts of the modern era. Commonly referred to as Lisbon's Overseas War (*Guerra do Ultramar*) or in the former colonies, the War of Liberation (*Guerra de Libertação*), these struggles played a seminal role in ending white rule in Southern Africa.

Though hardly on the scale of hostilities being fought in South East Asia, the casualty count by the time a military coup d'état took place in Lisbon in April 1974 was significant. It was certainly enough to cause Portugal to call a halt to violence and pull all its troops back to the Metropolis. Ultimately, Lisbon was to move out of Africa altogether, when hundreds of thousands of Portuguese nationals returned to Europe, the majority having left everything they owned behind. Independence for all the former colonies, including the Atlantic islands, followed soon afterwards.

Lisbon ruled its African territories for more than five centuries, not always undisputed by its black and mestizo subjects, but effectively enough to create a lasting Lusitanian tradition. That imprint is indelible and remains engraved in language, social mores and cultural traditions that sometimes have more in common with Europe than with Africa. Today, most of the newspapers in Luanda, Maputo – formerly Lourenço Marques – and Bissau are in Portuguese, as is the language taught in their schools and used by their respective representatives in international bodies to which they all subscribe.

Indeed, on a recent visit to Central Mozambique in 2013, a youthful member of the American Peace Corps told this author that despite having been embroiled in conflict with the Portuguese for many years in the 1960s and 1970s, he found the local people with whom he came into contact inordinately fond of their erstwhile 'colonial overlords'.

As a foreign correspondent, Al Venter covered all three wars over more than a decade, spending lengthy periods in the territories while going on operations with the Portuguese army, marines and air force. In the process he wrote several books on these conflicts, including a report on the conflict in Portuguese Guinea for the Munger Africana Library of the California Institute of Technology.

Portugal's Guerrilla Wars in Africa represents an amalgam of these efforts. At the same time, this book is not an official history, but rather a journalist's perspective of military events as viewed by somebody who has made a career of reporting on overseas wars, Africa's especially. Venter's camera was always at hand; most of the images used between these covers are his. His approach is both intrusive and personal and he would like to believe that he has managed to record for posterity a tiny but vital segment of African history.

The author operational in Cabinda, Angola
(Photo Cloete Breytenbach)

British national Al Venter has written more than a score of books on recent military history including *War Dog: Fighting Other People's Wars* on mercenaries as well as *Gunship Ace* (which covers the exploits of Neall Ellis, the world's most famous mercenary aviator). He spent much of his professional career reporting on wars for Jane's Information Group as well as for various news and photo agencies. These assignments ranged from visiting Beirut over several years to cover the Lebanese civil war from the Christian side and included the Israeli invasion of Lebanon and the taking of Beirut in the 1980s.

Others covered a spate of African conflicts that included the second army mutiny in Nigeria (as well as the Biafran war that followed), South Africa's border wars, the Rhodesia insurgency, the Congo debacle where he was arrested on charges of espionage, Mozambique, Tanzania's invasion of Idi Amin's Uganda, Portuguese Guinea, Somalia, Executive Outcome's mercenary operations in Angola, civil war in Sierra Leone and others. He was operational in El Salvador's guerrilla struggle and later, in the Balkans. At the behest of the CIA, he made a one-hour TV documentary on the Soviet offensive in Afghanistan in 1985.

Venter has written three books on nuclear proliferation, including *Iran's Nuclear Option, How South Africa Built Six Atom Bombs, Allah's Bomb* and another awaiting publication. He originally qualified as a Fellow of the Institute of Chartered Shipbrokers at the Baltic Exchange in London.

Nominated in the United States in 2013 for the New York MAS Arthur Goodzeit Book Award. This book is also to be published shortly in Portuguese in Lisbon.

PORTUGAL'S GUERRILLA WARS IN AFRICA

LISBON'S THREE WARS IN ANGOLA, MOZAMBIQUE AND PORTUGUESE GUINEA 1961–74

Al J. Venter

Helion & Company

Helion & Company Limited
26 Willow Road
Solihull
West Midlands
B91 1UE
England
Tel. 0121 705 3393
Fax 0121 711 4075
Email: info@helion.co.uk
Website: www.helion.co.uk
Twitter: @helionbooks
Visit our blog http://blog.helion.co.uk/

Published by Helion & Company 2013
This paperback reprint 2015

Designed and typeset by Farr out Publications, Wokingham, Berkshire
Cover designed by Euan Carter, Leicester (www.euancarter.com)

Text © Al J. Venter 2013
Maps © as follows – Africa 1974 © Al J. Venter; Angola at the end of the war in 1974 © Dr
Richard Wood; Portuguese Guinea © Al J. Venter; Coastal regions of Portuguese Guinea
© *Revista da Armada*; Mozambique © Dr John P. Cann.
Photographs © Al J. Venter unless noted otherwise

ISBN 978 1 910294 73 4

British Library Cataloguing-in-Publication Data.
A catalogue record for this book is available from the British Library.

Front cover: Portuguese marines on patrol in Guinea waters. (Author's photo). Rear
cover: When a vehicle hit a mine, there were invariably casualties, which was when the
air force would be tasked with uplifting casualties and flying them to the nearest
hospital. In this stretch of the "Hell Run" – from the Zambezi to Mwanza, on the Malawi
border – it would have been the clinic at Tete. (Author's photo)

For details of other military history titles published by Helion & Company Limited contact
the above address, or visit our website: http://www.helion.co.uk.

We always welcome receiving book proposals from prospective authors.

While the United States was fighting a bitter war in Vietnam in the 1960s and 1970s, Portugal battled an equally resolute bunch of guerrillas in a spate of insurgencies that stretched halfway across Africa. Very little was known of these conflicts at the time, because South East Asia tended to hog the headlines. While these tropical insurgencies might have lacked the intensity and sophistication of what was going on in Vietnam, tens of thousands of people were to die in Portugal's African wars. Ultimately, these conflicts would radically alter the political dynamics of the continent. Indeed, it was the beginning of the end of white rule in Africa...

A Luta continua!

Dedication

In the realms of recent African history, particularly with regard to Lisbon's role on the continent, one writer stands out above all others and that is my dear old friend and colleague René Pélissier. You have been a fount of knowledge and inspiration, which is why I dedicated this book, with thanks, to you René.

Former United States naval captain John Cann – whom we all know as Jack – also figures strongly as a friend, a colleague and a 'co-conspirator'. His breadth of understanding of Portugal's efforts in Africa encompasses much and we have learned a lot from his books. Thank you Jack.

Contents

Appendices

Glossary

A-76:	military radio set
AAA:	anti-aircraft artillery
ACIG:	Air Combat Information Group
AEB:	(South African) Atomic Energy Board

African National Congress: ruling South African political party, Socialist in orientation and in its day, closely allied to Portuguese opposition groups like Angola's MPLA and FRELIMO

AK, AK-47:	*Avtomat Kalashnikova* 7.62mm assault rifle
aldeamento:	Portuguese protected camp
ALN:	*Armée de Libération Nationale*—the military wing of the FLN nationalist movement
ALO:	air liaison officer
ANC:	African National Congress
APC:	armoured personnel carrier
APILAS:	Armour-Piercing Infantry Light Arm System, French portable one-shot 122 mm recoilless anti-tank rocket
AR-10:	7.62mm battle rifle later developed into US Army's M16
ARMSCOR:	Armaments Corporation of South Africa
Assimilado:	Africans overseas who had 'assimilated' sufficiently to earn full Portuguese citizenship rights
AU:	African Union (See OAU)
Bergen:	military-style multi-part backpack
BfSS:	(South African) Bureau for State Security, generally referred to in its day as 'BOSS'
BM-2:	Stalin Organs
BMP-2:	*Boyevaya Mashina Pekhoty*, Soviet amphibious tracked infantry fighting vehicle
BND:	*Bundesnachrichtendienst*, West German/Federal Republic of Germany Federal Intelligence Agency
BRDM:	*Boyevaya Razvedyvatelnaya Dozomaya Mashina*, 4x4 (converting to 8x8) amphibious 'Combat Reconnaissance Patrol Vehicle'
'Browns':	South African army personnel, or their uniforms (slang)
BSAP:	British South Africa Police, Rhodesian police force
BTR:	*Bronetransportyor*, 'armoured transporter', 8x8 armoured personnel carrier
C-4:	Common variety of the plastic explosive known as Composition C.

CAS-sorties:	Close air support sorties
CCB or Civil Cooperation Bureau:	Secretive quasi-military organisation formed in latter stages of apartheid rule in South Africa
Chef do Poste:	Local Portuguese administrator
CIA:	(United States) Central Intelligence Agency
CIO:	Rhodesian/ Zimbabwean Central Intelligence Organisation
COIN:	Counter-insurgency
Comintern:	Communist International, abbreviated to Comintern
COMOPS:	Combined Operations
Congo-Brazzaville:	The Republic of the Congo (*République du Congo*), also referred to as Congo-Brazzaville or simply Congo. Not to be confused with Democratic Republic of the Congo (Kinshasa)
CSI:	Chief of Staff Intelligence, South African military
CSIR:	(South African) Council for Scientific and Industrial Research
CT:	Communist Terrorist: term used for Chinese Malayan guerrillas by the British
DF:	Direction Finding
DGS:	(Portuguese) *Direcçao Geral de Segurança*, General Security Directorate
DHQ:	(South African) Defence Headquarters (in Pretoria)
DMI:	(South African) Directorate of Military Intelligence
DRC:	Democratic Republic of the Congo, formerly Zaire, formerly Belgian Congo, also called Congo-Kinshasa
DShK:	*Degtyaryova-Shpagina Krupnokaliberny*, Soviet 12.7mm heavy antiaircraft machine gun
D Tels:	(South African) Directorate Telecommunications
ECCM:	Electronic Counter-Counter Measures
ECM:	Electronic Counter Measures
EO:	Executive Outcomes, mercenary group that ended civil wars in Angola and Sierra Leone
ESM:	Electronic Support Measures
EW:	Electronic warfare
FAA:	*Forças Armadas de Angolanas*, the Armed Forces of Angola
FAF:	forward airfield
FAL:	The *Fusil Automatique Léger* (Light Automatic Rifle), a self-loading, selective fire battle rifle produced by the Belgian armaments manufacturer Fabrique Nationale de Herstal (FN).
FALA:	UNITA's military wing
FAP:	*Força Aerea Portuguesa* : Portuguese Air Force
FAPLA:	People's Armed Forces for the Liberation of Angola (*Forças Armadas Populares de Libertação de Angola*) – today *Forças Armadas de Angolanas*
FIA:	Field Intelligence Assistant

FLEC:	Cabinda Liberation Movement
FLING:	*Frente de Luta pela Independência Nacional de Guiné-Bissau/Front de Lutte de l'Indépendence Nationale de Guinée,* Struggle Front for the Liberation of Portuguese Guinea
FLN:	Algerian Liberation Group
FN:	See FAL
FNLA:	*Frente Nacional de Libertação de Angola,* National Front for the Liberation of Angola
FRELIMO:	*Frente de Libertação de Moçambique,* Liberation Front of Mozambique
FPLN:	*Frent Patriotica de Libertação National*: Guiné-Bissau liberation movement with headquarters in Algiers
G3:	7.62mm battle rifle developed in the 1950s by the German armament manufacturer Heckler & Koch GmbH (H&K) in collaboration with the Spanish. Adapted by the Portuguese Armed Forces
G-Car:	Transport Alouette helicopter
GOC:	JCFs General Officer Commanding Joint Combat Forces
GP:	*Garde Presidentielle*
GPMG:	General purpose machine-gun
GRAE:	Revolutionary Government of Angola in Exile (*Govêrno Revolucionário de Angola no Exílo*)
Grupos Especiais:	Portuguese Army Special Force units
Grupos Especiais Pára-Quedistas:	Paratrooper Special Groups (volunteer black soldiers that had paratrooper training)
Grupos Especiais de Pisteiros de Combate:	special units trained in tracking
GRU:	*Glavnoye Razvedyvatel'noye Upravleniye* – foreign military intelligence main directorate of the Soviet Army
HAA:	Helicopter Administration Area
HAG:	Helicopter Administrative Group
HC:	*Honoris Crux,* South African combat bravery decoration in various grades
HEU:	Highly enriched uranium
HF/DF:	High frequency direction finding (radio system)
HK21:	Heckler & Koch 7.62mm general purpose machine gun
HVAR:	High velocity aircraft rocket, also nicknamed during WW2 as 'Holy Moses'
IAEA:	International Atomic Energy Agency
IDI:	Illegal Declaration of Independence (British rendering of Rhodesia's UDI)
IFP:	Inkatha Freedom Party (Zulu-based)
IFV:	Infantry fighting vehicle
INSS:	(United States) Institute for National Studies

ISIS: (United States) Institute for Science and International Security

JARIC: Joint Air Reconnaissance Intelligence Centre; JOC command centre

Joint-STAR: United States Air Force E-8 Joint Surveillance Target Attack Radar System

K-Car 'Kill Car' (as in Rhodesian war): Alouette helicopter gunship armed with machine guns

Katyusha: Soviet 122mm multiple rocket launchers

KGB: *Komitet gosudarstevennoy bezopasnosti*, (Soviet) Committee for State Security. See also GRU

KIA: killed in action

LAW: M72 LAW (Light Anti-Tank Weapon), also referred to as the Light Anti-Armour missile

LZ: Landing zone

MAG: The FN MAG is a Belgian 7.62mm general-purpose machine gun

MANPAD: Man-portable air defence system (like the Soviet Strela)

MASH: (United States) Mobile Army Surgical Hospital

MBE: Member of the Order of the British Empire

MBT: Main battle tank

metrópole-províncias ultramarinas: Portuguese overseas provinces

MG-42:   A general purpose machine gun, originally German and much favoured by Portuguese ground troops in all three African theatres of war

MG-51:   20mm cannon

Mi-8:   'Hip' transport/gunship helicopter

Mi-17:   Development of Mi-8 'Hip' transport/gunship helicopter

Mi-24:   'Hind' helicopter gunship/attack helicopter

MID: South African Military Intelligence Division

MK: *Umkhonto We Sizwe* (Spear of the Nation) – ANC military wing (South Africa)

MPLA: Popular Movement for the Liberation of Angola or *Movimento Popular de Libertàcao de Angola*

MPRI: Private (mercenary) American military company

MRBM: Medium range ballistic missile, such as the South African produced RSA-3

NATO: North Atlantic Treaty Organisation

NCB: nuclear, chemical and biological (warfare)

OAS: *Organisation de l'armée secrete*: a short-lived, French dissident paramilitary organization that was founded in French Algeria

OAU: Organisation of African Unity, today African Union

OB: *Ossewa Brandwag,* anti-British and pro-German WWII organization in South Africa

OCC: Operations Coordinating Committee

OP:	Observation post
OPO:	Ovambo People's Organisation
OZM-4:	Metallic bounding fragmentation mine
PAF:	Portuguese Air Force
PAIGC:	Guerrilla group in Portuguese Guinea – *Partido Africano da Independência da Guiné e Cabo Verde*. Took power by force after the Portuguese had hastily departed
Panhard AML:	*Automitrailleuse légère*, light 4x4 armoured car, developed by South Africa into the Eland
Panhard EBR:	*Engin Blindé de Reconnaissance*, French-built, light 8x8 armoured vehicle
PATU:	Police Anti-Terrorist Unit (Rhodesian War)
PCA:	Angolan Communist Party
PIDE:	Portuguese International Police for the Defence of the State or *Polícia Internacional e de Defesa do Estado* –Lisbon's equivalent of the secret police
PKM:	A Soviet 7.62 mm general-purpose machine gun much favoured by anti-government guerrillas
PLAN:	People's Liberation Army of Namibia, the military wing of SWAPO
PLUA:	The Party of the United Struggle for Africans in Angola
PMC:	Private Military Company
PMD-6:	Anti-personnel mine
PNE:	Peaceful nuclear explosives
POM-Z:	Soviet anti-personnel stake-mounted fragmentation mine, much used in Africa
PPsH-41:	Soviet WWII submachine gun
PSYOPs:	Psychological warfare operations
RAD ALT:	Radioaltimeter. System provides the pilot with accurate indication of the aircraft's height above the terrain, usually in the range of zero to 2500 feet AGL (above ground level).
RAF:	Royal Air Force
RhAF:	Rhodesian Air Force
RLI:	Rhodesian Light Infantry
RPD:	Soviet-made light machine gun, similar to the Degtyaryov, 7.62mm calibre
RPG:	Rocket propelled grenade – either RPG-2 (used by guerrillas in Portuguese African conflicts), or RPG-7 more recently, with additional variations
RPK:	Soviet-made light machine gun, 7.62mm calibre
RUF:	Rebel unit (Revolutionary United Front) destroyed by the South African mercenary group Executive Outcomes
SAAF:	South African Air Force

SABC:	South African Broadcasting Corporation
SACP:	South African Communist Party
SACS:	South African Corps of Signals
SADF:	South African Defence Force (in apartheid era)
SAEC:	SA Engineers Corps
SAFARI:	South African Fundamental Atomic Research Installation
SAFMARINE:	South African Marine Corporation
SAM:	Surface-to-air missile, SA-6, SAM-8 et al
SANDF:	South African National Defence Force (in post-apartheid era)
SAP:	South African Police, changed to South African Police Services in post-apartheid South Africa
SAR&H:	South African Railways and Harbours
SAS:	Special Air Service Regiment
SDU:	Self-defence unit
SF:	Special Forces
SG-43:	The SG-43 Goryunov – a Soviet medium machine gun (equivalent of the American M1919 Browning)
SIS:	Secret Intelligence Service or MI6
SNEB:	37mm Matra rockets
SO1 Ops:	Staff Officer 1, Operations
SS:	Nazi SS or *Schutzstaffel:* originally a protection squadron or defence corps; a major paramilitary organization under Hitler and the Nazi Party
SSO:	Senior Staff Officer
STASI:	*Staatssicherheit*, East German Ministry for State Security
Sten:	WWII-era 9mm submachine gun
Stick:	(Rhodesian Army) – usually four troops on patrol
SWA:	South West Africa, now Namibia
SWAPO:	South West African People's Organisation
T-34 and T-55/T-54:	Soviet tanks supplied to Angola and Mozambique
TBVC States:	Transkei, Bophutatswana, Venda and Ciskei (apartheid-era regional entities within South Africa, ostensibly supposed to be independent of Pretoria)
TM-46 and TM-57:	Soviet anti-tank mines used by liberation groups
TNT:	*Trinitrotoluene* is a chemical compound best known as a useful explosive material with convenient handling properties
Tropas Especiais:	Special Troops, commonly known by the acronym TEs, which came into effect when one of the UPA/FNLA guerrillas defected to the Portuguese with 1200 of his men
TTL:	Tribal Trust Land
UAV:	Unmanned Aerial Vehicle

UDI:	Unilateral Declaration of Independence
UNAVEM:	United Nations Verification Mission in Angola
UNISA:	University of South Africa
UNITA:	*União Nacional Para a Independência Total de Angola*, National Union for the Total Liberation of Angola
UPA:	*Unià̀o dos Populacèes de Angola,* Patriotic Union of Angola
USAF:	United States Air Force
VHF:	Very High Frequency
WMD:	Weapons of Mass destruction
WO I:	Warrant Officer Class I
WO II:	Warrant Officer Class II
ZAF:	Zimbabwe Air Force
ZANLA:	Zimbabwe African National Liberation Army (guerrilla group)
ZANU:	Zimbabwe African National Union
ZAPU:	Zimbabwe African Political Union
ZIL:	Angolan *Zona de Intervencao Leste*
ZIPRA:	Zimbabwe People's Revolutionary Army (guerrilla group)

Foreword

In 1961, Portugal found itself fighting a war to retain its colonial possessions and preserve the remnants of its empire. The country was totally unprepared, as its leaders never believed that what had happened in other parts of Africa could happen to them. Portugal had been in Africa for almost five centuries, longer by far than any other colonial power, and its notion of the permanence of its empire drove it to defend its colonies or *ultramar* at all costs. For this small European nation, the importance of the colonies was captured in an editorial by Marcello Caetano in *O Mundo Português* (Portuguese World) that appeared in 1935: "Africa is for us a moral justification and a *raison d'être* as a power. Without it we would be a small nation; with it, we are a great country."

While other European states were granting independence to their African possessions, Portugal chose to stay and fight despite the small odds for success. When war was thrust upon it by the March 1961 uprisings in the north of Angola, it opened a new chapter in the lives of its citizens and the many others who would become involved in the 13-year conflict—one that would extend to three theaters, Angola, Guinea, and Mozambique, and exhaust the treasure and manpower of the country. The Portuguese army had virtually no experience or training for this sort of war and little or no experience of any sort in serious fighting. Few had seen a shot fired in anger. On the other hand, they were very brave and had the ability to live and fight under conditions that would have been intolerable to other European troops. They could go for days on a bag of dried beans, some chickpeas and possibly a piece of dried codfish, all to be soaked in any water that could be found—probably infected with bilharzia—then cooked and eaten in the evening. At night they would tie themselves up in trees to sleep. They were capable of covering on foot and through elephant grass and thick bush distances of over a hundred miles over a three-day patrol. They endured heat and humidity that took your breath away. The insects attacked them in "airborne waves" and poisonous snakes were constantly slithering underfoot. They learned how to fight and did so successfully for thirteen years across their three fronts. It was a remarkable achievement for a nation of such modest resources.

Al Venter was attracted to this war during the late 1960s and recorded his first experiences and observations on Angola in his *The Terror Fighters* (1969). Subsequent reporting on the other two theaters produced *Portugal's War in Guinea-Bissau* (1973) and *The Zambezi Salient* (1975). He immersed himself in these wars, writing from personal observation at the center of the action. His combat descriptions are riveting and remind the reader of General George Patton's famous observation, "Compared to war all other forms of human endeavor shrink to insignificance." This book brings together his earlier experiences and heretofore unrevealed ones in a broad perspective of a war that was overshadowed by the United States involvement in Vietnam and is now largely forgotten by non-Portuguese audiences. He combines vivid descriptions of the fighting, the daily lives of the soldiers in combat, and the larger campaign perspective through a broad range of interviews and observations as a seasoned war reporter. He further draws on personal papers and published sources to produce an informative, valuable and readable account of the agonies and successes in the progress of Portugal's guerrilla wars in Africa. While not defeated on the field of battle, Portugal ultimately had to recognize the futility of the struggle in 1974. Its decolonization proceeded at a rapid and ill-considered pace and brought peace to none of its former colonies. No one was happy with the outcome, and Lusophone Africa became a continuing battleground for local and international interests for decades afterward. Al Venter offers a thoughtful conclusion in this work on a nationally cathartic war that ended in tears both for a nation and its European and African citizens.

John P. Cann, PhD
University of Virginia
Charlottesville
21 October 2013

Acknowledgements

One of the problems related to books that an author has been working on for a very long time – and this, to me, has been about a dozen years in the making – is that one sometimes forgets who it was that gave you what.

With that thought in mind, I hope I am able to thank all my friends, colleagues and associates who made this very substantial mini-history of a bunch of very personal experiences as a war reporter into something of a reality. Clearly, there are some notables who, as the saying goes, are going to fall through the cracks.

Obviously, with the passing of years, the majority of military folk with whom I was associated in all three theatres of military activity in Africa – both men and women – must remain unacknowledged. The four principal players that I remember well and who remained friends after hostilities ended, have all taken that Long Walk that awaits us all.

This includes my dear old friend and fellow combatant in the Dembos north of Luanda, Dr Ricardo Alçada. And then I learned that my other good pal, Vitor Alves, with whom I spent time in the Angolan war, had also recently died.

Both men were serving as captains in the Portuguese Army in Angola when we first met. Both afterwards responded to an official invitation to visit me in South Africa and deliver a number of talks at universities on what Lisbon was trying to achieve in fighting for her African 'provinces'. That would have been almost half a century ago and my recollection of events is that in addressing students at Witwatersrand University, they gave a pretty good account of themselves, certainly enough to placate a large gathering that was demonstrably hostile.

Afterwards, I was to visit Vitor and his wife Theresa at their home at Oeiras on Lisbon's outskirts. I did so several times prior to the Carnation Revolution that unseated Portugal's civilian government and I'd sometimes get back to their flat late at night, more often than not to find Vitor in deep conversation with a bunch of his fellow officers. Though it was often past midnight when I got in, that didn't surprise me. What did was when I learned afterwards that Major Vitor Alves – as he then was – had been one of the principal planners of the military coup.

The individual who initially got me into covering these African struggles was a still-youthful colonel who went by the name of José Manuel Bethencourt Rodrigues and who was serving as military attaché at the Portuguese Embassy in London. That little episode is interesting, because by the time the putsch had taken place in the Metropolis, he had been elevated to a full general and managed to successfully turn the guerrilla war around in Angola.

From there, this no-nonsense and incredibly competent army officer went on to Portuguese Guinea, where he took over the reins from the fourth man whose friendship I cherished, General António de Spínola.

My first meeting with Bethencourt Rodrigues was inauspicious. I'd hitch-hiked all the way across Africa from Johannesburg and got stuck for a while in Marxist Guinea because of a border guard who wouldn't let me continue with my journey and cross into Senegal. That was in northern Guinea, near the small town of Koundara, which was perhaps a couple of hours' drive in a four-by-four from the border with Portuguese Guinea[1].

Because I was obliged to wait for my passport to be processed in Guinea before I could move on – and obviously, I was broke – I stayed with a couple of equally-broke Peace Corps volunteers. They offered me a bed and curiously, were able to fill a lot of gaps about the Soviet radio monitoring station that occupied a building about three doors up the street. Apparently this was one of the major communication links for the anti-Portuguese PAIGC guerrillas then waging war in the neighbouring territory.

Once I got to London, I told some of my friends in South Africa about the Soviet communications unit and then, out of the blue, Colonel Bethencourt Rodrigues invited me to visit his office in the embassy 'for coffee'.

Once there, he wasted little time in asking me all about the Soviet radio monitoring station in Koundara. I related what I could, that it was well staffed – and distinctive because of all the aerials that protruded from its roof – which was when he enquired whether I'd consider going back to Africa, at his expense, of course. The idea, basically, was to show a group of Portuguese soldiers where all this was happening.

We'd go in, probably by helicopter from the eastern border of the 'province' he confided, and being young, impetuous and more than a little stupid at times, I said yes. In fact, I welcomed the opportunity because it meant a bit of excitement from my hum-drum London job, there was money to be earned for my efforts and, most important, somebody else would pay for me to get back into the African sun for a 'holiday'. London in winter is always dismal.

In the end nothing came of it, though the colonel did thank me for offering. Then, a couple of years later, after I'd been working in Nigeria for a while, I found that I again needed a visa to enter Angola if I was to head south overland, as I'd done before. I contacted the good colonel in London, he asked for my passport, which was then returned to me in Lagos with the requisite visa in place.

Not long afterwards, I approached him again, this time to cover the war in Angola as an aspirant journalist. I did the same not long afterwards for Portuguese Guinea. From there on I regularly covered all of Portugal's conflicts.

I suppose I have that stroppy border guard in Guinea to thank for it all, and for this book ...

Closer to home, I have an enormous debt of gratitude to another member of the old guard, former Brigadier General Willem van der Waals who everybody knows as 'Kaas' because he was born in Holland. He spent 33 years in the SADF, starting his career in uniform with the South African 'Parabats' – an airborne battalion – and ending it as Director of Foreign Relations.

Kaas's strength lies in the fact that he spent several years in Angola as a vice consul at

xviii PORTUGAL'S GUERRILLA WARS

the South African Consulate General in Luanda, having stepped into the role when Jannie Geldenhuys left. And having been active in that vast West African country while Portugal was battling insurgency, he went on to write a fine book about the conflict titled *Portugal's War in Angola 1961-1974*. A comprehensive and well-balanced study, I'd originally published it a quarter century before when I owned Ashanti Publishing. The new edition was put out by Protea Books in Pretoria in 2011.

For my efforts, 'Kaas' played an invaluable role in reading this manuscript before publication and making numerous changes of fact and of language: he is fluent in Portuguese. It took a lot of time and effort and I thank you old friend.

The other individual who needs recognition is someone whose work on Lisbon's former possessions in Africa I have been following for decades. René Pélissier and I go back a long time. Indeed, with this work, he helped me complete its Bibliography, which is arguably one of the most comprehensive in print.

Over many years, I have exchanged notes with René, to the point where I and a lot of others regard him as the leading international authority on Portugal's overseas provinces: someone once referred to him as the Grand Old Man of Portuguese History. It is fitting that I have dedicated this work to him.

At the same time, another student of military history, former United States Navy aviator Captain John P. Cann – who prefers to be known as Jack – deserves a good measure of appreciation. He has written three books on Portugal's African wars – all listed in the Bibliography – and in the process he has done a marvellous job of recording great dollops of near-contemporary history that would have been lost had he not done so. So I am dedicating the book to him as well.

Unlike Brigadier General van der Waals, Jack Cann never served either in Portugal or in any of that country's African outposts, so the question begs: why his unusual and all-encompassing interest in a series of remote and isolated foreign wars? I posed the question and this was his reply:

> From my first contact with the Portuguese as a naval aviator on landing at Lajes Field in the Azores in 1966 in a P-2V Neptune, I have always had the greatest affection and respect for those people. Over the years, as I spent many hours at Lajes and at Sal in Cape Verde, it became apparent that the country was fighting in Africa, as we witnessed Portuguese jungle training camps and war-weary troops at both places.
>
> A decade later, in the late 1980s, I participated in a few exercises at the NATO headquarters in Lisbon and these expanded my positive feeling about the Portuguese Armed Forces. When I retired from the navy in 1993, I decided that I would write about these three conflicts in Africa as there was not much about any of it in English, and what little there was, was mostly denigrating screed.
>
> I knew that the Portuguese were not perfect, but much of what I found strained credibility. There was, I knew, another story of brave men and women and it needed to be told. So I began to craft it, but it was a complicated war that needed many books.

The more I wrote, the more I learned...it was an enriching experience.

Working in archives and interviewing veterans is time-consuming and often frustrating, but I would not trade the adventure for anything. The people whom I have met have become fast friends and that has been an unexpected bonus.

What more needs to be said, except that the publishers of this work are also responsible for putting out Jack's three books. Check them out on the Helion website (www.helion. co.uk), because each is a valuable contribution to recent African military history. Appendix C actually features an extract from his book, *The Brown Waters of Africa,* and it provides the reader with a sobering insight to these little-known guerrilla wars that collectively, were instrumental in eventually changing the political face of Africa. For a start, it heralded the end of white rule on the continent.

Others who need to be thanked include my old friends Fiona Capstick who is the most multilingual woman I know and fluency in the Portuguese language is only one of her attributes. There is also my old friend Manuel Ferreira who came up trumps with some of the photos linked to one of Lisbon's most illustrious combatants, Captain João Bacar and his *Comandos Africanos.*

Thanks too, to João Paulo Borges Coelho of the Eduardo Mondlane University in Maputo for allowing me to include his thesis on the role of African troops in Portugal's colonial wars. His paper was originally presented in April, 2002 at a symposium hosted by Brown University in Providence, Rhode Island and headed 'Portuguese/African Encounters: An Interdisciplinary Congress'.

An earlier version that focused on the Mozambican case was presented at the Second Congress of African Studies in the Iberian World, held in Madrid, Spain in September 1999. It was published as *João Paulo Borges Coelho, 'Tropas negras na Guerra colonial: O caso de Moçambique,'* in José Ramón Trujillo, ed., *Africa hacia el siglo XXI* (Madrid: Sial Ediciones, Colección Casa de África 12, 2001).

Photos came from many sources, quite a few from Jack Cann. Others I took myself while active in these wars and still more were retrieved from Portuguese military archives in Lisbon. South African lensman Cloete Breytenbach will recognise some of his own pix here, including the one of me on the back flap. Cloete and I covered the Angolan war together in the late 1960s.

On a more mundane, but no less important level, there are others who deserve mention.

Top of this list is my publisher Duncan Rogers who runs a pretty tight ship at Helion and Company, a British publishing house that has grown at a heady pace these last few years. When I first met Duncan a few years ago, the number of books he put out annually was something like 40. Now it is double that and growing steadily, which prompted a question recently – 'do you get any time to sleep, Duncan?'

The Helion editorial and production team has done a fine job in knocking all the bits together, helped in proofreading by Jerry Buirski, another good pal from Cape Town. It might be because Jerry is clinically deaf that very little slips past him when he casts his eagle eye over copy, but the fact that he had read about 1,500 books by the time he left school certainly helps. The man is exceptionally sharp on African history.

Two delightful people – dear friends – came to my rescue in the closing stages of this book. They are former SAAF Brigadier-General Peter 'Monster' Wilkins and his lovely wife Val. I stayed with them on Umhlanga Ridge in Durban while proofreading. They have always been a tower of support. 'Monster' is the author of Appendix B, which details SAAF support for the Portuguese Army in the final stages of the struggle in Angola. It says a lot that, after almost half a century in the air, he is still flying into some of the remotest outposts on the African continent.

A thousand words of thanks must also go to Caroline Castell who was with me for much of the final period of getting this work ready for publication.

I should mention that some of this work can be found in abbreviated form in some of my earlier books on Portugal's wars including *The Terror Fighters* (Purnell, Cape Town), *Report on Portugal's War in Guiné-Bissau* (Munger Africana Library, California Institute of Technology, Pasadena) as well as *War Stories by Al Venter and Friends* (Protea Books, Pretoria).

Many of the adventures of my second Trans-African 'safari' are recounted in *African Stories by Al Venter and Friends*, published in 2013 which I rate as one of my best works to date. It took me four months of the kind of African adventure that would be almost impossible to achieve today.

Finally, I have my very good friend and colleague Manuel Ferreira to thank for reading the complete book one final time prior to us going in a second edition. He discovered quite a few Portuguese language spelling errors and several of fact. We have made the appropriate corrections, for which I am deeply grateful.

The archetypal small wars [of Africa] largely follows the Maoist prescription of protracted war, always a difficult and insidious threat for any incumbent government to fight and win. And there are tried and proven solutions to gaining victory in these circumstances ...

From the Foreword, by General Bernard
E.Trainor, to John P. Cann's book
*Counterinsurgency in Africa – The Portuguese Way
of War 1963-1974*

Poverty of itself does not engender revolution. But poverty side by side with progress creates a new amalgam; the hope of social change stimulated even by a little education produces a new social phenomenon; the ambitious poor, the rebellious poor, the cadres of the revolution who have nothing to lose and see much to gain around them.

Robert Taber: *The War of the Flea*, Palladin,
London, 1970

The primary functions of guerrillas are three: first to conduct a war on exterior lines, that is, in the rear of the enemy; second, to establish bases; last, to expand the war areas. Thus guerrilla participation in a war is not merely purely a matter of local guerrilla tactics but must also include strategic considerations.

Mao Tse Tung

Prologue

If your intervention force is small, like Guevara's or the British in Sierra Leone, you are greatly at risk. So, inevitably, you have to bargain, seek allies, make deals. This means that you, too, have to work on the basis that you are an armed group with certain irreducible interests – that is, that you are just another piece in the factional jigsaw. The only way out of this is to dominate – if necessary, to suppress and destroy the factions.

R.W. Johnson: 'Playing with Fire in Africa'
The Daily Telegraph, London, August 29, 2000

Contemporary Africa has a predilection for violence not always evidenced elsewhere. Coups, insurrections and other forms of carnage are commonplace. People are killed, sometimes for the clothes on their backs, yet the international community tends to look the other way. Darfur, the Congo, Zimbabwe and the rest make the news these days, but almost grudgingly.

The Middle East and Central Asia have a history of conflicts, but these – with the notable exception today of Syria – are mostly brief, intense conflagrations like hostilities between India and Pakistan, or those involving Arab and Jew. We had Vietnam and the outrageous Pol Pot regime in Cambodia, but those countries are stable today, their troubles relegated to the history books. As we go to press, things are even looking up in Sri Lanka.

The same applies to regional wars in other corners of the globe such as in Central America and the Philippines where low-level insurgencies continue but seem to be contained.

That is not always the case in Africa. In Angola, after almost four decades of fighting, a peace of sorts has settled on the nation, but even there, another civil war is barely a whisper away, kept brutally in check by the routine excesses of a police state that include a brutal, black-clad para-military security group that everybody refers to as the 'Ninjas'; truly a modern African version of the SS. Small wonder then that the life expectancy of the average Angolan, well into the New Millennium, is barely 40-something.

The same applies to the Congo, which has been ablaze for decades. Mayhem has become part of everyday life in this vast Central African country, a condition that evolved within days of the Belgian Congo having been granted its independence in 1960 by Brussels and some years before the tyrant Mobuto Sese Seko seized power. That carnage – unbridled and unmitigated by any kind of reason – has continued ever since. The number of dead as a consequence had been estimated by authoritative commentators to be between five and seven million people, of which only a tiny proportion were military.

Even worse has been a series of military struggles that have blighted Khartoum since the 1950s. In reality, what is happening today in Darfur in the Sudan is an extension of a series of conflicts in the south of the country that have left more than a million people dead

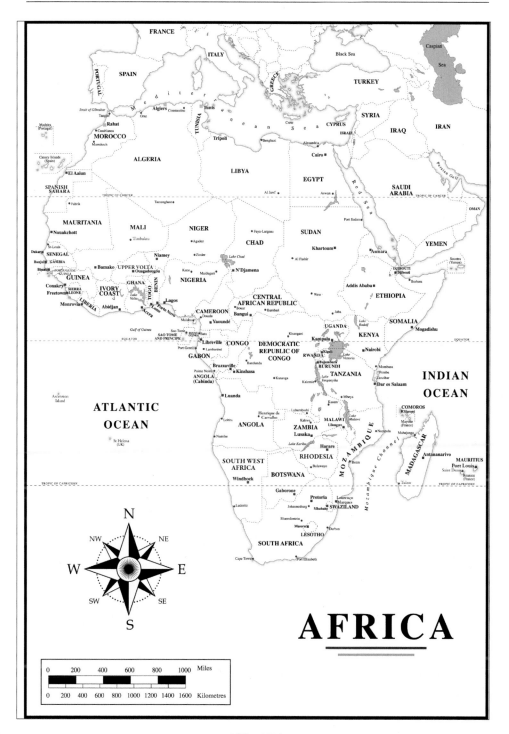

AFRICA

Africa 1974

Portuguese Prime Minister Antonio de Oliveira Salazar, for decades Lisbon's controversial leader who refused to bend to what Britain's Harold Macmillan termed Africa's 'Winds of Change'. He made the cover of *Time* on July 22, 1946 and was brutally castigated by Portugal's future NATO partner. The report stated that this little European country had 'produced no big spot news for 20 years' and went on: '...it might not for 20 years more if the God he strove so hard to serve spared Antonio de Oliveira Salazar. For Salazar distrusted news. He suppressed and distorted it for the good of the Portuguese who, he believed, were unfit for facts. After 20 years of Salazar, the dean of Europe's dictators, Portugal was a melancholy land of impoverished, confused and frightened people ...'. (Author's collection)

Portugal's first modern-day African revolution (there had been many over centuries past, all brutally subjugated) started with an invasion of a dissident guerrilla force from the Congo in 1961. Thousands of civilians, many of them white settlers and their families were slaughtered and photos such as this one were commonplace. (Author's collection)

Lisbon's links with Africa as a colonial power went back five centuries. This monument in Maputo, formerly Lourenço Marques, commemorated the Portugal's enduring relationships with its African subjects. (Author's photo)

and who knows how many more millions homeless or displaced.

Then you have Nigeria, currently struggling with a low-level insurgency that has festered for years. Hostilities have blighted this oil-rich West African nation that supplies the United States with more than 20 percent of its imported crude, and cut domestic oil production by about a third.

For the observer, the scenario for Africa is a sobering reality that appears only to get worse each time a new assessment is made. It will be even more so with a deteriorating international economic climate that will ultimately affect just about everybody on the planet, and Africa most of all.

Yet much of the violence that has ravaged this volatile continent during the course of the past half-century had its roots in a series of liberation wars launched in the early 1960s in Angola, Mozambique and Portuguese Guinea. All three countries were part of Lisbon's overseas provinces in Africa, or more appropriately, what the Portuguese liked to call their *metrópole-províncias ultramarinas*.

The first of these rebellions was launched in 1961 in Angola, when groups of rebels invaded the country from an already-destabilized Congo Republic. More upheavals took root in Portuguese Guinea in 1962 followed by Mozambique in September 1964.

Unlike Kenya's Mau Mau uprising of the 1950s, countered by stern military measures implemented by Whitehall, all three Portuguese conflagrations gradually evolved into fully

After the initial insurgent onslaught that caught Lisbon totally by surprise (though there had been warnings about an impending attack) the Portuguese responded with vigour and drafted thousands of troops and heavy equipment to Angola. Some of these were caught on film by the author at a Luanda parade some years later; the French-built Panhard armoured cars were often deployed on convoy duty. (Author's photo)

fledged military campaigns that involved tens of thousands of troops on both sides of a series of largely undefined 'front lines'. There were thousands of casualties during 13 years of guerrilla warfare and while agreements of sorts were eventually signed by the warring parties, the peace that followed was fragmentary.

What Lisbon's campaigns did do for Africa was to forever change the political face of this inordinately unstable continent. Effectively, Portugal's African conflicts were the beginning of the end of white rule on the continent.

A fascinating insight to this period in Angola was provided by John Miller, *Daily Telegraph* correspondent in Africa in the 1970s. He provided a chapter on the Portuguese territory for one of my books *War in Africa*, that was published in the United States and South Africa and which proved to be both incisive though possibly somewhat over-optimistic of things to come on the sub-continent.

An unusual commentator, John – who had become a good friend during his Cape Town sojourn – had spent a lot of time in Eastern Europe. Though he was guarded about his activities there, he spoke good Russian and sensed that there were a few common denominators between what he'd discovered for himself in Moscow and what was going on at the time in apartheid-dominated South Africa.

I quote from his chapter, which I've paraphrased, in part to bring it in line with timeline as well as style:

The architect of many of the earlier attacks in Southern Africa was President *Mwalimu* Julius Nyerere of Tanzania. He was heard many times to say that the white communities in Southern Africa 'must be eradicated, by force if necessary'. As a consequence Dar es Salaam became the principal conduit of war matériel used by various guerrilla factions in what was termed their 'liberation' wars. (Author's collection)

Luanda, the capital of Angola, Portugal's largest overseas territory, is a handsome city which need not fear comparison with any other city in tropical Africa. Because the Portuguese in Africa have their roots in Angola, it has a bustling business quarter and docks, an old-fashioned and curiously designed Governor-General's palace and government offices, a castle built in 1638 and still dominating the city – and São João, an old fortress, now a common prison.

On February 4th, 1961 around the grim walls of São João were fired the first shots in a war which has plagued Portugal ever since. In a swift surprise attack under cover of darkness, a group of Africans armed with machetes and shotguns attacked the prison. It is just another of the many ironies of revolutionary history that the group had hoped to free political prisoners and that there were none there at the time. In any event, a handful of prison guards drove the attackers back to the opulent Miramar residential district, where the richest of the descendants of the early Portuguese colonizers, civil servants and products of recent immigration cowered in their homes clutching pistols and sporting rifles.

During a long and confusing night the Africans regrouped and struck at the police headquarters. It was here that the first blood was shed. Eight policemen and 36 of the attackers were killed and 63 other Europeans and Africans wounded. Many more were to die the next day, when, at a series of funeral processions some white nationals who demanded reprisals went on the rampage.

President Nyerere took an active interest in his own military forces after he was almost
deposed by disgruntled troops in the 1964 army mutiny. When Nyerere appealed
to London for help, a swift British reaction followed, including the deployment of
the Royal Navy aircraft carrier HMS *Centaur*, Royal Marines 45 Commando as well
as British Army elements flown in from Aden. (Photo CameraPix, Nairobi)

The death toll during the two days was insignificant compared to what was to
follow that year – and every year since. African nationalism had tasted blood in
Angola, over which Portugal's red and green flag had fluttered for nearly 500 years,
and there was no going back. Inevitably a lull in the fighting was followed by a storm.

On March 15th, 1961, several hundred freedom fighters, many of them trained in
the Congo, and armed with machetes, cutlasses and homemade rifles, had launched a
series of attacks on isolated white settlements south of the Congo border and deep into
the coffee-rich Carmona province. In just a few days some 300 Whites and as many
Africans were killed (and often mutilated) on the fazendas, the coffee plantations.

Lisbon and Dr Antonio Salazar, the man of granite, were powerless to halt the
wave of bloodshed, for there were no Portuguese troops in Carmona Province, which
is the size of Portugal itself, and as few as 3,000 troops in two regiments in the whole of
Angola. Not surprisingly, considering the ferocity and determination of the freedom
fighters, the massacre continued for a fortnight. If it was not the biggest slaughter of
whites which has taken place in Africa in this century, it was not far short of it. What
is certain is that it passed almost unnoticed in the world press.

By the end of 1961, thousands of Portuguese troops rushed from Lisbon were
beginning to get to grips with the situation. The freedom fighters still attacked farms
and villages and laid ambushes from impenetrable bush, but the spark had not led to

The author took this clandestine shot of Dar es Salaam harbour while staying at the city's then-still-exclusive Kilimanjaro Hotel. There were several Soviet freighters berthed in the port at the time. (Author's photo)

a roaring inferno. What had happened was that some 2,000 Whites and an estimated 50,000 Africans had been killed.

War had come to Angola, where the Portuguese had dozed for five centuries – the long and lazy colonial siesta was over. The year 1961 marked the beginning of what has since become a continual challenge to the Portuguese to stay in Africa.

For twelve wearisome years the Portuguese, and those of mixed European and African descent, as well as the six million Africans, have been learning to live with their grim little war. And there were ever-present reminders of it. On every street in every town and village there were soldiers, white and black, swaggering and conspicuous in their jungle camouflage uniforms. The original 3,000 had become 60,000.

In Carmona Province each and every fazenda was surrounded by barbed wire, and day and night armed sentries stood in the obligatory high white towers. In the railway workshops of Novo Lisboa (Huambo today) workers fitted armour plate to pilot trucks travelling the long line to the east, or patched up sabotaged engines. Across the country the walled and guarded military posts bristling with radio masts were always on the alert, their heavy machine-guns well oiled and swivelling free.

And in Luanda on a Saturday afternoon, a slice on the 17th tee of the local golf course could mean trouble if the ball could hit a descending paratrooper. As it was, golfers played to the background of crackling small-arms fire from the nearby military range and the constantly rising and falling snarl of army helicopters.

Anti-Portuguese demonstrations were a regular event in the streets of Dar es Salaam at the time. Some prominent Mozambican leaders can be seen in the foreground - including Marcelino dos Santos - who eventually became vice president of his independent homeland. (Author's photo)

Overhead American Harvard trainer/ground support aircraft of World War II vintage simulated bomb and napalm attacks and the immensely useful French-built Noratlas troop carriers lumbered in, bringing the dead and the maimed, or simply tired young conscripts aching for the bright lights, bars and brothels of a Western-style city. And often Luanda golfers have to hold back their drives for fear of hitting the halftracks and trucks crammed with troops that are ceaselessly rattling along the road cutting through the back nine holes, and going God knows where.

But Luanda was 'safe'. It had not heard a shot fired since those dark days of 1961. The terse little communiqués of actions and ambushes, of who killed whom, how and where, hardly ever made front-page news in Luanda newspapers, and in any case, as in Vietnam at its worst, were seldom read.

The reality of a protracted anti-guerrilla war comes home to you, however, on the convoy run from 'safe' Luanda to Carmona.

There were two roads to Carmona. One swept south-east from Luanda to Salazar and then north. It was the best part of a day's drive and it was said to be safe from ambush. The other road, which struck north, was shorter, more direct – and dangerous.

The danger zone rolled north from Cuixita, an hour's drive from Luanda. Here swarthy Portuguese truck drivers came face-to face with the reality of a guerrilla war, with the fact they could just possibly die from a sniper's bullet, or a Russian or Chinese anti-personnel mine lovingly laid in a lousy road. But the job had to be done. And

Kwame Nkrumah's Ghana was also a major player in the liberation struggle, though the former Gold Coast was thousands of miles from where the action was then taking place. His symbol was the Black Star, to which *Osagyefo* (Redeemer) Nkrumah erected an edifice in a large square in the heart of the Ghanaian capital. (Author's photo)

every day for several years, heavy trucks taking food and supplies to hamlets along the route had to be marshalled, counted and protected.

The convoy run to Carmona began at seven in the morning and the 350 kilometre drive took all of 13 hours. When I joined it, a bearded African corporal was listing the truck numbers and pulling the convoy into line. Soon the lead army vehicle with a mounted and shielded heavy machine-gun and eight soldiers with their Heckler and Koch G3 automatic rifles eased away from the local bar where the soldiers had been having bad Portuguese brandy and better coffee and took up point position. Another similarly equipped vehicle roared and rattled down from the local military base to cover the convoy's rear.

For the first hour's ride to Ucua over twisting, bad road, the truck drivers fought to get behind the lead army vehicle. Horns blared as the trucks jumped the potholes and swayed from side to side. It was not fear so much as the one-hour stop at a hamlet with two bars, half a dozen stray dogs, the army and a house of camp-followers, which drove them on.

There the game ended, for the next 170 kilometres to Carmona was deadly serious business. The sergeant with the machine-gun swept the towering bush grass, jungle and hills while the rest of the platoon nervously fingered their weapons. Not far from the surface of the jaunt through classic guerrilla warfare country was the knowledge that someone could get killed if anyone were careless.

The convoy hugged itself through to Checkpoint Three. There it waited for

Agostinho Neto was the founder and leader of the MPLA, the largest Angolan liberation movement and eventually the country's first president after it had achieved victory. A mild-mannered son of a Methodist pastor, he left Angola for Portugal where he studied medicine at the universities of Coimbra and Lisbon. He was arrested by the Portuguese secret police and jailed for seven years for subversion. He married a Portuguese woman and returned to his homeland in 1959. The liberation war started a few years later. (Author's collection)

another convoy – this one bound for Luanda – to be cleared by a slip of a lad with a bundle of grenades at his feet and a clipboard in his hand.

To kill time and escape from the heat of the fierce midday sun, the truck-drivers slipped away up the hill to the Portuguese army 'farm', complete with a mini soccer pitch, and bristling with heavy machine-guns and updated bazookas. For an hour or two we drank beer with the three platoons who sat it out on the hill month after month with nothing to pass the time but a pack of cards, a battery-driven portable record player and the African women who sat passively on the grimy army camp beds.

This was what the war in Angola is largely all about: sitting it out, waiting for an attack which rarely came. This was what the Portuguese called 'terrorist-infected country'. It probably was. But because the freedom fighters could only hit the convoys or the military 'farms' at their peril, it could fairly be said that the Portuguese had managed to contain the war in Angola.

They controlled the densely populated, economically viable areas of a territory nearly the size of Western Europe. They were keeping the guerrilla movements at bay in the useless under-populated areas, and they were pushing through as rapidly as possible – for Portuguese bureaucracy had been a deadening hand in the past – the economic, social, cultural and medical reforms necessary for a counter-revolution against African nationalism.

The author visited all Portuguese overseas territories many times over the years and produced several books on hostilities in Angola and Portuguese Guinea as well as numerous reports for newspapers and magazines on four continents. From Bissau, he went on military operations along that country's northern waterways with Portuguese marines – the *fuzileiros* in their rubber boats - where this photo was taken.

And so it went on until the army mutiny in Lisbon of 1974 when Portugal hastily vacated its African possessions. That said, one needs to carefully examine the nature and extent of Portugal's wars in Africa to properly appreciate the consequences of these struggles, though this can be difficult since comparatively little has been recorded when compared to other military struggles of the past century.

In his dissertation on Portugal's African wars, William Minter stated: 'even in Portuguese, the written material for a more careful judgement is sketchy. The gaps in the history of the Angolan conflict are larger than the patches of reliable information or systematic analysis.[1] This is true both for the pre-1975 war against Portuguese colonialism and even more so for the post-independence strife.'

Look at the facts: Lisbon, a tiny nation of less than nine million people fought twice as long against its African foes as the United States did in Vietnam. Moreover, they did so in regions whose populations aggregated roughly 12 million, spread over regions half the size of Western Europe. Yet today, little more than a generation later, there might be one in ten thousand Americans who are even remotely aware that Portugal not only had colonies in Africa in fairly recent times, but were actually involved in a spate of military upheavals on the continent. Moreover, this was guerrilla warfare on a massive scale.

Brigadier General Willem (Kaas) van der Waals, the penultimate South African to

Monument to Africa 'breaking the enslaving chains of colonialism' erected by former Zambian President Kenneth Kaunda in Central Lusaka. (Author's Photo)

serve as Vice Consul tasked with military liaison in Luanda prior to the Portuguese finally leaving Africa, encapsulates it neatly in the preface to his book on Portugal's wars:[2]

> ... from the 1960s, revolutionary warfare, insurgency, guerrilla war and national liberation movements were to become the major form of strife on the Southern African subcontinent. This type of conflict in the Third World, symptomatic of the international Cold War scene after the Second World War, erupted in Angola in 1961. It was soon to spread to Mozambique, Rhodesia (Zimbabwe), South West Africa (Namibia) and eventually to the Republic of South Africa.
>
> 'While other colonial powers progressively retreated from Africa, Portugal weathered the storm for several years until its capitulation in 1974. This was followed by decolonisation at an unseemly and ill-prepared pace, the result [more than a decade] of costly warfare in three of its African possessions, stretching its material, human and moral resources to the utmost and creating a climate of psycho-political collapse. While not defeated on the field of battle, Portugal ultimately had to give way.

The Brigadier General goes on to say that the military coup in Portugal in 1974 and the withdrawal of its troops from Angola should have resulted in peace in that country. It did not. He declares that the ensuing chaos left a power vacuum and caused this area to become a physical and psychological battlefield involving international as well as regional

Captain Ricardo Alcada accompanied the author throughout much of his first visit to the 'Sector D' war zone in Northern Angola, colloquially termed the *Dembos* (jungle). After this first visit, Captain Alcada and Captain Vitor Alves (then commanding a unit at N'Riquinha in Eastern Angola, were invited to South Africa by the author on an official visit where they addressed students at Johannesburg's University of the Witwatersrand. Alves was later to become one of the leaders of the 'Carnation Revolution' – the army mutiny that ousted the civilian government in 1974. (Author's photo)

forces and influences.

The original accord initiated by the Portuguese stipulated that there be a power-sharing agreement between the three ethnic-based liberation movements in Angola, pending a general election. But that was soon breached and fighting between the factions continued for another 30 years.

What happened after independence in Angola in the mid-1970s, he tells us, is that 'with the United States paralysed after its mortifying Vietnam experience, the USSR moved quickly to capitalise from the situation in Angola, using its resources to install its own protégé, the Marxist-oriented MPLA, in power. The Portuguese buffer disappeared virtually overnight, and strategic Soviet bases were set up in Angola and later in Mozambique, from where the Soviets and their surrogates were to pursue an intensified revolutionary onslaught against the remaining white regimes in Southern Africa.'

This was all Cold War stuff and sadly, much of it still has to be properly recorded.

For all its problems, Lisbon did have material though discreet support from much of Europe, their NATO allies (including the United States, depending largely on who was in the White House at the time). There were also a variety of Western-orientated nations such as Morocco and one or two Middle East states – including anti-Communist Saudi Arabia – that provided Lisbon with a measure of covert assistance.

The war in Vietnam created enormous movements to end that conflict,
including the 'Peace' symbol. It quickly caught on among the largely
conscript army in Portugal's overseas possessions. (Author's photo)

Almost all weapons and aircraft deployed in the three overseas provinces had North Atlantic Treaty Organisation hallmarks and while NATO was not an active participant in Portugal's colonial wars, it was no secret that there were many American and European specialists who were able to spend time in the various operational areas. Washington tended to focus on war matériel then being supplied by communist states, in particular, some of the weapons being used against American Forces in Vietnam.

For their part, the rebels in all three Overseas Provinces got their succour from Russia, China, Cuba, Vietnam, Algeria and most Eastern European states, the majority channelling their wherewithal through Dar es Salaam in Tanzania and Sékou Touré's Guinea. As with Angola, Mozambique and Namibia's South West African People's Organisation (SWAPO), a good deal of assistance came from moderate liberal nations such as Sweden and Canada, as well as churches and philanthropic organisations throughout North America.

While hostilities in Africa continued, racial overtones remained a feature of the struggle, though it was never a convincing argument. At the beginning, the conflict was propagated by the various liberation movements as a confrontation between black and white. While that ploy had its adherents, it didn't work because the Portuguese had long ago reduced colour to economic, and to a lesser extent, social considerations.

While the Angolan liberation war was being countered in Angola, a major military upheaval was then taking place in the neighbouring Congo. The southern Congolese province of Katanga had tried to secede and in the north-west anti-government rebels were fomenting a revolution of their own. This prompted the CIA to create its own pro-Government air force that comprised WW2-era North American Aviation T-28 'Trojan' aircraft flown by renegade Cuban pilots recruited in Miami. (Photo courtesy of Leif Hellström)

What did soon emerge was that Lisbon was forced to increasingly rely on black volunteers, never in short supply. In line with this approach, some of the best counter-insurgent units in the Portuguese overseas empire were created from the bootstraps up, the majority predominantly black. There were African Commandos (*Comandos Africanos*) and Special Force units composed entirely of black soldiers, including their officers as well as African Special Marines, the *Fuzileiros Especiais Africanos*. The only white faces in the ranks of the guerrillas, in contrast, were their Cuban and Russian advisers and the very occasional Portuguese defector who had joined their ranks. There was also a bevy of British journalists who propagated the cause, including the British writer Basil Davidson. Occasionally a member of the French Left, customarily a follower of Regis Debray or some other revolutionary would appear among rebel forces.

In the eyes of the rebel central committees, said one neutral observer at the time, a white Portuguese would always be exactly that: a white Portuguese, even though, over the years, there were quite a few Portuguese soldiers and airmen who deserted and went across to the enemy. Curiously, the desertion figures for the Portuguese army in Africa were modest; there were only 103 desertions throughout the 13-year period of the war in all three African territories.

World War II-vintage bombers were also brought into the Congolese fray by the CIA, with the result that a large body of Katangese troops sought refuge under Portuguese auspices in Angola. These dissident soldiers were later to launch vigorous efforts to retake their homeland from Angolan soil. (Photo courtesy of Leif Hellström)

While the intent of a fugitive from the Portuguese army might have been sincere, rebel leaders considered these defectors of more value outside the fighting zone, preferably behind the Iron Curtain or, in the case of the PAIGC – the Freedom Army in what was to become Guiné-Bissau – under the control of the exiled, communist *Frent Patriotica de Libertacao National* (FPLN), with its headquarters in Algiers.

A constant preoccupation with enemy agents was a trait – not necessarily peculiar to the PAIGC High Command – that was almost certainly inherited from the Portuguese. In this regard, the movement's internal security could almost be equated to PIDE, the Portuguese secret police. Equally ruthless, an individual might easily be liquidated if even suspected of collusion with the other side.

Douglas Porch tells us in *The Portuguese Armed Forces and the Revolution* that as the war crept on, more and more good officers began to slip away, usually into the metropolis. He maintained that while some were politically motivated, many more were spurred on by economic considerations. Then there were those officers that failed to return from holidays abroad ... [3]

Then came the incident involving 15 engineering cadets – all of them regarded by the establishment as the 'cream of the Military Academy' – who, after completing their four-year course in 1973, walked across the frontier to Spain.

While the Portuguese were fighting for their African possessions, the Organisation of African Unity launched vigorous attempts at discrediting the Lisbon government for what it termed 'inhuman military actions'. There was always much fanfare and a huge press corps invited and entertained, such as on this occasion on the last night of an OAU Summit. Cape Town-based Pieter Seidlitz of *Der Spiegel* can be seen lighting a cigar; three places down to his right sits the rather bored author. (Official OAU photo)

Economic factors were destined to play as significant a role as politics in the outcome of Lisbon's colonial conflicts.

For a start, these were exceedingly difficult times: after Albania, Portugal was the second poorest nation in Europe. Yet by 1971, it had committed nine-tenths of its military resources to its wars in Africa.

The Cambridge History of Africa[3] is piquant when it declares that 'together with the conscription of settler manpower in Angola and Mozambique and of African service units and local militias (including 'commando' type units at special rates of pay), Lisbon then had in Africa a total force that was probably equivalent, by ratio of the Portuguese and American populations, to at least seven times the largest United States force in Vietnam.' In the same year, 1971, it says 'the Portuguese spent 40 percent of its national budget on military purposes'.

Captain John Cann, a former US Navy aviator who served in the Pentagon, subsequently wrote one of the definitive books on Portugal's African campaigns. What he has to say is instructive.[4]

For Portugal in 1961:

Shot from a helicopter gunship in Northern South West Africa at the height of South Africa's so-called Border War, this photo shows the kind of terrain the Portuguese encountered in their extreme southern areas of operation. The terrain was similar throughout the region – largely deep sand, few roads and with sparse rainfall for many months of the year. (Author's photo)

... to have mobilized an army, transported it many thousands of kilometres to its African colonies, established large logistical bases at key locations there to support it, equipped it with special weapons and matériel, and trained it for a very specialized type of warfare, was a remarkable achievement.

It is made even more noteworthy by the fact that these tasks were accomplished without any previous experience, doctrine, or demonstrated competence in the field of either power projection or counterinsurgency warfare, and thus without the benefit of any instructors who were competent in these specialities. To put this last statement in perspective, other than periodic colonial pacification efforts, Portugal had not fired a shot in anger since World War I, when Germany invaded northern Mozambique and southern Angola.'

Consider too that all three wars were great distances from the Metropolis. Portuguese Guinea – or as it is known today Guiné-Bissau – is almost as far from Lisbon as Nairobi is from Johannesburg.

Luanda, Angola's largest city and the major resupply point for the war in the interior, lies more than 7,000 kilometres from Portugal, or roughly speaking, the distance between Washington and Berlin. Mozambique, twice the size of California, lies another 3,000 kilometres further east, on the far side of the African continent.

On the south-western fringes of Mozambique's frontiers, the Portuguese were increasingly aware of another gathering storm in neighbouring Rhodesia. That guerrilla war steadily gathered pace as insurgents made their way southwards along FRELIMO-established conduits. As in Mozambique, a large proportion of government forces were black. (Author's collection)

Of all the European countries that established Imperial dominions in Africa, Portugal's colonial traditions lasted the longest. Lisbon was the first of the seafaring nations to establish a foreign base in Africa when it captured Ceuta, a tiny enclave in the north-west corner of Africa in 1415. It was also the last to leave.

These weren't the first attempts to colonise Africa. The Arabs – both from Egypt and the Gulf – had made serious inroads from the north for millennia. In fact, much of East Africa was ruled by Omani Arabs by the time the British and Imperial Germany arrived in Kenya and Tanganyika towards the end of the 19th Century. From the Dark Ages the Chinese had been intermittent visitors in their periodic global voyages of exploration.

Consequently, when Prince Henry's navigators first arrived in Africa in the early 1400s, they discovered a continent that had already had some form of contact with what might have been termed the 'developed world' of the day. Quite a few of their countrymen who followed in their wake were to put down roots in the new-found settlements.

Lisbon ended up ruling its African possessions for more than five centuries, eventually driven out by the combined forces of an impoverished economy, political impasse at home, coupled to the kind of domestic upheavals that had already characterised post-World War II developments in French Indo China, Malaya and Algeria.

And when rebel groups in the *ultramar* took up the cudgels, they did with a determination that was ferocious enough to take the world by surprise. For more than a

Soviet spy ships, such as this 'trawler' in the South Atlantic, were a regular feature of Southern African guerrilla conflicts. Moscow played a seminal role in monitoring radio communications in all three overseas territories and passing intercepts onto the various guerrilla commands. (Author's photo)

decade, it was these small bush wars that eventually bled Lisbon dry.

Portuguese colonial history, though tarnished by self-interest and, some might say, delusions of grandeur, was as illustrious a colonial chapter as anything launched over the centuries by Madrid in South and Central America, and by Amsterdam, London or Paris on the great unexplored continent that lay to the south of Europe. It was a historic epoch that was to have far-reaching and historic effects on the globe. For a start, it opened up trade between an isolated Europe and the East and once initiated, there was no going back.

Until other European states arrived with their so-called 'civilizing missions', the Portuguese were active even before Spain, Britain, the French, the Dutch or the Italians had established permanent outstations in their respective possessions, several motivated by a burgeoning trans-Atlantic slave trade. Lisbon went on to leave its identity – and its blood – in all its former possessions.[5]

In one respect, this ethnic footprint is still there. Portuguese remains the language of choice in all three of its former African colonies. The same holds for Brazil, where there are as many Ferreiras, Delgados, Rodrigueses, and Alcadas in the telephone lists of São Paulo and Rio as in Lisbon or Oporto. So, too with Portugal's other erstwhile colonies, like Sri Lanka and Goa in South Asia, Macao off the Chinese Mainland and Timor, within the borders of present-day Indonesia, since renamed West Irian.

It was Africa's Liberation Wars – *Guerras de Libertação* – first in Angola, then in Portuguese Guinea and finally in Mozambique – that brought this remarkable epoch to an end, and none too soon either.

France and the United Kingdom, Africa's two other major colonisers – if you don't count Italy and Spain – had already been made aware of the 'Winds of Change' in the late 1940s and 1950s. Most of their African colonies were consequently quietly prepared for

With a shoreline stretching from north to south of almost 2,600 kilometres, it was impossible for government forces in Mozambique to monitor all maritime traffic. Many insurgent infiltrations were accomplished by small boats coming through from Tanzania, such as this dhow. (Author's photo)

independence and in the majority of cases – there were dozens of countries involved – self-rule was handed over little more than a decade later.

Effectively, the Gold Coast became Ghana, Tanganyika was renamed Tanzania while Basutoland and Bechuanaland became Lesotho and Botswana. Overnight a host of brand new Francophone states were created, among them Niger, Chad, Upper Volta, Ivory Coast, the Central African Republic and others.

Lisbon, in contrast, resisted these changes with a fury. Power-sharing or even limited autonomy in Africa was never even considered an option in a colonial policy that was strictly in line with the *Estado Novo's* narrow vision of what some of its adherents believed was a divinely-inspired imperial mission. This was one of the reasons why the bureaucrats along the western shores of the Iberian Peninsula would refer to their African struggles as Colonial Wars, or more colloquially *(Guerras Colonial)*. Overseas War or *Guerra do Ultramar* also became part of the Lusitanian lexicon.

While the war raged in Angola, we'd hear the catch-phrase everywhere, on the radio, at public meetings and more often than not on billboards posted on every vacant space: *Angola é Nossa*! – 'Angola is Ours'.

In truth, as the nation was often reminded by the dictator Antonio de Oliveira Salazar, the three African 'provinces' represented a powerful motive for national pride. Then the wily old fox would subtly add that Angola, Mozambique and Guinea not only sustained Portugal's economy, but for centuries had symbolized a heritage of a great and glorious past.

As magnificent as Mozambique's tropical coast is, a myriad of tiny inlets, islands, lagoons and isolated beaches could not be adequately patrolled by government forces to prevent guerrilla infiltration. (Author's photo)

He was only partly right because he ignored the reality of history: while cultures might remain mired in the past, ideologies and the people who shape them constantly change.

More to the point for Salazar, who had an old-fashioned notion of what constituted the wealth of nations, he would tell his people that the overseas colonies were what made his nation great. Angola, Mozambique and, to a lesser extent Portuguese Guinea, all helped to provide captive markets for home-produced goods, ready sources of cheap raw materials and foodstuffs as well as an outlet for the homeland's surplus population.

Consequently, when Angola was finally invaded by a rag-tag rebel army that emerged out of the recently-independent Congo to the north, Lisbon retaliated by sending to Africa an inexperienced conscript army and as many aviation and naval elements as it could afford. Similar guerrilla struggles followed shortly afterwards in Mozambique and Portuguese Guinea. The conflicts soon escalated and were to evolve into a grim series of military campaigns that went on for half a generation.

Yet curiously, Lisbon's African travails received scant attention beyond its own frontiers. Were that to happen today, these military struggles would almost certainly get the attention they deserved, but in the 1960s almost everything was focused on Vietnam and, to a lesser extent Algeria. Nor were matters eased by Lisbon's reluctance to provide

IGUAIS
Ā FACE
DA PĀTRIA

IGUAIS
Ā FACE
DA LEI

SOMOS TODOS PORTUGUESES

Somos Todos Portugueses – We are all Portuguese – was the multi-racial watchword on a million propaganda posters distributed throughout Angola during the war. Everybody was, of course, but the guerrillas believed otherwise. (Author's photo)

journalists with the necessary facilities to report on them.

More salient, it was also a time of dissension at home, with a growing body of radical, left-leaning military officers who believed that the military campaigns should be terminated and Africa left to its own devices.

With time and numerous assignments to the colonies, I got to know some of the members of the junta that eventually overthrew the Lisbon government and it was interesting to glimpse the machinations of the revolt from the inside. Captain Vitor Alves, with whom I spent time operationally in Eastern Angola and Captain Otelo Saraiva de Carvalho, an aide to General António de Spínola and my escort officer while I covered hostilities in Portuguese Guinea, were among them.

While Captain Alves was relatively moderate as revolutionaries go (he was eventually to serve his country in the European Parliament), that did not apply to de Carvalho, who was both an insurrectionist and an anarchist. General de Spínola's aide was eventually jailed for sedition by the government that he'd helped to create.

There were many reasons why Lisbon eventually bowed out, with politics and economics featuring in roughly equal measure.

Lost in a quagmire of conflicting ideologies was Lisbon's initial impetus, in large part because the majority of the young conscripts who were called to spend first two and later

After almost a decade of war, some of the military commanders believed that a military victory – or rather, a series of military victories – was no longer possible. Which was why General António de Spínola, then in command in Portuguese Guinea, wrote his historic book *Portugal e o Futuro*, which suggested a realistic alternative to a seemingly unending military conundrum. His conclusion was that Portugal's African wars could only be settled at the negotiating table and the war-weary nation listened. *Portugal and the Future* (it was translated into English) became an immediate best seller and was to play a deciding role in Lisbon's civilian government being toppled. (Author's photo)

Portuguese forces towards the end were up against some formidable guerrilla forces, the majority totally dependent on Moscow and Beijing for enormous supplies of hardware. This unit, operating in Central Angola was under the command of dissident MPLA cadre Daniel Chipenda (bearded, taking the salute). Many of his men later defected to South Africa to become part of the crack 32 Battalion. (Author's collection)

three years in Africa, saw absolutely no sense in losing their lives in wars for which they had neither interest nor enthusiasm. The majority had never even seen Africa. Almost to a man, they couldn't wait for their military service to end.

In a sense, it was déjà vu, something similar experienced by the majority of American servicemen in Vietnam.

It was not surprising that all these interacting factors, together, eventually caused Lisbon's colonial empire to disintegrate in 1974. Within a year, the Portuguese Army, Navy and Air Force had packed their bags and were headed home.

Portugal's guerrilla wars in Africa were fought under horrendous conditions. They were made worse by a continent that has never been kind to the interloper.

Interestingly, things weren't nearly as bad in Angola, where generations of young Portuguese had lived and worked in this remote and remarkably wealthy bush country. Primitive it might have been, but Angola's natural resources included diamonds, gold and oil and offered undreamt-of rewards to those who persevered. More to the point, the always-hardy Portuguese appeared to adapt easily to adversity. Those who had been there for generations often enough understood conditions better than their black compadres, which

FLNA guerrillas in Angola – operating out of Mobuto Sese Seko's Democratic Republic of the Congo – were well equipped with military hardware, but decidedly inferior as a fighting force: they lacked adequate 'muscle' provided to their adversaries, the MPLA, by Fidel Castro's large Cuban army. (Author's collection)

was a reason why the war in Angola ultimately went a lot better than it did in Mozambique.

The majority of young conscripts taken off the streets and from homes in Oporto, Sintra, Coimbra, Figueira da Foz and elsewhere often faced a host of uncompromising options. Like many American GIs in Asia, the majority were still in their teens, thrust into a series of bitter conflicts that ultimately went on to claim more than 3,000 lives. There were another 13,000 casualties – apart from those who died in accidents or of disease.

Stuck in the African bush, sometimes for years at stretch, coupled to austere, harsh living conditions, as well as the prospect of contracting any one of dozens of tropical illnesses, their options were limited. Malaria, tick bite fever and other insect-borne diseases were always a factor and though Lisbon seemed to cope, they exacted a steady toll.

No wonder then that tens of thousands of young men of military age from the western fringe of the Iberian Peninsula voted with their feet. Most slipped quietly across the border into Spain and made their way to Germany, France, Scandinavia and elsewhere to find jobs and sit out the war.

I spent a lot of time with Portuguese units in the field, first in Angola where, on my first visit I was accompanied by Cloete Breytenbach, one of South Africa's best known lensmen (and brother to peripatetic Breyten, who vigorously opposed the apartheid policies of the white South African regime) and afterwards, in Portuguese Guinea. Cloete's third brother,

Colonel Jan Breytenbach, went on to become the founder-commander of South Africa's first Special Forces unit, the Reconnaissance Regiment. More popularly known as the Recces, very little about it has appeared in print apart from one outstanding book.[6]

My time spent with Lisbon's military in Mozambique was fragmentary and usually centered around units based at Tete, in the Zambezi Valley, or on the isolated road that linked Malawi with Beira.

We called it 'The Highway to Hell', and that it certainly was. About the only thing that was certain about travelling between the Rhodesian border post at Nyamapanda and Mwanza, at the southern tip of Malawi was that someone in your convoy was bound to be blown up by landmines.

Conditions everywhere were tough. In this regard, there is nobody better than Ron Reid-Daly – founder-commander of Rhodesia's illustrious Selous Scouts – to offer words of his own about the kind of circumstances that might have been encountered, especially along the southern approaches to the Zambezi Valley.[7] I deal with this matter in Chapter 23.

The Tete Region of Mozambique – through which the great Zambezi flows out of Zambia to the sea – rapidly developed into one of the most disputed zones of the war. The most important role of Portuguese forces there was to guard the strategic Cahora Bassa hydro-electric dam then in the process of being constructed.

Over several years, I was able to visit the place both by road and by small plane from Tete and, as I was to observe, the defences – and the minefields – were extensive.

I was to see the consequences of some of these encounters in the military hospital in Tete – it's all there in Chapter 24, which deals with the casualties of war – a grim experience throughout.

At the end of the war, early in 1974, after the cease-fire had been signed, I returned to the now abandoned air force base at Cahora Bassa by car. Travelling alone, it was a long, lonely road, situated some distance from where dam construction work was taking place.

Still intact, the place was deserted. It was almost as if the local natives, fearful of intruding on something that had been forbidden for so long, were not eager to disturb yesterday's ghosts. Hangers, mess halls, sleeping quarters and engineering shops were all intact but there was garbage everywhere. The only call came from a go-away bird precariously perched on an abandoned radar antenna. Flies descended on me as if there were no tomorrow.

In a sense, it was like something in those early British films made after World War II, where the main character would go back to one of the airfields where he'd spent time and found only faded photos on the window sills, broken cups and doors banging in the breeze.

It was much the same on the long journey between the camp and Tete, a distance of a couple of hundred kilometres. Mine was the only car, and because the road was tarred and I was struck by the insecurity of an isolated countryside, I travelled fast. I never encountered a single domestic animal along the way. At one stage I was stopped by a lone FRELIMO soldier who first apologised for halting me and then asked politely whether I would give

A latecomer in Angola's war was the Swiss-educated Maoist Dr Jonas Savimbi whose Ovimbundu tribal base from the south east gave him powerful territorial sway towards the end of the war, and after independence, against the Marxist MPLA government in Luanda. (Author's collection)

him a lift to town.

It wasn't the first time I'd given a revolutionary cadre a ride while travelling around Mozambique: I'd done so a few years before on the road between Tete and Rhodesia, only this one was a full-blown rebel commissar who waved me straight into his camp.

For my efforts he offered me a cold beer in the comfort of his headquarters.

Some idea of the intensity of these African conflicts, particularly in Portuguese Guinea, might be gauged from what has been listed in the record books as 'The Battle of Como Island'. It was a series of grim battles that involved Portuguese land, sea and air forces and provides a valuable insight to rebel determination to win, at all costs if necessary.

By early 1964, the PAIGC had captured Como Island. A counterattack by Portuguese forces was swiftly repulsed and even the deployment of F-86F Sabres by the *Força Aérea Portuguesa* from Bissau were unable to change the outcome of the battle. On the contrary, it soon became almost impossible for the Portuguese troops to operate anywhere in Guinea at any distance from their well-fortified bases.

For a while the anti-guerrilla campaign stuttered along. A few *colons* were moved to safety – usually under control of the regular army – but very little else happened that might disturb the connection between the local population and the insurgents. The war thus developed negatively for the Portuguese from the start.

As it became clear that a better-organized operation was needed in order to liberate, Como Island, the headquarters in Bissau prepared 'Operation Tridente', which was to involve army, naval and aviation elements. The battles that followed were fierce and progress was slow, with the Portuguese suffering heavy casualties to combat, disease, and malnutrition.

After 71 days of bitter fighting, the island was cleared of rebel forces – but at a terrible price. As Jack (John) Cann told me:

'Operation Tridente' and the several islands of Caiar, Como and Catunco, [these efforts] were bound to be obvious to the PAIGC, as one of such size cannot be concealed.

The native gossip channels would have tipped the enemy to the entire operation, so there was no reason to stick around. There were a few insurgents and some shoot-ups in the interior canals, particularly the Canbanca do Brandao, but there were no big prizes to be had.

The Quitafine Peninsula was easier to use as a staging point for operations further inland, as it had closer proximity to Guinea and thus easier access. The three islands were frankly out of the way and were never really in play again.[8]

During the course of 'Operation Tridente' the Portuguese Air Force flew 851 combat sorties. These were partially detailed as follows:

- F-86F Sabres: 73
- T-6 Harvards: 141
- Dornier Do-27: 180
- Auster: 46
- Alouette III Helicopters: 323
- PV-2 Neptunes: 16
- C-47/Douglas Dakotas: 2

This effort was in vain. Barely two months later, the rebels recaptured some of their original positions on the island, in part because the Portuguese Army had to re-deploy forces to fight elsewhere. This time, there was no counterattack: due largely to the PAIGC establishing new important positions in the south of the country, especially on the Cantanhez and Quitafine Peninsulas where considerable contingents of the Portuguese Army at Catió and Bedanda were encircled and put under a siege. As a consequence, Como lost much of its strategic importance.

Besides, in October 1964, the FAP was forced to repatriate all 16 of its F-86Fs based at Bissalanca because of pressure from the United States. By deploying Sabres to Africa for use in counter-insurgency operations against the rebels, Washington maintained that Lisbon

When the end of hostilities did come, there were many residents of Angola and
Mozambique who opposed the change. This pro-Lisbon demonstration took place in
the streets of Lourenço Marques, soon to be renamed Maputo. (Author's collection)

was endangering NATO defences along Europe's Atlantic coast.

Peculiarly, the USA had nothing to say about the deployment of F-84Gs Thunderjets
to Angola.

The eminent French historian René Pélissier should have the last word in introducing this
volume. No other writer in modern times has devoted so much time and effort towards
chronicling Portugal's wars in Africa. And in doing so, he gives us a timely warning:

Truth, he tells us, is at a premium in contemporary as well as historical Portuguese
Africa.

> One needs to tread warily between censorship by the antagonistic parties and a great
> deal of rumour. There are such controversial questions as political support, prison
> camps within and outside Angola, military activities and casualties, to be dealt with.
> Any study of [these African] problems must be an exercise in scepticism: one cannot
> rely entirely on any document, any allegedly dependable informant, and any statement
> by the official information services of one side or the other.

Though the colonial war in Angola had ended, another version of conflict was just starting, that of CIA and South African-backed, ostensibly pro-Western UNITA against the MPLA government, by then, with some clandestine Portuguese assistance, firmly ensconced in Luanda. Washington provided the Stinger missiles that destroyed this Angolan Air Force helicopter in the east of this vast country. (Author's collection)

What then is left from which to assemble the facts? Little that is entirely indisputable; each time one seems to have unearthed an element of truth, some new information comes to light to invalidate it.

He goes on to stress that the researcher's task is a thorny one:

In a Latin country such as Portugal and in a part of Africa like Angola, verbiage proliferates but is rarely applied to the letter. Hence weight will be given to a law, a party programme or a speech only if the author has personally been able to observe that it has had some effect on the ground.

In any case, in a country where it is the exception for anyone, black or white, to speak freely to a foreigner without trying to preach the government or party line, one cannot hope to attain a level of authenticity comparable with that in a country where information is free. So, in good faith but with no illusions as to the paucity of the information available, the reader is offered a middle-of-the-road account of events which later historians with access to the archives will invalidate or confirm ...

PART 1: PORTUGAL'S WARS IN AFRICA

February 4 1961 is commemorated as the 'Day of the Revolution' against Portugal's presence in Africa. There were many uprisings in the five centuries that Portugal had been in Africa, but this insurgency was different. It was far more intense and brutal than anything that had gone before. Large groups of guerrilla fighters entered Northern Angola from the Congo and took the population by complete surprise; the violence that followed was horrendous. Almost overnight, Lisbon was faced with a major war, followed soon afterwards by uprisings in Portuguese Guinea and Mozambique.

Brigadier General W.S. Van der Waals
Portugal's War in Angola 1961-1974

1

Tete Convoy in Mozambique

Notes from a diary, 16/18 February 1973

While Portugal fought its military campaigns in Africa, the town of Tete – a strategic African settlement dominated by a huge suspension bridge across the Zambezi River – came to represent one of the last of the embattled outposts of an Imperial tradition that had lasted half a millennium. When I visited the place in the early 1970s, what was going on in this vast land on the east coast of Africa was a chapter of recent history about to close.

I'd gone through Tete with Michael Knipe –the London *Times*' man in Southern Africa at the time and we were to discover an archetypal Portuguese-style settlement that could be found in many parts of the southern half of the continent. Critical times these were, in what European pundits would term 'Africa's Liberation Wars'.

But for the great Zambezi, Tete could have been mistaken for Luso in Angola or Cacheu in Portuguese Guinea where the first of Prince Henry's navigators made landfall on African soil for fresh water in their bid to discover a sea route to the spice islands of the East.

By the time we arrived, it was clear that the ongoing conflict in the adjoining region had been tough, especially for the hardscrabble black population where, apart from the military, opportunities to earn those few extra escudos were sparse. Almost all of the town's Portuguese civilians had left a year or two before, in part, because normal commercial activity had ended. More likely they'd been intimidated by the war. More often than not, hostilities would start at the edge of town, almost as soon as the sun disappeared over the jungles to the west.

With all the soldiers and military vehicles about, there was no mistaking that armed rebellion was on Tete's doorstep. Worse, nobody in uniform was prepared to say how this complex socio-military conundrum would end.

As hostilities gradually became more intense, mines began to take a bigger toll. There wasn't a day that we didn't spot vehicles towed in from the bush or hauled back to town on low-loaders after they'd been blown up or ambushed. Many more trucks were destroyed by landmines than in enemy ambushes, their cargoes either removed or, when oversized – like mining equipment or industrial plant – abandoned, hopefully to be recovered another day. The rebels would see to it that it rarely was.

Such was the nature of insurgency in this remote corner of tropical Africa that fringed the Indian Ocean, a very different kind of war compared to what was going on just then in South East Asia.

Moving through Mozambique in the late 1960s and early 1970s was always an experience. The region was remote and because of the isolation, there were few independent

In the riverside town of Tete – it lies on the south side of the great Zambezi – just about everything began with the bridge, which led to the Tete Corridor the road north to Malawi. Landmines were a serious problem for us all. (Author's photo)

observers either willing or able to chance their luck in an unforgiving corner of Africa. Communications were invariably a consideration, especially in the interior: most times they simply did not exist. There were phones, but they didn't always work. Faxes and cell phones were not yet on the market. You considered yourself lucky to get a call through to Europe or America once you'd left the comfort of Mozambique's big cities of Beira or Lourenco Marques, though a fat bribe helped if you were prepared to use military equipment.

Getting about was always problematic. You either travelled in convoy or you didn't go anywhere. Between towns of the central regions and the north, that was something that happened perhaps twice a week. Even then, if the guerrillas had been active, delays were commonplace, sometimes as long as a week. Much depended on the competence of local garrison commanders.

Compared to Vietnam, the number of combatants deployed by the Portuguese Armed Forces in Mozambique was modest. Equipment fielded by both sides in this harsh unforgiving African hinterland was not nearly as sophisticated as that deployed in South East Asia by the Americans, or for that matter, by the French before them. In all of Mozambique – a country almost twice the size of California, and curiously, roughly the same elongated shape – there were only a fraction of the number of combat helicopters you were likely to find in a single Vietnamese city like Da Nang or Hue while that war raged.

For the isolated scribe covering the African beat, the crunch centred on the fact that Vietnam was where things happened: South East Asia was constantly in the news. Then as

A Portuguese Army Berliet heavy truck with troops onboard played the role of escort at the front and rear of our columns, with one or two troop carriers taking up positions in-between. (Author's photo)

now, sadly, Africa had already been relegated to backwater status by most European and North American editors

Our road to Tete, overland from South Africa, was circuitous. After crossing the Limpopo River, Knipe and I spent a week in Rhodesia – then also at war. The intention was that he would return to Johannesburg from Mozambique while I kept on heading north. I would travel the length of the Tete Panhandle – first to Malawi and on to Lusaka in Zambia (then another black African country technically at war with the 'White South') my final destination being Mobutu Sese Seko's Zaire, or what had formerly been called the Congo.

But like others on the road, we had to wait for the next convoy and for three or four days, Tete became home. It was a distasteful sojourn in the town's only hotel, the Zambezi, where the plumbing didn't work and meals, such as they were, an unappetizing and often unsanitary grind where you competed as much to catch the eye of the one of a dozen waiters standing around as with the flies on your fork.

There was little to do in that heat that was both soporific and enervating and if you hadn't packed a reasonable supply of books, you were left staring at the walls of your hotel room. Not that it mattered much because there was no air conditioning either. A film or two might have helped, but the only movie house had been shuttered and even if it hadn't been, whatever might have been on offer would have been in Portuguese anyway, and without subtitles.

Most times when we did hit the town – always after dark when a light breeze came off the river – we were left to make our way past a succession of people who seemed to do little more than drink cheap wine, or thugs who would offer us a local girl for the price of a cocktail. The Portuguese military presence was everywhere, the majority in their wavy-coloured battledress who made the best of their off-hours in the torpid, dust-choked streets. Army trucks trailed endless little sandstorms in their wakes as they trundled through town and that didn't help either.

Wrapped around a dirty crossroads on the banks of a the third biggest river on the African continent, Tete could easily have passed for a film set depicting the early years of the great American trek to the west. The only difference was an occasional, modern-looking building and a communications aerial on the tallest hill that overlooked the town. There was nothing to remind us that the settlement was one of the first inland trading posts established by Portuguese mariners who first sailed up this great waterway in their shallow-hulled galliots in the 15th Century.

Much of what happened in Tete centred on the couple of thousand men of the 17th Battalion, as well as the three or four helicopters and ground support squadrons that made up the bulk of the town's defences. Essentially, it was a captive market, for the troops had nowhere else to spend what little they earned.

The colonial gloss and glitter of Lourenço Marques – Maputo today – lay more than 1,000 kilometres to the south.

For those who took that extended overland leg southwards, there were still more military convoys for the first leg of the journey, at least until you reached Beira – Mozambique's second city – as I was able to do on my way back home more than a month later.

There were big plans afoot for Tete, we were told in the first in-house briefing with Tete's military commanders. One of the biggest hydro-electric dams in Africa was being built across a gorge on the Zambezi River, more than 200 kilometres upstream. That construction, we were assured, promised long-term dividends, but as we now know, it was only completed after the war ended. By then the majority of the Portuguese had decamped, bags and baggage, back to the *metrópole*.

At that stage, getting the dam finished on schedule had become a formidable task, especially since it was to be the biggest man-made body of water in Africa, second only to Egypt's Aswan. For their part, the insurgents hurled everything they could muster at both Portuguese civilian and military interests in efforts to halt construction. Along the way, an awful lot of lives were lost.

Twice each day, starting at dawn, lurching open trucks that carried two platoons left Tete to guard the shipments of supplies, men and equipment headed towards the gorge. That was the easy part, because the road was tarred and the threat of mines were minimal. But that did not stop the ambushes, which seemed to keep an intermittent pace with the convoys and would take an almost inevitable daily toll.

The Moatize Junction was a compulsory stop while the road was 'swept' in both directions, for us heading north and for a southbound convoy heading our way. Moatize was then one of the country's major sources of coal and has since become one of the biggest coal mines in Southern Africa. (Author's photo)

Tete's Barracks Square was where all military activities were coordinated by the military. Writing about the place, British writer James McManus recalled that it looked 'absurdly Beau Geste'. From there too, patrols around town would set out before dawn each day and check routes leading in and out for booby traps and mines which, we were to discover, were sometimes responsible for the first casualties of the day.

Security in and around Tete was tight and strangers were invariably regarded with suspicion. We fell in the latter category and it came as no surprise that journalists like Knipe, James McManus and I, though tacitly accepted because we'd made the long haul north, were not made overly welcome. In any conflict, we were already aware, the Fourth Estate is routinely regarded with suspicion and the Portuguese military establishment was no exception.

In my case, I was fortunate because I'd previously covered the war in Angola. Also, I'd been given an informal letter of introduction to the local commander and that opened all the doors. Having experienced combat on the west coast, and then transferred my allegiance temporarily to Mozambique, it didn't take long for me to be accepted as 'one of them'. The trouble was that it invariably happened after the metal cap of the first bottle of Aguardente had landed in the bin.

In spite of the booze and bonhomie, talk about the guerrilla role in the conflict remained guarded, especially in the presence of us scribes. Reports of actions and casualties were a given, but there was never any serious talk about the adversary: it was almost as if the

The consequences of an ambush along that stretch of road a
few weeks earlier. (Photo *Revista da Armada*)

guerrillas didn't exist. Casualty figures were always 'secret' and when there was an 'incident', such discussions in the officers' mess were usually conducted in whispers.

The general approach to the war was different to what you'd find in other conflicts such as in the Congo, Algeria or neighbouring Rhodesia. One got the idea that many Portuguese officers liked to think – and some actually believed – that it was all a rather temporary affair, a bit of trouble with local savages that would soon be over, we were told often enough. The gesture was patronizing and that annoyed because we'd all done time at the sharp end and in this, Mozambique was very different from what I – and others – had already seen in Angola and Portuguese Guinea.

There, at least, the Portuguese Army didn't ignore the threat. Rather, they got to grips with it.

The convoy left Tete at dawn. In a straggling line astern, the trucks rumbled across the river and were halted briefly at what passed for a tollgate at the far end of the bridge.

There were machine-gun emplacements at several points along the structure, some illuminated by a string of searchlights that continually swept across the water below.

One by one, the sleepy-eyed drivers paid the fee and moved the last 20 or 30 kilometres of metalled road to Moatize. There, under military supervision, we would assemble for the

Not all of Mozambique's roads were mined. This stretch leading from Tete towards
Beira was tarred and the occasional ambush was the only concern. (Author's photo)

remainder of the trek to the Malawi border, almost 200 kilometres to the north.

Some of the trucks in our column were bound for Blantyre, the capital of Malawi,
a tiny country that straddled the north-western border with Mozambique. Others were
headed further north, where they would again cross into Mozambique territory and where
hostilities were at their most intense.

The majority of vehicles travelling with us were ten or 12-wheelers, including a number
of low-loaders from Johannesburg factories that hauled freight bound for the Zambian
Copperbelt. The drivers were a motley bunch, mostly professional haulers, some white, the
majority African.

There were few among them who were indifferent to what lay ahead. Their guffaws and
uneasy, conscious swaggering as they gathered in groups prior to us setting out were typical
of travelling groups under strain. They'd all survive, they confidently told each other and
they'd smile and nod their heads. What a way to earn a living, one of them chuckled.

There were many opinions about what lay ahead, as might have been expected in an
area where there were landmines buried in the soft, gravel-topped laterite shoulders along
the route and where Portuguese and insurgent forces had been making almost daily contact
for almost a decade of war. The enemy was out there, waiting, the drivers would tell each
other. Then the banter would start again: who would drive behind whom, which drivers
were considered lucky or had experienced this kind of thing before and had come out
unscathed. Anybody who had done six or eight trips across this narrow strip of no-man's-

land without being hurt automatically earned great respect from his colleagues; he was the man to watch, they'd say quietly among themselves.

Somebody pulled out a bottle of South African brandy and everybody took a swig. A few Portuguese soldiers nearby barely noticed, and if they did, they said nothing. There would be no policing on this stretch of road.

There were many views about what lay ahead. Quite a few of the drivers had been shot at or mortared and just about everybody knew somebody who'd been hurt. Not too many killed, it seemed.

'One man he die last week...Mulatto...his truck he go...boom...very big mine!'

That came from a swarthy trucker from Madeira. His observation was lost on many because of his poor English and nobody made any comment. Most of the drivers continued doing what they'd been busy with or looked deep into their cups or tin mugs. Other drivers kept drinking, even though the sun had barely clipped the thorn and baobab trees clustered to the east beyond the railway station and coal dump at Moatize.

The man who spoke had a lot to say during the three-day convoy run. He'd done the trip often enough he told us, and made the point that he preferred to travel somewhere towards the rear of the column.

'Better others hit the *minas*,' he'd quietly comment, going colloquial when nobody else was listening. All we knew about him was that he was bound for a settlement in the interior which had been attacked often enough in the past. His cargo was his own business and he said so; that security thing again.

Apart from two buses packed with Africans on their way home from South African gold mines, there were about 35 trucks assembled at Moatize. Some were taking cargoes through to Zaire and sported Rhodesian plates. These would be replaced by Zambian tags for the final leg of the journey.

There were two private vehicles on the road with them, our Land Rover that had Dutch registration, as well as a medium-sized English car on its way to Zambia. The driver, a youngster from York was under contract on one of the copper mines and had returned from long leave in Britain with his vehicle. He'd been forced to head east and cross at Tete after waiting for six days at the Kasangula Ferry in Botswana; he said he'd rather risk landmines and ambushes six hundred miles to the east to taking his chances with President Kaunda's undisciplined Zambian Army in an unstable hinterland where South African forces regularly intruded.

He'd made that choice after reports had come across the river of drunken soldiers having fired on another civilian car which had tried to cross southwards.

A woman travelling as a passenger had been wounded ...

Portuguese bureaucracy and a tendentiously aggressive enemy eroded our schedules from the start. We were told the journey would take eight hours. It lasted three days. On that first morning, we were all left standing in the sapping heat of the Zambezi Valley for four hours

A squad of Portuguese Army sappers sweep the road for landmines. (Author's photo)

before we eventually pulled out.

An hour before leaving, a bunch of civilian officials – they were in khaki and displayed rank – approached the convoy. The bureaucracy that followed quickly became tiresome. Names were checked against lists, vehicles against registration plates, passports perused, cargoes vetted, instructions issued and questions asked. Weapons, tape recorders or radio equipment?

'Anybody with binoculars?' somebody queried. There was no reaction, even though one of the drivers sported a 400 mm tele-lens for his Nikon camera.

Finally the civilians were required to sign a document, in triplicate, which exonerated the Lisbon Government against claims in the event of any kind of military action. The final paragraph, in good English, indemnified Lisbon against losses that might be inflicted on us by the Portuguese army and air force.

We signed...anything to avoid delay.

At this stage Erico Chagas, a young Portuguese army lieutenant introduced himself. He'd been watching us from a distance and only then did we understand why. He needed to get to Munacama, he told us. He would travel with us, admitting that the Land Rover offered the most comfort. There was no question of him asking permission: it was already a fait accompli.

Young Chagas was to join his unit, about 30 minutes by road from Zobue, one of our destinations in the north. Born in the Mozambique capital and educated in South Africa, he spoke good English. We gathered that he'd been fighting for two years and, on the face of it, was clearly professional in his approach to all things military; the young man was tough

Soviet anti-personnel mines such as this one were a constant worry for those of us in the convoy. They were often laid at random, right alongside the road at likely stopping points and casualties sometimes resulted. (Author's collection)

and seasoned both by Africa and by conflict. As we were to discover later, Chagas liked to say that he'd seen and done it all.

We were happy to have him onboard: with a Portuguese Army lieutenant in our vehicle, we'd be spared further inspection.

The young officer was casual about most things, including the prospect of combat. It helped that he was as familiar with the bush as his native trackers. As to being ambushed while travelling in convoy, he was dismissive. Of course we'll be ambushed, he declared impassively, 'but the bastards never come very close...much of it is just noise'.

'Mines, yes! But ambushes...ha!'

His comments were derisory, and sometimes contentious. The *terroristas,* as he called them, rarely caused any real damage, he said. 'They don't aim, so the shots are almost always high. And anyway, he suggested, it is old law. Unless someone is firing specifically at you, chances are that somebody else will be hit ... '

He was explicit that we travel towards the rear of the column. He pointed at the truck belonging to the Maderian. 'We stay behind him. He knows the tricks.' The man from Maderia had already spaced himself well down the line. It was his contention, we learned, that the more wheels that passed over the track before us, the better. 'Let others take chances,' he reckoned.

More instructions were issued by our escorts, who had called us all together. Chagas translated.

We were to stay between 50 and 100 meters behind the next vehicle. If the truck ahead of you was hit, the explosion shouldn't affect the truck immediately behind, though sometimes a front and not real wheel detonated a mine, which often enough caused casualties among those in the cab. The military spokesman stressed that each vehicle should follow exactly in the tracks directly ahead; as he said, slowly and distinctly 'not to the right of it and not to the left, but *on* the tracks of those who have gone before.'

Because of the dust, this might sometimes be difficult, one of the other officers conceded.

Should one of the vehicles be blown up, it then became the responsibility of the troops escorting the column to search for more landmines, because they were rarely laid singly. And when that happened, he declared, nobody was to exit his vehicle and move about.

'There are landmines for trucks,' the officer declared, with Chagas keeping pace with a good translation, 'and there are landmines for people. Consequently when the terrorists lay a bomb for a vehicle, they hope that some inquisitive person might get out and walk about to find out what was causing the hold-up'. That had happened often enough before and there had been casualties, he disclosed.

By now some of the Rhodesian drivers had edged closer to better hear Chagas' translation: few had more than a basic understanding of the language.

The officer continued: 'Remember all of you, and this is important. With landmines, all casualties are serious'. He added that it often meant calling for a helicopter to evacuate the victim...'but there are times when there are no helicopters available...so the man can die.'

He told us that while there would be several officers travelling as passengers to re-join their units up-country, the convoy would be in charge of a sergeant, a wiry, intense little man whom he brought forward and introduced to the gathering.

'His name is Vieira. Officially it is Sergeant Vieira and he knows this business very well. When he tells you to do something, you listen. You do not argue, even if you think he might be wrong. Follow his instructions carefully and without delay because there are sometimes very good reasons for doing things in a hurry.

'This is a war, people, not a tourist jaunt and this man will lead you all through to the other side...*Boa sorte*!'

The most impassive of the drivers gathered around in Moatize that morning were the black Rhodesians. They'd heard the same story often enough, both prior to hostilities and now that conflict had enveloped much of the region.

We got to know some of them in the days that followed and they were a resolute bunch. Riding shotgun was their way of putting bread on the table and though they weren't happy with the risk, they didn't complain. We were to discover that there were moments when they possibly knew the ropes a little better than their youthful Portuguese Army escorts.

Often deployed by insurgent groups early on in this guerrilla war was what the Chinese had originally labelled the 'box mine'. Functionary and primitive, it comprised a stock of gelignite or TNT inside a wooden box (easily constructed in a forest environment) with a simple pressure-triggered detonator attached to the lid. Step on the box or drive a vehicle over it, and boom! (Author's photo)

Some had lost colleagues on this road and each one was out to ensure that mistakes of the past wouldn't be repeated. Their heavy vehicles, many with their company names painted on them – Swifts, Watson's Transport, United Transport, Heins and others – stood at the vanguard of the procession.

A 10-ton Albion truck from United Transport's Malawi office headed the civilian column. The driver said it was carrying Caterpillar spares and was headed for Zaire. He'd travelled the route for almost two years, he disclosed and for reasons of his own, he preferred to travel right up front.

By 10 that morning, the first army trucks that would provide our escort rumbled past. It was a hefty Berliet, heavily sandbagged around the driver's cab. Because the hood had been removed, we could see more sandbags fitted around the wheel cavities.

We only learnt later that Portuguese convoys rarely moved about with their hoods intact. Too many troops had been decapitated by these steel sheets that were sometimes blown sideways. It stayed that way until this rough and ready antidote was semi-officially implemented.

A short while afterward, another squad of troops arrived, all in regulation camouflage uniforms. Each was armed with Heckler and Koch G-3s, standard issue in Lisbon's African war zones and most times casually slung over their shoulders. There were also some MG-

Standard Portuguese Army Unimog troop carrier. The soldiers sat facing
outwards so that they could retaliate when attacked. (Author's photo)

42 LMGs around. A few more troops had mortar tubes, a bazooka or two and here and
there, bundles of shells neatly slotted into canvas carrying bags that they humped over their
shoulder like back-packs. Just about everybody had additional belts strapped onto their
webbing with grenades and extra ammunition.

The newcomers seemed a lively, animated lot, though there were those among them
who were clearly nervous; they stayed that way until they got into the swing of things. One
or two looked as if they still had a couple of years to go to make 18, never mind the ripe old
age of 20.

The unit sergeant-in-charge – he was also to take his orders from Vieira – was 22 and
had already been in Africa for two years. Over a couple of drinks on the second night out
he told us that in a stupid patriotic moment he'd voluntarily cut short his university studies
to fight but just then, couldn't wait to get home.

A short while later more army trucks roared past and pulled up nearby. An officer
disembarked and barking into a walkie-talkie gave somebody at the other end a string of
orders. We were ready to move, said Chagas.

The column rolled forward, a sandbagged Berliet in the van. One of the Unimog troop
carriers moved into position towards the middle of the convoy, about five vehicles ahead
of us. Its soldiers were clustered around a heavy machine-gun mounted on a fixed tripod

A Soviet TM-46 totally destroyed this army truck. (Author's photo)

on the back. An imposing width of steel plating swung about as the weapon rotated on its pivot. Moments later there was a clicking of bolts down the line as soldiers tested their weapons.

With another Berliet bringing up the rear, we were relieved to be on the move, but it was a tedious process, covering perhaps 20 kilometres that first day. Almost from the start, there was evidence of conflict in the area to the north of Moatize.

Barely five minutes from the railhead, our cherished tarred road ended abruptly, making for a smooth transition on a relatively level surface to rattling corrugations and potholes that might have swallowed a goat. Once on the dirt, huge swathes of dust enveloped just about everything – trucks, soldiers, civilian cars and their passengers, up our noses, into our ears and across the windscreen that needed to be wiped every ten minutes or so.

The 'brown-out' seemed to be suspended above ground for the duration and in that heat, thirst became our most constant companion.

Minutes later we passed an abandoned, broken-down villa, its faded, off-white walls pock-marked by shell holes and splinters of who knows how many actions. It was a scene symptomatic of all of Portugal's wars in Africa and is still the kind of scenario you're likely to see these days on CNN in news reports on rural Afghanistan.

A significant difference between rural Africa and Asia was that the bush around us was a spurge of tropical overgrowth that sometimes hung over the road for kilometres at a stretch. It was so thick that the guerrillas might easily have taken up their positions within touching distance of our vehicles and we probably wouldn't have known the difference.

Minutes later, another building came into view, also partly blown apart. Chagas

though obviously it had happened.

One area, near a bridge that had been partly demolished by FRELIMO guerrillas, provided a few answers. The remains of a burnt-out truck – its cab ripped apart by what must have been an awesome blast – lay on its side alongside the road. Alongside the dusty track – yards away – were the wrappings of a bunch of army field dressings, together with empty plastic plasma bottles and wadding. Some of it was tinged black with coagulated blood ... there were flies everywhere.

The dressings were relatively fresh, which suggested that it might all have happened a day or two before, probably on the southbound convoy and certainly before the last rains, which would have washed away all this evidence.

The next time we stopped, one of the troops told us what had happened. He'd been on that southbound convoy and had been ordered by his lieutenant to join us on the way north again, in part because it was his job to search for mines. He explained that a black Rhodesian driver working for a transport company out of Salisbury had been caught in the blast. His legs were badly mutilated and he had large gashes in the head and arms. Because he was losing blood, they radioed to base for instructions. Fortunately the air force had one of its gunships deployed in the area and they pulled him back to Tete. The driver lived, we heard later, but he went on to lose a leg.

Noteworthy, the soldier said, was that within a couple of hundred yards of the incident, several dozen more landmines were uncovered in an operation that involved dozens of soldiers and took more than a day. The bombs were mostly anti-personnel, but there were no more casualties. 'Not that time,' he smiled. The truck had toppled over onto its side after two more TM-46s had been detonated *in situ* during that operation.

Then for us, on this hot February morning, the inevitable happened. Quite suddenly, we were involved in an event that might have had serious consequences for one or more of the vehicles if a Portuguese Army scout, perched precariously on the roof of the lead French Berliet, hadn't spotted something on the road ahead.

There were human tracks in the road that had caught his attention, we heard afterwards, and that in an area where there hadn't been anybody living for who knows how long.

Having stopped the column and dismounted, the soldier moved slowly ahead, as close to the edge of the road as the bush would allow in case anti-personnel bombs or booby traps had been laid. That was when he spotted wires. Moments later, a volley of shots rang out from a gully on the far side of the convoy: it was automatic fire and it came in bursts.

For three of us in the Land Rover, squeezed as low onto the floorboards as our bulk would allow, the conflict had suddenly become interesting. None of us had any idea where the shooting was coming from or who might have been the target. Seconds later the rattle of more shots rang out from another position towards the rear. This was what the Portuguese drivers had earlier referred to as *Flagelacau,* a whipping burst of gunfire and a quick getaway.

As the firing continued, our military escort retaliated with enthusiasm. From both

Landmines were a perennial problem for government security forces. The devices were brought in from Tanzania and often carried overland – sometimes hundreds of kilometres - on the backs of civilians who were opposed to colonial rule. (Author's collection)

ends of the convoy they ripped off a stream of tracers in a broad arc across the bush. The heavy machinegun on the Unimog followed, together with several dull mortar plops. Then, every few minutes, three or four more ...

Though we'd been ordered to stay put, it didn't take us long to emerge from our cramped vehicle and we found ourselves close enough to watch a clutch of detonations a few hundred yards away in some heavily foliaged jungle country. By then tracer fire had already ignited several fires in the dry brush and within minutes the entire area was enveloped in smoke.

Sergeant Vieira, our youthful sergeant meanwhile moved through the periphery shouting instructions. He ordered a squad of black soldiers to take up positions along the length of the column; they were to lie prone in the bush, he told them and face the direction from which the first shots had been fired, Lt Chagas explained.

'*Terroristas*', he muttered dismissively.

Several of the troops took their chances and opted to cross stretches of gravel that hadn't been cleared in search of better vantage points.

Because of the problems ahead and the uncertainty of the strength of the guerrilla force, the next hour or two saw a lot of movement up and down the length of the column. There was so much movement along the road that some of the troops barely bothered with following in each others' tracks. The mine threat had become secondary, though Chagas reckoned that some had almost certainly been laid in the area.

One of the officers from the lead Berliet came down the line and indicated to our lieutenant that the insurgents had laid an as-yet undetermined minefield ahead, which was when we were ordered to get back in our vehicle and stay put. The entire area first had to be cleared, he explained. Worse, it could take the rest of the morning.

There were several more bursts of automatic fire from the insurgents. Then they fired several clutches of mortars which usually landed way off target behind us. It had taken us almost half a day to get this far, but by then we'd almost become accustomed to the sound of gunfire, especially since enemy volleys would be answered with enthusiasm from our lines.

The army eventually cleared the minefield, though it took hours longer than anticipated. A total of 14 mines, two round metal TM-46s and a dozen anti-personal bombs were detected and detonated. There were no casualties – on either side in all probability – because by now I'd set no great store in the ability of the troops guarding us. It was a job they had to do, but they displayed little relish.

For our part, we gambled on the notoriously bad marksmanship of the enemy.

While Lieutenant Chagas viewed most of what was going on around with what appeared to be an amused detachment, his approach was very different when we moved a few paces from the vehicle. It didn't matter that that was our only option in heat that had become

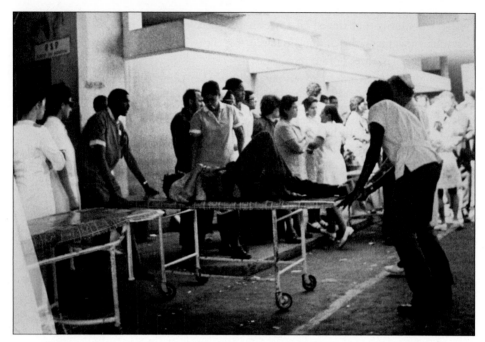

Many casualties resulted during the course of these upheavals, both to white and black citizens of Mozambique. (Courtesy The South African Argus Group of Newspapers)

crippling. When we found the shade of a large fever tree preferable to the Land Rover, he marched briskly across to where we had taken up station.

'You are taking chances,' he said sternly. 'Unnecessary chances ... this area hasn't been cleared ... and we don't know where *they* are.' We had no option but to return to the truck.

Then he surprised us all by going off towards the head of the column, in a huff, we thought. He returned with a smile on his face, telling us that he'd asked permission for me to come forward so that I could watch the demolition process. I was the only news gatherer in the group, so the request made sense, he reckoned. Moreover, I'd watch the goings-on from the gun platform of the lead Berliet, he stated. Apparently he'd explained to the lead commander that I'd covered the Angolan War and that I wanted to 'compare notes'. I grabbed my Nikons.

The system that the Portuguese Armed Forces employed to clear mines was basic, though clearly not without risk. A number of trained soldiers – black and white – would spend several minutes assessing the situation on the road ahead. If they felt that the surface might conceal mines, a stick of four would disembark and walk slowly ahead, using their steel-tipped wooden lances about the length of a golf club to probe the soil. It was soft, recently-disturbed soil that would customarily indicate mines.

The lances were named *picas*, after the Iberian bullfight probe, a curious anomaly at a time when there were any number of electronic mine detecting devices available. Yet, I was to see that throughout all of Lisbon's conflicts in Africa, these primitive handheld staffs were always regarded the most reliable means of detecting these insidious weapons that remain as much of a threat in the New Millennium in some parts of the globe as they were 30 or 40 years ago.

It was interesting that the convoy had onboard a variety of electronic gear for the purpose, all with NATO designations. But this equipment was rarely unpacked from their bulky, suitcase-sized containers, one of the officers explained, because they were all but useless along roads where huge amounts of metal debris lay about. That included cans, tin foil, spent cartridge cases, spare parts and the rest – all discarded over the years by minor armies of transients like us.

It took our group about 90 minutes to find seven mines; a large anti-tank bomb surrounded by six APs. All were PMD-6 antipersonnel mines; rudimentary pressure-activated blast devices and each in its own little wooden box.

We were aware that the PMD-6 had already been widely used in Cambodia, but because of Mozambique's vast distances, the insurgents had taken to manufacturing some of these devices themselves. The forest provided the wood, while explosives and detonators were brought into the war zones from Tanzania on peoples' backs.

Not all landmines deployed by the guerrillas were primitive. The insurgents soon notched up significant losses among Government troops by using larger TM-57 anti-tank mines. Also deployed were PMN 'Black Widow' mines and the deadly POM-Z, both anti-personnel devices already well blooded in Vietnam.

In the final stages of these heady African colonial conflicts – as in Rhodesia and South West Africa afterwards – RPG-7s had begun to supersede the more ubiquitous RPG-2s

Midday brought up the short distance to the Portuguese Army para-commando camp at Muxoxo.

For at least an hour before we reached the base, the unit's pair of helicopters provided air cover against further insurgent forays. Camouflaged Alouette gunships would move at a fair pace above the bush, sweeping low and often doubling back to previous sites, their heavy machine-guns strafing suspect positions. The pilots would sometimes wave as they passed.

Muxoxo offered few surprises. The dilapidated building at its centre had once been a farmhouse and was surrounded by neat rows of army tents that housed the garrison. We welcomed the opportunity to buy warm Manica beer at five times the going rate in Lourenco Marques. In the milieu of the Portuguese shopkeeper in Africa, passing trade has always been lucrative.

The men at the camp had a fairly large area to patrol, at least by today's counter-insurgency standards. They were backed by their handful of helicopters which air-lifted small units to wherever intelligence reports indicated the guerrillas might be working, or possibly concentrating assets. The unit averaged about four operations a week, mostly when road convoys were expected.

Muxoxo was strategically placed and responsible for security on that section of the rail link between Moatize and Caldas Xavier and these activities often took heli-borne sorties long distances towards the south-east. These were short, swift 'search and destroy' hits which sometimes offered unexpected surprises.

During our brief stay, two captured FRELIMO insurgents were brought in. One was an old man hardly able to walk, obviously malnourished and definitely no belligerent. Yet both admitted they'd been linked to a rebel sabotage unit that had been operating near the rail town of Goa. They had been taken while preparing food for their compatriots in the bush, men, whom they admitted, had been responsible for a spate of attacks on the railroad which winds its way to Beira at the coast.

Ultimately, it had been a squad of Portugal's crack *Comandos Africanos* that had scored and subsequently dealt with a larger group of insurgents that had been spreading mines about in the region. Several hundred anti-personnel mines were seized but curiously, not a single anti-tank.

The two captives were first interrogated then fed. More interrogation followed before they were flown to Tete for a more professional session, after which they would probably be transferred to one of the prison camps in the south, Chagas reckoned. After doing some independent news gathering of his own, the lieutenant told us that the men would probably be of some use to the security forces.

'They claim they were shanghaied. Had they offered any resistance they said they would have been shot,' he explained. 'Trouble is' he added, 'they all claim that ... but the truth is, they probably would have been killed had they not cooperated ... '

It was late afternoon when we finally made contact with the southbound convoy at the road junction to Xavier Caldas. The crossroads was marked by a primitive wooden signpost on which none of the directions were discernible.

We were again warned again that the area had not been cleared of mines and that we should be circumspect. Spent cartridge cases littered the area and its approaches.

While approaching the intersection, we'd crossed a small river which had been prominently signposted in Portuguese: *Zona Armadilhada*: *Minefield*, it read, in both languages.

This deterrent was Portuguese and had been laid in a bid to prevent the guerrillas from setting charges at the base of the bridge and possibly destroying it. As somebody mentioned, the measure was decidedly two-edged since it also prevented anybody travelling in our convoy from getting water at a time when stocks were getting low. Water shortages onboard the buses, we knew, was already critical, especially among the children.

The oppressive heat which had followed us across Africa from the Zambezi Valley hardly made matters any easier. Even so, a handful of passengers did make an effort. In a small column some of the men and boys traipsed single file down a path towards the river, each one stepping carefully in the imprint of the man directly ahead.

Temporary helicopter base in the bush, something that the South Africans were to emulate in their own guerrilla struggles in South West Africa soon afterwards. (Author's collection)

One of the older soldiers later told us that the week before, a civilian had tripped a mine. He hadn't been killed, but it did underscore some of the privations that those who had few resources faced when moving across this corner of East Africa.

'He needed water very badly – not only for himself, but also for his family. So he set out on his own in spite of warnings from the troops. As he stepped near the water his foot triggered something that shot a small mine about six feet into the air.' It was later determined that the device was similar to the notorious South East Asian 'S mine', or what the Americans liked to call the 'Bouncing Betty'. Lisbon's opponents used these munitions to considerable effect throughout their colonial conflicts.

Apparently, the man who had tripped the mine while going for water was lucky that eventful day. The mine detonated almost within touching distance of where he stood, but it was apparently facing the wrong way. The victim was concussed by the blast, but not a single shard of shrapnel penetrated his skin.

We waited an hour for the oncoming convoy to arrive. From the start we could see that conditions were much harder in their sector than in ours. A number of times we heard detonations in the distance. Gradually distances shortened.

Chagas came back not long afterwards to tell us that the approaching column had taken a casualty. He wasn't specific, but said something about a mine. Moments later an evacuation helicopter veered over our heads and prepared to land in open ground near the crossroads. Ours was the first convoy the pilot reached and he had no way of knowing which of the two columns had triggered the bomb.

Having established that much, the chopper lifted off again, leaving a dense cloud of dust whipped up by its rotors. We watched as the helicopter sped northwards barely a yard above the tree-tops. A minute or two later he was on his way back to base, this time at a higher altitude and making directly for Tete Military Hospital.

When the oncoming convoy eventually did reach us, the word went out that a man had been killed. He'd been second in the line in the unit's main *pica* squad, his point man having apparently stepped over an anti-personnel mine. The soldier behind was not so lucky and he took the full impact of the blast.

Three other members of the *pica* squad were lightly wounded but they were able to continue with their duties even though their leader was limping badly from a large cut on his thigh. In Vietnam, a wound like that would have meant immediate evacuation to the base hospital. With the Lisbon's Army in Africa, such matters were accepted in the line of duty.

Portuguese troops weren't awarded Lisbon's version of the Purple Heart because there wasn't one.

We travelled halfway through the night to reach Mussacauna. The road had been cleared by the oncoming convoy and it was essential to cover the prodded ground as quickly as possible before the insurgents laid more nines. The same held for the convoy that passed us and was headed in the opposite direction. They'd want to cover as much ground that we'd cleared before more mines were laid.

But we weren't quite fast enough. A heavy Monsoon-like downpour provided the drivers with the almost impossible task of following exactly in the tracks of the vehicles ahead and within an hour, two more vehicles were blasted. These were heavy trucks, one from Johannesburg, the other from Salisbury and both carried cargoes destined for the mines in Zambia. What made it ironic was that the insurgent groups who'd laid the mines were actually using Zambia as a base. The mines that had destroyed the trucks had actually originated from there. Now these same guerrillas were helping to disrupt the economy of one of their allies ...

There were no more incidents that night. The mines had been detonated by the back wheels of both trucks, giving credence to reports that the insurgents where using a more sophisticated type of landmine that had recently been brought in from South East Asia following the de-escalation of American military involvement there. Only much later were we to learn that these were ratchet mines.

A curious name, ratchet mines used by the Viet Cong were usually set to detonate after a pre-determined number of wheels had passed; sometimes 10 or 12, often double that. The fact that the trucks involved were well down the column when they were blasted, underscored this development. It could have been us.

One of the vehicles was travelling in our column barely 100 yards ahead of where we kept our position in the column. That happened about a mile out of the village of Capirizanje,

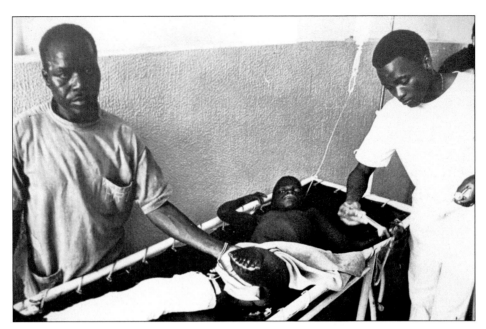

It was the innocents who suffered the most from anti-personnel mines laid near populated areas. This youngster had just emerged from surgery in a Mozambique hospital after he had trod on a mine and the blast removed most of his leg. (Author's photo)

our next stop on the long road north. A heavy downpour was pelting down when the blast ripped through one of the open windows of the Land Rover and the column halted.

For a long time we sat in silence, accepting that it would have been foolish to get out and see what was happening. Only when the convoy started to move again and we carefully followed neat rows of new tracks created through the bush around the stranded vehicle, could we see that a set of back wheels on one of the low-loaders from South Africa had been shredded.

Not long afterwards we passed a quarry alongside the road, illuminated by lightning as we passed. It was one of those African thunderstorms for which the Zambezi Valley is known, the water sometimes coming down in spurts big enough to fill a bucket overnight. Three or four flashes of lightning told us that the area had long ago been abandoned. Some of the trolleys that had probably been part of the facility lay on their sides. A few yards away, a wheelbarrow without its wheel rested upside down in the mud, more reminders of a conflict that had already spanned half a generation.

Mussacuana arrived unheralded. We'd climbed steadily in the mud and muck and suddenly, just before midnight, there were lights ahead. The rain had lifted minutes before and as happens so often in a region only a few hundred miles from the Indian Ocean, the settlement in the mountains above Capirizanje lay swathed in mist. The ground was sodden, for it had poured here as well.

A soldier on guard in an improvised machine-gun turret shouted a greeting. We replied in English and he turned his back on us.

At least the beer would be cold ...

3

A Bitter War in Angola

'The Portuguese Forces (in Africa) are to be congratulated, for the enemy whom it is their mission to destroy is a worthy adversary. Its commanders are well versed in guerrilla warfare, and they use to best advantage a difficult terrain [which] they know like the back of their hands'

Diario de Noticias (Lisbon)

On my flight in 1968 from the Angolan capital of Luanda to the Dembos – a vast expanse of jungle stretching all the way north to the Congolese frontier – we were taken in by a Portuguese Air Force Noratlas freighter. The plane swung inland from the sea minutes after take-off from the city's Presidente Craveiro Lopes Airport and we levelled off at about 600 feet. The road was apparently too precarious for such a long ride, we were told.[1]

Although we were later to traverse great distances in road convoys and exposed to our share of snipers and mines, I never ceased to marvel at the way in which the pilots took these lumbering transports into tiny bush air-strips which sometimes hardly looked capable of accommodating a Piper Cub. This was a war of improvisation, we soon discovered, and even though Portugal was one of the poorest of Western countries with a population of only nine million, the nation seemed to manage very well.

We found it interesting that the Nord Aviation 2501 supply planes – similar in construction to the Fairchild C-82 and C-119, came from France, a nation ostensibly opposed to Portugal's military role in Africa. They were originally part of a NATO arms deal that included several dozen Alouette helicopters which, converted into gunships, ultimately ended up dispatching almost as many black revolutionaries as Portuguese soldiers dealt with on the ground. This was a significant development, contrary to all that France was supposed to stand for, since Paris had recently divested itself of a score of its African colonies.

The popular call from the Elysées at the time was emotive: 'France and Francophone Africa are one,' de Gaulle had said. But such sentiment didn't appear to extend to killing machines like helicopter gunships or Mirage fighter-bombers that France supplied to the apartheid government in South Africa.

As with the Alouettes (of which Pretoria had scores, later supplemented by dozens of Puma helicopters) all were operationally deployed against dissident black people.[2]

Angola at the end of the war in 1974. Many of the place names were
changed by Luanda's new revolutionary MPLA government.

In the early morning haze, the Angolan capital disappeared fast behind us. Coastal swamplands and civilization gave way rapidly to uneven, triple-canopied jungle below. We continued at almost tree-top level for five minutes before the plane lifted slowly for a row of mountains to the north.

Occasionally, a tall palm broke through the green, felt-like foliage. For some minutes our plane flew perilously close to these forest giants. There were moments when it almost felt that we might be able to put out our hands and touch them.

We were barely ten minutes out of Luanda when the four paratroopers on board started preparations for a supply drop.

'Enemy so close to Luanda?' I asked through the intercom.

Captain Moutinho, our pilot, shrugged. 'We have come a long way since the war started seven years ago. But we still have our problems'. Our target was Quicabo, a Portuguese military post in the mountains north of Luanda, I'd been told in the pre-flight briefing back in the capital.

Below us the terrain had suddenly become rocky. The jungle was broken by blue-gray fingers of granite which reached out hundreds of feet into the air. Silent and erect, they were mute sentinels to the insurgency being fought around them. For the guerrillas, I was to learn later, these rocks offered excellent vantage points. What a pity, were my thoughts, that it was ravaged by war.

'The area below is thick with *terroristas*', Captain Moutinho said, turning away from his controls. 'This is the notorious sector you have heard so much about, the Dembos. It starts here, 50 miles north of the capital ... like Vietnam, heh?'

Lights flashed on the instrument panel indicating that the paras in the rear were ready. Each of the four men wore a harness with a chute, a safety precaution, one of them explained. It had happened before, he said, and though the crew had seen the man's parachute open, he was never to be seen again. With the rear doors open, the roar of twin engines made speech difficult.

The captain explained that seven crates would be dropped onto Quicabo; two during the first couple of passes and three the final time round. The last drop would be difficult because by then the insurgents might have the drop on them and it was not unusual to return to base with holes in the fuselage. But they had their orders, the captain said, because the consignment contained the camp's fresh provisions for two or three days, additional medical supplies as well as the mail.

'The mail, that's the real priority and it's the first thing that goes out that cargo door in the rear. We cannot afford to make a mistake with that lot. It's more important than everything else in this plane—including ourselves', Moutinho added. He sported a wicked little half-smile as he spoke, but the man was deadly serious.

'Our approach height will be around 500 feet, but this varies because the camp is small and, as you can see ... the mountains. That gives us almost no opportunity to manoeuvre.'

We had been told back in Luanda that in this sector, most fresh supplies were dropped by air. The roads were notoriously bad and the guerrillas active. It sometimes took a convoy as much as a day to cover a 30-mile stretch and in the rainy season, it could take twice that. Convoys were often attacked four or five times in a single outward journey and there were always casualties, which made work for the helicopters.

The return trip was even worse. The enemy had observed trucks heading north and were ready for them on their return.

'It's a bad war', the pilot commented. 'All this business to drop a few packages on a camp ... we stick our neck out every time ... you will see for yourself.'

The captain was a veteran of the early days of Portugal's war in Angola. He had also flown American-built F-86 jets for two years in Guinea further up in West Africa where his country was involved in a second war. I was to learn some years later that he eventually ended up at the controls of a DC-6 in Mozambique, but for now, he'd only recently been transferred to transport command and hated it. 'Now I drive a taxi in the air', he scoffed.

The Noratlas dipped to port to avoid a row of granite peaks ahead as Quicabo stood out sharply on the verdant slopes. The base looked as if it was perched on an ochre-coloured mine-dump.

'You can't miss that kind of target', the pilot shouted into his mike.

'What if something goes wrong?'

'Don't even think about it ... perhaps one of the Alouettes will reach us before they do ... '

Both the pilot and the co-pilot were armed with service revolvers and bush-knives—one strapped under each armpit in specially-adapted camouflage service vests that Portuguese airmen donned while on operational duties in Africa. The handguns were American: Smith and Wesson .38 calibre snubbies and were generally regarded as little more than a token protective measure.

Meantime, the military post loomed up ahead and we were going in fast as well as losing altitude. For a moment or two the jungle seemed ominously close. Captain Moutinho sounded a buzzer and the drop began.

Three times the Noratlas circled the camp. It seemed as if all 200 beleaguered men below had turned out to watch. A group near the perimeter waved.

During the twists, turns and directional changes that followed, mountainside slopes sometimes slipped by only yards from our bulky wingtips. At times, granite peaks towered above us as we swung up and around to prepare for another approach. Two of the men on board became sick from the gyrations.

'We had it easy on that run', the pilot said to us after the drop and we'd settled back. He had turned the plane around and we were heading north again. 'It's much worse when the slopes around the camp are covered in low cloud. He called the Angolan mountain mist *cassimbo*, a native Bakongo name that had been adopted by the Portuguese.

He intimated that they sometimes had guerrillas firing at them from some of the high points around the base during their approach runs. According to the co-pilot, the conditions that day were the best they'd seen for weeks.

Fifteen minutes later the transport plane landed on the long uneven gravel airstrip at Santa Eulalia. We had arrived at Comsec D—centre-point of the Portuguese counter-guerrilla campaign in northern Angola.

Santa Eulalia, our destination and effectively, the operations center of Sector D, lay about half an hour's flying time from Luanda.

Once on the ground we found ourselves in a fairly substantial military base that had been a hilltop settlement before the war. Apart from a fairly large African compound around the base, the 'town' was complete with its local government functionary or *Chefe de Posto* and a trading store. The entire panoply was dominated by the Catholic church.

The plane was met by a delegation of uniformed types and we were led to a row of prefabricated bungalows in the middle of the camp. This was military headquarters to Brigadier Martins Soares and his six staff officers, almost all still in their early twenties.

There was garbage lying about everywhere outside and the Brigadier apologized for the filth. The place had just recently been recaptured from the rebels, he told us, and the rebels had used the church as a barracks for their soldiers. There had been other changes since the Portuguese Army had retaken the town.

Santa Eulalia was surrounded by a double barbed-wire fence more than eight feet high. Arc-lamps with protective wire covers punctuated the perimeter every dozen yards or so. Machine-gun turrets at six or seven vantage points stood out sharply against the jungle. With squat brown buildings in the middle, the place looked like one of those army camps built round Kuala Lumpur during Britain's Malayan Emergency in the 1960s.

The headquarters and its garrison of 300 on the edge of the village was the stock pattern of most Portuguese Army camps in Angola. Built in 1961, soon after the first wave of attacks swept in from the two neighbouring Congos, the Portuguese had managed to stand their ground for a while, but sheer numbers eventually forced them to pull back to Luanda. All that had taken place barely a year after the two countries had been granted independence, the one from Belgium and Congo-Brazzaville from France.

There were other similarities to the earlier conflict in South Asia. An elaborate system of bunkers and tunnels wound past the command post, all the way to a variety of outer defenses. If the camp was attacked, my escort explained, it was easy to send reinforcements to any position if defenses needed to be bolstered. The youngster was an *Alfares*, in the Portuguese Army, a rank roughly equivalent to that of a subaltern in the British Army, or a Lieutenant JG in the United States.

Because of enemy snipers – there were sometimes quite a few of them, the young officer explained – he and his colleagues were able to move in comparative safety between the central control position and any other building in the camp, including the hospital. Casualties could be brought back from the most forward positions through sets of interleading tunnels.

'We find the tunnel system effective. As in Vietnam, the enemy often creeps up in the darkness and will fire a salvo of RPGs or mortars before they disappear again. Half an hour later they'll try again from the other side. The bush was so thick in the surrounding terrain

The original caption to this photo, taken by Brigadier-General W.S. "Kaas" van der Waals - who served in the South African diplomatic legation in Luanda - was 'Terrorism starts where the road ends'. In fact, this was a road-building effort in Angola's Mayombe Forest in Cabinda.

that even with arc-lamps it was difficult to see more than 50 yards beyond the fences,' he explained.

While Santa Eulalia had experienced that kind of attack perhaps four or five times in the past weeks, other, more remote Portuguese positions in Sector D had similar problems and by all accounts the tunnel system worked well. The only problem, one of the officers told me afterwards, was that the interiors were damp and badly lit and had to be cleared of poisonous snakes each morning.

Going through the tunnels towards evening, we found the tunnels stifling, especially in this tropical environment where humidity registered 100 percent on most days during the rainy season.

As the largest military component in the region, Santa Eulalia was actually two camps in one. A second section had been set aside near the landing strip where air force personnel were billeted. Though fenced off and patrolled by the army, it didn't make sense since it was obviously a duplication of essential duties. I was to discover during subsequent visits in Angola and Mozambique, that such inter-service anomalies became more pronounced as hostilities in the three overseas provinces dragged on.

Once could hardly avoid noticing that the three services appeared to have as little do with each other as possible. Elitist Blues would sometimes hardly acknowledge the presence of the Browns, even if there were officers present. The Portuguese Navy regarded itself as several cuts above the rest.

The place had originally been a coffee estate and even with the war around it, production went on, which was just as well since the Dembos produced some of the best coffee beans in Africa. As we observed when flying in, there were thousands of neat rows of stubby coffee bushes that spread out in all directions in a succession of patchwork patterns. If a piece of land could nurture a couple of trees, somebody used it to plant coffee there.

It wasn't easy, the Brigadier explained. The economy couldn't be left to rot because of the war and one of his jobs was to provide escorts for those who kept the jungle at bay. The owners and workers, black and white, were armed and when not under escort, were responsible for their own safety.

Each farm in the area – almost like the Rhodesian anti-insurgent Agri-Alert system that was to follow further towards south-east Africa not very long afterwards – was linked with military headquarters. When an alarm was sounded, the troops came running.

That was the idea in theory. In practice just about everything depended on the strength of the attacking force and if landmines had been laid. Another feature in common with the subsequent Rhodesian war was that it was not uncommon for the guerrillas to fake an attack on a farmhouse and then turn their attention to ambushing the troops as they approached.

Farm-owners often dealt with small attacks on their own, and though the situation was fraught, those involved soon managed to establish a basic system of priorities. Though geographically very different from other African conflicts, the pattern of hostilities in Angola was akin to what had taken place in Kenya at the height of the five-year Mau Mau emergency in that East African state less than a generation before.

Brigadier Martins Soares, a tall, slim, unassuming soldier, might easily have been mistaken for a bank official back in the Metropolis where he and his family maintained a home. He'd been fighting insurgents in Africa for as long as there had been a war in Angola.

When the first cross-border invasions took place, he'd been Governor of the Province of Luanda. The situation became desperate fairly soon in those critical early months, it was his job to organize effective counter-measures in a bid to save the country from being overrun. He'd clearly been successful, at a time when the national army was makeshift and there was almost no air support. It was obvious that this quiet, affable tactician was highly regarded by his men, as he was in Luanda when I was told that I'd be embedded with his unit.

'That there were attacks in 1961 at all is partly our fault,' he told me at lunch the day we arrived. 'We'd been warned six or eight months before by the Portuguese Embassy in Leopoldville that there was trouble brewing. That was long before the first bands of these irregulars pushed across the frontier which, as you will see, is nothing but jungle and still more jungle.'

In Lisbon too, the military, ignoring the politicians, was very much aware that something was afoot. Which was why, about 18 months before the first attacks took

As with American forces in Vietnam, Angolan guerrillas often forced government troops to use the most basic means in order to achieve an advantage. This was tough going on young soldiers who had grown up in Europe and who had little understanding or interest in what was going on in Africa. (Author's collection)

place, the Portuguese Army General Staff initiated a project named *O Exército na Guerra Subversiva* or 'The Army in a Subversive War'. As he explained, a large part of the problem initially faced by the army was that like the British in Malaya and Kenya – and the French in Algeria – almost nobody in any responsible position at the start had any hands-on experience of guerrilla warfare.

Another aspect, Brigadier Soares disclosed, was that the country had 3,000 miles of land boundaries with its neighbours, and almost all of them – except to the south – were hostile to the Portuguese presence in Africa. Compounding issues still further was the fact that almost all national boundaries throughout much of Africa were little more than a series of lines drawn on maps at a convention of Imperial Powers in Berlin in the 1890s.

He explained that early intelligence reports indicated that certain dissident elements had been formed into what was termed a 'Freedom Army'. They were well armed and while training was regarded as cursory, the early insurrectionists were certainly not the disorganized rag-tag band of brigands that some media portrayed them to be.

'But we ignored most of these reports. Though the intelligence coming in was constant, almost all of it was dismissed as alarmist and here the civil authorities were especially culpable. They dismissed it all as hogwash. Even Lisbon suggested that the malcontents involved were little more that a jumble of black people intent on making trouble ...

'The officials back home even argued that the invasion scenario was preposterous. There were those who maintained that African people had neither the initiative nor the ability to undermine the security of the state. But if it were to happen, they declared, as it had often enough in the past five centuries, then obviously the army would deal with them. That was the kind of sentiment being voiced from on high and which countered my every move to prepare for trouble.

'But by then there were some of us who began to take things more seriously, especially when the first reconnaissance groups started to cross the frontier and some of their people were caught. That usually happened after they'd got drunk at a local store and spoke too much, or perhaps they'd threatened a local store owner after being short changed in buying beer or perhaps cigarettes ... these things happen, and all too often too ... ' the Brigadier said.

Among early reports – together with information gleaned from early captures, he explained, were suggestions that the rebels were not acting on their own. There were consistent reports that they had support from abroad. In fact, I knew six months ahead that many of their men had been trained in foreign armies and when these groups began to appear with sophisticated weapons, it was clear to us all in Luanda that this was no minor Saturday afternoon uprising.

Holden Roberto's army entered Angola in their thousands. They covered hundreds of miles between the border and the capital within weeks.

'Suddenly we were in the thick of it ... the entire civil and military establishment was caught completely off guard,' the Brigadier said.

'The few police and troops that we could muster could do nothing. Remember, when this was first happening, we had only 8,000 men in the security forces, and that to cover all of Angola, a country twice the size of Texas. Of them, only about 3,000 were Portuguese nationals.

'The rest were all black and suddenly, through no fault of their own, their loyalty was regarded as suspect, largely because this was essentially a racial issue. The rebels were making a play of the fact that they were all members of an ethnic African political organization and were only demanding their rightful dues from Portugal, a European country with colonial aspirations. Never mind that they were murdering black and white civilians wherever they encountered them in their sweep towards the south. People were being slaughtered in their thousands ... '

In their purge of the established order, Roberto's FNLA – the National Front for the Liberation of Angola – laid waste to farms, buildings, administration centers, towns and settlements that were inadequately protected and a good deal more with it. They swept aside all opposition before them and anybody encountered along the way that wasn't 'for the cause' was slaughtered.

Even infants weren't spared: there were dozens of instances of babies having been sliced open and stuck on stakes. These barbaric gestures were supposed to serve as warnings to others.

The Portuguese Air Force made wide use of the Nord Noratlas freighter to move
men and equipment around in the overseas territories. (Author's photo)

At one logging village in the north, eight Portuguese men, women and children were
fed lengthwise through circular saws.

One of the Angolan revolutionaries, describing the event afterwards in Kinshasa to
Pierre de Vos of the Paris newspaper *Le Monde,* said, *avec un large sourire* (with a broad
smile) that once the Portuguese had been bound, 'we sawed them lengthwise'.

'Those were the scenes that greeted us in the early days. It was enough to make a man
throw up his hands in horror and ask what had become of humanity,' the officer said.

Brigadier Martins Soares was candid about his country's shortcomings and the effect these
ultimately had in fostering revolt:

'We'd become accustomed to years of unopposed rule. We also presupposed that when
the troubles came, those indigenés in our sphere of influence would rally with us and we'd
counter the menace together. After all, we'd ruled effectively for God knows how many
generations, though we didn't take into account how the world had changed after World
War II.

That shortcoming, he declared, pounding the table with his fist, 'was a critical mistake
that will ultimately affect this entire continent.' Though the Brigadier didn't yet know it,
it also signalled the end of white rule in all of Africa. It was only a question of time, he
reckoned and in retrospect, he was astonishingly perspicacious in making that prediction.

As he said, it was actually asking too much that Portugal should have been excluded
from what Jean Paul Sartre liked to refer to as the 'Liberation Equation'.

What happened then was that government forces were simply no match for those huge
mobs on the march that were sometimes thousands strong. Trouble was, they'd had a whiff
of blood and were eager for more.

'They stormed through hastily erected barricades as if they weren't there'...

The brigadier maintained that the reason for early rebel successes was basic. Many of the so-called Freedom Army soldiers believed they were inspired by the gods of their forefathers. Also, they were under the spell of their witch-doctors and were told that the bullets of the enemy would be turned to water. 'They really believed that they were invincible and that nothing could stop them ... I learnt very quickly that it is difficult to stop a man who thinks like that ...

'They would rush headlong into battle, screaming and firing their weapons. Others followed behind wielding spears and machetes, fearless and utterly ruthless.'

The cry as the insurgents attacked was always *'Mata! Upa! Mata! Upa!'* which, loosely translated, meant Kill! Upa! Kill! Upa!

UPA, he explained, referred to the Patriotic Union of Angola or *União dos Populacèes de Angola*, Holden Roberto's liberation group that organized the invasion in and around Leopoldville.

It was more than a month before the Portuguese found their feet again. The brigadier held on with what few resources he had at his disposal and everyone gave a hand. He had butchers and plumbers and nurses in Luanda manning the barricades and in between, his NCOs were instructing these people how to handle firearms. In fact, he added, there was a group of students at one of the higher educational establishments, black and white, that became quite good at it. They would sometimes venture short distances into the bush after the rebels.

Believing they were in the clear, the attackers were often caught unawares, usually high on liquor or drugs – or both – and in the process of sharing the booty they'd appropriated from the civilians they'd just murdered.

One of the significant problems facing Lisbon in those early stages of the insurrection was the lack of modern weapons by government forces serving in the overseas provinces. When hostilities started in 1961, the Portuguese forces were barely equipped to cope with the demands of a major counter-insurgency conflict. It was standard procedure, up to that point, to send old and obsolete military hardware to the colonies. All the good stuff was retained for NATO use.[3]

Thus, the first military operations in Angola were conducted using Mauser rifles, some of which dated back to the turn of the previous century. Communications were another issue: almost all the sets available were World War II vintage.

Obviously, Lisbon needed to act quickly. The Wiki website tells us that within months Lisbon had clinched a deal with West Germany and started domestic production of the Heckler & Koch G3 as the standard infantry rifle for the Portuguese Army, though Fabrique Nationale FALs – also in 7.62mm NATO caliber – were issued in limited numbers.

For their part, Portuguese Special Forces – mainly the Parachute Regiment – was set on the AR-10, until a collapsible stock version of the G3 rifle became available. The MG42 machine-gun was issued until 1968, when another Heckler and Koch variation, the HK21 came into production and was made available to the forces fighting in the *metrópole-*

províncias ultramarinas.

Support weapons included outdated American Bazookas, as well as 60mm and 81mm mortars. These were later supplemented by 120mm mortars and howitzers. Some of the heavy equipment went onto Panhard AML and EBR armoured cars, the Fox and, in the final stages of the conflict, the Portuguese-built Bravia Chaimite, an 11-man armoured personnel carrier or APC, customarily with a .50 Browning mounted on the turret.

Though deployed mostly in urban security duties, Daimler Dingos, small, two-man armoured scout cars, were always in the background during official parades. The majority of these vehicles were deployed in convoy support roles.

One of the immediate consequences of the insurrection was that it forever changed Angola's social structure. If there had been racial differences among some members of the community, blacks fighting alongside whites to preserve the national hegemony quickly dispelled prejudice.

Soon, Angolan civilians of all races generated the kind of pioneer spirit that hadn't been seen in the colonies for generations. Civilians were doing patrols and their women helped out where they could. Many society ladies who hadn't done a hard day's work in their lives

Angola

The Fortress of São Miguel that overlooks much of Luanda was built almost a century before the Dutch first settled at the Cape of Good Hope in 1652. This massive structure has always played a significant security role in the city's history, and became a Portuguese Army headquarters during the Colonial War. (Author's photo)

These old guns were placed in defensive positions centuries ago, but never fired in anger. They are still there today, overlooking the *Ilha* or island, which is connected to the mainland by a causeway. (Author's photo)

Military parade in the heart of Luanda a few years before Lisbon decided to end it all. These events were showcase efforts, put on as much to impress the locals of Portuguese Army prowess as to boost civilian morale in Lisbon's largest city in the *ultramar*. (Author's photo)

Portugal's traditional links with Angola were a constant propaganda theme, in the towns, cities and in military camps in the interior. (Author's photo)

Portuguese Army column along one of the main roads through the
mountains in the Angolan interior. (Author's collection)

The sign is explicit – there are landmines
half a pace away. An exaggeration, of course,
but it does emphasise the enormous threat
the troops faced when moving around
in the interior, especially on roads that
had not been swept. (Author's photo)

The hill on which the strategic settlement of Nambuangongo in Sector D is perched, viewed from the almost exclusively black village below. The guerrillas captured the town early on in the war and the Portuguese fought hard to win it back. (Author's photo)

The jungle reaches of Northern Angola – commonly referred to as the Dembos (bush) – is one of the most difficult terrains anywhere in which to fight a guerrilla war. For a start, it is almost impossible to build good roads in this kind of swampland environment. (Photo Peter Wilkins)

A gathering of troops together with some heavy artillery at a frontline
position in the Angolan bush. (Author's collection)

Portuguese Army soldier with his G-3 rifle on one of the bridges
leading to the interior of Angola. (Author's collection)

This army truck carrying soldiers and ammunition for one of the camps in the Dembos was part of the convoy to which the author was attached while moving in jungle terrain north of Luanda. (Author's photo)

Brewing up at one of the jungle stops in the interior of the Cabinda enclave. (Author's photo)

Much confusion as a patrol prepares to leave a base camp for the bush. If it is to be a follow-up operation, additional supplies and adequate ammunition must be taken along. As the war progressed, Portuguese foot soldiers rarely stayed over in the bush at night if they did not have to. (Author's photo)

In the field, the guerrillas had a singular advantage over Lisbon's troops – they could live off the land. This photo shows a group of UNITA soldiers with the results of a hunt hung up to dry for use on future operations. (Unknown source)

One of the youthful officers in charge of a squad of Lisbon's crack *Comandos Africanos*, a Special Forces unit that achieved good results against the guerrillas in Central Angola. (Author's photo)

On patrol with a small element attached to *Comandos Africanos*. Towards the end of the war, the majority of these specialist fighters in Angola were black. In Portuguese Guinea they were preponderantly African almost from the start of that guerrilla campaign. (Author's photo)

Army column waiting for orders before moving off into 'Injun Country'. (Author's photo)

A bunch of guerrilla mortars as well as RPG-7 rockets and launchers were typical of the hardware recovered during regular Portuguese strikes in the interior of Angola. Almost all of this hardware was of Soviet origin, much of it shipped into Africa through the Tanzanian harbour of Dar es Salaam. (Author's photo)

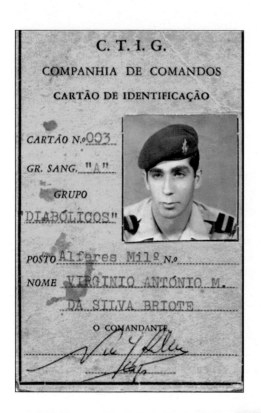

C. T. I. G.

COMPANHIA DE COMANDOS

CARTÃO DE IDENTIFICAÇÃO

CARTÃO N.º 003

GR. SANG. "A"

GRUPO "DIABÓLICOS"

POSTO Alferes Milº N.º

NOME VIRGINIO ANTÓNIO M. DA SILVA BRIOTE

O COMANDANTE

An official military identity card issued to Portuguese troops fighting in Africa. (Author's collection)

The POMZ was the standard Soviet stake-mounted, anti-personnel fragmentation mine used in almost all of Africa's guerrilla struggles. It – and several variations of the weapon – were also extensively deployed against Western forces, first in Korea and later in Vietnam. This one –without its explosive charge – sat on Al Venter's desk for many years. (Author's collection)

A strongpoint on the outskirts of a military base manned by almost 100 Portuguese soldiers at N'Riquinha in Angola's extreme south-eastern corner. Close to the Zambian frontier, the unit was commanded by Captain Vitor Alves, one of the plotters in the army putsch that ousted Lisbon's civilian government in 1974. (Author's photo)

Portuguese soldiers raid a suspect guerrilla camp in the African interior. (Author's collection)

The average soldier who arrived in Africa to fight Lisbon's wars was not yet out of his teens. Harsh conditions and a tough regimen quickly matured them into a reasonably competent fighting force, though for the majority of conscripts, their hearts were elsewhere. (Author's collection)

Military parade on one of Portugal's national holidays in Angola. It was always ceremonial and grand, part of the old custom that traditionalists said would never die. It ended abruptly after a decade of hard fighting. (Author's photo)

Cabinda, the tiny oil-rich Portuguese enclave that lay north of the Congo River, saw much action in the early days, the guerrilla group FLEC that was active there receiving almost all of its support from a Socialist-orientated Congo-Brazzaville. (Author's photo)

The heavily-defended military convoy that took us almost all the way through Sector D in the jungles of the north. We had two French-built armoured personnel carriers for our protection, and while we were consistently sniped at from the foliage, their guns were never used on the enemy because it was impossible to spot them through the thick jungle that often encroached right to the edge of the road. (Author's photo)

Two locals we encountered along the way in Cabinda are questioned by Angolan troops about an insurgent presence. Of course, they didn't know what we were talking about ... (Author's photo)

Northern Angola is a difficult region to traverse, which is why it remained undeveloped over the centuries. The discovery of oil which made Angola one of the biggest producers on the African continent changed everything. (Photo Peter Wilkins)

Convoy with supplies heading for an isolated outpost in the jungle with its APC protection. (Author's collection)

One of the many T6 Harvards deployed operationally in Angola over farmland in the north. The canopy has been left partially open for ventilation. (Photo *Revista da Armada*)

Unlike more sophisticated wars – as in Vietnam and, more recently, Afghanistan – convoys in Angola were largely improvised. Troops were allocated to them for protection and they travelled wherever they could find somewhere to sit. (Author's collection)

The Angolan flag, adopted when this vast country achieved its independence from Lisbon, symbolised a version of the Soviet hammer and sickle against a largely blood-red backdrop but that also included some black, symbolically, the colour of the majority of its people. (Author's photo)

found themselves working 72-hour shifts in the city's clinics and hospitals. Upper crust or not, they scrubbed floors and swabbed blood in improvised operating theatres.

'These are the tough people who built this country—and but for them, Angola would be lost today, said Brigadier Soares. By then he had been in Angola for more than a decade and he knew his people.

Once it became apparent to Lisbon that the country was faced with a good deal more than a short-term uprising by small groups of dissidents, a form of universal conscription was enforced by the Portuguese government, both in Europe and in the colonies. All fit young men in their early twenties were called up and required to spend time in Africa fighting an enemy that the authorities said, was a direct threat to Portugal. Thereafter, military service was enforced straight out of school, unless a student opted for university; he would do his time in uniform after his studies were done.

Initially, because no one knew how long the emergency would last, there was little or no opposition to military service. Officials in Lisbon were talking about months—perhaps a year. That was March 1961. Nobody was to know that Lisbon was faced with than a decade of hard fighting. Portugal was to wage three separate wars in Africa – in Angola, Mozambique as well as Portuguese Guinea – twice as long as the Americans fought in Vietnam.[4]

'There was no question that the rebels had the upper hand from the start. They held on to it until our people were able to send reinforcements. But these all had to come from Lisbon, where endless decisions had to be made within a bureaucratic morass that sometimes defies description. That meant still more delays. And remember, Europe is thousands of miles from Luanda and the men and equipment still had to arrive by sea … in the end it took a lot of time.'

At times, he disclosed, it was touch-and-go whether the revolutionaries would actually be able to take Luanda. At one point they reached the outskirts of the city and it was only the presence of loyal African troops who pushed them back.

'Many of those same black soldiers who saved Luanda are now in command of their own units in this very same jungle that you see around you.

They were brave men and Portugal does not easily forget,' he declared, gesturing with a sweep of the arm towards the mess bar for more *vinho tinto*.

Much had changed by the time we arrived in Sector D. A good deal of the country to the immediate north of the camp – stretching away towards the west and the coast – was either impenetrable jungle or swamp. It was known to the Portuguese military authorities – and to the insurgents, who soon enough became familiar with the more common day-to-day military terminology – as Sector A.

Added to that improbable scenario were tropical diseases like malaria, cholera and sleeping sickness, all of which were rife.

Even more pervasive was hepatitis which would sweep through some camps like the plague. It was only discovered later by the Israeli Army that the disease became endemic if the camp kitchens were not kept spotless. Animal fat residue, it became apparent to IDF specialists, was the principal cause of the disease, especially if allowed to accrue on cooking utensils.

The nature of hostilities too had altered from the early days and it didn't take the Portuguese Army long to establish its own parameters for combating insurgents.

'These days, said Brigadier Martins Soares, 'we patrol where we can. But it is impossible to create a no-man's-land in this vast jungle region as the Americans might have done in Vietnam. If you clear the bush one week, it grows a foot high the next,' he said. He reckoned that the terrain in which his units operated was possibly the nearest thing to a Ho Chi Minh kind of trail in Africa – all two or three hundred miles of it.

Of the roughly 6,000 rebels in Sector D at the time of our visit, the staff officer reckoned that almost all had originally come down this ragged barely discernible bush path from the Congo. Because of the almost uniform heavy overgrowth, the route used by the insurgents was almost always obscured from the air.

'It takes them roughly six weeks to cover the distance, but that is not the only threat. More of these dissidents had come in from the south-east, originally from their bases in Zambia and that's more than six or eight hundred miles away. Or they may have been coerced into joining the insurgent army in the sector itself: it is simply a matter of putting a gun to a man's head ... '

Another officer explained: 'They go on down the trail with everything they need on their backs – their weapons, ammunition, explosives, food, medical supplies, propaganda handouts for the locals – few of whom can read anyway – together with anything else that they may think might be needed to wage war. They're extremely efficient at moving stuff in bulk – one group even managed to haul a 500-pound aerial bomb into the sector, carried all the way on a litter between them.'

He admitted that such tasks obviously demanded enormous effort, though he was puzzled by the bombs, which he maintained were used by the insurgents as mines. It beat him why they'd try to move such large cargoes when 20 smaller ones would have done just as well, especially since the country – as we'd observed from the air – was extremely difficult to traverse.

Also, there were few roads in the early days and almost no bridges across most of the rivers, almost all of them fast-flowing.

'A large bomb will blow up a large vehicle; so they bring these monsters down in the hope that they would blow up our Panhards. They've never succeeded yet ... far too big and bulky ... we spot them every time. Who knows what it all cost in suffering to get these things that far down the line.'

Most of the men garrisoned at Santa Eulalia were employed mainly in tactical and support roles by other Portuguese units in the vicinity.

These French-supplied Panhard armoured cars were the mainstay of many Portuguese Army installations in all three overseas provinces during the war. (Author's photo)

With about two dozen trucks and a couple of helicopters on hand for emergencies, the garrison was mobile. Like several other Portuguese Army units in the region, their main task – apart from running convoys – was protecting the local African population.

The camp at Santa Eulalia had its own clinic, surgical theatre and dental unit. Soldiers further afield who needed more advanced treatment than the unit medic might be able to provide, such as root canal treatment or an appendectomy, were flown into the camp by light aircraft or helicopter. More serious casualties were airlifted to the military hospital in Luanda, usually on special litters fitted to a single-engine aircraft. Or they'd also be taken out by helicopter, which landed on a concrete slab behind the clinic which was used after-hours as a tennis court by the officers.

The camp doctor was an unusual character, the kind that one sometimes encounters in remote corners of Africa. He was noted for being a repository of remarkable stories which invariably involved the kinds of things that can go wrong with humans who work in a totally unforgiving tropical environment.

One of his patients, a former waiter from Coimbra, had been brought in on a stretcher a short while before we got there. He'd contracted a form of elephantiasis, his body, arms and legs grossly swollen. It had apparently been caused by a mosquito-borne virus, leaving the soldier with a grotesquely swollen face. To somebody who wasn't familiar with the symptoms, it looked like he'd been severely beaten round the eyes.

'It took an insect the size of a flea to do that to him,' the doctor explained, showing me the photos. 'All we could do was dose him up with the usual drugs and hope for the best.'

Antibiotics had so far had no effect, he added.

It was aspirin, strangely enough, that eventually cured the man, and it happened quite by chance. On the second day, the patient complained of a headache.

'It was really severe and had us worried for a while because he'd already been dosed with just about every drug we had on the base. So as a desperate measure, we gave him aspirin because there was nothing else.

'Within hours the swelling had subsided. A week later he was back with his unit.'

This kind of thing goes on all the time in the jungle, one of the reasons why the British had such a high casualty rate when they originally fought communist terrorists in Malaya.

On one return trip from one of the remoter military camps in the jungle, we brought back with us in our aircraft a young soldier who'd been bitten in the face by an insect. It should have been nothing – troops get bitten all the time – but then it turned bad and the infection affected both the soldier's sight and hearing.

By the time the Santa Eulalia medical team started to work on him, the soldier was only half-conscious. The senior doc was even considering getting him out of the bush to Luanda, which he would have done had his condition deteriorated any further. After he'd almost died in the night, they knew that they would have to ship him out, which they did. But by the time he got to the capital the man was fine ... he walked off the plane with no support whatever, and we'd put him in there on a stretcher ... .

'We don't get that kind of case very often', said a young smiling intern from the Algarve, but it certainly keeps us busy ... there are always extraordinary things happening to people in this remote region'. Nor was it all snakes and scorpions, though there were enough of those around.

The doctor wished all his problems were that simple. Quite a few tropical afflictions he'd encountered were killers. Bugs, viruses and bacteria seemed to get hold of the men and rip them apart — physically and psychologically.

'You can imagine the problems the other side has with these issues since they have few of our facilities. When we hit their camps, we rarely find anything but the most rudimentary when it comes to medicine or equipment. But then again, they're much more accustomed to this primitive environment than our boys.'

Still, he added, the other side suffered, sometimes badly. Their medical techniques were archaic and logistics simply didn't allow for the same kind of treatment, though guerrilla barefoot doctors were fond of dosing with penicillin – whatever the ailment.

The insurgents suffered from a serious lack of trained medical staff. By some accounts, the few African doctors that might have been available for the cause scoffed at the idea of traipsing around the African bush in search of casualties. They would argue that should they do that, there was a fair chance of them being used for target practice by the Portuguese Army. Nobody could argue with that kind of logic.

One or two Algerian doctors were attached to enemy units, but even they were wary of crossing south from the Congo.

'Sometimes we'll get a medical man with the enemy that will come through to Sector

D. The army shot up a group a few months ago and among the dead they found a doctor from Nigeria, a London-trained trauma specialist, we heard later. He was apparently a good man, very focused.

' ... as if Nigeria hasn't enough of its own problems without still getting the few trained medical specialists that they can boast of slaughtered in a war that is of absolutely no interest or consequence to their country', the physician mused.

4

Bush War in West Africa

' ... the guerrillas are rather good at demolitions, I must say. There is a road which
runs between Gago Coutinho and a place called Chiume, about 48 kilometres west
of the Zambian frontier, north-south ... you have to cross in any case marching into
the country, and I did so in both directions. They were carrying out a rather good
demolition operation when I was there and they blew up five trucks ... the explosives
were obviously put together very well indeed, by men who had been trained in the
work and they were effective.'

> Basil Davidson, speaking in 1971 at Ned Munger's Africana Institute,
> California Institute of Technology, Pasadena.

The briefing at Santa Eulalia lasted well into the evening and was initially handled by
a baby-faced lieutenant with his left arm in a sling. His shoulder had been creased
by an AK bullet in an ambush the week before, we were told.

'It could have been a lot worse,' the young officer admitted: 'we were caught in an
ambush in some heavy jungle country and the bullet ricocheted off the gun turret onboard
the Panhard that I'd commandeered as a command post ... it happened during a routine
convoy run south of here. In good English he elaborated on some of the problems faced by
Comsec D Command.

'The enemy enters northern Angola from an area along the Congo frontier, roughly-
speaking between Matadi – that country's major port – and Kinshasa, the capital.

'Many of the rebels who arrive in Angola from Congo-Brazza cross the river at night
in shallow-bottomed dug-outs [*pirogues*] and though we had problems in the past, naval
patrols have been quite successful in stopping some of these infiltrators. But if you've
seen the river, you'll know that the Congo is wide – miles across in places. Also, there are
thousands of floating islands constantly being carried downstream by the current.

'It is easy to hide in those matted reed or papyrus islands if you see the lights of a patrol
craft approaching and it's physically impossible to inspect each one of them ... that would
need thousands of men', the officer suggested.

Once across the frontier, it took the average insurgent about six weeks to reach Sector
D.

We were shown our position on a map of the area. Also pin-pointed were other camps
in Sector D—Zala to the north, Zemba lying further towards the south and the pivotal
crossroads settlement of Nambuangongo slap bang in the centre. There were four other
Portuguese military bases in the area, each responsible for the security of a segment.

As soon as the revolutionaries had flooded into Angola from the Congo in the early stages of the war, the small hilltop hamlet of Nambuangongo in the *Dembos* was chosen as the new rebel capital. (Photo Manuel Graça)

Nambuangongo, he told us, was a most interesting place, with a history that went back to the earliest days of the war.

'Nambu', as the troops liked to call it, had been the original headquarters of the insurgent army in Angola. They'd taken it by force, killed everybody there, including a number of logging people and their families who had taken refuge at the home of the local *Chefe de Posto*. Fighting in the vicinity of the camp had not only been fierce, but consistent, and it had been that way since March 1961, the lieutenant said.

At which point another officer, Captain Ramos de Campos took over and told us that the guerrillas still tried to retake the hilltop base from time to time. They had come close to doing so several times, he reckoned, especially when most of the troops are away from base either out on patrol or on convoy duties.

It was at Nambuangongo, he explained, that the rebels had achieved some of their best successes in the past. Their political commissars would talk about 'our most glorious victories against the Fascist colonial forces', an expression regularly used on the guerrilla radio station broadcasting out of Brazzaville.

Apart from terminology, said de Campos, you couldn't really scoff at that notion, because early on, they'd actually pushed government forces all the way southwards to the outskirts of Luanda. There was a time, several months in fact, he said, when they were masters of just about all they surveyed ... from the Congolese frontier south.

'But no longer ... these days we have a tight grip on the place. But that doesn't mean we can be lax'.

He explained that it was part of an insurgent master-plan to recapture Nambuangongo, 'snatching it out from under us again would be regarded as quite a significant victory and frankly, so it would be too.' Portuguese losses in the environs of the camp were still comparatively high, 'so they're still at it, literally as we speak.'

Another officer at the briefing was Captain Virgil Magalhan. His job was to outline guerrilla tactics, which was when he called for the blackboard to be rolled in.

Using a pointer, he detailed how the war had entered a new phase, how the insurgents liked to lay their ambushes, the types of their weapons and mines they were equipped with and where their main camps were believed to be situated.

The sector experienced about four or five actions a week, he declared. Most were ambushes on patrols or convoys. As opposed to the early days when they attacked in bands often 200 strong, they now concentrated in groups of about 20 or less. What was also different was that some of the men that had come through from the north had been trained outside Angola— in Zambia, Congo-Brazza or further afield. Quite a few had been to Russia, Cuba, China, Tanzania, Algeria, Egypt and elsewhere.

'As for ability, they're a mixed bag, which actually holds for most of Africa's so-called Liberation Wars. The majority of fighters are indifferent, reasonably well-trained, but lacking either focus or purpose. That said, their section leaders can sometimes be pretty good when it comes to tactics and the use of more advanced weapons like heavy machine-guns or mortars. The balance, thankfully, are dismal. They've been taught, but they learnt nothing ...

'Still, they persist and recently they tried a new gimmick,' he elaborated. 'While they'd previously restricted their attacks on camp sites to the dark hours, they'd resort to making the occasional daylight mock attack on a particular area. A group would make a show of strength near the forest, perhaps half a mile or so from one of our bases, while snipers hidden on higher points would attempt to pick off the officers.

'This is something also used by the Vietcong, but the aim of these clowns has always been deplorable. Not all of them, mark you, because we've had some men killed, but even then they are rarely accurate at anything more than a 100 or possibly 150 yards — which is one of the reasons why our casualties have been so light'. Things could change, radically perhaps, he added, but that was the situation at that time.

It was notable that in spite of the threat, Portuguese officers – in all three services – quite often displayed rank in the various operational areas. With the potential threat of attack omnipresent, one would have liked to think that they might have discarded their epaulettes and gold braid, or at least used muted shades which would not have been difficult to distinguish from a distance, very much as Western military forces do in hostile areas. Granted, they removed all rank on patrol or while on convoy duty but by then, the insurgents knew exactly who the officers were. They had their own means of monitoring activity in Portuguese Army military bases. No doubt they also used some of the domestic

African staff as informers; it had always been the African way.

There was a good deal of speculation in the camps visited on the kind of training received by the insurgents. It was a consistent theme in most of the operational sectors.

The perception among the majority of Portuguese troops was that as an enemy, the guerrillas were an inferior element, though to this outsider, that didn't make sense considering the number of troops the rebels had succeeded in tying down. The argument, as presented, applied as much to basic tactics as to accurately firing their weapons.

In truth, it was a fundamental misconception that had obviously cost lives in the past, for while the ability of the majority of African guerrillas was nothing to shout about, there were some brilliant and innovative combatants within their ranks. Nino, – later General Nino (who was to become President of Portuguese Guinea) was among them: he successfully 'ran rings' around the Portuguese Army in what has since become Guiné-Bissau.

The common denominator among them all was that in the choice of weapons, the insurgents tended towards the AK-47. Functional under all conditions and ubiquitous, it was the weapon of choice among most revolutionary armies in Africa and it is still that way today, well into the New Millennium. Going solely by results, the Kalashnikov has proved remarkably effective over more than a half a century in other wars in Asia and the Middle East. The Viet Cong and anti-Israeli Arab forces like Fatah, would use nothing else, nor AQIM – Al Qaeda in the Maghreb – in the recent war in Mali.

Even today, Hizbollah, the Iranian surrogate force in Lebanon, prefers the AK to anything that the West has to offer.

It was notable that apart from AKs, RPDs or Simonov Soviet-manufactured rifles, Portuguese forces occasionally came up against the occasional 19th Century blunderbuss that fired just about anything. The opposition wasn't averse to including nails and small chunks of iron or rock.

'It's the irregular stuff that causes the damage', said Captain de Campos. 'These antique pieces can sometimes rip holes the size of saucers in a man's chest.'

He was right, of course. I had seen the effect of these old guns in parts of Tanzania and Zambia in the past, where local Africans use them to hunt larger game like buffalo and, occasionally elephant. Given the chance, any game ranger would confiscate the lot. More often than not, the museum pieces would wound and not kill. The animals would then wander off into the bush and be left to die, sometimes weeks later.

Yet consistently, the guerrillas most times lost more of their own men in actions than did the Portuguese Army because they weren't using their carbines to good effect. Even though they might initially have had the advantage of surprise in an ambush, it was the same almost each time when there was a contact.

The AK would be put on full auto and firing would continue until the magazine was empty: obviously most of the shots went high. This failing appeared to hold good for Mozambique and thereafter, the Rhodesian War. In their bush wars that followed the

Nambuangongo from the air after the settlement had been
retaken by Portuguese forces. (Photo Manuel Graça)

departure of the Portuguese, the South Africans had similar experiences.

Nonetheless, the insurgents would work to a series of systems that had strong Soviet overtones: almost everything was done 'by the book'.

They would choose a stretch of road with good visibility for some distance in both directions. If the area was heavily foliated, they'd attack from a position above the road, firing down on the convoy. This gave them the advantage of being able to escape. There was a perpetual fear of gunships among the rebels and even if they did manage to mutilate a patrol, they would rarely hang about and finish the job.

Captain de Campos told us of an ambush he'd experienced a short time before. 'Just before I'd been promoted to captain, I was based in a village a few miles from Terreiro, a small coffee-producing area in Sector F, just north of here', he explained.

'The sector had been reasonably active, but at that stage it was fairly quiet, and had been so for a while. We thought that the main insurgent force might have passed us by. It was a Friday morning, shortly after the week-end supplies had been dropped and I had to go into the village to see what fresh provisions I could get for the men. We try to eat fish on Fridays, not easy in this bush country, but not impossible either.'

The captain chose seven men and set out in two jeeps, his own leading. Driving into town he kept his foot down hard on the accelerator. The road was good for this kind of mountainous country and he was eager to get back in time for lunch.

'We came round one of the many bends in the road, fairly close to town. As we turned sharply and dropped into a dip in the road, they opened fire from a position above us ... let rip with everything and the noise was awesome. It was actually a good spot for an ambush.'

'That's when you start reacting instinctively; I had to get us out of this mess, All eight of us simultaneously jumped off the jeeps, firing into the grass immediately ahead.' It was standard procedure, he reckoned. It was also a precaution that could sometimes result in some of the insurgents lying next to the road becoming casualties.

But you had to know what you were doing, he warned. On your own in heavy bush country and away from the vehicles, it could quickly become a one-on-one issue; the ambushers would sometimes slash at anybody nearby with their machetes. He used the word *catanas,* as the Angolan long knives or pangas were called by local people.

'It took a little while, but we eventually got clear of our attackers after emptying a few magazines and hurling all the grenades we had in the group...must have been about a dozen. Only when we were in comparative safety of the elephant grass, did I call for casualties from my two corporals. By then I'd heard the whistles used by the enemy officers and knew that our attackers had pulled back.

Details of the attack were interesting, and the captain answered all the questions put to him, especially with regard to extricating his men.

'One of the men in the second jeep had been hit in the thigh — a bad wound that bled profusely. A dumdum bullet had blown most of the flesh away on the upper leg exposing the bone and that meant we had to get this guy back to base immediately or he would have died on us from loss of blood.

'Now had the terrorists stuck about a little longer with harassing fire, they could have done some real damage. But they, as the saying goes, shot their bolt and were off.'

The captain estimated the attacking force at about 20 to 25 strong. They were well dug-in about 30 yards on the rise above them. Their position was not easily defensible, but they had the advantage of height; they could see pretty well where the all the Portuguese were positioned after they'd disembarked.

'All we had was tall grass ahead and a road behind', said the captain, 'and clearly, they didn't use the opportunity as they might have done.'

'We saw afterwards that they'd initially broken a path through the thick bush and were able to disappear down this jungle trail as soon as things got rough. Only one of their number was left behind—an African irregular who had taken a blast from one of the grenades that killed him.

Several blood trails indicated that one or more of the attackers had been wounded. More important, they hadn't managed to remove any of their used cartridge shells. 'It's the unwritten law among these people – they bring back their empty shells to base ... if they can manage to do so, of course.'

The Portuguese were puzzled in the beginning, but then captured rebels admitted that they were only issued with more ammunition if they could produce their original casings. That prevented them throwing away good ammunition and claiming they had been in an action.

'Also, they rarely fired their guns indiscriminately ... it might attract a nearby Portuguese patrol.' The old shells were often used again, sometimes many times over. Back at base they were reloaded and reissued.

The captain mused: 'It's a question of economics—African economics'

Another aspect of the ambush which the officer noted was that the attackers had left behind a dead comrade. They probably didn't have enough time to move the body, he thought, 'and in any event, we were coming up fast.'

Essentially, he explained, by not leaving casualties behind, the idea was to deprive their adversaries of evidence of casualties ... all of it was psychological, he suggested.

'Often, after an action, we'd find blood traces where we knew one or more of the wounded had sheltered. But then we wouldn't be able to establish whether it came from someone KIA or wounded.'

The rebel army in northern Angola by the time I arrived in Sector D was estimated at about 6,000 regulars. Their numbers were more preponderant than the strength of the Portuguese Army, though with conscription back home having taken effect, things were improving.

Apart from the insurgent army, there were two or three times that number of African civilians who lived in the jungles and among the mountains of the sector, many of them caught in the perennial crosshairs of conflict.

Though not part of the regular insurgent movement, civilians provided useful support when needed, customarily acting as porters or bearers. They'd also be tasked with taking out the dead and tending the wounded in their villages if the casualty couldn't be hauled back to their own lines.

The majority of these irregulars might have been innocent bystanders to start with, but that was no longer the case. Early rebel successes had given many of these tribal people the desire for more of the same, often as a result of tribal associations or simply because they were sympathetic to what the rebels referred to as a just cause.

Living permanently in the jungle, they were able to harbor groups passing through. They'd feed, and if necessary, hide those guerrillas operating in the vicinity of their villages or, in the lingo *sanzalas*. These were often large enough to house makeshift field hospitals.

Life in the primeval forests around Nambuangongo, Santa Eulalia and the other strongpoints was fundamental to the kind of tropical existence that had evolved over centuries. It was possible for locals to grow fairly large crops of their more popular cassava root (manioc) in any one of thousands of jungle clearings. The root is pushed a few inches into the earth by hand. Fertile ground, lots of rain and a hot tropical climate sees the plants through to maturity. Crops can sometimes be harvested every other month, or the tubers, not unlike potatoes, might be left in the ground for harvesting later, either by the villagers or the rebels.

Local inhabitants also grew small quantities of maize or sorghum to supplement their diet. When a rebel group intended to stay in an area, villagers might plant beans for variety. Meat was always scarce, especially in wartime where a rifle shot might draw attention.

Captured ELNA guerrillas who were persuaded by the Portuguese to continue
to fight the war, but against their old compadres. The tall man on the left was
killed in a contact soon after he posed for this photo. (Author's photo)

'We see these communities from the air from time to time, but mostly there is nothing
we can do', the captain stated.

He wasn't overly critical of the role played by these civilians. In most cases, he said, they
had little option but to help when ordered to so by a bunch of armed newcomers. Whether
their hearts were in it or not was another matter. If they didn't assist, they could be accused
of siding with government forces. Then it was not only the individual at risk, but his entire
family. And those pointing a finger needed little proof: a bullet behind the neck would end
the argument.

'We have exactly the same problem as the Americans in Vietnam and the British
experienced in Malaya', he explained as he waved his hand across a map.

'The guerrillas are now doing the same here in Africa ... trying to win the support of the
civilian population'. For a variety of reasons, it would seem that they have succeeded quite
well, he declared.

We travelled by road convoy between Nambuangongo and Zala – the northernmost
Portuguese army camp in Sector D. Our guide and translator was Captain Ricardo Alcada,
a lawyer from Lisbon with a coruscating mind that all too often disguised a twinkling sense
of fun.

On his second voluntary tour of active duty in Angola, this enthusiastic young officer had been drafted into the army in the dark days of 1961 and had seen some of the worst excesses of the insurgent-led campaign. That effort – and some of the massacres he'd witnessed – hardened his approach towards any kind of compromise with an enemy that he utterly despised. He'd quite blandly refer to them in mid-sentence as barbarians.

As an infantry officer, his makeshift unit –quite a few postings to Africa from Portugal were piecemeal, with the men being slotted into available posts – had played an important part in stemming the tide of the invasion from across the border. He'd done his time and was proud of the consequences. When our paths crossed, he'd been back in Angola about six months.

'The war has changed a lot in the four years I've been away', he told me as we charged down one of Nambu's hills in an open jeep that seemed to be held together by screws, fishing nylon and a couple of bolts.

'I had to re-assimilate just about everything I'd been taught before. Even my approach to ambushes was different when I returned ... which meant that I had to be much more careful ... more cautious than before ... landmines, of course.' As officers, he suggested, they were required to think three moves ahead and, more often than not, attempt to do something totally new.

'One of our colonels called it experimenting with guerrilla war, which he believed was essential. With time, he'd tell us, the enemy became familiar with the manner in which we operated, our deployments, our weaknesses, our clever old wiles.'

Since he had been back in Africa, Captain Alcada had narrowly avoided being killed twice, both occasions in ambushes close to the camps to which he'd been posted. Both times, he candidly admitted, was because he had been careless. He put it down to lack of foresight in believing that conditions were still the same as before, when he left Angola in 1963.

'On one occasion, I was temporarily seconded to another unit. We were in the vicinity of a *sanzala* – a village in the jungle. It didn't occur to me at the time that those people had possibly set a trap, or that they could be anywhere nearby. We hadn't seen a trace of the enemy for days.

'After casually scouting around, I entered what appeared to be a makeshift camp with some of my men: I'd intended talking with the chief and was taken to a hut where four elders were sitting, one of them quite senior. I had barely settled down on my haunches when a group of terrorists opened fire on us all from the opposite side of the jungle. Not one of the soldiers was hit, but they did manage to kill one of the old men and wound some of the others ... idiots!'

'They'd surrounded the lower side of the village, carefully avoiding the rest of my patrol ... just kept on firing for a minute or so and then rushed off into the undergrowth.'

There were no grenades ... nothing big ... just rapid-fire. Probably AKs, he concluded afterwards.

'I got up afterwards, with four men still on the floor and it took a little while to sort out the wounded from the dying. I had been lightly grazed across the back, but you can imagine how I felt: I was incredibly lucky – could easily have been one of them.

'Anyway, that was another of my "lives" used up. They're getting scarce now so I'll have to watch my step', said Alcada as he quietly chuckled. His sense of humour, I was soon to discover, was quite infectious.

'Just goes to show', he exclaimed afterwards. 'Can't take anything for granted in this war. One minute you see the bastards—if you're lucky. The next you don't ... but by then they might have you in their sights.'

Captain Alcada, who I got to know well after the war and whom I subsequently hosted in my Cape Town home, often referred to the war as a bagful of tricks. It was his favourite expression, having a good feel for the English language. Fully bilingual, he'd spent a few years at one of the better English schools when he was young.

In spite of media opprobrium – British newspapers and the BBC especially, were coming down hard on Portugal because of their ongoing colonial wars – Captain Alcada still had a fond regard for the British and their traditions as well as their casual, beer-imbibing lifestyle. That might have been one of the reasons why rugby maintains a rather special niche in the minds of so many of the Lisbon and Oporto upper set. Like many Portuguese officers, he also spoke passable French.

'This is not a proper war', he would say, usually impatiently and after a few drinks. 'It's a game— something lethal ... and incredibly so.

'Call it a game of chess with variations of Russian roulette. You never know when you're going to collect the next bullet. And remember, we're fighting this war in their backyard, not ours – Angola is their turf,' he'd declare, head high and more often than not with a sweep of an arm for effect.

He liked the analogy with regard to chess. It was the one game to which he was addicted. I'd often marvel, sober or after a gutful of drinks, how he'd take on any number of his fellow officers and thrash them all.

Then he'd start to ruminate. In Vietnam, he maintained, the Americans had systems, codes, statistics and the rest to go by. Some battles were fought by computer. 'Here in Africa, we Portuguese and our enemies put most things down to chance ... every move we make is a gamble', calculated most times, but a gamble, nonetheless,' he asserted.

Alcada spoke forcefully, often with the aplomb of somebody far senior than that of a lowly captain in the infantry. He typified the traditionalist, the sort of person who yearned for an era when the world was ruled by kings, archbishops and princes and by friendly, if not always-benign dictatorships, in part because he was a product of just such an environment.

His background suited him well; Ricardo was part diplomat, part doctor of law. In Lisbon he had been secretary to the Under-Secretary of State and I thought it peculiar that he should have chosen the more difficult route by returning to Africa in a bid to make his mark.

On one issue Captain Alcada was outspoken, and vociferously so. He believed that there were too many ethics involved in the war in which he was engaged, too many rules,

Coffee was the mainstay of many of the settler farmers in Angola's high-lying regions, particularly in the north of the country. While the war went on around them, locals still tried to bring in the crop. (Author's photo)

he would tell us. His view was that in order to win, you needed to institute a no-holds-barred campaign, much as the Germans had done. Then, almost disparagingly he'd throw Churchill at you: 'In the struggle for life and death there is, in the end, simply no legality,' was the quote and it was word perfect.

After reflecting a few moments, he'd add a rider; 'the bastards we're up against had no compassion when they came across the frontier and slaughtered our women and children. Now only one criterion remains paramount—for us to win.'

Alcada suggested that the only way to ultimately achieve victory was to get the Portuguese army into the jungle; 'Tackle the enemy on his own turf and at close quarters'. Also, he deplored the American concept of what was termed 'limited attrition'. One of his theories revolved around what he termed 'pace of hostilities'.

There was no such a thing as pace of hostilities in wartime he would say. You needed to do what was necessary and in as short a time as possible ... kill or be killed ...

'That is why my unit has been so successful in this area. We fight the enemy in his own environment ... and we beat him every time. The policy of wait-and-see is pointless—the Americans are proving that under similar conditions in Vietnam. The French army proved it in Algeria.'

And of course, with time, Captain Ricardo Alcada was proved correct, even though his own country gave up all its possessions in Africa.

More's the pity that Captain Ricardo Alcada didn't have Iraq to underscore the kind of logic that made him something of a maverick among his fellow officers. Most of them deplored their African postings and, indeed, I encountered very few who couldn't wait to get back to the Metropolis.

In contrast, the still-youthful captain loved it ...

5

The Conflict in Depth

' ... they didn't need logistical support. Gatherers since kids, they could live out of nothing, with a special ability to find food and water. We really had good operational results with them and we never had a desertion from the ranks of the *Flechas*'.

Oscar Cardoso's testimony on the *Flechas,* one of the African Special Force units created in Angola after the war began: Antunes, *Guerra de África:* 1: 401.

At Nambuangongo, after we'd arrived, I was to discover that the Portuguese Army had implemented a bold and somewhat optimistic program of rehabilitation of former enemy combatants.

Lieutenant-Colonel Joâo Barros-e-Cunha, the garrison commandant, showed us over a village where most insurgent veterans who had come across were housed. With its distinctive tall palms, banana-leaf huts and kids playing around in the dirt, the village looked a little incongruous against a military backdrop, with the camp and its gun emplacements towering on the hill above.

The philosophy of using turncoats to fight for what was essentially a European-orientated cause – a concept, incidentally, that was later applied by the South Africans in their own Border Wars units like with Koevoet, the police counter-terrorist unit and 32 Battalion, and with considerable effect – was that every man taken prisoner was given an option. He either worked with them, the colonel explained, or 'swish', he drew his hand across his throat in the traditional cutthroat manner.

The choice was straightforward, he maintained: defect and start to work with the security forces against their former comrades or face the consequences. No trial, no questions, no answers.

He admitted afterwards that while that was what happened most times, it wasn't the case with every suspect brought into camp. There were quite often innocent civilians taken prisoner but they could usually be easily spotted. Rebel military types usually wore some kind of uniform that was nothing fancy, but different from the rest. They all had boots, issue types made in East Germany and customarily with a chevron imprint on the soles, which set them aside from the bulk of the populace.

'Might sound primitive to you, but these people don't need coddling: they're killers, one and all and we act accordingly', the colonel maintained.

'We're at war against an enemy that is as mindless as it is brutal. The rebels never once showed compassion towards any of the Portuguese soldiers they captured, never mind civilian women and children mindlessly slaughtered at the start of it all. Their grossly mutilated and tortured bodies that we discovered afterwards – and are still finding – bear witness.'

Colonel Barros-e-Cunha waved towards an orderly and told him to get our meals ready; as always in the Portuguese Army, the only intrusion ever allowed when serious issues were being discussed was food. He went on, deeply committed to an issue that had affected his notion of how the war should be fought.

'As you will see while you're with us, we do things differently. We offer the hand of friendship to these people—partly because it is a Christian gesture and partly because we know they can help us win the war.'

He explained that while some of his colleagues differed with his approach, it was pointless killing everyone who opposed Portuguese rule. Granted that there were masses of civilians who had been turned against the government, but equally, many innocents were caught up in a cause which they simply did not understand because most were unlettered.

'Essentially, the people in the bush throughout Angola are hardly likely to be able to comprehend the intricacies of modern-day politics that includes socialism, communism, capitalism or even Fascism ... most wouldn't be able to tell one from the other ... they are primitive folk with their own gods and customs ... their world is the bush and the ability to survive.

'What they have been told is that Africa is theirs. And so it is. They've also been told by the political commissars who move about with rebel units, as much to keep their own people in check, Soviet style – as to indoctrinate the locals – that we are imperialists who have illegally seized their country.' The nuances could be interpreted in a dozen different ways in as many countries', he argued, using the deprivations of the American Indian and the Aborigines in Australia as examples.

'How do you expect a simple tribesman in this jungle to counter that kind of logic?' he queried. He ignored the political reality that that shortcoming almost certainly lay with the Portuguese themselves: the colonial tradition in all three provinces only allowed for the most basic levels of education, though he conceded that with the war, this was changing fast.[1]

The Colonel went on: There were reasons why some of the insurgents that had been captured were given a chance.

'In exchange for their lives, we require them to tell us everything they knew about their former colleagues. They must give us names, places, codes, signals, dates of training, future and past programs. Also, they need to explain all the documents in their possession.

'Some of them give us a story of sorts, but they can't lie ... we've enough experience to know when a man is telling the truth. If he doesn't come clean, then he's used up the chance we offered him ... and he'd been warned...for him it's over.'

The real moment of truth follows immediately afterwards, when the captured insurgent is expected to lead the army to his former headquarters and detail everything that went down in the operational area in which he had been active. This sometimes took in lengthy deployments of six months or more, but there were good dividends in the end.

A squad of youthful Portuguese soldiers doing their national
service in Angola. (Author's collection)

'It is here where the final showdown comes', he declared. 'The man takes a patrol through the jungle to his various hide-outs. He shows them the camps and other places he has used while he fought against us. He knows – and more to the point – *we know* that he's going to be spotted by his old pals ... they're watching us from the jungle all the time.

'By then they'll be aware that they have been betrayed by this compadre, so there's no going back. Ever ... '

As the Colonel explained, if the prisoner did try to return to his old haunts, he'd be shot by his former comrades. There was no need to explain why.

'Overnight, this former enemy combatant becomes our man and let's face it, he's a useful adjunct because he's trained, he's better educated than the rest and he clearly understands his changed circumstances. We are so confident that he will continue to help us – for he has no alternative – that we give him a gun with which to protect himself. Not just any old gun, but one of the modern automatic weapons that our own people use, the G3 in 7.62mm calibre ... as good, if not better than the AK with which he was originally issued.

After lunch we ambled down the hill towards the compound housing former insurgents and the commandant smiled at a group that had been gathered together to greet our party. His attitude towards these former enemy troops was avuncular but friendly. They seemed to be fond of him, greeting us with smiles all round and waving or saluting the officers in our group.

One of the men was brought forward. His name was Alberto Imbu, a tall lad, perhaps 20 years old.

Imbu might have been younger because it is difficult to tell a man's age in the bush: a 13-year-old often looks 18 or older and it was no secret that many of those captured were barely 14 or 15, all of them armed. It was the same in old Stanleyville (today Kisangani) in the Congo: some of the worst brutalities were perpetrated by children not yet into their teens.

Imbu had an automatic Sten slung casually over his shoulders. His dark glasses – a requisite badge of office among so many African insurgent movements – glistened in the sharp light as he spoke to us in fluent Portuguese. He could also speak French, having been taught the language by Algerian revolutionaries at Tclemen.

Yes, he had been captured by the Portuguese, he explained, with Captain Alcada translating. It had been in March 1967. He remembered it because it had been an important day in his life and the action in which he'd been badly wounded had been rough.

As one of a group of 18 insurgents who had attacked a coffee-farm late one night, he told us, three of his comrades had been killed in the same contact by Portuguese troops who came up shortly afterwards. For a short while they had been trapped, with a fast-flowing river behind them and, it being night, none of his colleagues were prepared to take the chance and swim for safety. That was when they took most of the casualties, including quite a few wounded.

He'd been patched up at one of the local hospitals after he'd indicated a willingness to cooperate and had subsequently led the authorities to his former camp. That gesture resulted in Captain Alcada's squad killing still more of his former comrades.

No, he replied when I asked him, he had no regrets. He had his wife and children at the camp below and was confident that he could look after himself.

Was this his original wife? No comment. And his children? Again no comment. All the while as he spoke, Imbu patted the elongated magazine on the Sten.

We were later told that this man had shown great courage in several recent actions and had been made a section leader, to which Alcada added, 'he's a good fighter … , tough, knows the ropes'. I only learnt afterwards that his name had been put forward for a decoration for a brilliant piece of work in destroying an enemy supply column some months before.

'These former gooks are a very good second arm to our forces', the captain told me later, though he admitted that the possibility of some of them being double agents was not impossible. 'We infiltrate their units, they ours … '

We were discussing problems linked to employing erstwhile hostile elements to handle tasks that might be problematic, such as being entrusted with sensitive intelligence. There were easily more than a thousand of these turncoats in the Angolan war, he admitted, and while they were a priceless adjunct, there were very few Imbus within their ranks. Most were basic foot soldiers, former insurgents that were illiterate and not all that motivated, whatever the cause.

'But they know the jungle. They are familiar with many of the foibles of their old buddies.' Most important, he declared, 'they know every ruse and that is invaluable'.

The captain told me of a 16-year-old he'd captured on one of his raids. 'We'd caught this young fellow—only a boy—about 10 miles south of Zala. He'd been a member of a pretty competent group of insurgents operating in the area. We were lucky to catch any of them alive—they'd been trained by the Chinese and had been instructed to fight to the proverbial last, he added.

'Having taken him in that battle was only half the battle won. His colleagues knew we'd got one of their people and they were going to do their best to get him back—or at very least try to kill him before we could get to work on him. Consequently, they were right on our tail as we headed home. At one point our lead scout came in and told us that they were perhaps 30 minutes behind us.

'The trouble was, we still had a difficult march of several hours to get to the road where, hopefully, we'd be picked up. Bottom line was that we'd have to move quickly. I'd already radioed base and told them what we had ... asked for a helicopter but there weren't any available. I'd considered an ambush, but we didn't have the numbers ... this was a large force we were up against ... also, they were all MPLA ... knew all the tricks in the game'.

'So here were we, in the depths of the African bush, running for our lives. Meanwhile, this little shit was making things difficult for us.

'At first he refused to walk fast, as we required of him ... he'd drag his heels between the two soldiers delegated to march on either side of him. Then he complained that he couldn't keep pace because his arms were bound. Granted, I was aware that he'd fallen face-forward a few times because the undergrowth was vicious and sometimes reached right across the paths we were following.

'Our guys pushed him ahead anyway, clipped him across the head when he became difficult but none of it helped. He obviously knew his buddies were on our trail.

'I knew that if we didn't improve our pace, the guerrillas would double around, as they often liked to do and we'd be ambushed. These people knew their own back yard and all the short cuts. We were in a fix, which was when I thought that perhaps I should do the obvious and whack the guy.

'Eventually I took the boy to the side and spoke to him. He'd been educated in a mission school so he could speak fluent Portuguese. I told him that he was holding us up and that if he continued playing games, I'd kill him ... .simple as that! He was placing us in jeopardy, I said, and rather he died than we did.

'The little bastard was sceptical to begin with. He'd heard stories about us needing people like him. He kind of suggested that we wouldn't simply kill somebody for not cooperating, and that we needed him more than he needed us. At that point I warned him that he was wrong, adding that I was more interested in saving the lives of the men with me than anything he might be able offer.

'But even this didn't have any effect on him and he refused to talk. He just stayed sullen and stared into space.

'At that point I told the sergeant to cut his restraints, so he would clearly understand

Portuguese officers discuss tactics under the wing of a Dornier spotter
plane on the Nambuangongo air strip. (Author's photo)

that this was no idle chatter.

Things improved a little once his arms were free, but he still answered in spurts. He said
he was going to die anyway and that there was no difference whether it happened out there
in the jungle or later at the hands of some of the Portuguese torturers who were waiting for
him. "Death was inevitable—one way or the other", were his words. He was either a very
brave young man, I concluded, or a very stupid one.

'Well, when you have something like this on your hands in the middle of nowhere and
the enemy is breathing down your neck, the consequences are usually terminal. I told him
so. Again he looked past me and stayed mute.'

That was when captain Alcada took a chance. He asked the boy whether he would
believe anything he said? *Anything*?

'I asked him whether he'd accept the word an older man, an officer. This caught him by
surprise. "What do you mean?" he shot back.'

Alcada told the boy that if he came voluntarily, he, as a fellow-soldier, would promise
him his life. On the other hand if he kept up the charade, it was over. By coming of his own
free will, the captain said he would personally take up his case.

'I gave him my word—one soldier to another – were the words I used. Obviously I'd already overstepped the line by making a declaration of faith with the enemy. Everything went quiet for a moment because just about everyone in the squad – apart from the men that had taken up positions on the periphery – was listening.

'We could see that he was hesitant ... more puzzled in fact, probably by me treating him as an equal, though I'd imagine that my right hand fiddling with the pistol on my belt must have played a role in him finally making a decision. Which was when he answered: 'yes, I'll come!' That astonished us all.

The young insurgent had been told by everyone he'd ever met while under training that the Portuguese were a crafty bunch of bastards, so it was a big decision. Alcada also accepted that the boy wasn't stupid: he'd been offered his life instead of being shot, a pretty realistic option under the circumstances.

'We lost more time so now we had to move fast. I told the youngster to get himself together and move off, right behind me. I said I wasn't going to bind his arms again, which was about the best thing I did because that in itself was a gesture of sorts.

The captain's patrol didn't make contact with the enemy again, probably because they moved at the double for the rest of the long haul. Before nightfall they were back in camp.

I was to learn only afterwards that that young fellow was actually in Nambuangongo when we were there, helping to build the new school. He also had one of the young conscript officers helping him with his secondary school studies.

Alcada: 'He's bright. Probably go far. If he keeps on like this, he'll probably make university, especially since I'm on his case. It's a debt of honour, I suppose...

After a month covering that African conflict, that event in a remote military base in the Angolan jungle was one of the few positive things to emerge in a war that seemed to offer little for either side. We subsequently heard that whenever Alcada passed though Nambuangongo, he'd spend a little time with his young protégé and if circumstances allowed, would take him books and magazines. When his second two-year period of duty was over, he promised the youngster that he'd look into the prospect of more advanced studies in Luanda—or perhaps even Lisbon.

I never heard the outcome of that little episode, or perhaps captain Ricardo Alcada wasn't telling. When I saw him in Cape Town afterwards, he told me that Imbu – the young guerrilla fighter with the Sten gun that we met on the first day – had died in a road ambush three or four months after our visit.

In the six months that captain Alcada had been back on active duty in Africa, he'd been in about a dozen contacts with the enemy. These were major actions he said, not just the kind of casual shots that ring out from when a convoy passes. Each time he'd either been ambushed, or he'd set one.

During this time, his group, 166 Company, had killed 15 and captured 37. They had also taken more than 50 weapons, almost all automatic and mostly of Russian and East European origin.

Pedra Verde – the 'Green Rock' – was a significant guerrilla redoubt in the *Dembos* north of Angola until it was retaken in September 1961 by government forces. It was a difficult action across high ground that cost lives on both sides of the line. (Photo Manuel Graça)

Since he had returned to Africa, his group hadn't lost a man in action, and there were quite a few wounded. One of his corporals was killed in a road accident and another badly wounded in the shoulder and evacuated to Luanda. Lighter wounds were treated at the field hospital.

'They'll get better sooner or later and are perhaps wiser for the experience', he commented with characteristic aplomb when we discussed casualties.

The captain was proud of his record. Though his adversaries might disagree, he had good reason to be. The fact that he had taken a number of prisoners underscored his often-voiced theory that the Portuguese should take the war to the enemy. He was dismissive of any kind of prevarication or what some Portuguese officers liked to call 'alternative action', which was largely defensive-based.

Alcada had been operating mostly in an area between Zala and Nambuangongo. This area, he said, was slowly being cleared of insurgents, though I was not sure how anybody could really be certain of what was going on in some of the most forbidding rain forest on any continent. The jungle stretched more than a thousand miles northwards, all the way

Pilot's-eye-view of an army base in Angola's embattled Sector D. (Author's photo)

through the Congo and on to the Central African Republic, Gabon and beyond. It was the same throughout: a dark, overwhelming hinterland that had never taken kindly to human incursion. The area around Nambuangongo was no different.

The captain believed otherwise. He thought he knew what was going on in his modest fief and was proud of his role as a counter-insurgency tactician. He would comment succinctly that the secret was in getting your hands dirty. 'Remember, this is never pleasant work. It is not, as you Anglo-Saxons say, *nice*. But it is war and lives are lost. You've to get out there and do what needs to be done to win it.'

He had his own views on the outcome of the kind of modern guerrilla conflicts being fought at the time, both in Africa and Asia. The captain was outspokenly critical about what was going on in Vietnam where, he said, the Americans, because of Washington politics, were fighting a rearguard action.

He maintained that the hostilities in which Portugal had been thrust could only be won if the conquest was both military and political. You have to achieve victory both in order to win at all, he would stress, though he was never prepared to discuss the role of his own politicians in his African struggle.

The French in Indo-China, he would say, lost both militarily and politically; it was an utter disaster. In Algeria they beat the FLN in battle, hands down as the English say. But then they went and lost the sympathy of the civilian population. That too, was a debacle.

The FLN at Evian were a broken military power, but De Gaulle was shrewd enough to realize that he could never win the Arab population to his cause. 'That's why he pulled out', the captain added.

There were two examples of modern guerrilla warfare he reckoned, where the insurgents were beaten both at political and military levels; in Malaya against the communists and in Kenya against Jomo Kenyatta's Mau-Mau.[2]

'And that's exactly what we are trying to do in Angola—follow the British example and get the upper hand in both the military *and* political spheres. The first we are accomplishing, of that you see the evidence here in Nambuangongo, Santa Eulalia and elsewhere in Angola. But it's a race against time and the MPLA for the second.'

Trouble was, he added, there were other nations involved in this fight. The idea of having South African troops in Angola would cause a flurry in Third World politics, especially among the Afro-Asians.

'But the Afro-Asian powers say nothing about foreign powers helping the insurgents ... if you examine this war carefully, you will see that we are fighting, one way or another, just about every major power.

'The war started with dollars. The Americans thought that by backing Holden Roberto they would chase the Portuguese out of Angola within months—like New Delhi did, when the Indian Army overran Goa. What they still don't realize is that we, like De Gaulle, knew long before the final strike, that Goa was lost.

'We couldn't possibly win against a nation of 450 million people which has the backing of every major power in the world. But here in Africa, things are different.

'The Americans now accept that they might have made a mistake, but they're still allowing money into the Congo from a number of organizations in the United States. There are American church and social groups and others in Britain and more in European and Asian countries passing on money to guerrilla groups—over and above what they receive from Iron Curtain states.

'The rebels wouldn't be able to keep on with the war but for this financial aid', Alcada maintained.

'Fortunately, a lot of it seems to be finding its way into private pockets and no doubt effecting the resources of the 'Freedom' armies, but then, let's face it, that's the African way, *n'est-ce pas?*'

It was his view that that since the Organisation of African Unity [African Union] had taken over the finances of the rebel group UPA, the amount for their war effort had decreased. 'Last year Roberto complained bitterly at one of the OAU conferences that he was receiving less financial assistance now than his people got in 1965.'

'Obviously there are a lot of people cashing in on this war—but then we don't mind—the more the merrier', he quipped.

6

The Enemy

While the military plays a key role in counterinsurgency, at heart it remains a political struggle. Consequently, the job of the armed forces is not necessarily to deliver an outright military victory, but rather to contain violence, protect people from intimidation, deny guerrillas access to the local inhabitants and their supply of food and recruits, gain the people's confidence with psychological and social initiatives, and through these activities produce enough respect among the insurgent leadership to induce political negotiations.

John P. Cann:
Counterinsurgency in Africa: The Portuguese Way of War 1961-1974

I
t was the charisma, determination and more often than not, the ruthlessness of individual revolutionary leaders that made so many African liberation groups function. If not always practical or efficient, they most times got themselves and their co-conspirators going with a lot more intent and determination than the colonial defenders that opposed them.

The political leader Kwame Nkrumah was among the more prominent of the political firebrands to emerge after World War II, though very much in a 'self-absorbed' class of his own, writing absurd books and fostering revolt among his neighbours. Not long after he took charge he told the nation to refer to him reverentially as *Osagyefo* – the word signifies 'Redeemer'. Shortly afterwards he took his modest West African state into nationhood to become the Republic of Ghana.

His counterparts in East Africa, *Mzee* Kenyatta of Kenya, Uganda's Milton Obote and *Mwalimu* (teacher) Julius Nyerere of Tanganyika (which, with the amalgamation of Zanzibar, soon became Tanzania) were revolutionary figures that became respected heads of their fledgling nations. For a while, anyway ...

Obote unfortunately – like Robert Mugabe and the tyrant Jean Bedel Bokassa of the Central African Republic – soon hoisted their colours as almost certifiable psychopaths. While the Zimbabwean leader and Obote ended up murdering tens of thousands of their own people, Bokassa was the kind of basket case who liked to cut the ears off recalcitrant children 'to teach them lessons'.

In an absurd ceremony that might have done ridiculous justice to the Court of Louis XIV at Versailles (a function attended by many African Heads of State as well as the entire Bangui Diplomatic Corps) he eventually crowned himself Emperor. Even for Africa in the 1970s it was crazy, yet nobody had the temerity to say anything because that would have

Holden Roberto (left) was the designated leader of the Western-orientated FNLA guerrilla movement and because it operated in opposition to Agostinho Neto's Marxist MPLA, it soon became the most prominent CIA surrogate force in the Congo. (Author's collection)

been regarded as 'racist'.

The madcap Idi Amin Dada, a former heavyweight boxing champion while serving with the King's African Rifles in East Africa, followed. A cruel, ruthless man, Amin presented himself to the world as a ridiculous caricature and, like Mugabe, managed to discredit African people in the eyes of the world.

During his 'reign', he volunteered himself as King of Scotland, so that the Scots, as he would say 'could be free of British rule' – a theme which resulted in a brilliant film that went on to win an Oscar. Then he would send telegrams to the Queen of England, insulting and taunting her. He even challenged the president of Tanzania to a boxing match.

From 1977, Amin officially adopted the title 'His Excellency, President for Life, Field Marshal Al Haji Doctor Idi Amin Dada, VC, DSO, MC, Lord of all the Beasts of the Earth and Fishes of the Sea ... ' and on and on and on.

While these contemptibles made headlines – sometimes hilarious and more often than not, ludicrous – they were fortunately in the minority. Quite a few personable black leaders were to emerge and some, like Nelson Mandela and Léopold Senghor of Senegal, went on to become much-revered international icons of moderation and progress. Eduardo Mondlane of Mozambique's FRELIMO might have enjoyed that same kind of status had he not been murdered by his lieutenants whom, it was said on good authority in Dar es

Dr Agostinho Neto's MPLA – the Popular Movement for the Liberation of Angola – was thoroughly Marxist and Kremlin-controlled. In a real sense, the situation was regarded by most as an adjunct to the Cold War, with Washington supporting Holden Roberto's FNLA. And when they were not able to 'deliver the goods' Jonas Savimbi's UNITA became the recipient of CIA largesse (including Stinger missiles during the subsequent civil war period). In truth, the MPLA was far more focused and driven than any of the other guerrilla groups in the country, with women playing important roles both in and behind the fighting lines. (Photos from author's collection)

Salaam diplomatic circles, included his successor, Samora Machel.

Another leader assassinated by his own was Laurent Kabila – those who knew him reckoned he had the intellect of a demented army corporal. Ché Guevara met the man on one of his revolutionary 'fact-finding' missions to Africa and in his diaries, referred to him as a buffoon. Yet Kabila had the ruthlessness and the basic atavistic guile to lead his bunch of crazies through the jungles of the Congo to eventually oust the equally manic Mobuto Sese Seko.

The same with Foday Sankoh, leader of Sierra Leone's Revolutionary United Front, the rebel group that spent time cutting the hands and feet off children and brutalising women. Considered a blunderer by his peers while still in the Sierra Leone Army, he was as cunning and brutal as any 20th Century anarchist. Sankoh and his bloody-minded lieutenants, usually high on drugs or local gin (and often both), went on to set Sierra Leone ablaze for almost a decade.

It was British forces, led by then Brigadier David Richards, who used good dollops of force to terminate that revolt and in the process displaying the kind of courage and good judgement that allowed him to achieve the ultimate honour of being appointed Britain's Chief of the Defence Staff.

In this regard, in many respects, Angola was no different. Those who led the uprising were a diverse lot, some brilliant, others patently lacking in skills, But all were vehemently dedicated to the most passionate cause of all: that of ousting the Portuguese from their homeland.

For a long time, the revolutionary whip hand in Angola was jointly held by Holden Roberto's UPA *(Uniao dos Populacoes de Angola)* and the MPLA or, more commonly, the Popular Movement for the Liberation of Angola or *Movimento Popular de Libertàcao de Angola)*. UPA was eventually to transmogrify into GRAE, and finally into the FNLA, neither of which came to much.

How different was the MPLA, headed by Dr Agostinho Neto, a charming young intellectual who nursed the radical, pro-Moscow movement through its most difficult years. Under his leadership, things were a lot different. A man clearly ahead of his time, there are many party stalwarts in Luanda today who maintain that Neto was murdered by the Soviets while being treated at a Moscow clinic, in part because he'd reached a stage of his political evolution when he began to show a predilection for drawing closer to the West.

Daily Telegraph correspondent John Miller had his own take on Angolan revolutionary movements 40 years ago, and considering developments in that country since then, his views, in retrospect, are instructive.

As he stated, during the 1950's the winds of change were blowing through Portuguese Africa just as they were throughout the English or French-speaking Africa. They were fanned as much by the willingness – for many different reasons – of international bodies to support conflict in the area, as by a growing African awareness of the possibilities of

A bunch of UNITA guerrillas at the end of the colonial war in 1974. Blooded
against the Portuguese Army, they were ready to continue with another military
struggle in a bid to oust the MPLA from Luanda. The photo was taken by South
African Army Brigadier Philip Smit, who acted in a liaison capacity with Dr
Jonas Savimbi at his Jamba headquarters in the south-east of Angola.

independence.

Even though he was sceptical about the eventual outcome of this liberation war, I
quote Miller in detail:

> The toughest African fighter against the Portuguese presence in the decade of the
> 1970's will almost certainly be a card-carrying, gun-hawking, mine-laying member
> of the MPLA.
>
> The Popular Liberation Movement of Angola was born at a secret meeting in
> Luanda in 1956. By any unbiased standards the MPLA ringleaders were communists
> who had successfully built up a following among discontented intellectuals in Angola,
> and as a subversive movement it had to operate clandestinely. This it managed for
> three years until PIDE, Portugal's ubiquitous secret police, smelt out some of the
> MPLA leaders and arrested them.
>
> Threatened with the destruction of its cadres, the MPLA moved out of Angola to
> Conakry in the Republic of Guinea and to Paris, and eventually to Brazzaville.
>
> Initially the change paid huge dividends. The movement was brought into close

contact with many Angolan refugees and with others with a militant anti-colonialist, anti-Portuguese nationalist spirit. The drawback was that such contacts also resulted in political infighting, backbiting and petty squabbles. It took the appearance on the scene in 1962 of Dr Antonio Agostinho Neto – poet, physician, one of the first of the contemporary Angolan nationalists, and an escapee from metropolitan Portuguese prisons – to give the movement influence and impetus.

Dr Neto quickly realised that the movement needed to break out of its pro-communist image, and one of his first moves on becoming MPLA president was to seek the aid of the United States. In fact, ever since, while his ragged regiments pick their way through Angola as a symbolic gesture of 'control' over huge areas, he had been flying from one capital to another seeking moral, military and financial aid. In a way, Dr Neto has achieved much: a blessing from the Pope, a handful of dollars from the World Council of Churches, kroner from Sweden and undisclosed but not really substantial guns-without-butter support from Russia and China.

His failure has been to bring any kind of unity to the anti-Portuguese [liberation] movements. It is fact, not Portuguese propaganda fiction, that the bitter rivalry, the unrelenting radio campaign of mutual recrimination, remained in full stride while he was at the helm and afterwards. In the shifty and shifting world of the fight against Portuguese 'colonialism' dog still ate dog.

What was just as true, and more worrying to the Portuguese, was the fact that MPLA fighters were better equipped than those of the other movements. The days of machetes and homemade muskets were gone – forever. The trophies of war of the Portuguese (after a surprise attack on an MPLA base in eastern Angola) were more often than not Simonov and Kalashnikov light and medium machine-guns of recent make and of Chinese and Russian origin.

The MPLA had other things going for it. It was then the most-favoured son of the Organisation of African Unity's Liberation Committee, and it operated from safe sanctuaries in Zambia and the Congo (Brazzaville).

In Kenneth Kaunda's Zambia, the MPLA's recruiting and staging points were Balovale and Kalabo, with Sikongo the major arms dump and supply distribution centre. Operations in Northern Angola were carried out from Dolisie in Congo (Brazzaville), and from Bango on the rare occasions Dr Neto felt it was safe to strike at the oil-rich enclave of Cabinda.

Dr Neto claimed he had some 5,000 fighters in Angola constantly rotating from these safe bases. He might have been right – for one certainty of the war at the time was that the Portuguese High Command did not really appreciate the true fighting-strength of the MPLA units specialising in hit-and-run ambushes.

What was undisputed in the propaganda war which was carried on side by side with the 'other' war, was that the MPLA was a pocket of resistance in the Dembos mountains north-east of Luanda – difficult terrain encompassing an area of about 200 kilometres square – and that it roamed relatively at will in eastern Angola, a huge,

Meantime, as it became clear that Lisbon was pulling back to Europe, huge numbers of guerrillas had gathered along Angola's northern frontier with the Congo. These FNLA troops were soon to cross swords with the MPLA whose forces had been bolstered by thousands of Cuban troops flown in from Havana. (Author's collection)

arid, under-populated area which the Portuguese would be powerless to control even if they had wanted to.

The best the Army could do was to organise sorties with halftrack personnel carriers from eastern Angola's fixed garrisons – which the MPLA kept well clear of – or hopefully hit an area with the small French-built helicopters overloaded with *Tropas Especial* commandos who had become experts in this kind of bush warfare.

Meantime, Neto had grown weary of Moscow's insistence of putting the party ahead of the individual. Shortly afterwards he was heard to say that after years of fighting and untold numbers of deaths, the guerrilla struggle was going nowhere. The Portuguese were of a similar mind and had already put out feelers for some kind of political settlement.

In spite of initial misgivings, it was the MPLA, with enough Moscow-led coercion and Third World subterfuge to do justice to any communist revolutionary group, that eventually wormed its way into a position to take over the Angolan Government once the Portuguese had left for home. Curiously, the movement was assisted by the most senior Portuguese officer in Angola, Admiral Rosa Coutinho, the man subsequently dubbed 'The Red Admiral'.

Coutinho had been a communist for years and though he played a prominent role in

Angola's war, nobody was in doubt in later years where his true allegiance lay.

These weren't the only players during that critical pre-independent phase. During the course of the war there were numerous splinter groups and off-shoots with such illustrious titles as CPA-CNE, FLEC, FLJKP and, of course, UNITA, arguably the most successful African guerrilla group of the 20th Century.

UNITA – the Union for the Total Liberation of Angola or *União Nacional Para a Independência Total de Angola* was led by a burly Geneva-educated Maoist by the name of Jonas Malheiro Savimbi and initially he marshalled his insurgents in the east of the country. As an Ovimbundu tribesman he had originally started campaigning among the primitive bush people in his own back yard and after he had produced results, this charismatic insurgent leader moved further afield. Eventually he achieved a powerful following throughout the country.

At his best, in the post-independent period, Jonas Savimbi managed to gain control more than 90 per cent of the Angolan interior. It was only the big cities which eluded him in the end, though in the heavy fighting which endured for years, huge tracts of some of the conurbations– like the lovely old city of Huambo, previously Nova Lisboa – were reduced to rubble

Savimbi – who had spent time in China and spoke seven languages, four of them European – waged a series of vicious wars for almost 40 years, first against the Portuguese and afterwards, with strong South African support – both army and air force – against the communist-led MPLA government.

He was killed in 2002, after being lured to a meeting by foreign agents, believed to be either former diamond-dealing Israelis or, more likely, some of the South African Special Forces operatives with whom he had been linked during the early days of the Angolan Civil War.[1]

There is no question that UNITA left its mark on Angola like no other liberation group on the African continent. The MPLA might have taken over the government but they would never have achieved that much but for the machinations of the Soviets and a clandestine group of Portuguese communists – Admiral Coutinho included – who had supported Moscow from the start.

The UNITA guerrilla group carried out its first attacks late in 1966, by preventing trains from passing through the Benguela railway at Teixeira de Sousa on the border with Zambia. In fact, it was UNITA irregulars who twice derailed the railway in 1967. That angered the land-locked Zambian government which shipped its copper through the Angolan port of Lobito and Zambian President Kenneth Kaunda responded by kicking all of Savimbi's 500 'Freedom Fighters' out of his country.

Jonas Savimbi then moved to Cairo, Egypt, where he lived for a year, before secretly returning to Angola through Zambia where, word had it, he worked with the Portuguese military against the established government order.

During the Portuguese epoch in Africa, all these freedom groups operated from neighbouring states and were headquartered either in Kinshasa or in the Zambian capital.

In President Sékou Touré's Marxist Guinea, it was *La Voix de la Revolution* in central Conakry that broadcast the official party line to the masses. This radio station also sent out coded messages to PAIGC guerrillas operating in the neighbouring enclave. (Author's photo)

In the case of groups opposed to the Portuguese presence in the oil-rich Cabinda enclave, they chose Brazzaville.

UPA – later to be renamed GRAE and then FNLA or Front for the Liberation of Angola – achieved prominence early on as a guerrilla group and was headed by Holden Roberto, the man who engineered the first full-scale attack into Angola from the Congo in March 1961. Most of his succour came from Western-orientated countries as well as pro-African movements in the United States, Britain, France and Belgium. Other countries that helped financially and militarily were Tunisia, Ethiopia, Israel, the United Arab Republic, and in the final stages, India.

Founded in 1954 as an illegal independence party within Angola, UPA was largely tribal-orientated. Its power rested with the half-million Bakongo people of northern Angola and though other tribes were involved, all senior positions were delegated by Roberto who was said to enjoy the support of clandestine CIA-funded groups including dissident Cubans based in Miami.

Holden Alvaro Roberto (alias Jose Gilmore, Roberto Holden, Ruy Ventura, Onofre, etc.), was born in 1923 near Sao Salvador, a town close to the Congolese frontier. While still an infant, his family moved across the border into the former Belgian Congo where the

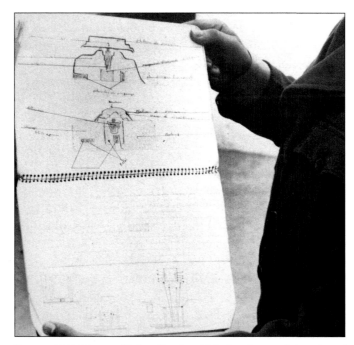

Captured MPLA guerrilla handbooks which date from training abroad
show the mechanics of a Soviet anti-tank mine. (Author's photo)

future leader received most of his secondary education.

Prior to his revolutionary interests, he worked in the Finance Department of the Belgian Administration in Leopoldville (Kinshasa), Stanleyville (Kisangani) and in Bukavu in the Congo's Eastern Province. During this time he retained close links with family interests in Angola and consequently spoke fluent Portuguese, French, fairly good English and a little Flemish—as well as his native Bakongo.

This 'Freedom Army' leader admitted that most of his early support came from the American Committee on Africa and the Ford Foundation, largely as a result of the efforts of the late Eleanor Roosevelt and former Under Secretary of State Mennen Williams. He credited much of his success, as well as moral support from abroad to the man who remained his 'guiding light' until his death—Patrice Lumumba. Both men were on first-name terms with Nkrumah, Roberto having worked in Accra for a while from 1958 onwards.

Above all, it was Washington that gave UPA/FNLA the impetus it needed to get its revolution functioning. One Belgian diplomat I met afterwards in Kinshasa, maintained that but for CIA money, the movement would have floundered years before. It was his view that the United States feared the growing influence of communist-backed MPLA and fostered the UPA image as an effective counter to the more radical Congo (Brazzaville) and Lusaka-based opposition.

After more than seven years of fighting, Roberto's party took its first of many serious knocks in July 1968 when an Organization of African Unity [African Union] resolution withdrew recognition of his Angolan government-in-Exile. OAU leaders stated in Addis Ababa that in future they would channel all military and financial assistance to the MPLA, already in strong opposition to UPA/FNLA. The reason for the choice, the media was told, was that the MPLA appeared to be the more successful guerrilla grouping in Angola.

Indirectly, Lisbon concurred that it was the better choice. By the time I arrived in Luanda for the first time in the late 1960s, Portuguese military authorities admitted that the MPLA threat was the most serious they had encountered since the start of the war. They made no bones about it: the MPLA, together with the Conakry-based PAIGC movement operating in Portuguese Guinea were the most effective guerrilla armies in sub-Saharan Africa, was the most significant theme of my first briefing.

Of concern to Lisbon throughout, was the fact that the MPLA got almost all its weapons from the Communist Bloc. The Mosin-Nagant bolt-action rifle was an early starter, followed by Soviet SKS and AK-47 automatic rifles as well as PPsH-41 submachine-guns.

It was interesting that a number of Portuguese units, including several Special Forces groups, actually preferred the AK; they regarded it as superior to their own G3s. The same held for South Africa's largely Portuguese-speaking 32 Battalion, but for different reasons. Many 32 Battalion operations were clandestine cross-border raids into Angola. The unit often used former Portuguese Army camouflage uniforms together with Kalashnikovs in bids to confuse locals that they were the MPLA

Angolan guerrilla movements also made extensive use of the Degtyarev light machine gun together with the DShK as well as heavier weapons like the SG-43 Gorunov. Support weapons included Soviet mortars, recoilless rifles, the RPG-2 and, when more readily available, the RPG-7. In anti-aircraft weapons, the ZPU-4 was top of the list, supplemented towards the end of the war by Strela-2s ground to air guided missiles, more commonly called SAM-7s and introduced into the Guinea theatre in 1973. The weapon appeared among Mozambique guerrilla fighters a year later.

SAM-7s or Man Portable Air Defence Systems (MANPADS) were actually successful in shooting down several Portuguese Air Force Fiat G-91 support jet fighters in Guinea and the consequences had a lasting effect on morale among government troops. Once the insurgents had proved that they had the wherewithal to knock sophisticated aircraft out of the sky, Portuguese Air Force bombing and strafing raids were immediately halted and only very sporadically used in the final stages of the war.

Shoulder-fired SAMs are relatively inexpensive and, at less than two metres in length, easy to use. Operated much like a rifle (as is the RPG-7) early versions of the MANPAD were effective up to about 4,500 metres and for the guerrilla operating under primitive conditions, the ultimate offensive weapon.

Two Rhodesian civilian airliners that had taken off from Kariba towards the end of that conflict were shot down by SAM-7s while still in the Zambezi Valley.

As with the MANPADS, most of the MPLA's arms, ammunition and equipment was – and is still – of Eastern European Bloc or Chinese origin.

It was the same with training. MPLA cadres were put through their paces by Soviet,

Chinese, Cuban, Algerian and—in a few instances—North Vietnamese guerrilla veterans. The Vietnamese were put to good use in breaking the language barrier, especially since many rebel volunteers had originally come from Francophone Africa. Since Vietnam was formerly a French colony, the choice made good sense.

The individual behind the MPLA, the movement that made the most decisive anti-Portuguese gains in what is termed by historians as the Liberation Period, was Dr Agostinho Neto, a former Portuguese national and Lisbon-educated poet and intellectual. For a long time early on, he operated from an office in downtown Lusaka, though his movement's military wing had previously operated from Congo-Brazza. Increased French influence later forced the movement southwards.

Ultimately, the Zambian government's militant stand against newly-independent Rhodesia was the deciding factor for Kenneth Kaunda's support. The country's geographical position between three of the four European-dominated Southern African states made the former British colony an excellent staging post for a variety of insurgent groups.

Daniel Chipenda, a competent but testy revolutionary who later fell foul of the elders of the founding party was initially the MPLA representative in Dar-es-Salaam. His job, early on, was to coordinate training and supply programmes with other liberation groups in Southern Africa. It was a significant posting because a large proportion of the military hardware used by the MPLA – as well as Mozambican and Rhodesian liberation groups was channelled through Dar es Salaam harbour.

Chipenda used his position to good effect since it was said he was working for both the CIA and South African Military Intelligence.[2] Which was why it came as no surprise when he formed his own political and military grouping that he called the Chipa Squadron or in the lingo, *Chipa Esquadrao*. It was this band of fighters that went over to the South African Army almost en bloc after the Portuguese had pulled out and was moulded into the crack 32 Battalion, an elite Special Forces group.

Throughout the insurgent struggle, Neto maintained a host of representatives in Europe – both East and West – as well as in Peking, Havana, Cairo, Lagos, Dar es Salaam, Conakry and Algiers. His links with FRELIMO, the Mozambique insurgent group once headed by another American favourite, the late Eduardo Mondlane, were close. Following the murder of Mondlane by unknown assassins, Dr Neto was said to become more reclusive and even isolated from the party. He is said to have feared, correctly, as it transpired, that he might eventually suffer the same fate.

Compared to earlier periods, a new kind of political awareness started to emerge in the Portuguese territories in the early years of the 20th Century.

Civil disobedience, while not widespread, caused Lisbon to pass the Portuguese Colonial Act in June 1933. While it recognized the supremacy of Portuguese over 'native people' and accepted that locals could pursue all studies including university, reality was very different. While some Africans from the 'Provinces' did manage to enter universities

Marcelino dos Santos became a moving force within the FRELIMO guerrilla movement in Mozambique. He is seen here talking business with a member of the Chinese diplomatic mission in Dar es Salaam. Shortly afterwards the insurgents received several shiploads of weapons. (Photo courtesy of the late Mohammed Amin of CameraPix, Nairobi)

in the Metropolis, they were never encouraged to do so.

After World War II – in which Portugal remained neutral [it sided with Britain in the Kaiser's War] many Portuguese settled in Angola. That flow became a flood in the 1950s, vigorously encouraged by the dictator António de Oliveira Salazar.

That was roughly when a group of young, reasonably-educated black enthusiasts led by Viriato da Cruz and others formed the Movement of Young Intellectuals in Luanda in 1948 and went on to promote a largely ethnic Angolan culture. The body was taken over by aspiring nationalists who sent a letter to the United Nations that called for Angola to be given protectorate status under UN supervision. Many of these dissidents were arrested by PIDE, the Portuguese secret police and quite a few died in detention after being tortured.

Five years later, Angolan separatists founded PLUA, the Party of the United Struggle for Africans in Angola, the first of several organisations that advocated a total break from Portugal. At that point, one of the moving forces in the Angolan political spectrum, Mário Pinto de Andrade, stepped up to the podium. Together with his brother Joaquim, the two men formed the Angolan Communist Party (PCA).

In December 1956, they engineered a merger between the PLUA and PCA to form the Popular Movement for the Liberation of Angola (MPLA), which ultimately led the country to independence. This was no small task since it took more than a dozen years.

Black FRELIMO guerrillas are given instruction in a bush camp in the handling of a Chinese-supplied machine-gun. (Photo courtesy of the late Mohammed Amin of CameraPix, Nairobi)

Even here, there were tribal overtones. Most of the support for da Cruz, Mário Andrade, Ilidio Machado, and Lúcio Lara came from Luanda and the preponderant Mbundu people of Northern Angola. For centuries the Mbundus had been the most important tribal kingdom in a region which included much of north Angola as well as huge swathes of the Congo. From the earliest days of Empire, Lisbon assiduously cultivated good relations with these people, and in particular, its titular heads or chiefs.

With time though, these relations soured. By the early 1950s the Portuguese could no longer count on the support of the Mbundu Royal Household.

The big 'breakthrough' arrived in January 1961 when Angolan peasants in Malanje Province boycotted the cotton fields they were forced to harvest. The workers burned their identification cards and attacked Portuguese traders in what was subsequently referred to as 'Maria's War'.

In a typically ham-fisted manner, Portuguese military commanders in Angola responded by bombing several dozen villages with napalm and killing 7,000 Africans. Weeks later the dissidents upped the ante by storming a police station and São Paulo prison. There were seven policemen and 40 Africans killed in February 1961, effectively signalling the start of limited hostilities against the colonial regime.

Conditions deteriorated further when the government held a state funeral for the deceased police officers. Incensed by the deaths of their compatriots, all of them white, enraged Portuguese citizens massacred still more Africans during a march through the streets of Luanda. Militants attacked a second prison on February 10 and the Portuguese again retaliated brutally.

John Marcum, the American historian and political scientist reported:[3]

> ... Portuguese vengeance was awesome. The police helped civilian vigilantes organize nightly slaughters in the [Luanda slums]. The whites hauled Africans from their flimsy one-room huts, shot them and left their bodies in the streets. A Methodist missionary... testified that he personally knew of the deaths of almost 300.

Within weeks the government pushed the MPLA out of Luanda and into the Dembos region of the north where the MPLA established their '1st Military Region'.

UPA/FNLA leader Holden Roberto had meanwhile launched his combined military incursion into Angola in March 1961, at the head of what was variously estimated to be between 4,000 and 5,000 militants. His problem was that very few of these irregulars had been trained. While there were some automatic weapons, the majority were armed with ancient blunderbusses and machetes (pangas). Nonetheless, such was the vehemence of the mob that the Portuguese authorities were taken completely by surprise.

UPA went on to seize farms, government outposts, and trading centers and murdered everybody that the rabble encountered along the way[2]. At least 1,000 whites and an unknown number of Africans died in this uprising.

Commenting on the incursion, Roberto said, 'this time the slaves did not cower ... they massacred everything ... '

It took months for Lisbon to regroup and finally make an effective stand, all the while taking more casualties. But traditional Lusitanian doggedness persevered and finally government forces – backed by limited air power – started to have an effect. Portuguese Forces took control of Pendra Verde, UPA's last base in northern Angola, six months later.

In the first year of hostilities there were roughly 2,000 Portuguese and 50,000 Africans killed. Between 400,000 and 500,000 refugees fled into the neighboring Congo, or as it was soon to become, Zaire. UPA militants used the opportunity to draw as many refugees into their movement as cash and facilities allowed and continued to launch attacks from the safety of the adjacent country.

The violence throughout this period was unbridled and included intra-factional brutality. A UPA patrol took almost two dozen MPLA militants (their supposed allies) prisoner and executed the lot in October 1961 in what subsequently became known as the Ferreira incident. That wasn't the first time that UPA and MPLA exchanged blows, but the event sealed a growing enmity and sparked still more bloodshed.

Gradually the MPLA proved to be the more forceful of the two liberation groups, largely because its leader Agostinho Neto, a dedicated communist, was receiving arms, equipment and training from the Soviet Union. By then the CIA had recruited Holden

Anti-Portuguese guerrillas in attack mode. (Photo courtesy of
the late Mohammed Amin of CameraPix, Nairobi)

Roberto, but he was both ineffectual and a drunkard. It didn't help his cause that Cuba entered the fray shortly afterwards. Neto met with the Marxist leader Ché Guevara in 1965 and soon got funding from Cuba as well as the German Democratic Republic.

In May 1966, Daniel Chipenda – then a member of the MPLA – established the Eastern Front, significantly expanding the group's reach. When that effort collapsed, Chipenda and Neto blamed each other.

As a combatant, the author joined Chipenda's extended force in Nova Lisboa in the mid-1970s. By then the South African Army had already invaded Angola from the south and he was eventually forced out of the city after receiving death threats. The messages, usually delivered by small boys picked at random off the streets, warned that if he didn't leave town, he would be killed. Venter complied with alacrity.

During the late 1960s the FNLA and MPLA ended up spending as much time at each other's throats as they did fighting the Portuguese. It got so bad that MPLA forces eventually assisted PIDE security agents in hunting down FNLA hideouts.

Born in September 1922 at Lcolo e Bango, south of Nova Lisboa in Angola's central provinces, young Neto was educated to secondary level in Luanda. From 1944 to 1947 he worked in the Portuguese Health Services in Angola. It was then that his zeal and initiative prompted the authorities to allow him to study medicine at Coimbra University in Portugal, but five years later, in 1952, he was imprisoned for taking part in popular demonstrations against his hosts. Although freed shortly afterwards, he was imprisoned again from February 1955 to June 1957. Agostinho Neto qualified as a doctor in 1958.

Dr. Neto's MPLA was originally established in Luanda in 1956 as an underground movement advocating equal rights for all people in the country irrespective of race, colour or creed. Prior to its exile to Congo (Brazzaville), it merged with a number of political groupings that had been declared illegal by the Portuguese authorities.

An early leader of the party was the noted 'African' philosopher Mário Pinto de Andrade, who lived outside Africa for most of his life. During the course of his studies at Lisbon, Frankfurt and Paris, Andrade joined both the Portuguese (underground) and French communist parties. He had meantime undergone political training in Moscow, Warsaw and Peking.

The date the MPLA commemorates above all others each year is February 4. It was then, in 1961 – almost six weeks before the first UPA attacks had taken place in northern Angola – that a small band of MPLA guerrillas attacked a prison near Luanda and managed to free a number of political prisoners.

Dr. Neto always maintained that the large-scale UPA/GRAE attacks were premature. Had Roberto waited a few months, he says, their joint attacks would have had a far more devastating effect on the Portuguese security forces. Luanda might even have fallen to the insurgents, he maintains.

MPLA also liked to claim responsibility for opening Angola's 'second front' in the east, near the Zambian border—an area of infiltration that the Portuguese military authorities in Luanda admitted to me was already larger than Rhodesia's by the late 1960s.

Most of the preliminary training that MPLA and UPA/GRAE/FNLA recruits underwent was, for a number of years completed in Zambia, Kinshasa, Congo (Brazzaville) and Tanzania.

A number of insurgent training camps were pin-pointed early on in various African states bordering on Southern Africa and these included Dolisie and Pointe Noire in Congo-Brazza; Kinkuzu, a large UPA/FNLA camp some miles from Kinshasa; Tanzania's Kongwa, Bagamoyo and Nachingwea as well as Sikongo in the Barotse Province of Zambia.

Many of the brighter young MPLA trainees were sent for advanced guerrilla training at military institutions in Algeria, Cuba, Russia and China. UPA/GRAE graduates, on the other hand, receive their post-graduate terrorist training in Ethiopia, Cairo and India. The huge guerrilla training base at Tclemen, Algeria, is regarded by many as the ultimate in training camps in Africa—a terrorist-style African West Point.

A major factor in favour of the Portuguese in the Angolan struggle, Portuguese military leaders maintained throughout, was that UPA and MPLA – while opposed to Portuguese domination, we also at war with one another.

Of the two, MPLA guerrillas were by far the most resilient; tough, wily and dangerous. As one officer commented, 'they have been well trained ... they know what they want and they know how to get it.

UPA/FNLA, in contrast, while a reasonably effective guerrilla force in its day, had

Zambia's President Kaunda with Ehtiopia's Emperor Haile Selassie who provided training camps for anti-Portuguese insurgents in the Horn of Africa. (Author's collection)

been weakened by a lack of discipline that seemed to stretch all the way up the ladder of command to headquarters in Kinshasa. Holden Roberto ruled largely by decree and preferred the good life in the Congolese capital, especially since it was being subsidised by Langley. He ended up a chronic alcoholic and was one of the few of the old guard who were to die in their own beds, of heart disease, in 2007.

There were other differences. Whereas MPLA men would ask villagers for food and pay them for their efforts, UPA fighters would demand it as their right and make no recompense. More salient, MPLA cadres rarely touched the women of their hosts—something apparently drummed into them while they were in training. UPA men had no qualms about demanding solace from the wives of local tribesmen. In one area, an officer told me, a UPA officer had shot a tribal chief because the chief had objected to his men taking three young virgins of the village for their pleasure.

'That would never have been allowed in any area controlled by Neto's crowd', he said. The philosophy behind the MPLA strategy was basic and involved a simple maxim: help us now and once in power, you will not be forgotten'. This was where the Chinese and Cuban influences immediately became apparent, Brigadier Soares maintained in one of his briefings.

MPLA units, he stated, were implementing the Chinese communist dogma that before it was possible to win a guerrilla struggle it was necessary to win the confidence of the civilian population. 'They must move as freely among the civilians as the fishes in the sea', Mao Tse Tung wrote.

Perhaps the best illustration of MPLA efficacy and where they made headway, the brigadier said, was that when their young men returned to an area after being trained abroad, they spent time organizing the villagers to tidy their living quarters and make more equable sanitary arrangements. It was healthier for the entire community, they would explain. They would also encourage the young men of the villages to help their women grow more crops, something unheard of in stratified tribal circles where it had always been females who were responsible for tending to the needs of the family and growing things.

Applying simple administrative principles was usually enough to impress any village chief who had lived in the jungle most of his life. In any event, to these simple African folk, enthusiastic young MPLA guerrillas were more reliable than either the usually-obnoxious Portuguese government functionaries with whom all had had fleeting contact or their grab-all UPA adversaries.

It is worth mentioning that shortly after the first UPA incursions into Angola's north, Lisbon did initiate a few moderating measures in a bid to bring the mass of the population back into the fold. Cautious at first, these first measures soon took on lives of their own.

The *assimilado* program was begun, whereby certain colonials (of colour) could be 'assimilated' into Portuguese society. The gestures also opened the way for qualified black combatants to achieve commissioned rank within the armed forces. A growing body of black civil administrators in government service – of whom more were required each year to manage the affairs of this vast country as the war progressed – was also wooed with promises of high office.

Similar programs were instituted in Mozambique and Portuguese Guinea and it was all concurrent.

But as the saying goes, it was too little and far too late. There were already dozens of French and British independent African states represented in the United Nations and their voices about universal equality for the black man were being heard. Also, former Portuguese dissidents were returning home as guerrillas and spreading the word: with a bit more effort, they told the populace, Angola, Mozambique and Portuguese Guinea might soon be theirs.

Nor had events that had taken place at roughly the same time in the United States under President John F. Kennedy been lost on Lisbon. Premier Caetano and his ministers tried to institute vaguely similar moderating policies in the overseas territories, but few were followed through by an entrenched colonial hierarchy who regarded concessions to black people as a form of weakness.

Nor was it all a one way street towards egalitarianism. It might be recalled that President Lyndon Johnston was not a consistent advocate of racial equality and his explanation of why he backed the Civil Rights Act of 1957 explains some of it, especially since these sentiments would be uttered by the ruling establishment in Lisbon shortly afterwards. I quote Johnston verbatim:

> These Negroes, they're getting pretty uppity these days and that's a problem for us since they've got something now they never had before, the political pull to back up their uppityness. Now we've got to do something about this, we've got to give them a little something, just enough to quiet them down, not enough to make a difference.

Road to the North

An important aspect of colonialism in our country, and in other Portuguese colonies as well, is Portugal's underdevelopment; the social, economic and cultural backwardness of Portugal.

Amilcar Cabral, the first insurgent leader in
Portuguese Guinea, today Guiné-Bissau

It took us almost a day to travel between Nambuangongo and Madureira on our way to Zala in Angola's heavily tropical north. The country between the two military posts was mountainous and covered in forest that was both forbidding and verdant. Fast-flowing streams cut across the road at almost regular intervals. It was the kind of terrain that was admirably suited for waging a guerrilla struggle.

'This is the nearest we have come to Vietnam-type conditions in Southern Africa', one of the convoy officers said to me as we left headquarters, which had also played a prominent role for the guerrillas when they held the high ground. 'This and portions of Cabinda where swamp covers much of the lowlands', he added.

'Not the kind of country in which to wage a war ... you can hardly get about and when you need top cover, there usually isn't any because the helicopters are being used elsewhere,' he stated.

We travelled on one of the lumbering old Panhard armoured personnel carriers that the Portuguese army used to protect civilian trucks, which, at first glance, seemed better suited for European roads than one of the remotest regions of Africa. It was a pleasant experience, though, Cloete Breytenbach and I perched atop the turret and enjoying the view. We would not have had it otherwise because it was stifling inside the machine.

Our escorts – a couple of dozen men – followed in their troop carriers and sat crouched, eyes intent and with their weapons ready. Ambushes were a regular occurrence, we were assured.

There were three APCs in the column—one at each of the extremes and another towards the centre which was for our use. Like the soldiers, we wore regular army camouflage. It was necessary, we'd been told because once out there, anything unusual drew attention and a couple of Gringos in civilian garb certainly would have been.

'You must look inconspicuous. If they think you're important, their snipers will go for you ... not the best shots, but then you don't want to take chances. Nor do we ... '

Another of the wags in our party said that if the gooks were actually aiming at us, we were quite safe. 'They're terrible shots ... you'd be lucky to be hit ... it's the fellow next to you that's got to be worried', he quipped.

By all accounts, snipers were more of a problem than the Portuguese were prepared to concede. Captain Alcada told us later that they constantly targeted officers if they had the chance and, as in any war, he suggested, people doing that kind of thing tend to improve with time. He'd been targeted several times because even though he'd removed his epaulettes, he always travelled on the van and it was clear to everybody who was in charge.

I could see my beard worried him a little. It was out of character and it was only then that I realized that I was the only person in any of the camps we'd visited that had one.

Although the area we moved through was very much a part of northern Angola and immediately adjacent to the Congolese frontier, I'd found the nights unusually cold for the tropics. Getting up in the morning was almost as bad as a cool London dawn; it could be cold, misty and miserable.

It was the altitude, of course, much the same as at Eldoret in Kenya, on the Equator – where, over the years, I was to spend many days with Hoffie Retief and his family who eventually decamped to Malindi. Not an evening went by without the servants lighting a large log fire; as soon as the sun dipped, temperatures plummeted.

This part of Angola was a lot different from East Africa. It was tropical and heavy undergrowth encroached everywhere. If not constantly kept in check, the foliage would soon envelop roads and buildings, within weeks, in fact, if not regularly pushed back. Roads not regularly used by traffic, soon reverted to bush and had a distinctive mist which the locals call *cassimbo*. It often enveloped the countryside after sunset in what locals liked to call 'the cool season'. By nine in the morning the sun would have caused it to dissipate, but until that happened, nothing moved on the roads. In fact, it was noon before the last of the previous night's dew had evaporated and until then, each time we passed under a cluster of trees, drops would rain onto our shoulders. After ten minutes or so, many of us would be soaked, especially those travelling ahead.

The leather straps on my cameras turned a disgusting green within days of arriving in Sector D and no matter what I did, it stayed that way until we returned to normalcy. It was still a lot better than the Cameroons, I reckoned at the time, where the humidity allowed mushrooms to grow on the carpet of your hotel room.

Apart from our three Panhards and the accompanying troop carriers, there were about a dozen trucks in our convoy hauling an assortment of arms, munitions, supplies and replacement troops to outposts in the interior. We were travelling relatively light because much of the equipment had already been off-loaded further south, at Cage, Canacasalle, Nambuangongo and elsewhere. What was left would be delivered to Madureira and Zala.

'Zala is the end of the road—thank God', our driver commented. He was relieved that we were almost there. It had taken him two days to get that far from Luanda—a distance of about 150 kilometres and thankfully, there had so far been no mines.

On the way back, he said, they picked up all the coffee in the surrounding farms. His

Two squads of Portuguese soldiers head out into the bush onboard their
German-built troop-carrying Unimogs. (Author's photo)

group did the run five or six times a month, but less in the rainy season.

'Then it's hell ... '

We'd arrived in the middle of Angola's dry season and as he pointed out, it was bad
enough. Also the roads were in pretty bad condition. Under normal conditions they would
have been scraped every few months or so, but the war had stopped all that. Consequently,
tropical downpours and the constant movement of heavy traffic would sometimes create
holes and culverts in the dirt that could swallow a jeep.

Our column fared no better. There were times when we'd be reduced to a crawl, slower
than an average man's walk. Then we'd amble alongside our vehicle until it picked up speed
again. In several places, we skirted huge boulders in the road.

'We should really get something done with what's left of these roads', the captain
suggested, but though they'd tried, the rebels intensified their activity each time they
spotted heavy equipment arriving from Luanda. Then there would be mines all over the
place and the casualties would mount.

'The war has been getting hot again, so the authorities haven't been able to get down to
it this season', he said. In other sectors they had managed to keep roads in a reasonable state,
as I was later to see in Cabinda and in the east, but the Dembos had a slew of problems that
were all its own.

Almost like clockwork the convoy would be ordered to halt. Then we'd wait for the
stragglers and the officers would order out perimeter defences to prevent attack.

Every third or fourth vehicle in the convoy was a German-built Unimog (Mercedes) personnel carrier with a bunch of Portuguese soldiers sitting back-to-back. All the troops onboard faced outwards, almost reminiscent of famous Robert Capa photos of the Spanish Civil War. The Mercedes was much-favoured among Franco's Nationalist forces, but then, they got them free from Hitler.

Convoy routine, though pretty basic could also be tedious. There was a sergeant who was in charge of each of the troop carriers and he sat next to the driver up front and we'd constantly hear them barking orders.

'He's ordering them to keep their heads up; which means that some of the soldiers have nodded off ... it happens all the time, the captain explained. The dreary road, the monotonous jungle terrain and the dust made the men drowsy and for some, sleep came easily.

Our transport was more casual than most. Either by accident or design on the part of colonel Joâo Barros-e-Cunha at Nambuangongo, the men around us could almost all speak some English, with one or two of the men quite fluent. It was clear from the start that they enjoyed the change, posing for the camera whenever the lenses appeared. Thrown in among them was a pair of *estrangeiros* taking photos, asking questions or passing smart-arsed comments.

The trip could be interesting. Conversation along the line of the column was interrupted every 15 or 20 minutes or so by a radio operator in one of the Panhards calling up another section of the convoy.

'*Echo ... Lima ... Nove. .. Dois. .. Zero.*' His staccato voice would echo across the jungle.

If there were any enemy about, they would easily have picked up his voice, not that it would have mattered as there seemed to be more wisecracking among the men than sitreps.[1] It went some way towards easing tension.

The men would shout at each other from one vehicle to another and several times, almost as if on cue, the men would start singing and the rest of the column would follow in unison.

The hit of the day that year – even in Portuguese Africa – was Tom Jones' *Delilah* and surprisingly, while travelling on these jungle roads, in the back of beyond of the universe, everybody seemed to know the words. These were melodies probably not unfamiliar to many of the insurgents in the bush around us. That ditty would be followed by *It's Not Unusual* and other songs made famous by that Welshman.

For all the bonhomie, this was a country at war. At one stage as we approached Madureira, a mountain-top post in the heart of the coffee country, a couple of shots rang out from one of the ravines ahead. More followed at one or two-second intervals.

'Get your head down ... behind the barrel', the captain ordered, pointing towards the Panhard's turret. Some of the troops around us slipped quietly into the tall grass next to the road. Nobody said a word as we waited.

Radio clatter started up again. '*Echo ... Lima ... Nove ... Dois. .. Zero,*' the operator calling. Even the troops on the far side could follow.

After five minutes of intermittent talk the convoy rolled out again. Captain Alcada explained that somebody had fired a clip into the first Panhard and that a patrol had been sent out to scout around.

'That's exactly what these clowns often hope for. They fire a few shots, then we send in a patrol—slap-bang into an ambush...they're waiting for us.'

'When it happens to my guys, I've taught them never to follow any tracks ... always stick close to the bush ... make your own paths if the bush allows, and unfortunately, it often doesn't because it is so dense. It's the AP mines that I worry about and those bastards have got a lot of them ... .'

Though circumstances would vary, the insurgents would never hang about. Once things were not going to plan, he explained, they'd pull out, principally because of fear of encirclement, which I thought, considering the formidable bush on both sides of the road, to be impossible anyway.

I was only to learn later of the terrible price both soldiers and civilians were paying in this war as a result of the indiscriminate use of mines. There wasn't a Portuguese Army base that didn't have at least one victim who had lost a foot or had a leg blown off.

And that, almost half a century ago, was only the start of it ...

As we approached Madureira, Captain Alcada showed us where he'd made his first real contact with the war.

It was a lonely spot in a valley, on the outskirts of what had once been a delightful little logging settlement. As with the rest of Angola's north, the forest crept right up to the road. Nearby stood the burnt-out remains of an old farm house where we could still spot patches of whitewash against the few crumbling moss-covered walls that remained. There was something about the place that was foreboding.

It was late April 1961, he told us. He was a young *Alferes* then, in charge of his own platoon. 'We came down this stretch of road towards Nambuangongo in the early hours, a bunch of us, travelling in a column of three jeeps ... no Unimogs then.

I'd been ordered into the first one by my superior and I couldn't argue ... we were already aware that there were landmines just about everywhere, but then somebody has to lead the way and that's usually the junior officer.

'As we came out of the darkness to this spot I felt uneasy. I still don't know why, but I'd asked our driver to slow down. Then we emerged from around that corner', he said pointing at a cluster of palms.

'In the road ahead of us was the head of a woman on a stake.'

In Alcada's book, this was symbolic, a warning of sorts. The head, with long black hair matted with blood had been purposely placed there by the enemy.

"They were pretty damn bold in those early days and that face, pitted already by rot and dirt and the insects clinging to it kind of took us by surprise. I'll never forget it ... I can still

Convoy duties in the interior – often a tough regimen that could take days to traverse some of the toughest roads in Africa. (Author's photo)

see the dark cavities where her eyes had been ... what was left of her jaw was hanging askew'.

The woman had obviously been Portuguese. It didn't take them long to discover that she'd been the wife of the man that ran the farm and he'd also died in that first attack.

' ... never found her body. God only knows what medicine they used it for ... .her husband, we learnt later, together with a couple of young kids were also missing, presumed dead, as more civilized people used to phrase it.'

That was the night, Captain Alcada continued, that really got him going in this war. It was his first real baptism in a conflict that ultimately claimed many of his contemporaries.

Later, over a couple of beers we talked about it and this young officer admitted that nothing else had shaken him up quite like that experience, either before or after. 'There have been others since—some far worse. But that one had a special significance. It was revolting.

'My immediate response was one of rebellion. I suddenly wanted to murder ... to kill everything black, man woman or child. I wanted to do to them what they had done to her. At the same moment I had to pull myself together ... I had three black soldiers under my command in that same patrol.'

Captain Alcada admitted that to control his instincts was no easy task. 'I knew that I still had to satisfy this primitive lust for blood and I did it another way'.

'I took an oath. I knelt down and made the sign of cross, very much as the Spanish

Conquistadores probably did when they first went after the Incas, though for very different reasons. I swore that I would avenge these deeds and that I would do so with enough enthusiasm to become a name to be feared among these people, though to me just then they were more like fucking animals.

'I would become a deadly hunter of people, those who had started the war. At the same time, I would retain my integrity and that of my flag – to the best of my ability, at any rate.

'Also, though this had become personal, I would fight my war justly and fairly. Unlike some of my colleagues, I would take prisoners and not shoot them out of hand. But I also promised myself that I would kill more *terroristas* than any other Portuguese officer who served in my command.'

Not normally an effusive individual, Captain Alcada's revelations had been instructive. I found it demonstrable how one man coped under powerful emotional pressures. I was also aware that the captain had garnered a reputation that had followed him back to the Metropolis as a war hero and that he had probably done more than his share of killing, though he was never to talk about it with me.

Captain Alcada was a good, if ruthless officer. He was also tough but fair on his men. Somehow, he'd managed to achieve a balance between how he might have reacted and how he eventually responded when faced afterwards with similar problems.

Several times in the years that followed, we'd meet, both in South Africa and in Portugal. Each time he'd be reasonably forthcoming about what new experiences he'd had. He wouldn't tell me everything, but enough for me to ponder on, sometimes for a long time afterwards. While almost all these events involved bloodshed and some were horrendous, he admitted, he'd always managed to keep his emotions in check.

He'd like to call it 'keeping my cool', which was when I told him he'd been reading too many American books about Vietnam, which was when he admitted that he had.

I recall him telling me that night in the mess at Madureira of how, eight years after seeing that woman's head on a stake on a jungle road, rebel headquarters in Kinshasa had put a price on his head.

'Not the highest bounty for some of the men fighting alongside me,' he declared with a smile 'but enough to tell me that I might have accomplished what I originally set out to do ... '

Madureira was then one of the smallest mountain-top military camps in Sector D. The road to the garrison wound two or three times around the mountain before you reached the gate of the encampment topped by two machine-gun turrets.

Surrounding slopes were covered in neat rows of metre-high coffee bushes and the ordered pattern of the plantations in the vicinity stood out vividly in contrast to the jungle below which had recently been cleared up to the barbed wire and the adjacent minefield.

This Portuguese army post was possibly one of the most beautifully situated in Angola. Like Nambuangongo and Santa Eulalia, it had previously been a coffee estate. The old farmhouse, standing at the very pinnacle dominated the countryside for almost 50 kilometres in all directions. On a clear day, one of the officers joked, you could see forever...

The jungle splendour was staggering. Faraway in the distance resplendent greens blended almost imperceptibly with blues and yellows and purples. Evening brought out a shower of reds and oranges in profusion. Unnamed mountain-tops towards the horizon provided more ragged contrast. Had this been Kenya or Sarawak, the setting would have been a tourist attraction of note. The sunset alone compared with anything I'd experienced elsewhere in Africa.

The war that had blighted these images was stamped on the scene, almost indelibly. Four trucks stood ready in the central parade ground and troops with an assortment of weapons – rifles, automatic weapons, grenade launchers and mortars crowded around. They were being briefed. To complete a Malayan Emergency-type scenario, there were more heavy machine-gun turrets on the periphery.

'This is where the action is', said the young captain who commanded a company of soldiers that had been posted to Madureira for two years after we had exchanged greetings. 'You have come to the centre of the war,' he added. Then he suggested we move to the mess.

A patrol of 40 men were going out that afternoon, he explained. It was nothing definitive, but some of his people had picked up the trail of a large enemy squad that had entered from the Congo, probably overnight. His troops weren't after the men as much as the stuff they were reported to be hauling through, probably on their way further south. There had been one captive and spoke of about 30 or 40 mines. They were of metal, which headquarters had deduced, suggested anti-tank.

In the insurgent group, it had been reported, there were also about a dozen mysterious parcels, carried in slings between pairs of men. The contents hadn't been identified but it was Madureira's job to search and destroy. If possible, they were to discover what new 'secret weapon' the enemy was introducing into Angola.

'They'll try rockets next, probably 122mm Katyushas, like the Vietcong have been using around Saigon', Ricardo commented. He added that there were already RPGs galore ... they were in every contact, he added.

It is worth mentioning that the RPG-2 of the Portuguese wars in Africa soon gave way to the more sophisticated RPG-7, both originally of Soviet extraction. Though the 'bark' of the RPG-7 is worse that it's bite – unless it is armour-piecing because it cannot penetrate heavy steel – these rocket propelled grenades have been used to good effect by just about every insurgent army in the world. I gathered afterwards that South African scientists had reverse-engineered several versions, with the intention of producing them in quantity in South African factories.

RPG-7s were also used in the Battle of Mogadishu in October 1993. Thousands had been secretly shipped from Yemen to the Somali warlord Mohamed Farrah Aideed (by al-Qaeda, one report maintained). He used them to ambush an assault force of about 160 men travelling in a dozen vehicles and made up of US Army Delta Force and Ranger teams. Of the almost 20 aircraft involved – including a number of Blackhawks – two were shot down by concerted RPG-7 fire.[2]

The Portuguese Army patrol left soon after lunch. We weren't invited along because they'd be out overnight and we hadn't been issued with sleeping bags.

The troops were to be taken out seven or eight kilometres by road and would then continue on foot. A party of paratroopers had been dropped several kilometres to the north and between the two groups – in a kind of pincer movement – they hoped to cut off the guerrilla group before they buried their loads and bombshelled. Captain Alcada said it was a favourite rebel ploy; the tactic that followed had become standard Portuguese Army practice.

As soon as the gooks thought the odds were against them, he added, they'd bury their supplies and heavier weapons and disappear into the bush. 'They knew the area very well. Also, they've got some locals to guide and track for them – so there won't be any problem finding the cache later.'

Alcada was confident of the eventual outcome of the sortie. He'd done it himself often enough before, he told us. It was no secret, he reminded us, that ZANU and ZAPU insurgents then clandestinely entering Rhodesia from Mozambique and Zambia were using similar tactics.

Huge supplies of arms, food and water were being ferried across the Zambezi or brought into the country overland from entry points such as Beira and Nampula. This stuff would be buried at predetermined spots with about a day's march between each supply drop and would be made use of by other bands of infiltrators who followed later. The objective was to get as much equipment into the territory as possible. It gave succeeding units a measure of independence from outside sources of supply and allowed for a wider field of operations.

The captain in charge at Madureira told me that there were about 3,000 African civilians in his area, which stretched about 10 kilometres in all directions. Of them, about 300 were guerrillas, many of them veterans and armed with automatic weapons. There was no question that the majority of the civilians were sympathizers: if they acted otherwise they would be quickly dealt with.

'It's tough, with this well-trained hard-core that we're targeting, but then things are difficult in these mountains', he explained. More pertinent, they were holding the civilians as hostages. We're made aware of that because once we've knocked the terrorists around a bit and perhaps killed some of their leaders, villagers come to us and tell us what has been happening. In contrast, if they attempt to escape, they'd be shot. And so will their families … something used in Algeria as well.

Obviously, they're all aware of this, so they stay put – for the time being. Meantime, we wait'.

The Captain made the point that the region in which Portuguese forces were operating was severely stressed economically. All the old jobs had gone, except for those around the base where coffee was still being harvested, though he had to provide enough guards to

The road through the *Dembos* north of Luanda was always tough and demanding. The elephant grass was sometimes taller than the vehicles in which we travelled, which allowed the guerrillas many opportunities for ambush. (Author's photo)

keep the workers safe. He was aware that most of the civilians were eager to return to a more settled way of life, but hostilities made this impossible.

'They want the work. They also need to produce their own crops without it being taken from them by rebel squads passing through. Most of all, they really miss the occasional shindig where they haul out the *pombe*[3] that had been prepared by the women during the week and where they can dance around the drums after dark.

'They want to get drunk and kick up their heels without worrying about somebody arriving from the jungle unannounced and perhaps getting themselves shot.

'We see it often enough when a group of civilians arrive from the jungle. The beer comes out and they sometimes celebrate for a week.'

The captain's unit was called Cobra. Each man in the camp wore a flash on the right shoulder of the uniform displaying one of these reptiles with its hood raised.

'That's us—the way we think and the way we operate', one of the younger officers declared after we'd been briefed.

An African officer, he'd been born in Beira in Mozambique, all the way across this vast continent on the Indian Ocean. Before conscription he'd spent two years studying economics in Lourenco Marques, the Mozambique capital. Like his contemporaries, they'd almost all completed their mandatory period of active service and he had only five months of military service to complete. 'Then I'm going home', he declared, a huge smile creasing his face.

'It'll be a great day when I get on that plane again and this time I'm going the right direction', he reckoned.

On the wall of the officers' mess the word *cinco* (five) had been pencilled in above one of the dates. On the month following the word *quatro* (four) appeared above the same date and so on until the unit's final five months of service in Africa had been notated. All else had been torn off the calendar because after those critical five months nothing would matter anymore, the men reckoned. At least they would be out of the army, even though it might take a while because many of the soldiers would have to return by sea and that could take weeks.

This simple action typified the approach of most conscripts fighting in Angola. All that mattered was how much time they still had left to serve. Once finished with the ordered, stultified rigmarole, the majority reckoned, life was for living again.

While at Madureira, one of the Portuguese Air Force spotter planes circled low over the camp a number of times. The pilot flapped his wings acrobat-fashion to attract attention. He wanted to land and this was his way of telling us, though I would have thought it would have been easier to use the radio.

Madureira, like most other camps in the sector, has its own landing strip, even though the post was perched on the topmost crest of a mountain. The air strip lay a few kilometres further down in the valley and the pilot had to warn the base beforehand. Troops would then be sent down the line to secure the runway.

'The men have to ensure that the aircraft is not attacked on touching down, which has also happened before', the young African officer explained.

Departure was another matter. I did so several times and each time it seemed to get hairier. Much worse than Lesotho's Matekane Airport, the strip was not only inadequate; it was about 100 metres too short for any kind of conventional take-off. Only the smallest planes could land, and while the pilot might arrive with two passengers, he could only take off with one.

Once pilot and passenger had been strapped in, the man at the controls would back his aircraft towards the furthest edge of the jungle, furiously rev his engine and release the brakes. The little plane would race forward, pick up speed and if there was enough forward momentum, it might even lift off. More often than not, the plane would hurtle over the edge. In theory, the plane might have gained enough speed to dip down and right itself over the edge of the precipice. It was a dangerous experience, but it made for a good few yarns at dinner parties afterwards.

As one pilot wryly commented, 'The mountains here have their own rules ... it is better to take off downhill and downwind because in these parts, the hills are likely to outclimb you ... '

It was also at Madureira and Zala that the Portuguese waged their first helicopter campaign against in this insurgent conflict in 1966.

UPA/FNLA units had been causing a lot of problems and at one stage, were attacking army convoys almost at will. They'd lay their ambushes and strike, withdrawing into the bush immediately afterwards. Things went on this way for a while, but then casualties started to mount because the rebels knew that Portuguese troops weren't able to come in after them. Military Command in Luanda finally decided to deploy ten choppers in the region for a week.

'We had them running between here, Zala and Nambuangongo and the results were good', another officer explained. Distances are short and when a patrol spotted rebel activity in an area, he'd radio in and the helicopters would strafe the area with their 20mm guns,' he said.

'One week became two, and then a month. After four months, the guerrillas were reporting serious casualties ... we were able to monitor their radio messages back to the Congo,' the youthful lieutenant told me.

'We'd always have at least two choppers and their crews standing by. If needed, they'd take in some of the commandos – our Special Forces – who had been detached to us from Luanda. They'd be dropped by the helicopters and unlike the usual run-of-the-mill troops, these guys would go hunting; they'd go right into the bush after their quarry.

'Sometimes they'd be dropped behind an attack area as a stopper group, perhaps two hundred metres from the road. In this way, hopefully, all avenues of retreat would be cut off. Or the rebels would be caught in a crossfire.

'We killed 37 that first week—apart from dozens wounded or taken prisoner', the officer said.

'So you see Sir, we like to fight this war a little differently to what they do elsewhere' said the lieutenant afterwards in the mess.

He admitted that there was much internal debate among some of the officers about whether conditions in Africa were different from elsewhere. In the end, it took one of the American military attachés on a rare visit to the front to explain what was really happening.

His comments were direct and from what I gathered, they didn't please many senior officers. For a start, as an accredited diplomat, he'd not requested permission to address a serving group of officers in this foreign war, which was considered mandatory in most countries. More significant, there were those in Lisbon who always maintained that what was going on in the 'overseas territories' was unique, in part because they always held that these were temporary 'inconveniences'. The wars would be suitably dealt with in time, was the consensus. They were wrong, said the American colonel.

The diplomat, a strictly military man, had apparently experienced South East Asia for himself over several years. What he had to say had a significant impact on many of the Portuguese Army officers that he addressed and, with the benefit of hindsight his comments might be as applicable to what is going on with al-Qaeda today in some of the world's trouble spots like Iraq and Afghanistan.

A single Soviet TM-47 anti-tank mine caused this kind of damage.
Everybody on the vehicle was killed in the blast. (Author's photo)

Like Vietnam, he declared, the 'seek and destroy' war in Angola had no front lines. The enemy could be anywhere and anybody at all. He – and increasingly, she – was an extremely elusive enemy. This adversary was also becoming a much more efficient factor which needed to be dealt with much more efficiently than was currently the case.

Moreover, like Vietnam, the war in Angola was not isolated. It was very much part of the Cold War effort by the Soviets, which, he pointed out, was one of the reasons why the Portuguese Army in Angola, Mozambique – and Portuguese Guinea especially – were using the same equipment with which some other NATO countries were equipped, like American F-86 fighters and the Fiat-built Aeritalia G-91 attack jet.

Like Vietnam, this was a war that was being fought by conscript armies. American enlisted men served 365 days in Vietnam. Portuguese troops were in Africa twice as long.

Earlier in the war, the American pointed out, there were a lot of rudimentary PMD-6 antipersonnel mines in their distinctive little wooden boxes. As he observed, these pressure-activated blast devices had since fallen out of favour with the guerrillas on both continents because wood rotted in the tropics and the mine mechanism would shift.

The war had been upped many notches since it began, was the Colonel's view. As in Vietnam, helicopters had become a means to an end, though unlike the Americans, there wasn't a Huey Cobra in sight. More serious was a recent development in Portuguese Guinea where Moscow had introduced the first shoulder-fired anti-aircraft guided missile, the SAM-7.

These devices might soon find their way into the hands of one or more of the Angolan insurgent movements, or even terrorist groups abroad, he warned. As we are now aware, the American diplomat was right.

In November 2002, al-Qaeda operatives tried to destroy an Israeli-owned Boeing 757 passenger jet with 261 passengers and 10 crew onboard at Mombasa International Airport, in the largest harbour city in East Africa.

Incompetence coupled to bad judgement caused both missiles to go wide. But later that morning a suicide bomber did ram a truck loaded with explosives into one of that city's Israeli-owned seaside complexes.

A dozen tourists and staff were killed in the attack.

Our convoy reached Zala in Sector D the following day. Zala, a magic name in the Congo among the rebels, was the 'end of the line' for guerrillas infiltrating southwards from the frontier. With its huge airstrip and long, uneven approach road though some of the harshest bush country that we'd experienced, Zala military base lay at the northernmost tip of Sector D.

Because of a narrow defile through the hills, insurgents heading further south had to pass close to the Portuguese garrison. For weeks, while travelling from the Congo, they'd held their fire. On reaching Zala they often liked to celebrate by making their presence known, more often than not letting rip with a clip or two. Because the jungle in that region was especially dense, few of the enthusiasts would have penetrated close enough to hit the target.

Still, as one of the officers explained, it was the gesture that counted: they were signalling their achievement and in all probability, they were mighty proud of it.

'We come under fire fairly often', the camp commandant told us through an interpreter. 'But it's usually a case of exuberance. They'd reached the "promised land".'

The presence of so many insurgent groups transiting that northern reach required vigilance on the part of the Portuguese Army, and obviously the presence of helicopters helped. Guard duty was usually double strength and night patrols around the camp numerous. There wasn't much activity by the defenders: they just dug in and waited.

One of the African stewards at the camp was an insurgent who had been captured three years earlier. His name was Alfredo and he'd been a minion of one of the insurgent generals who'd been captured alive. By some account, this 'senior commander of the Liberation Forces' needed little coercion to switch sides.

Lisbon offered the general respect, amnesty as well as a squad of turncoat rebels to do his bidding. A monthly salary – much more than he'd been getting in his old job – was part of the deal that was clinched with a party and a document signed and witnessed to that effect. Having compromised himself and his headquarters by betraying half a company of men, he was sent further up the line to the necessary, but not Alfredo, his former steward.

We kept him here because he was valuable. He could read and write in French and

Portuguese and understood enough of the Bakongo language to be useful. Also, he knew his old boss and we'd show him some of the communiqués and ask his comments, just to be sure the general was doing what was expected of him.

With time, Alfredo proved himself exceptionally useful since he had one great passion—interrogating captured terrorists. He spoke their lingo and it provided him with the kind of authority he'd previously lacked. In fact, with no training, he was thoroughly adept at what was required of him since he had seen his former master at work in the past both questioning and torturing captured Portuguese. He also appeared to take pleasure in the measure of trust engendered by his new masters.

One of the officers explained that Alfredo would have made the ultimate spy if they could depend on him to return if they let him loose across the border again. 'But he's his own kind of man. Here we can keep an eye on him and we're aware of some of his tricks. If we let him go, we'd never see him again: he'd do the turncoat thing with his old bosses and would probably be that much the stronger for it. Here in Zala, he does the job, even if he is a little brutal sometimes.'

Apparently Alfredo would spend an hour or two with a man in a room. By the time he came out he knew his history, where and by whom he'd been trained, who his grandmother was and exactly what the prisoner had been expected to achieve in this area.

'We've got much valuable data about how the enemy works over a period of time, so he stays. He has a bank account in Luanda and every few months or so, he'll go down on one the flights for a weekend on the town ... got a wife there too. When the time comes for him to report back at the airport for the return flight he's there ... never missed a plane ... yet.

I was to hear from one of my Portuguese friends after Lisbon had abandoned its overseas territories in 1975 that Alfredo was one of thousands of Africans who were subsequently allowed to make new homes for themselves and their families in the Metropolis. He'd settled in the heart of Lisbon and loved it.

8

Mixed Fortunes of War

'... Sometimes in Africa a heavy machine-gun can be as effective as ten tanks elsewhere ...'
Lt-Col Tim Spicer, former chief executive of Sandline and author of
Unorthodox Soldier

Of all the soldiers we were to meet in Angola, Chaplain Lieutenant Jorge, a Roman Catholic priest, was probably more intimately associated with the problem of refugees than anyone else in the country. In June 1968, he was awarded the silver medal with palm clusters for bravery under what was termed 'exceptionally dangerous conditions in the field'.

His story was not only interesting, it had an almost Walt Disney resonance about it; single-handed, almost, he'd managed to rescue several thousands of people from their abductors in the jungle near Sao Salvador in the north. With a platoon of commandos, it had been his job to follow a group of civilians estimated to be about 6,000-strong and who had been taken hostage by the rebels. If they were to be forced to cross the Congolese border, the majority would be irrevocably compromised; many of the males of whatever age would end up waging war against the Portuguese.

Though small numbers of Kazombo tribal folk had managed to escape from the main body, they, in turn, had been captured by Portuguese forces following up.

The Kazombos told the Portuguese that the rebels in control numbered perhaps 400, not all of them armed. More important, the entire column was critically short of food and quite a few of the civilians had already died of starvation. Privations apart, the guerrillas were vigorous in their efforts to hustle these people across the border. Apparently they were headed for an area just east of Matadi, the main Congolese port and an often-used refugee transit-point.

With that information in hand, the Portuguese High Command ordered that a company of Special Forces be dropped into an area adjacent the frontier, hopefully, just ahead of the convoy. Two more companies of soldiers set out by road from Sao Salvador with the intention of creating a pincer movement and trying to cut the main body off.

Had the Portuguese forced the insurgents to fight, the results might have been catastrophic. In the heat of battle, in those primitive circumstances, it would have been impossible to distinguish civilians from guerrillas. Moreover, as with irregular struggles in other parts of the globe, 'human shields' had already become a reality and Angola was no exception in the late 1960s.

Such confusion would result not only in unnecessary deaths but also in many of the guerrillas using the disorder to escape into the jungle. This had already happened twice earlier that year under circumstances that were much the same, though this was the largest group of civilians yet.

Padre Jorge volunteered to approach the improvised jungle camp on his own in a bid to make contact with the elders. He was familiar with the area from which they had originated and could speak their native Bakongo. As a priest, he was confident that he might be able to persuade the villagers to force a halt to the march, even though it would take time and effort, and possibly, several such visits. Essentially he needed to win confidence within a community that was not only terrified of what was taking place but distrustful.

His logic was that with a Portuguese Army right behind, any kind of delaying action might compel the insurgents to abandon their charges and high-tail it, possibly into the arms of the waiting commando unit. And while they might kill some of the dissenters, they couldn't murder them all. Anyway, if any real shooting started, the army would move swiftly.

On his first night, Lieutenant Jorge tentatively approached a small party of villagers camped on the edge of the larger group. It was a risky venture, he knew, because he could just as easily have been betrayed. Having been taken by road some distance towards the camp by his own troops, it was still a two hours march through the bush on his own, much of it in the dark. Because the guerrillas posted guards, he couldn't use lights, though it helped that the moon was full.

Eventually he was able to creep close to a group that he discovered had originally come from Quitexe, a village near Carmona where he'd previously been stationed. Some of the men recognised him as they had been educated in the local mission school.

A couple of dozen of the villagers were initially sceptical, which was to be expected, the lieutenant conceded, but they could see that he was unarmed. He talked a while and then told them briefly why he had come. He offered them his blessing and said he would return the following night.

On the second visit, the priest talked most of the night. By now the group had been joined by some of the headmen from other nearby camps and, as might have been expected, that made the situation still more hazardous. Their guards, everybody knew, weren't stupid, though it helped that everyone took turns in keeping a lookout.

The priest told them that the Portuguese were right behind. They were ready to attack the people holding them hostage. The priest promised safe passage to all who agreed to return to their former homes. They would be helped financially by the government to re-establish their *sanzalas* as well as their schools. Since everybody was aware that the entire area had been laid waste by the guerrillas after they had been abducted it was a reasonable offer. They'd have a market for their crops and the presence of soldiers to protect them in the fields.

Most important, he told me, the Portuguese authorities understood that they had not voluntarily joined their abductors.

In their native tongue, he warned that there was a good likelihood that some of the

Every unit had its crest, proudly displayed on the parade ground. This kind of symbolism had much to do with trying to maintain morale among troops sent to Africa for years at a stretch and who had very little interest in what they often referred to as 'this foreign war'. (Author's photo)

civilians might be killed. His people, he explained, were ordinary soldiers. While they might be efficient fighters, they simply had no means of distinguishing between their abductors and civilians, especially since few of this particular group of rebels wore uniforms. Each time prior to leaving them he would offer all those present blessings.

The priest returned on the two following nights. The last time one of the elders asked that they start with prayers and not end with them. The priest complied.

As he recounted these events afterwards, Chaplain Lieutenant Jorge admitted that he'd reached the conclusion very early on that whatever the outcome, this would probably be one of the events of his life.

'I can only believe that my faith in God and in the basic goodness of these people helped me through. I admit that there were moments when I wavered: it seemed incomprehensible that I would succeed. If I'd been caught, they would have cut my heart out, end to the story', he told me earnestly.

On the fourth night he was brought before the council of headmen. The meeting had been arranged beforehand and it went quickly.

'It was a terrible night of thunderstorms and lightning. You could have fought a battle near by and not have known the difference. I arrived about two hours after dark and I knew immediately that this was when I would either save these people or be killed myself. By now I was certain that the enemy must have been aware there was something afoot.

'Five chiefs sat in a row, all men of importance because they carried their office with the dignity for which the Kazombo are known.' They all spoke in Portuguese, as was the custom with these formal events.

They asked only one question for me: 'How do we know that you are telling the truth? How can we be sure that we won't all be killed if we return?' It had happened before, I knew, and I couldn't argue. But I also told them that those events had taken place in the early days of the war.

'I could only give them my word. I said it was the word of a man of God'. The group went into a huddle for a few minutes and their leader emerged. He didn't smile or have much to say except that they accepted the offer to return to their homes. At which point he asked what the next step should be.

Some real problems then emerged. There were still more than 5,000 refugees in the group that stretched over several kilometres. How to get them out of the control of their captors? The chaplain said that there would have to be a plan as simple as pie since these were not sophisticated people. He told the headmen that they had already had something in place, but that its implementation – with such a large number of people that included some very old and very young – would have to wait until the following day.

'The idea was for the villagers to create conditions suitable for a small-scale sit-down strike the following morning at dawn. They'd argue that they couldn't go on, that there were too many sick and too many of their number were either dead or dying.

'This would give me enough time to get back to my troops and organize the unit so they could strike simultaneously. It was a tight schedule, with only about an hour to spare either way. There would be only one chance to make it all happen.

'We would attack simultaneously—from all sides', he said.

Meantime, the civilian leaders quietly went to work, though with a determination that he said surprised him afterwards. All the men fit enough to fight brought out what weapons they had—mostly *catanas* – long knives or machetes – a few spears and a few kitchen implements. The others had hoes, or had fashioned crude spears from pieces of dried wood. A few settled for wooden clubs.

The attack started at first light. The Portuguese forces held back only long enough for the civilians to make an initial impact. They then rapidly moved in.

There had been a good deal of shooting to start with. Quite a few villagers were killed, but it was the preponderant numbers of the captives together with the efforts of the army troops that turned the tide in the end. It took about an hour before the rebels were overwhelmed, though many did manage to escape into the bush.

Always a favourite tactic of rebel leaders in Third World struggles (and more marked in the early days of the Angolan war), was to move entire civilian communities, or more colloquially, *sanzalas,* out of their rural settlements and into the jungle.

In Uganda, as we approach the end of the first decade of the Millennium, the Lords

Resistance Army is still taking hostages by the score, in part to bolster their numbers. In the process entire villages are being massacred, largely among communities that reject the demands of the self-appointed LRA leader.

The same has been taking place in Darfur in the Sudan and with the Tamil Tigers in Sri Lanka.

In Angola, each time, the rebels took hostages, they would force these primitive communities across the border at gunpoint; it would be a lock, stock and cooking pot affair. If they could manage to haul along a few goats, they would take those as well; they'd need fresh meat along the way in any event.

The guerrillas had good reason for dominating the civilian population. By shifting local African communities into their domain, they were taking a large proportion of the work force out of the economic equation and that often included almost all the labour needed by Portuguese-controlled farms and plantations in order to survive. It was something that Mao had successfully incorporated into his overall plan against the Japanese, and, subsequently, against Generalissimo Chiang Kai-shek.

The immediate effect of this guerrilla tactic was to bring the economy of a region to a halt and in so doing, Mao's people were astonishingly successful. So too, coincidentally, were ZAPU and ZANU guerrilla groups in Rhodesia's seven-year bush war. Essentially, it was the reverse of the 'protected villages' agenda that the British had instituted in Malaya and which was ultimately instrumental in bringing that emergency to an end.

The Portuguese tried it themselves with their so-called *aldeamentos* programme [in Rhodesia protected villages were called 'Keeps'] but in Angola and Mozambique, these Latin administrators were neither as thorough nor as systematic as their European counterparts. The bottom line was that the programme known as *reordenamento rural* looked fine in theory but didn't work as well as it should have in practice.

In spite of enough barbed wire to encircle all of Africa, coupled to untold numbers of machine-gun turrets and patrols, the rebels had almost as much access to these 'gated' civilian communities as before. Most times they'd wait until the workers went out early in the day to till their crops: contact would be made and food, medicines and the rest would be passed along.

Taking a civilian community hostage, and setting off into the sunset with thousands of people was a different proposition.

At one stage during the height of the 1963 campaign, these measures had such a severe effect on coffee production in the north that there were shortages in most centres in Angola, never mind the collapse of the export market. This was a time when espresso could only be had at black-market prices, despite a world glut of the bean.

More important, by taking into custody a large group of civilians, the insurgents would have had access to a steady flow of new recruits. While able-bodied men were shanghaied into the rebel army, so were young boys barely into their teens. There were promises of food, bounty and the glory that would await them once they had conquered the country. Women in the party were obliged to cultivate crops for the group, though, as we were to see with South Africa's expatriate ANC military camps in Angola, Tanzania and elsewhere, they served other purposes as well.

In theory, had the rebels managed to ferret the entire Angolan population—at that stage nearly five million people—into the Congo, they would probably have succeeded with their objective. What they hadn't bargained for was deteriorating social and economic conditions to the north.

After independence in 1960, the Congo took a series of mighty knocks, not least the mutiny of the *Force Publique*, on which the security of the nation depended. Within months the country was in the hands of a small but ruthless band of anarchists, among them Patrice Lumumba, friend and confidante of Holden Roberto who headed the UPA/FNLA faction of Angolan rebels.

The immediate consequence was that almost the entire white population fled. That was followed by the collapse of the country's financial, commercial and industrial sectors. No money, no factories and no production meant no jobs.

The country never recovered from that exodus because the Belgians were even more remiss in educating their subjects than the Portuguese had been. By the time Brussels handed over power to the Congolese in 1960, there were only six university graduates in the entire country.

Consequently, even at the height of the war, Angola – with some exceptions like Sector D to the north of Luanda – was still a better place in which to live than the former Belgian colony. Then – and now, as we have since witnessed – the Congo was being disrupted by civil and military unrest.

As one army officer put it: 'We had war, yes. But if civilians came to us, we gave them protection. In the Congo a man had to be mad to ask the *Armée National Congolaise* for any kind of assistance. They'd rob you first, then protect you with a grave.'

And in all likelihood, as one of the officers succinctly commented, 'they'd get somebody else to dig it first and throw him into the hole as well...' He was joking, of course, but point taken ...

The Congo seemed always to have been in turmoil. Since the 1960s, there were many violent changes of government, Leopoldville had been renamed Kinshasa and unemployment peaked. There were times when food was in such short supply that there were riots in the streets. Mobutu's soldiers – a vicious a bunch of thugs – didn't hesitate to use live ammunition to put a stop to it all.

Add to that conundrum the perpetual fear of cross-border napalm and bombing raids on wandering bands of Africans by the Portuguese Air Force and it was small wonder many former Angolans chose to stay put in and around Leopoldville.

Others, disenchanted at what they found in the Congo, took their chances and went back into the bush. There, they'd wander about for a while, cross the frontier again and return to their old homes in Angola. Those caught doing so were shot by self-appointed bands of armed youths, the dreaded *Jeunesse* who patrolled these undermarcated frontier regions and thought nothing of killing a man because they wanted to get at his pretty wife.

Zemba was the nearest camp to Santa Eulalia. It lay about 20 kilometres to the south-east.

The country in between, like most of the terrain south of the Dembos, was thinning out, in part because of the logging and because the rains had been bad for a year or two by the time we got there. There was more open grassland than jungle across much of the terrain we covered. We flew across to the camp in one of the Portuguese Air Force Dornier Do-27s used in spotting roles in the sector.

Overlooking Zemba from the south was a massive bald mountain that stood out starkly from the surrounding country. It was a bit like Rio's Sugar-Loaf, or some of the larger 'gomos' in Zimbabwe.

'That's a very bad mountain,' said our pilot, a young air force pilot who seemed to be coming to grips with some of the navigational vagaries that his colleagues encountered in Africa. He explained that the insurgents often climbed half-way up and fired down into the camp.

'I like to keep clear of the place. There are dangerous cross-currents around the peak. Once the *terroristas* opened fire on me with some heavy stuff as I flew past – somehow they'd hauled a machine-gun up the foothills and into the surrounding bush and ended up giving us a few headaches. We bombed them, but I don't think it did much good ... too much jungle', he explained.

He told me the mountain had once been used by local tribesmen for ceremonies or sacrificial purposes. That was before the Portuguese colonized the area, but it was still considered sacred by the animists who live in the vicinity.

'They also slaughtered a number of Portuguese civilians on the rock in the early days of the war. We don't know what they did to them, but the heads of some of the women were found stuck on stakes', he said.

The atmosphere and lifestyle at the Zemba military base differed markedly from what went on at headquarters. You sensed there were things afoot that were not immediately apparent. For a start, the camp played host to a large contingent of Portuguese Special Forces.

At Santa Eulalia you got the impression that the place was run with a quiet efficiency, the kind you'd expect to find in a large office block in any city. At Zemba, in contrast, there was something indefinable about the place, especially since the war was only a rifle shot away. Situated on fairly high ground, everybody came into the sights of a rebel sooner or later.

Apart from the paratroopers, the rest of the troops at Zemba appeared a fairly independent bunch of conscripts, bustling about on one task or other. They were alert and very much aware that the place had seen some serious fighting in the past. A Portuguese journalist who visited the camp a short while before, wrote that ' ... the men [at Zemba] carry themselves like lithe, wary animals. At any moment you expect to see them break into a sprint and rush for the nearest machine-gun turret.'

He suggested that it could have been because the base came under fire as often as it did. Since the start of the campaign in Sector D, Zemba had been fired on virtually every week.

'Yes, we have things a little tougher than at Santa Eulalia', Captain João Salvatori told us shortly after we arrived. 'But that's the way it goes in this war that is not really a war. He smiled at our reaction and said he'd explain later.

This still-youthful professional soldier, originally from Lisbon and who admitted to having joined the army to experience the extent of Portuguese possessions in the world, was Zemba's commanding officer. It was a temporary posting because the camp rated a lieutenant-colonel, but he'd gone to Luanda on a staff course.

After lunch, Captain Salvatori led us towards his operations room, situated in a bunker not far from the base living quarters. It had been constructed partly underground to avoid enemy fire which had been much more severe in the past and included heavy mortars. Even so, there was one wall left open to the elements – the enervating tropics demanded some kind of improvised air conditioning in an environment where you were already bathed in sweat before you got out of your bunk in the morning.

The Captain spent an hour detailing the kind of war that he fought. He told us that the sector was much more active than other bases in the sector, in part, because they suspected the presence of a major terrorist headquarters in the vicinity of the camp.

'We know it's there, fairly nearby, but we've never been able to pin-point its exact location, not even with the help of captives. Also, those people are pretty good and they're never permanently based. In fact, they can pick up everything and move it a day's march away if they chose to do so – radio equipment, supplies, prisoners, the lot.'

'What we do know is that they like to keep themselves on the move. One day their command post will be behind that big mountain nearest us, the following day behind the next ... all very shrewd ... '

The forces facing his men were largely MPLA, a very different proposition from the unruly UPA rabble. They knew what they were doing, were adequately equipped and supplied and in his view, streets ahead of the rest when it came to insurgency.

'But it ends there, because I doubt whether they plan very far ahead. They have their own systems which are known only to their leaders. We have not been able to make a breakthrough yet, but it'll happen with time.' It was interesting, he told us, that this particular bunch of irregulars drew heavily on the experience of the Vietcong in such matters.

'We have about a dozen vehicles here', the officer explained. 'We patrol the surrounding area either on foot or we go out in trucks – Unimogs, German built, but assembled in Portugal. As the country is a little more open than further north, we have a slightly less chance of being ambushed, but it happens, more frequently than I would like' At the same time, he suggested, the same conditions allowed the insurgents to maintain better look-outs.

'What we really need here, of course, are helicopters – permanently stationed at Zemba, about half-a-dozen of them. But that is not going to take place any time soon. With half a dozen Alouette gunships I could change the course of this war in a week', the captain reckoned.

I'd heard the same argument from a number of Portuguese officers, both in Luanda and in Sector D. I was to hear it subsequently in Cabinda and on the eastern front, near the Zambian and Caprivi borders. There wasn't a senior Portuguese Army officer who did not believe that helicopters were the ultimate weapon of war for this kind of struggle. It was almost as if it had been purpose built for counter-insurgency use, some of them would argue. Which was what the Americans were proving just then in Vietnam, they would add mournfully.

The trouble was, with three African wars, that kind of sophisticated equipment was expensive for a small, impoverished nation like Portugal. It was also in exceptionally short supply in Angola[1].

'It's ridiculous really, each time the guerrillas attack, they disappear into the bush the moment we make a stand. They're gone before we can bring our men up—never mind calling for reinforcements. With helicopters we could be over the enemy position within minutes ... we might drop men behind them and cut off their retreat.

'Then they would be forced to fight', a staff officer added.

Captain Salvatori: 'Give me three decent battles involving these aircraft and we will give them enough to talk about for a year in the Congo or wherever else they drag the survivors to.'

The captain was confident that in any evenly-matched engagement, his men could kill in the ratio of six to one. 'Six terrorists killed for every Portuguese casualty—killed or wounded.

While his critics might have regarded him as possibly over-confident, this was the actual statistic then being applied to Portugal's military campaign in Mozambique.

In the subsequent Rhodesian bush war, it was eight or ten times that.

The Portuguese Army at Zemba followed strict patrol procedures. Groups of about 30 soldiers were sent out daily into the surrounding bush, usually led by an officer with three sergeants to assist.

They stayed out from three to five days, sometimes longer, depending on whether contact was made. Other times they'd follow guerrilla trails through the bush. As spotters, there were customarily black Portuguese soldiers at the van since they excelled in such things: most had grown up in the bush and were able to follow a 48-hour old trail for days at a stretch.

'We keep another squad ready for any eventuality—including attacks which sometimes come out of nowhere', the officer explained.

I asked him about the black troops. They clearly served in the majority of camps that we'd visited. In Luanda a large proportion of the troops wandering about the city on

West German-built Dornier DO-27 spotter planes were a valuable asset, both in locating enemy positions and in supply or casualty evacuation missions. (Photo Richard McIntosh)

furlough were African. It seemed peculiar to find black troops in Portuguese army uniform when the enemy was the same colour as themselves, was the thrust.

Africans were conscripted in Angola like anybody else, including local Europeans, the officer said. Like their counterparts from Portugal, they were required to spend two or three years in uniform[1]. They wore the same uniforms, earned the same money as soldiers from Europe, lived in the same barracks, and, when wounded, were evacuated as any other troops might have been. He stressed that there was no colour bar or segregation and certainly no apartheid.

'It's not as strange as it might seem,' the officer said. 'Remember, these people have lived under the Portuguese flag for more than five centuries. They would not consider themselves anything but Portuguese.' He suggested I ask them myself.

Integration, as I was to discover, was indeed complete. The two races lived in comparative harmony, under conditions that were a lot more amenable than might have been the case in the United States in the 1960s or 1970s, or even years later.

As one young *alfares* put it to me through an interpreter, the two groups simply had to trust each other. Their ideals – right or wrong – he said, were based on 'a mutual conviction'. This was a dependence that not only worked quite well, but simply had to for the community to survive in the long term.

Another time, a black-faced junior officer who had learnt his English at a mission school when his parents had spent time in Zambia asked me: 'what else am I but Portuguese?'

He went on: 'I speak from experience because I have seen things beyond these borders. I am aware that the British and the South Africans may not be able to understand the fact that I am as Portuguese as the next man in this camp, but these are my colleagues and they accept me ... we fight together and occasionally we die together'. At which point he just smiled.

The youngster wasn't exactly pleased by my approach. In retrospect, he probably had good reason. His fellow soldiers had taken his blackness for granted, but as an inquisitive journalist, I had not.

The fact remained, the three Portuguese armies in Africa were more multi-racial than any other comparable military element in recent history.

History has some interesting footnotes about multiracial African units. There were black troops from Senegal and Equatorial Africa in the French Army during both world wars, and they were almost all white officered. The same with the King's African Rifles, whose two divisions included East African, Ghanaian, Nigerian, and South African troops. All saw active service not only against the Germans but also against the Japanese in Burma and their combat record was exemplary.

The Ugandan leader Idi Amin had made sergeant in the King's African Rifles in Kenya and by all accounts, was regarded by his white superiors as a fine NCO. It was only when he took power that he went berserk, or as the saying goes, absolute power corrupts absolutely ...

Before that, during World War I, there were thousands of locals recruited by Imperial German forces in Tanganyika under General Paul von Lettow-Vorbeck. He and his *Askaris* ran the allies ragged throughout East Africa and only surrendered after the war was over in Northern Rhodesia, or what is Zambia today. Among those on his tail were thousands of South Africans who, for part of the time, were commanded by General, later Field-Marshal Jan Christiaan Smuts, or 'Oom Jannie' as he was affectionately known to his people.

What was interesting about the German experience in Tanganyika in World War I, was that all the black troops were locally recruited, particularly the *Askaris*. Once Portugal got involved in her own colonial wars, this was regarded by the tacticians in Lisbon as highly positive.

One of the more interesting statistics to emerge from that 1915 bush conflict that covered an area larger than France was that General von Lettow-Vorbeck's troops were composed of 2,200 Europeans, 11,100 regular African soldiers and 3,200 irregulars. All were ranged in two dozen companies, each with roughly a dozen whites and 300 Africans.

It was one of the classic campaigns of World War I has and been the subject of several war histories. The one that stands out is *They Fought For King and Kaiser* by James Ambrose Brown, originally published by Ashanti in Johannesburg in 1997, a stunning read.

In Portuguese Africa, it took the 1961 invasion from the north to give black soldiers with the right educational qualifications the opportunity of becoming officers. The respect these men receive from their charges, black or white, was no different to that of any officer with a European background. If there was a difference, the Portuguese military code dealt with it, and very smartly too. There was detention barracks for insubordination.

An interesting aspect of camp life at a remote posting like Zemba was that it was reasonably well-stocked with just about everything the soldiers needed. Food was adequate, so was reading matter and, later, weekly films were the norm.

While wine came with the meals, they could buy local Cuca bottled beers at the canteen at a third of the price in town. If they preferred Aguardente – the local triple-distilled 'fire water' or even scotch – it was also available.

Despite the otherwise austere tropical backdrop, Zemba's officers' mess had been made into a cosy little 'home-away-from-home' for those using it and I found it was one of the most comfortable in the region. Exotic Portuguese sea dishes were a once-a-week must, as they were elsewhere in these remote operational areas.

Though hundreds of clicks from the sea, we were offered *bacalhau* and cuttlefish, both prepared in the traditional Iberian manner, in wine. I enjoyed my very first *presunto*, a delectable wafer thin smoked Parma-like ham at Zemba and ended one meal with the fondue-like *queijo de azeitao*.

I could just as easily have been at one those delightful little street-side restaurants in the Belem District back in the *metrópole*.

To some, it could be a good life if you didn't weaken and the Portuguese took a certain pride in being able to offer their guests the best available under the most primitive surroundings.

Although Lisbon was fighting a series of African bush campaigns that, like Vietnam, was claiming lives by the day – though not nearly as many as the Americans were to suffer – mealtimes were always a ritual. Officers questioned about these superficial gastronomic luxuries in the bush would maintain that food was their one link with the civilization to which they had been accustomed. In a way, I suppose it made sense.

'Two years out here in the jungle with few women about and we're left with only our wine and our food ... the guitar and music follow afterwards ... Fado', our host chuckled.

Another officer, a little more ebullient than the rest admitted that food had actually been the undoing of more than one encounter with the enemy. 'They know that if they have to make a mark at all during daylight hours, the best time to hit us is during the lunch break, which can sometimes last two hours. Defences are slackest during meals and the siesta hour immediately afterwards', he confided.

He told us of an attack on Villa Teixeira de Sousa, a railway town in the east near the Congolese frontier. It was a typical example of the kind that took place, he suggested.

The entire population and the local garrison had just sat down to their Christmas lunch – the usual celebratory affair, but much more so on the devoutly Christian Iberian Peninsula – when the first mortar bombs started coming across.

They hit the native quarter first. 'That gave the others some warning and they were able to get to their weapons. Had the enemy initially attacked the European sector they might have done a lot more damage ... it could have been a catastrophe', he confided, because there were women and children from the town in the party, he said.

During the visit to the camp we were taken on a number of patrols. I'd requested the experience to provide me with an insight as to how the Portuguese Army operated on foot and was seconded to a unit headed by a captain together with a 30-man squad to escort us out. This was the same group of soldiers that routinely worked together.

'These troops remain in the same detachment for the duration' he told me. Each man had a specific function. He also had to be familiar with the duties of the two men immediately in front of him and to the rear. If one of them was incapacitated, wounded or killed, he would automatically take over their roles, be it with the mortar or radio, or feeding the machine-gunner with additional belts.

Procedures were standard. On patrol, the men moved about in single column, usually allowing for a good space between individual combatants to avoid bunching. An individual was required to hump everything that might be needed and enough food and water for five days in his pack. They were also tasked to carry one extra item, which might be a collapsible stretcher, extra mortar bombs or perhaps the weapon itself. Several in the group hauled knapsacks with bazooka shells. At that stage rifle grenades had only begun to make an appearance in Portugal's wars.

Three machine-guns were issued to each patrol. Each gunner 'spoke' a reasonably fluent sign language with his hands; he was expected to understand, given the sign, whether to proceed left or right, pull back or advance. Or perhaps stay where he was and maintain a defensive position.

Ancillary touches included canvas boots with rubber soles. Since the countryside was heavily foliated, most units could march as silently as the enemy, though talk was never tolerated on the move.

It was ideal type of country for clandestine guerrilla operations. There were no twigs to snap on the track that might alert someone listening and few rocks on which to stub your toe. The foliage all around was an almost incandescent green, and the rest was putrefying; the eternal cycle. The British writer Spencer Chapman had it right when he originally penned his classic work *The Jungle is Neutral*.

While his book deals with the war against Japan in the Far East several decades before, many of the precepts on which this erstwhile academic elaborated, applied equally well to Portugal's African campaigns, particularly in places like Portuguese Guinea and Sector D in Angola. It is worth a read because the book delineates some of the parameters involved in these remote and mostly isolated conflicts.

For instance, metal items that might knock against each other during the march were bound with strips of cloth. When a patrol stopped in a clearing for a hastily prepared meal or a short rest, few soldiers had anything to say. Nor was there ever a fire lit. The men just did what was needed and got it over with. Always, there was a third of the squad standing guard, always on the fringe of the clearing.

During a five-day patrol through heavily overgrown jungle country a patrol might cover as much as 100 kilometres. They sometimes managed a good deal more in the east of the country where there were more clearings and the forest gave way to savannah.

Most times, the group would follow specific paths, risky because of mines but essential if there was to be any progress. On the immediate trail of a group of insurgents, they would try to follow alongside, rather than on the already broken trail, for obvious reasons.

They did this to avoid booby traps, the officer said. 'But sometimes the undergrowth is so thick that we're obliged to follow in the tracks of the enemy. That's when I start to worry ... .'

His adversaries used a variety of ruses, he explained. These ranged from Chinese anti-personnel mines similar to those used by the Vietcong, to improvised mines made from a grenade 'If it's a straightforward grenade, you've got perhaps three or four seconds to get clear', the captain stated. 'If it's an OZM-4, then that's it!'

The OZM-4, he explained, was a metallic bounding fragmentation mine, the original 'Bouncing Betty'. Designed to kill the person who sets it off, this cylindrical mine body is initially located in a short pot or barrel assembly and activation detonates a small explosive charge, which projects the mine body upwards.

The officer said he'd been lucky. He'd had a few scrapes, and added that it was strange, 'but when you've tripped a wire, you just knew it immediately. Everything else swings into slow motion, almost like it happens when you're in a car that rolls...'

Even worse, a tripped grenade could sometimes signal the start of an ambush and then things can get serious.

'You've rehearsed the signal a dozen times with the boys. With so much at stake it seems almost inadequate ... you just hope the guys behind you have dived as low into the bush as you're doing at that moment ... '

During the course of the previous eight months, the captain had had two encounters that involved hand grenades that had been used to prime booby traps. Both times he and his men had been lucky ... 'we had only minor injuries and there were no ambushes.'

A colleague in Mozambique, in contrast – also a captain, attached to the *Comandos Africanos* (an elite, mainly white-officered, African unit) – had both his legs blown off by a mortar bomb that had been attached to an anti-personnel mine.

'It took both his legs off just below the knee, and everything between them as well ... also an ambush. The others were in a very strong position overlooking the killing ground and they hit them with RPG-2s, mortars and grenades.

'Reports later stated that it was the worst battle of the month in the East African territory. Government forces took 13 casualties, five killed and eight wounded, two critically, including the captain ... bad for a patrol of 20 men', he reckoned.

The captain had since learnt to walk again with prosthetics. The President of Portugal awarded him the highest military honour and the newspapers were full of it at the time.

9

Cabinda: the War North
of the Congo River

'One of the most significant aspects of guerrilla warfare is the manifest difference
between information available to the guerrilla and that available to the enemy.'

Ché Guevara, on his return to Cuba after visiting
several African conflicts, including the Cabinda Front

The war in Cabinda – the oil-rich Angolan enclave north of the great Congo River, differed radically from guerrilla campaigns being fought against the insurgents in either the Dembos or, for that matter, in the east near the Zambian or Katangese frontiers. Things were also very different to what was going on at the time either in Mozambique or Portuguese Guinea.

If the Dembos was regarded as forbidding, this northern region, lying adjacent to the equator, was much more so. Conditions weren't helped by an overwhelming, almost-asphyxiating tropical heat that made people listless, somnolent and insecure. It was the kind of environment that within days, would cause all the clothes in your suitcase to grow a kind of scum-coloured mold that sometimes proved difficult to deal with. It was also a time when air conditioning – as you and I know it today – was still waiting to happen throughout much of West Africa.

Perspiring, out-of-breath, European-born Portuguese troops were aghast within minutes of stepping out of their aircraft when they first arrived, largely because they had never experienced anything like it. Few were likely to recall that early navigators had given Cabinda and French Equatorial Africa – including nearby Congo (Brazzaville) and Gabon – the unflattering handle of Fever Coast. British traders in Nigeria were more colourful in their use of idiom and 'White Man's Grave' lingered for decades after quinine was found to be a reasonable counter to malaria.

As with British Forces in Malaya in the 1950s – and the French and Americans in Vietnam – it didn't take these young soldiers long to get used to it all, for no better reason than they simply had to. In any event, conditions were light years from today's much vaunted humanitarian approach to human frailties under fire that often includes a range of specifics for any kind of stress disorder. To the majority in those faraway days, PTSD might have been a galaxy in the firmament.

A soldier who suffered mental trauma or who was possibly emotionally unstable in those days, was much more likely to find himself in the brig for malingering than before

An early photo of the war when the Portuguese first moved in to retake the
jungle north from an invading guerrilla force. (Author's collection)

the unit doctor.

The concept was adequately illustrated when American General Patton struck a GI at a
hospital in Sicily. The soldier had no physical wounds, but he was just as much of a casualty
as those who did. It says it all that in the First World War, only 30-something years before,
such people were often placed before a firing squad for cowardice in the face of the enemy.

In Cabinda, the actions of small guerrilla units arrayed against Portuguese authority were
dictated first by the jungle and then by their weapons, the need for food, the deployment of
their adversaries and finally, instructions from military command in Brazzaville—in about
that order of priority. The result was that this jungle campaign differed radically when
compared to similar military struggles then being waged by the rebels further towards
Angola's south.

It was a two-edged sword. The Portuguese faced the exact same privations, only they
were better organised. This was one of the reasons why Lisbon was so successful in the oil-
rich territory, a tiny spit of land about the size of Vermont and completely surrounded by
independent African states that were virulently anti-Portuguese.

In the years before I got there on my 'official' visit in late 1960s, the Portuguese army
managed to recapture all the territory that had formerly been under insurgent control in
the enclave. It was no easy task, because following the initial onslaughts of March 1961,

rebel insurgents managed to occupy more than 90 per cent of the enclave. They did this in a single, concerted sweep towards the coast from about eight or nine different entry points, the entire operation dictated by an MPLA chain of command then headquartered in Brazzaville.

The guerrillas overran villages and towns in the north-east and, as with the Dembos further south, they brought all commercial activity, logging, oil drilling and agriculture to a standstill. They were even more successful in routing an ill-prepared Portuguese militia and police north of the Congo than they'd been to the south of it and stopped just short of the capital, Cabinda, itself.

It was only a concerted effort by the Portuguese army, backed by whatever air support could be mustered that enabled the authorities to reverse this tide.

It took another four years before the country was manageable again. Although the insurgent threat in Cabinda thereafter remained negligible, largely because the MPLA was replaced by other, less determined liberation groups, you still needed to travel in convoy between all the major centres.

As a journalist in transit, I saw a little of the initial struggle when I briefly passed though Cabinda Airport in December 1964. At the time the place was ringed by machine-gun turrets and American-built T-6 Harvard trainers with loads of rockets, bombs and machine-guns were landing and taking off. The atmosphere in town was tense and the man in the street projected a nervousness that I had only previously seen in the Congo and at the height of the OAS-FLN fracas in Algeria.

Unlike my visit three years later, few Portuguese Army officers appeared to have much time for anything but the war. There was a real threat of being driven out of the enclave, which today ranks potentially as the fourth or fifth largest oilfield outside the Americas.

Major Mathias concisely summed it up: 'It was close ... too damn close ... the terrorists never realized how close to victory they really were.'

It has always been this apparent lethargy or lack of interest – or rather, ignorance of what was going on strategically in an operational area – that almost consistently let insurgents down. Patently, they lacked the infrastructure for an efficient intelligence set-up, not only in Cabinda but also in Sector D and in the east. This should never have happened because the East German intelligence specialists trained scores of MPLA cadres. These shortcomings, critical under the circumstances, repeatedly caused the guerrillas to play into the hands of government forces.

In Cabinda, they caught the Portuguese authorities literally, with their pants adrift. Yet as hostilities in the enclave progressed, they were not even aware of the damage they had caused. Nor did they have either the leadership or the initiative to launch that final push. Even Lisbon conceded afterwards that the rebels were a hairsbreadth from snatching victory, saying that perhaps it was the heat.

A reason for this, put forward by military strategists who studied Portugal's wars in Africa in more recent times, was that throughout their African campaigns, the Portuguese were tardy in releasing anything specific about what was going on in their African military theatres of activity. The Lisbon-based Lusitania News Agency would make its weekly declaration about casualties, promotions, retirements from the three services and possibly something notable about an action that might have warranted a decoration for bravery, but little else.

The media railed, the government gave the stock retort of 'no comment' and the military authorities were castigated by the international press corps. But then the Portuguese always seem to always have marched to the beat of a different drum.

Remember, this was a time when just about everybody and his brother could arrive in South Vietnam and, on demand, be given press accreditation by the Americans. All you needed was the price of a ticket to head for Saigon and become a 'war correspondent'. North Vietnam was much more sensible and played it like the Portuguese, and almost no foreigners covered the war from Hanoi.

When the Falklands War came along, the few British journalists who managed to cover the war were initially astonished at the level of media control instituted by their minders. If they didn't like military censorship, one and all were told, they were free to go. In the end, it worked very well.

For better or for worse, the Portuguese were remarkably successful in keeping the war out of the news, and here Vietnam also helped. Through the medium of television, half the world was able to watch this South East Asian conflict from the comfort of their living rooms, and as might have been expected, nobody gave Africa a second thought. Why should they? They already had a surfeit of helicopters going into combat, jungle patrols and all the blood and guts and gore of a real war.

There were some newsmen allowed to visit the fighting zones in Angola, Mozambique and Portuguese Guinea, but all were carefully screened. Apart from Portuguese scribes, Jim Hoagland of *The Washington Post* got into Portuguese Guinea, in part because of diplomatic pressure from Washington. The same with Peter-Hannes Lehmann of *Der Spiegel* and perhaps a few dozen others over more than a decade.

Those of us based in South Africa found things a lot easier, largely because Lisbon relied on Pretoria for advice as to who was acceptable. In any event, it was a simple matter to travel from Rhodesia to Malawi on the open road, and there were no restrictions. Long before you reached Tete on the Zambezi River in Mozambique, you were able to see aspects of the military dimension from up close.

On my part, having already covered the troubles in the Congo and Biafra, my bona fides were taken for granted. But even then, I was only allowed limited access.

Major Mathias conceded that the 'security blanket' as he would phrase it, was a complete reversal of the immensely successful Biafran propaganda programme which was handled by a public relations concern in Geneva.

The Swiss company MarkPress helped create universal support for Biafra's millions of starving children. Indirectly, according to Frederick Forsyth – who covered that debacle from the beginning – the emotional storm generated by hordes of little ones with bellies swollen from kwashiorkor and dying by the hundreds each day ended up being ghoulishly

A Portuguese soldier gives one of the locals a drink from his
canteen in the Cabinda jungle. (Author's photo)

beneficial to the Biafran leader, Colonel Odumegwu Ojukwu. The same kind of thing
took place afterwards in Ethiopia, only this time it was my old pal Mohammed Amin who
spread the word with his heart-wrenching pictures that eventually got him acclaimed by
the Queen, President Reagan, the United Nations and others.

The first book to appear in the West from the Portuguese perspective, *The Terror
Fighters*, was written by this author. On the guerrilla side, the radical British writer Basil
Davidson went in several times with the rebels and produced some notable volumes of his
own, including *The Eye of the Storm*.[1]

By far the best must still be *Angola*, written by Douglas Wheeler and another old
friend, René Pélissier. That work was published by Pall Mall in London in 1971, though
Portuguese Africa (Penguin) by J. Duffy rates good mention.

In Lisbon's African campaigns, by releasing only essentials and remaining almost totally
non-committal about just about everything else, the media played a relatively insignificant
role as these African hostilities progressed.

On the one hand, the Portuguese public was spared many of the gory details, though that kind of obscurantism ended up being defeatist. When the 1974 revolution took place, the entire nation was taken by surprise because they had no idea how bad things really were, in Portuguese Guinea especially. On the other hand, there was a limit to marginalising issues indefinitely, especially since the casualty lists spoke a language of their own.

On a more fundamental level, by saying nothing about a major insurgent strike in a sector—an attack that may have been months in the planning and which cost a mint in equipment and men – Lisbon was consistent in maintaining the upper hand in strategy. The lack of any news about guerrilla successes must have a severe effect not only in demoralising the rebel command but also on their men in the field.

'Put it this way', said the major. 'The insurgents hear nothing for weeks or even months about their great battle. They have no means of finding out either because radios in the jungle are at a premium, and the few that there are cannot be operated because the operator has been inadequately trained or the batteries have been drained by jungle damp.

'Even worse, had somebody in Brazzaville known the true story, somebody might have been able to organise a follow-up activity that may have delivered a coup de grâce in a particular sector.'

Major Mathias continued: 'This is basic incompetence, nothing else. For now a new bunch of guerrillas is going into battle not knowing what to expect. They have heard claims of victory, but these cannot be substantiated either by displaying captured Portuguese soldiers, or even by showing photographs of installations or equipment destroyed.'

It was all very well to broadcast weekly reports of 68 Portuguese soldiers killed in this action and 14 aircraft downed by the intrepid comrades in another – Brazzaville Radio was regularly putting out that kind of propaganda – it was something else to show proof.

Like the old adage, said the major: 'one picture is worth a thousand words.'

'So when one has had years of this drivel, even the most seasoned supporter of Freedom Army ideals becomes sceptical. This was one of the reasons why so many former Cabinda nationals have returned to their homes from across the border ... they didn't know whom to believe in the end...'

Another officer attached to the Cabinda commandant's staff said that perhaps the biggest single cause of desertion among the guerrillas was the number of wounded who were ferried back across the frontier. Most were taken out of Cabinda on primitive litters, often with arms or legs blown off. Others were brought in suffering from third degree burns as a result of napalm, though Lisbon consistently denied use of this weapon.

'Our pilots see these convoys moving through the jungle ... they report in, but the order comes back: let them go.

'The fact that they take their wounded back to base does us a lot more good than harm. Anyway, we're not keen to stretch our own medical services by treating people who would have little compunction in castrating Portuguese troops they find wandering about the jungle, which has happened often enough in the past', the officer suggested.

Anyway, he added, the Cabinda people were weary of war. 'They've had almost a decade of it and all they want now is peace. They also resent many of the demands made by the terrorists—and that is why local chiefs have been willing to co-operate with the Portuguese authorities in recent years.'

On a broader canvas, there was little doubt that the war in Cabinda had wound down considerably from the intensity of the earlier years. There had been almost no insurgent activity within 50 kilometres of the town for some years.

The few sorties that took place were restricted to the far north, though occasionally the insurgents would ambush a patrol or a vehicle. Often as not they were happy to enter the country, wander about for a few weeks and return home again, with the usual stock of hair-raising exploits and conquests which were dutifully repeated on Brazzaville Radio.

For all that, the Portuguese authorities in Cabinda had one persistent problem which had caused problems over the years—the ill-defined frontiers with the two Congos. These are what we know today as the Democratic Republic of the Congo with Kinshasa as its capital and the quasi-Marxist Congo (Brazzaville) on the north bank of the river they both share.

Even before the war, smuggling was a major commercial industry in the enclave. Traders from Brazzaville and Leopoldville would bring through quantities of cheap watches, cameras, silks, French perfumes and other items that were heavily taxed in the Portuguese provinces. In return they would go back with stocks of canned goods, condiments, raw coffee and goldware which could be sold for as much as 200 or 300 per cent profit in the former French and Belgian colonies.

Similar frontier problems exist today, Major Mathias said; only now it becomes more serious when a Portuguese patrol is on the trail of an insurgent band and they eventually catch up somewhere near the border.

'What does a man do then? We know vaguely we are near the frontier, but that's hardly the end of it. We go on and, if we can, we destroy. The insurgents invariably claim that we had acted against the precepts of International Law and that we had sent our troops into Congo-Brazza or Congo Kinshasa territory. But who is to prove one way or the other in the middle of an undefined, uncharted jungle?' the major asked.

He said that similar problems existed along the frontier with Zambia. More than once, President Kenneth Kaunda, the Zambian president, had taken the matter up with the United Nations. 'Then we'd have the wrath of the world on our shoulders for a week. And nobody stops to think for a moment that it could be the other way round.

'The terrorists are given carte blanche to cross any border they please to attack our people ... the Portuguese are never able to retaliate...'

Frontier problems in Africa were a heritage of the colonial era and in the 21st Century, they still are.

There are other difficulties involved in border claims elsewhere in Africa, like the Bakassi Peninsula, currently in the public eye. One is a tiny stretch of land that straddles an isthmus between Nigeria and the Cameroon claimed by both countries, to the point

Portuguese marines coming ashore after an operation. (Author's collection)

where their armies have moved closer. The dispute goes back well into the last century when the scramble for Africa by the former European colonial powers was intense, the only difference between then and now is that Bakassi holds rich deposits of oil.

There is a plenitude of such issues facing contemporary African governments. Lines of longitude and latitude defining frontiers were drawn arbitrarily across the map of Africa over conference tables in the various European capitals, with little regard for natural or geographical limitations such as rivers, mountains and deserts.

'The hardest hits were the tribes, and in Angola's Bakongo people, we have a typical example. Half the tribe lives in northern Angola, the other half in the Congo. A similar problem exists here in Cabinda', the major explained.

'There are few of the local population who have not got at least one member of the family living in Congo-Brazza. Everyone living on this side of the border can trace family links with someone over there.'

I was to see this later for myself. Many of the African villagers I met near Dinge and Belize in the interior spoke fluent French as well as Portuguese and their native tongues. A number had been educated by the French, as in the case of Corporal Mavungo, a Portuguese war hero.

Corporal Vicente Mocosso Mavungo, a native of Cabinda and a corporal in the Portuguese army was awarded the Cross of War, Third Class, for bravery while under enemy fire on Portugal Day, June 10, 1968. The action had taken place almost a year before and at the Luanda ceremony, Mavungo and other war heroes had been the toast of Portuguese newspapers on three continents.

Altogether 25 Portuguese combatants from the army, navy and air force – including four more Africans – received their decorations from the heads of the Portuguese Armed Forces in Angola. In order of merit, Mavungo's decoration was the fifth highest awarded by the government that day.

Corporal Mavungo's story was indicative of the way the Portuguese fought their wars in Africa. The event took place during a classic guerrilla ambush in tropical forests so dense that the Unimogs the troops were escorting had their lights on. In parts, tropical foliage completely covered the road, cutting off almost all the light from above. Conditions were ideal for an ambush, the squad had been told by their sergeant earlier, to which he'd added, 'so be careful ... '

In charge of a handful of troops on the second of four Unimogs, Mavungo took up a position behind a heavy .50-calibre machine-gun fixed to a tripod on the rear of the truck. There were no Panhards for back-up and under those conditions there would certainly be no top cover, even if there were any helicopters available.

Most of the men on the vehicles sat with their legs hanging over the side but it wasn't a comfortable ride because they continually had to give way as large clusters of bush sheered past. Meantime, the jungle darkened still more.

It suddenly became light as the trucks skirted a mangrove swamp and a pungent odour of putrefaction enveloped the convoy. Moments later a black swarm of tsetse flies arrived. Everybody cursed because it was stifling. Sweat speckled the faces of the men and they constantly had to swat both mosquitoes and flies, which eventually became so plentiful that even with the heat, the driver and his mate turned up their windows. A minute or two later, the column was in the jungle again and most of the insects disappeared.

According to Corporal Mavungo, they travelled like this for another five minutes or so when a group of guerrillas opened fire from a well-constructed hide to the immediate right of them.

Almost simultaneously a powerful explosion ripped open part of the roof of the cab of the first truck in the line. The vehicle lurched to a halt in a crash of splintered glass and screams while the driver of Mavungo's truck – taken completely by surprise – drove into the rear of the vehicle ahead.

The corporal's two comrades, one on either side of him, fell off the truck and were dead before they hit the ground.

The other two men still alive on the rear of the Unimog, joined their corporal at the base of the machine-gun. They could hear the two men in the cab groaning, though they weren't sure whether they'd taken hits. The ambush had been well planned.

By now there were only two vehicles countering the guerrillas firing from the nearby jungle; the last two trucks in the column had swiftly reversed and were out of sight. So much for back-up, thought Mavungo. The men on the back of the lead truck were still

The war became a rather relaxed affair when there was supposed to be no enemy around. The convoy would halt in a clearing and food and drinks would be hauled out. (Author's collection)

firing, though it was sporadic, because some of those men had been wounded.

For a few moments a single thought echoed though the corporal's mind— how many of the enemy were there?

His training had long ago taught him to shift the safety catch of his G-3 to 'rapid-fire' in an emergency. Within seconds he had used up two clips, spraying the jungle in the immediate vicinity of the truck. He spotted green tracers bouncing off the bodywork around him. This was MPLA, he thought.

A grenade exploded to the rear of his Unimog. Something hot touched the corporal's back high up, between the shoulder-blades. The touch turned to fire as blood trickled down his spine. He had been hit. He had never been wounded before.

The firing slackened a little after he'd emptied another magazine into the jungle and just then, a searing pain shot across his cheek as a fragment of hot metal grazed his face. He cursed in his native Kikongo. Spasms of a racking, throbbing pain pushed all other thoughts from his mind. Another explosion nearby brought his predicament into sharp focus once more. He was out of ammunition, which was when he moved towards the grenades on his belt.

As he pulled the last pin and hurled the khaki-coloured canister that looked more like a can of shaving cream than a bomb, he jumped from the truck. Moments later he felt for the grenades of the two dead soldiers, found them and took their ammunition clips as well.

10

Cabinda and an ongoing Guerrilla Struggle

Wartime armies are made up of professional soldiers and of civilians in uniform. Neither civilians nor soldiers are necessarily warriors, for the former may regret their peaceful callings while it is not unknown for the latter to prefer the dull round of garrison life to the excitement of campaigning. In truth, all too few of either category make warriors, yet it is warriors who win wars.

Brigadier Peter Young DSO, MC,
Head of Military History at the Royal Military Academy, Sandhurst

Two young officers were designated by the commandant to travel north with us: Victor Marques, our official interpreter, and 21-year-old Tony Martins, already a veteran of the war.

Both men had been in Cabinda almost two years and were due for discharge; clearly, they enjoyed the interlude. It was a change from an otherwise dreary and uneventful existence which had been forced on most of the troops since the insurgents had been driven northwards.

'We'll travel by jeep, driving during the day and staying over at various army camps en route, which is something that has already been formally dealt with by our brigadier,' he told me. He also suggested that there was little likelihood of any kind of action. 'That's long past', Tony declared and we had to take his word for it. Photographer Cloete Breytenbach and I consequently travelled the first 150 kilometres through rugged bush and jungle country with only two G-3 carbines and a clutch of grenades between us.

The two officers formed an interesting contrast. Marques was an arts scholar who had spent several years at Coimbra University. His bearing and polished mannerisms indicated that he was the scion of a well-placed family in the Metropolis. Like the rest, he'd been conscripted to spend two years in Africa and he loathed it. Obviously the Cabinda posting hadn't made life any easier and he had a unique take on his predicament

'If I'm going to be struck in Africa for ten percent of my lifespan, then surely, I'd have preferred to be where the action is,' he commented after a liquid lunch. 'Then at least there would have been interesting things to talk about ... there would be risks, yeh! But then life's a fucking risk ... '

Tony Martins was different. He seemed to relish the uncertainty of war. Born in Angola, near the South West African border close to a South African farming community – which

Cloete Breytenbach took this photo of the author while on operations in Cabinda.

was where he learnt his English – he pulled out a photograph of his aged grandmother early on in the trip. It surprised me that she was black: 'pure, authentic African', was the way he described her.

He was very close to her, he said fondly ... 'a really lovely soul'. Among the words he used to describe her was something affectionately Portuguese that I don't recall.

Grandma had married one of the early Portuguese traders and it was no surprise that Martins was immensely proud of his mulatto origins. He was actually quite passionate about Africa generally and would call it 'my oyster,' adding that he had only peered briefly under its shell. The exploration he dreamt and often talked about was still to come ...

It was interesting that quite a few years later, after Lisbon had capitulated, I was to bump into Tony – by now a civilian – among a large group of refugees gathered together in Sá da Bandeira, later renamed Lubango by the new MPLA government. Not at all despondent – though the future looked bleak because he and his family had lost everything – the former lieutenant was heading south towards South Africa where he'd make a new life for them all, he said.

Sanguine, even in adversity, the prospect of a good scrap in the jungle, coupled to the indeterminate esoterics of guerrilla warfare had become integral to Tony Martins' life in the Portuguese Army.

If there was no trouble in an area he'd go looking for it elsewhere and often led his patrol for days along the Congolese frontier in search of insurgent groups. He'd find them too, intimating that it would happen, even if he inadvertently strayed into what he liked to call 'enemy territory', though he never went so far as to explain whether it was Kinshasa's Congo or that of Brazzaville.

It was Africa, and that was all that mattered, he'd chuckle quietly and change the subject or order another Cuca.

Once, he'd chased a group of insurgents onto Congo-Brazza soil. The guerrilla group, about 15-strong believed they were safely across the border, stopped running. But not Lieutenant Tony Martins. He and his men destroyed half the group before they knew what had hit them and brought back the rest to Cabinda in shackles.

It caused a rumpus at the time. Both he and his commanding officer were furiously blasted by Luanda. The lieutenant ended up in the guard house for a while, though nothing ever appeared on his record, nor did he lose any rank. The furore was eventually taken all the way to the United Nations and Lisbon's representative at the General Assembly was obliged to admit that it had all been a mistake.

'Anyone would have thought I'd started the Third World War. It was a huge incident', he claimed, adding that next time it happened, he wouldn't be bringing back prisoners ... .

The following month, not altogether unexpectedly, he was decorated for bravery in a similar kind of action. Again, he'd gone quietly across the border, linked up with some locals who were being persecuted by a bunch of *terroristas*, who pinpointed an enemy camp and promptly ambushed one of their patrols.

During the course of a firefight that lasted about half an hour, he'd deliberately drawn enemy fire while some of his men crept around and caught the insurgents in a crossfire.

'You see, you never know what they want. The one minute they jail me ... the next they give me a medal', he exclaimed, gesticulating as he spoke. He also explained that the military code in the Portuguese Army made provision for prison sentences for officers found guilty of disobeying orders or insubordination and that it was not at all difficult to land in the brig.

Most of the officers maintained that discipline had to be of the highest order in Portugal's African wars. Officers were often alone in the jungle with their men for weeks or months at a stretch. Decisions regarding safety and movements rested with them alone. They were their own masters in the jungle and if high standards were not maintained, chaos would ensue, was one of the arguments.

The fact that the My Lai incident had taken place a short while before seemed to have certainly had an effect on disciplinary issues in this African war, even though Vietnam was halfway across the world. Undoubtedly, the massacre of innocent civilians was the last thing that Portugal needed at a time when it was at the receiving end of opprobrium from almost the entire international community.

Censure motions in the UN and in Europe were regular events, but as with Pretoria, Lisbon – and, more recently, Tel Aviv – those countries learnt to live with them.

Cabinda patrol in the Mayombe Forest area. (Photo Brig Gen "Kaas" van der Waals)

The road leading north out of Cabinda town was a good one. It was surfaced as far as Landana, a seaside village that had been a popular weekend holiday spot before the war for many of the Americans working in the enclave. After Landana the road led inland, to the forests of the interior and the Congo (Brazzaville) frontier.

The area along the coast between Cabinda and Landana was oil country in the traditional American sense. The bustling, gum-chewing, cussing influence was everywhere. Every few kilometres or so, huge oil-drills stood naked and erect, incongruous alongside tall palms and mahogany giants. There was an atmosphere of industry about this untamed land and the Americans had created it, as they had elsewhere in Africa and the Middle East.

In some places the oilmen had established caravan camps. These were temporary homes away from home which they had brought in from the States for their wives and families while they worked in the tropics. Some were surrounded by three-metre barbed-wire fences and spotlights.

Tony said they were a typical American precaution, not for their own protection, but to keep Portuguese – whom they regarded as largely bucolic -and recalcitrant Africans *out*. He was never shy to reciprocate some of the anti-Portuguese sentiments he'd encountered among a few of the oilmen, but generally he found them an amenable lot.

In all, there were about 500 Americans working in Cabinda at the time. Had there been no war, it would have been many times that. There were a lot more based on the offshore oil rigs that characterized this stretch of the West African coastline as far north as Nigeria, together with another thousand or so expatriates in Cabinda under contract to the Yanks.

Gulf Oil had been drilling along the coast for a dozen years before they finally found oil in commercially exploitable quantities, and when they eventually did, it was a bonanza. Although they were obliged to suspend operations during the worst of the terrorist raids in 1961, the machine-gun muzzles were barely cold before the oilmen moved in again.

Along the road to the north we passed numerous traces of many of the battles that so viciously blighted the region after the 1961 invasion.

Every 35 or 40 kilometres the derelict remains of a Portuguese army camp would emerge against the skyline. Their gates would long ago have fallen off their hinges, their observation posts and machine-gun turrets fallen into disrepair, but nobody had removed the barbed wire and there was no mistaking the original purpose of these installations gradually being enveloped by an encroaching jungle. Some were totally covered in creepers and lianas.

Most of the camps had been abandoned because there was no longer any need for them, Martins told us. The last shot fired in anger south of Landana was in 1966, two years prior to our trip.

We visited what was left of one of the camps, delightfully situated on the edge of a cliff and overlooking the sea. It must have been a plum posting in its day because a breeze from seawards kept temperatures down. A few hundred metres below stretched one of the loveliest palm-lined beaches in Africa, almost tailor-made for Club Med.

This paradise in miniature evidently had its problems. Crudely nailed above the entrance of one of the ramshackle buildings was a sign which read, in Portuguese, 'Hotel of Slow Death'. The witticism manifested the frustrations of hostilities in the tropics, as did the three-metre snake that guarded the entrance to what must have been a barracks building. Martins dispatched it with a single shot to the head from his sidearm, a Browning Hi-Power 9mm Parabellum.

Shortly after we'd passed though Landana we arrived at Cabinda's infamous 'Bridge of War'. There had been some brutal fighting in the area early on and it also marked one of the stages of the long trek south by some of the Portuguese refugees.

Apart from the battle, its main claim to fame was that the bridge was never taken by the enemy, which meant that in order to cross southwards, which they did in great numbers over the years, they had to go some distance upstream and use boats, pirogues or barges.

Straddling a narrow, swampy outlet to the sea, the structure looked typical of the many Bailey Bridges erected by British Army engineers in World War II, only this one had been built by the Portuguese after the insurgents had partly destroyed the original bridge in 1963. By the time we got there, it was being guarded at both ends by a detachment of black and white soldiers and they took our names, passport details and the number on our jeep as we passed.

'From here on', said Lieutenant Martins seriously, 'we don't know what lies ahead'.

'That's why they take our details, which are passed on to the next camp up the line. If we don't arrive, they come looking for us, or what's left of us,' he joked.

We halted on the far side of the bridge while Tony briefed us on the historic battle.

By all accounts, the Portuguese Army fought for almost a full day in the area around the bridge, one of the rare occasions that the guerrillas were prepared to match blow for blow in a stand-up battle against government forces.

'Across the border in Congo-Kinshasa and Congo-Brazza they still talk about the "army that disappeared" and even today they don't know the true story.' The jungle had jealously guarded its secrets, was the phrase he used.

Lieutenant Martins: 'The battle started at dawn. There were about 300 troops on either side, facing off across this channel. The bridge was in the middle, or what was left of it after it had been mined.' Earlier, the Portuguese had tried a dangerous tactic.

'Before dawn, and in complete darkness, a small party of commandos had moved around the edge of the swamp in rubber boats and were dropped off every dozen metres or so. It wasn't long before our troops were positioned all the way around the swamp. The idea was to make it look like they had surrounded the rebels,' he explained

In theory the Portuguese *had* surrounded the enemy, but with only a few dozen men. It was a dodgy ruse because the commandos were cut off from the main body and might easily have been overrun by the insurgents if the truth were known.

'But when battle was launched at a predetermined time just as it became light, it sounded as if an entire Portuguese brigade had arrived. They fired guns, threw grenades, even hurled mortar shells.

'The enemy held on for many hours, often giving as good as they got. But they hadn't been prepared for this kind of concerted action and eventually their firing wavered, probably because they were running short of ammo.'

It was late afternoon that the main group broke and ran, but they had nowhere to go but into the swamp. 'Our boys mowed them down...

'The handful that got away either drowned or were taken by the crocodiles. We didn't even have to bury their bodies.'

The lieutenant estimated that Portuguese casualties numbered about six or eight—all killed in the first hour of the battle when the insurgents were still carefully directing fire. He had since studied details of the onslaught and doubted whether the rebels would ever make the same mistake twice.

In his two years in Africa, Martins had been responsible for the death or capture of 23 insurgents, a figure he was reluctant to initially reveal, but we prised it out of him on the fourth night at a mess dinner that ended with a recorded concert by Amalia Rodrigues. Even in darkest Africa, Fado ruled.

The lieutenant's tally of kills were confirmed afterwards by Major Mathias, who noted that more than half were accounted for during sorties into Congo-Brazza.

Jungle stop in Angola. Perimeter defences were sometimes lacking,
but then the guerrillas were also lax. (Author's photo)

Though not exactly a fan or admirer of the former Cuban guerrilla Ché Guevara, Lieutenant Tony Martins, for reasons of his own, held the man in great respect.

'He and I would have been on opposing sides had we met, but that doesn't prevent me from admiring the man. Before he was killed he was one of the greats in unconventional warfare ... we studied the same kind of tactics ... probably had the same kind of mind when it came to inflicting damage to the enemy.'

Ché had visited Congo-Brazza during 1964 and spent a while at Dolisie, an insurgent training camp about 40 clicks north of the Cabinda frontier. That meant, Martins believed, that more likely than not he'd entered the territory on a reconnaissance sortie.

Ché was that sort of operative, Martins believed; he wouldn't have passed up the opportunity. 'He probably even got a few Portuguese soldiers in his sights, though he never actually went into battle in the enclave'.

Dolisie, he explained, was a major MPLA base staffed largely by Cubans, so it all made sense.

Part of our journey to the north passed through one of the great natural tropical jungles of the world, Cabinda's magnificent Maiombe forest.

At the time, the Portuguese claimed that only sections of the Amazon were denser, as does the present Angolan government. 'You get lost in there and you're a goner, Martins warned. Since World War II, a number of aircraft had gone down in the forest near the

Congo-Brazza border and some of these wrecks had not yet been found.

Maiombe starts about 50 kilometres north of the 'Bridge of War' and forms part of a jungle chain that stretches from the Congo River near Boma, through Cabinda and Congo-Brazza all the way to the Maiombe Plateau in Gabon, a distance of almost 1,000 kilometres.

I had seen parts of it while visiting the jungle hospital of the late Albert Schweitzer at Lambarene a year before he died in 1965. It had taken me two days of travelling rough on an open boat up the Ogówe River from Port Gentil at the coast and along the way I was told that the river cut through a section of Maiombe.

The growth on both sides of the Ogówe – a relatively short river, but in places, because of the rainfall, as wide as the Congo – was awesome. Much of it, I gathered, had always been impenetrable to man. Apart from more forest giants than I'd ever imagined before, the terrain was interspersed by mangrove swamps that seem to stretch halfway across Africa in a solid, unyielding mass.

Extraordinarily dense undergrowth along the river seldom allowed a glimpse of the bank, and one could only speculate what would happen should our boat hit something and sink. A hundred or more metres above, towering mightily, the tallest of the forest giants reached upwards and outwards towards the sun.

There wasn't a tree that wasn't covered in creepers, moss, fungi and other tropical growths, an orchid collector's dream. When looking at it from the river, it seemed impossible that living creatures could survive in that murky forest which was almost pitch black at river level.

But there was plenty of movement, even if we rarely spotted an animal.

Monkeys chattered away at our passing craft, birds screeched and chirped among the tall branches and occasionally we heard the distinctive grunt of a larger animal, a leopard or wild boar perhaps? Never mind huge communities of hippo, crocs or the snakes that we constantly spotted slithering across the water.

The biggest attraction of Maiombe before the war – and since – was the gorilla population. There were thousands in the forest, the Portuguese reckoned, although they were getting scarce on the Congolese side as a result of hunting which was mostly indiscriminate. In Cabinda, the forest was simply too thick for any kind of commercial tourist activity, and, of course, there was the war.

There was an orphaned baby gorilla at the officers' mess at one of the bases in the interior when we arrived, called Chica. But for hair that covered her entire body, she might have been human. Her mother had apparently been shot by a soldier near Belize as she scratched for food in the undergrowth close to an army camp and Chica had been adopted by one of the men. She knew almost instinctively that milk and sweet things would appear whenever he was around.

Tough, hardened jungle fighters dropped everything when he was not and Chica would grimace and scream. It was a noise that could be heard half-way across town.

The little gorilla had numerous needs apart from constant love, care and attention. She would cling to the arm of an admirer with the strength of a man, but left on the ground on her own, she would clasp her hands and feet together and move forward on her elbows screaming. Simultaneously she would urinate and defecate.

Once cleaned up, she was again a favourite with the men.

Dinge camp, our destination in northern Cabinda, was like most military establishments in Angola. The garrison was about 200 strong, but there was rarely more than half the complement in camp at any one time. The bulk of the men spent their time patrolling the surrounding jungle as well as the Congo-Brazza frontier which was only about 20 kilometres away.

Although the men had not seen action for a while, the commandant explained that it was necessary to maintain optimum security precautions.

'When the rebels arrived before – in 1961 – they caught us off guard. We won't allow that to happen again', he said. His fears were based on regular reports of another imminent guerrilla invasion, which, by the end of the war never came.

Dinge was surrounded by several machine-gun turrets, but these were manned only during daylight hours. The jungle in the vicinity was too dense to depend on searchlights after dark.

'There are too many bushes and trees growing near the edge of the camp ... we cut them back, but weeks later they are there again, which happens in the tropics,' he explained. 'So, if we were to depend solely on lights and machine-gun turrets, the enemy would be able to crawl through the forest right up to the fence before they attack. They would be on top of us before we knew where we were.'

For that reason, the commandant explained, a number of 24-man patrols were always in the outlying bush, his concept of an 'early warning system that seemed to work quite well'. As at Zala, the men would station themselves in a relatively cosy position in the jungle – usually just off one of the larger tracks – 'and wait for the enemy to arrive.' It was also reasonably secure because the bush was too thick for the guerrillas to creep up from behind.

'It's far more effective this way. Also, the enemy knows our system. They're aware that if they want to attack, they have to pass through our outer perimeter first,' he reckoned.

He said the men had almost no trouble with wild animals. 'They smell and see us long before we are aware of their presence. They steer clear of the most terrible animal of all— man', he added with a sardonic touch.

It was dinner-time when we arrived at Dinge and the sun set shortly afterwards, disappearing quickly over the horizon as it does in the tropics. In the few minutes before it became dark in Cabinda, the horizon would often change colour perhaps four or five times. At Dinge it was even more impressive. The surrounding rain forest and swamps seemed to create their own diffusing prism, which added a new dimension to a dying sun.

Even the soldiers would sometimes halt in their tracks at sunset. They had been there almost two years and it continued to awe.

Dinge had other attributes. Standing in the centre of the parade ground was a machine-gun turret, but it held no weapon. There was no sentry peering out from under its low roof. Instead, its focus was a porcelain statue of the Virgin Mary which looked fixedly out over the barracks.

'That's our Virgin Mary of the Machine-Gun Turrets', one of the men explained.

It had been consecrated by a priest and was dedicated to the people whose lives depended on this form of defence, he said reverently. Though it seemed odd at the time, the gesture appeared to make good sense to these deeply religious people, especially since Portugal has a history of patron saints. So why not one more to guard over present circumstances, asked the camp padre after we had broached the subject. Particularly since machine-gun turrets had almost become a way of life since an army of guerrillas fomenting revolution in Angola had appeared on the scene.

In other respects, life at Dinge was casual. When the men were not on guard duty or patrol, they could do what they wished. A reveille bugle blew at six, but few of the men stirred before eight. A few of the officers slept through until ten some mornings. All that was expected of the men was that they did the duties and watches assigned to them.

The commanding officer, Major Domingos de Mageliaes Filipe, allowed his men a reasonable amount of leeway with regard to the stringencies of routine. Two years living on top of one another, he said, and you couldn't expect the spit and polish of new recruits.

That said, the morale at Dinge was low, dismally so. The war, or lack of it, had had an effect and fist-fights between the men were regular. There were few extra-mural activities and little of the organized sport we'd seen in Angola proper. This unit had a month to go before they returned to Portugal and, I was assured, it would be an agonizing four weeks.

Like all Portuguese Army camps, the men – the majority of them white – had lived in close contact with each other for far too long. They knew each other almost as well as if they had been married and a new face was a rarity. Few cared to even begin to understand the idiosyncrasies of his buddies in his platoon and there were no surprises.

Day-to-day activity fluctuated almost solely between the barracks and security duties. Occasionally some of the soldiers would muster a group and go into the local village about 400 metres up a jungle track, which consisted of a bar, a shop and a few houses. Portuguese army food and wine had long ago become insipid and a snack in town – plantain perhaps, some yam and a jug of palm wine – made for a welcome change. And the local girls, of course, who charged by the half-hour in some palm-roofed, poorly ventilated shacks out back.

'What we really need is a little action. The men are bored', one of the lieutenants told me. In Sector D and the east it was not so bad, he said, but here, with only the monotonous jungle noises for company it was terrible.

'And to make matters worse, we can't get drunk all that often – just haven't got the money for it', he added moodily.

While camp life at Dinge was not typical of what I found at other military establishments in Angola, its troops did represent a cross-section of the Portuguese army. They had no real reason, apart from boredom, to complain. Materially they were reasonable well looked after.

Corporal Mavungo, hero of an insurgent ambush in the enclave of Cabinda north of the Congo River was decorated for bravery with the Cross of War. Curiously, through he was serving in the Portuguese Army, his home language was French. (Author's photo)

They were reasonably well fed, adequately clothed – though they were issued with two uniforms which had to last them for the duration – they had more than enough free time in which they could do as they pleased. Some men employed their time judiciously and several studied through correspondence courses. To others, it was too much trouble to do anything.

Having been uplifted to Africa, quite a few of the men had broadened their horizons and had seen more of the world than abysmally low wages in Metropolitan Portugal would otherwise have allowed. Some of these youngsters, who seemed to have adapted easily enough to African conditions, had never ventured further than their native villages before.

A number received their first pair of boots on joining the military. Quite a few started eating three square meals a day for the first time in their lives the morning they entered training camp. All seemed to have taken spartan living conditions in their stride and were capable of fending for themselves. These were the sons of fishermen, wine-farmers, Lisbon taxi-drivers and, very occasionally, of university professors or professional families.

Among the busiest soldiers at Dinge were the motor mechanics. Theirs was the job of keeping the garrison's seven trucks in running order. All except the ambulance were not only old but also dilapidated and required constant repairs. Cabinda rarely received new equipment—most of it went to other sectors where the enemy was more active.

The ambulance was certainly the busiest of the lot. In their policy of creating better relations with the local African population, the Portuguese helped where they could.

Medicine played a prominent part in the fulfilment of this ideal.

This was demonstrated while we were at the camp. At about 2am one morning the duty transport officer was called from the bungalow where we had been billeted for the night. An African woman had been in labour for the past 36 hours and there had been complications. The camp doctor had been in attendance and decided that the only way to save the life of the mother and her unborn child would be to take them through to Cabinda as soon as possible. It meant a journey of almost 200 kilometres, and in the dark.

It took a brave man to drive his ambulance to Cabinda, never mind at night. He had to cross some of the worst roads in Africa. He also knew that if there were guerrillas in the vicinity, he would be ambushed. The insurgents would have heard the vehicle coming for miles before they saw it, giving ample time to prepare for an ambush. They were not to know that it was an ambulance, though it wouldn't have been the first time they would have fired on a vehicle carrying the distinctive red cross.

As it happened, the driver got through without incident. He saved the life of the mother and her boy, who was born later that morning. We subsequently heard that the child was named after the driver of the ambulance – a simple gesture and nothing to do with winning hearts and minds.

Also at Dinge, an extraordinary story emerged about the early days of the war, told to us by the padre.

The camp had originally been a logging base. The old saw-mill still stood intact in the jungle near the barbed-wire fence, only now it was gathering rust and creepers. The original owner of the plant had been away when the terrorists struck, but on being told about the attacks in a radio broadcast, he rushed back to protect his family. It was too late.

When got to the veranda of his house, the heads of his three children were neatly arranged alongside each other on the porch. Their hacked bodies, the eldest eight years old, were discovered in one of the bedrooms. All three had been butchered.

His wife had been strung up by her feet in the living room; she'd been brutally raped and slit open from gullet to groin.

'The man lost his mind', the priest explained. 'He rushed back to his truck, collected his hunting rifle, a pistol, found a shotgun somewhere and set about killing every black man he encountered. Obviously these were not the people who had committed these grisly deeds and some had even worked for him on the mill. By then those responsible had moved on in search of other targets'

'He'd notched up a tally of more than a dozen innocents killed by the time the authorities caught up with him.'

Trouble was, said the padre, the last thing the farm-owner could understand was why he'd been taken into custody. Black people were on the rampage, he roared. They had destroyed his family, his life, his very existence. They, in turn, should now be destroyed, he argued.

The man had never quite regained all his senses. He was never brought to trial and at the time we were in the area, he was believed to be in Luanda working in the docks.

Last heard he was living with a mulatto woman.

11

Why Portugal Lost her Wars in Africa

In the late 1960s it was Portugal – after Israel – that proportionate to population had the highest percentage of people in arms in the world. Lisbon showed an annual increase of 111 per cent between the 49,422 that were officially listed in 1961 and the 149,090 documented in 1973.

T he question remains: why did Portugal lose its wars in Africa? For more than five centuries, Lisbon maintained the most dominant colonial presence on the continent. Yet, by 1974, she had lost all in a series of bloody military campaigns that lasted half a generation.

The more immediate issues are clear. When her colonial wars began, Portugal was on the lowest rung of poor European nations, with a population a little more than nine million. Yet she had colonial responsibilities that stretched around the globe. Apart from the three *metrópole-províncias ultramarinas* in Africa, there was Goa in India, Macau on the east coast of China and what was to become East Timor. None of the three Asian dominions were of any size, but each required a presence, both civil and military.

Additionally, the African conflicts were not centralised, such as the wars faced by the French in Algeria or the British in Kenya during the Mau Mau emergency. Rather, Portugal was sucked into a half-a-dozen different rebellions on eight or nine different fronts. One major military campaign in Angola's north became two when ZIL (*Zona de Intervencao Leste*) was initiated, first by the MPLA and later by Dr Jonas Savimbi's UNITA. Several smaller revolutionary groups, each eager for a slice of the pie, operated out of the Congo and though largely ineffectual, they still needed soldiers with guns to counter their advances.

Similarly, there were two fairly large and sophisticated groups fighting for territory in Portuguese Guinea, the PAIGC in the south and based largely in neighbouring Conakry and FLING out of Senegal.

One large guerrilla group was responsible for almost all hostilities in Mozambique, territorially, one of the biggest countries in Africa. And while the war started in the north, it soon moved to regions adjacent to the Zambezi Valley.

None of these uprisings were small fry. Instead they required an army, that with irregular African service units and local militias (including 'commando' type units at special rates of pay) and a police force that was quasi military anyway, ended up to close to a quarter million men.

There were naval components in all of them, including a sizeable force on Lake Malawi in a bid to interdict seaborne infiltration from both Tanzania and Zambia. And finally, leading the defensive thrust, the Portuguese Air Force – after South Africa and Egypt – fielded the biggest strike capability on the continent.

The actual numbers of operational aircraft were never constant because there were simply not enough technicians to keep them all airborne. Which meant that if the books showed six or eight Douglas C-47s in Mozambique, there might only be two or three airworthy at any one time. The same with the Fiat G-91 jets.

Lisbon's helicopter units appeared to be more fortunate, in large part because the Alouette gunships were rugged enough to take a battering from ground fire, unless the guerrillas managed to separate a tail boom or hit a gearbox, which also happened now and again.

Still, there were massive gaps in the deployment of Lisbon's troops and fewer helicopters in all three overseas provinces than you are likely to find in any large American city. While the Portuguese Air Force had ordered Aerospatiale Pumas, a dozen of these were destroyed on the ground in a single night after being delivered from France, by a radical anti-war group opposed to Lisbon's presence in Africa. That meant there were only a handful of government troopers in any of the theatres of African military activity and only two for all of Mozambique.

Cumulatively then, all this military activity spread over an area almost half the size of Western Europe needed manpower, something that became more acute as the conflicts dragged on and one of the reasons why the Portuguese turned increasingly towards using indigenes to assist with the fighting.

More significant, while a trusted member of NATO, Portugal's assets were embarrassingly sparse when compared to what her adversaries were getting from the Soviet Union and China. In a sense, this was an African version of Vietnam, only Portugal was no America.

Historically, development of the 'Overseas Provinces' had always been pitifully slow. The accent had always been on cheap labour, which, in part, meant keeping the populace relatively uneducated. And while the majority spoke Portuguese – as they still do today, a generation after the bloody transition, and there was great emphasis on what was termed the Great Society, there was little real authority vested in the provinces. Anything of importance was invariably referred to the 'motherland', the ultimate power, which, in any event, was a dictatorship.

René Pélissier, an academic authority who has written extensively about Portugal's wars, makes the point that economic exploitation of the workers 'was often brutal'. He illustrates his thesis by explaining what contributed to the Baixa de Cassange 'Cotton Revolt', the least known, yet, as he says, the most comprehensible of all the rebellions of 1960-61. Essentially, he declares, the rebellion was an act of defiance against the system of obligatory cotton cultivation for which Cotonang – a Lisbon headquartered monopolist company – had the concession in the region east of Malange.

Pélissier goes on: 'Censorship was such that it is not known precisely when and where the revolt started. The causes were numerous: the local population was forced to cultivate

From the very beginning of hostilities in 1961, the nature of conflict in Angola was both tough and demanding on man, machine and on totally inadequate and often outdated equipment. Overnight, this society was obliged to face a threat that would change 500 years of Portuguese colonial rule in Africa. This photo was used on the cover of Brigadier-General W.S. van der Waals' book *Portugal's War in Angola*.

cotton, to the exclusion of foodstuffs in certain areas ... the 31,652 producers of the Malange district were obliged to sell their whole crop at a price fixed by the government well below that of the world market ... moreover, to the east of Malange there was a veritable 'cottonocracy' that relegated the rural African to the role of being merely a provider for the company.'

He tells us that the annual income of an *indigena* family under this regime in 1959-60 was $20 to $30 *or roughly two dollars a month*, which by any standards, was unconscionable. As he says, 'this can justifiably be called exploitation; it was, indeed, denounced as such by some members of the Portuguese administration'.

Moreover, the African colonies were subject to the bidding of legions of functionaries who – with the military or the law just outside the door – oversaw everything, from local government, administration of the civil service, education, health, trade, commerce, industry to utilities and the rest.

In theory, Angola being an immensely wealthy region, there should have been an abundance for all its citizens, whatever their colour. In practice, Portugal's African population were relegated to a level of second class citizenship that would sometimes make conditions in apartheid-ridden South Africa appear conciliatory by comparison. Forced labour was commonplace, so were public beatings.

Rule of government was not only brutal, it was repressive and exploitative. Forced labour was exacted on a massive scale: many of the country's roads were built with prison labour. The Portuguese secret police, (PIDE, the so-called International Police for the Defence of the State or *Polícia Internacional e de Defesa do Estado*) – later replaced by the DOS, *Direcao Geral de Seguranca* – was almost a government in itself. Its methods were often cruel, and in some respects could compare with those of the Nazi SS or Iran's Sawak during the rule of the Shah.

Additionally, while everybody was supposed to be governed by a single, universal set of laws, there were very different criteria for Portuguese nationals and ethnic Africans.

Blacks could be arrested at the whim of the local *Chefe de Posto* for trivial offences. Not paying the mandatory head tax or perhaps using bad language in the presence of a Portuguese lady could result in a jail term. Similarly, anybody encouraging labour unrest for better wages was charged with sedition and sent to prison. Since the entire country was ruled by decree, any kind of political activity, black or white, was ruled illegal.

Severe laws were imposed by harsh and uncompromising bureaucrats. Often mindlessly brutal, they were rarely made to account for their actions, even when there were lives lost. Coupled to that, black wages in Angola, Mozambique and Portuguese Guinea were among the lowest on the continent.

As might have been expected, living conditions throughout this expansive overseas empire were dismal, for black people especially. Lisbon would always argue that in the long term, it was better for all because nobody starved. Nor did they, but by the end of World War II, this political scenario was also a clear-cut recipe for revolt.

Portugal's empire came into being directly as a consequence of the successful efforts of Lisbon's Prince Henry the Navigator to discover a trade route to India.

While other European nations had previously preferred the more ponderous and dangerous overland road to the east, through the Levant and age-old Persia, the Portuguese, to give them their dues, looked at the alternative option. That was by sea, around the Cape.

To take this giant step – which, in its day, was every bit as momentous as man's first flight to the moon – they needed along the way, a succession of supply stops for fresh victuals and water, which is why they established overseas trading stations in Angola and Mozambique. These eventually expanded and were ultimately settled by Portuguese nationals who, by the time war ended, numbered more than 300,000.

The frontiers of the various African states had been drawn up by all the European countries with interests in the continent around a negotiating table in Berlin towards the end of the 19th century. These included Britain, France, Portugal and Spain, Amsterdam's colonial interests having long ago been superseded by London.

Putting down roots in Africa –after having first to placate it – was never easy. Tribal leaders were traditionally suspicious of strangers bearing trinkets, and for good reason.

First Portuguese reinforcements sent to Angola after the invasion in a
ceremonial march through Luanda. (Photo Manuel Graça)

Africa had always been a ready source for slaves and though East Africa was the first region to be subjected to this pernicious influence that was mainly Arab to start with, the word got quickly around, especially since slaving forays had taken place deep into the interior of a continent that was already being referred to as 'dark' by early chroniclers. Consequently there were vigorous attempts by some African leaders to prevent the establishment of a permanent European presence, especially on the periphery of their tribal kingdoms. But the early Portuguese explorers were a resolute lot and they persisted.

Once the first colonists had settled along the coast of Angola and Mozambique and early settlements like Luanda, Bissau and Lobito became towns, black leaders not yet under the 'protection' of Lisbon would do what they could to prevent these newcomers from taking more land. Attempts at countering the settler influence went on for centuries, especially in Angola.

Nor were other African colonies immune from rebellion. In Southern Africa there were numerous uprisings among the tribes, first by the Xhosas and their allies and subsequently by the Zulus, insurrections that later spread northwards into Matabeleland and what became known as Rhodesia.

Some tribes sought protection from Queen Victoria. The always-resourceful Sotho people urged British dominion status for their mountain kingdom when they felt that Boers on the move northwards from the Cape were starting to encroach on traditional land, which is how Basutoland, afterwards Lesotho, came into being.

It was a time for rebellion in Africa; in the Gold Coast, in Benin, Nigeria, in some of the French colonies and against newly arrived North Europeans in German South West Africa (Namibia today) and in the *Kamerun*.

The bloodiest uprisings might well have been the notorious maji maji rebellion in Tanganyika which went on for more than a year.

As the history books recount, the Nyamwezi Chief Isike – from the central Rift Valley region around Tabora – fought a grim rearguard action against the Kaiser's soldiers that started in 1891. Rather than surrender, he blew himself up in the armoury of his fort in January 1893, which, in turn, paved the way for the maji maji war that followed a dozen years later.

For five centuries, there were any number of uprisings by locals in the Portuguese territories and all failed. Except for the last, which was sparked in 1961 by a murderous uprising among Bakongo people of Northern Angola and the Congo. Thousands died in the violence that followed, including 2,000 Europeans.

According to René Pélissier, the events of 1961 were to shake the Portuguese out of their lethargy and dreams. It also awakened unfulfilled hopes in the Africans, and, at the same time, brought down on a whole racial group – the Bakongo, and on a good proportion of their neighbours, the Mbundu, as well as on other *assimilado* cadres – the horrors of war and repression.

For the Portuguese, says Pélissier, it marked the end of colonial tranquillity; for Africans, the beginning of an ordeal. For all it was the year of terror.

But he warns, it is useful, first, to expose certain errors. 'The Portuguese were not taken totally unawares by the events themselves. What caught them off guard was the racial massacre that followed in the north. It was not the rebellion, but its intensity, its suddenness and its bestiality, which nearly brought about their loss of Angola.

The settlers were expecting trouble, as is shown by their arming: in 1959, Angola imported 156 tons of arms and ammunition; in 1960, 953 tons (six times as much); while, in 1961, this dropped to 424 tons and, in 1962, to 145 tons. It was certainly not to hunt elephants but to resist the Africans if they were to rebel that the Portuguese stocked their arsenals.

In spite of the threat from within and without, Angola in 1960 was, militarily speaking, a no-man's-land. Even allowing for reinforcements (denied by Portuguese sources), it can be estimated that on the Portuguese side there were only 15,000 to 20,000 whites, mesticos and Africans in the army or para-military organisations: a derisory force to hold a country that might spread into simultaneous, nation-wide revolt.

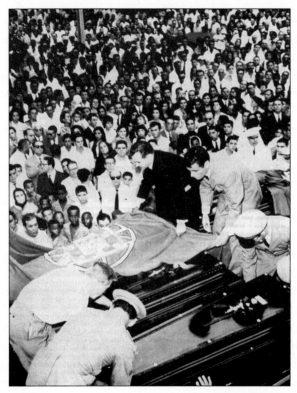

Funeral of the seven policemen who were killed in MPLA's ill-fated Luanda
uprising of 4 February 1961. The white community brutally turned on African
people in the city and many innocents were murdered. The event was a dramatic
precursor of the civil war that followed. (Photo Manuel Graça)

He concludes with the comment that it must not be forgotten that:

> if Angola failed to achieve independence by armed revolt in 1961, it was because only
> a small minority if its peoples and elite dared to demonstrate anti-Portuguese feelings.
> Whether through fear, lack of interest, ignorance, incompetence or loyalty, the
> peoples to the south of the Cuanza hardly budged; if only the nationalist chiefs had
> found there as favourable a terrain as they did in the north, it is virtually certain that
> the Portuguese would have been swept from Angola, or at the least confined to their
> strongholds along the coast.

With the benefit of hindsight, it is astonishing that of all the European colonial powers,
Portugal's grip on its African territories over the centuries – ruthless, intractable and totally
impervious to change as it was – proved to be the most durable. As old timers in Luanda
and Lourenco Marques would mutter, it wasn't perfect, but after a fashion, things seemed
to work.

They'd contend that after all, this was Africa. Pressed to elaborate, as I often did in

Early Portuguese Army bush operations in the jungles north of Luanda. (Author's collection)

some of the little restaurants in those two cities, they'd confide that the real problem lay with the indigenes. One and all they'd argue, the locals knew no better. There would be no mention of the impact of white rule on African health, welfare and dirt-cheap workforces, and that African lives were stunted by the requirements of capitalist enterprise.

In some ways it was a very different approach to how other European administrators conducted their affairs. Both London and Paris made serious efforts to improve their understanding of Africa and frame their policies accordingly. In Nigeria, the British went on to institute Indirect Rule, largely to avoid tampering with historical, religious-based systems that had been secure for centuries.

They'd also learn the local languages, which was how those white Kenyans who had learnt Kikuyu, eventually managed to counter most of the advances made by the Mau Mau.

To many of those involved in countries like Northern and Southern Rhodesia (Zambia and Zimbabwe today), Nigeria, Uganda, Sierra Leone and elsewhere, co-operation with indigenous rulers ultimately proved the best way to retain control at minimum human and material cost.

Lisbon did things differently. With time, Portugal's three African colonies – on paper, at least – became what politicians in the Metropolis would like to call 'one big, happy, friendly family'.

It was a splendid idea, except that the colonies were African, often proudly so. The majority of people there had tribal origins that were impossible to ignore, something that was often lost on those in charge. We are also aware that the system of government imposed on these societies, were insensitive. While never mindlessly as brutal as the excesses imposed on the people in the neighbouring Belgian Congo – and which Joseph Conrad masterfully captured in his denunciation of colonialism in his *Heart of Darkness* –the Portuguese, though not racists per se, could sometimes be cruel to people of colour.

Being Africa, things also tended to move very slowly. Inexorably, the tribal system tended to generate its own laws of cause and effect and these people have long memories.

The Cambridge History of Africa tells us that 'on the eve of the Second World War, the *Pax Euopeae* was firmly established in Africa.[1] At one level it was a seemingly tenuous peace, dependent on a handful of European administrators ruling over vast and populous areas with only a handful of African soldiers or para-military police at their disposal.

Nigeria, for example, had only 4 000 soldiers and 4 000 police in 1930, of whom all but 75 in each force were black.

Just how thin on the ground the European administrators were, can be seen from the fact that in this corner of British West Africa in the late 1930s, the number of administrators for a population estimated at 20 million was only 386: a ratio of 1: 54 000. And that included those in the secretariat.

In the Belgian Congo the ratio was 1: 38 400 and in French West Africa 1: 27 500. It should also not be forgotten, that in parts of the European empire, the colonial imprint was still very light. Many Africans had never personally seen a white man, while in Mozambique parts of the territory were not even administered by the government but by concession companies.

More salient, those same 'concession companies' were motivated solely by profit.

Despite all these disparities, it took a while but the master-servant labour system in Portuguese Africa became entrenched. Those who knew no better accepted social dominance as the norm. Also, life in the Overseas Provinces was unquestionably mixed, to the point that relations between the colonisers and the colonized gave rise to the old maxim: God made man white and God made man black, but the Portuguese made the mulatto.

Then, quite suddenly, arrived the age of *Uhuru* – the Swahili watchword that shook East Africa 'as in a whirlwind'. To the majority, it signified freedom.

'Freedom of the masses' Kenyan President Jomo *Mzee* Kenyatta would proclaim with verve while he waved about his ubiquitous oxtail that also served as a fly swatter. Almost overnight a novel and thoroughly radical concept was being espoused from one end of Africa to the other, and as my old friend Chris Munnion commented early on, it didn't take any of us long to realise that African politics were in an state of flux, alarmingly so.

The 'winds of change' in Africa became a part of that equation soon afterwards and it was not too long before a plethora of independent states came into being: countries like Gambia, Nigeria, Gabon, the Cameroons, Burundi, Chad, Sierra Leone and the rest. But not one under Portuguese rule. Of all the European colonial powers, the Portuguese proved the most intransigent. Sharing power, simply put, was anathema.

There were few people in the Metropolis who were not of the mind that no matter what, the nation would survive without any kind of political change. What was happening in parts of West, Central and Southern Africa would be referred to in the state-controlled press as a 'passing phase'. Lisbon's African possessions were part of a culture and a great historical tradition was the theme. For all its faults, ran the concept, Portugal and its Overseas Provinces had even eclipsed Iberian domination of the New World.

Indeed, Angola at that time was regarded by some as the 'future Brazil of Africa'.

What Lisbon had not initially factored into the colonial equation was communications. What was going on elsewhere in Africa, could obviously not fail to have an impact on the peoples of Angola and Mozambique. How else when Lisbon suddenly had to deal with a number of former British and French colonies now in control of their own affairs, several their immediate neighbours?

These included Senegal, Malawi, Congo-Brazza as well as quite a few, including Guinea, Tanzania and Zambia that were passionately opposed to any kind of Portuguese colonial presence on the continent. All three countries were later to wage hostilities against Lisbon. They also permitted revolutionary groups to operate from their soil.

Even this, some Portuguese colonists believed they could deal with. And they probably could have, had those belligerent neighbours acted on their own. But this was the time of the Cold War and both Moscow and Beijing believed that ultimately, they had good prospects in Africa.

One of the architects of the African revolution that eventually changed the modern face of Southern Africa from white to black was a modest African academic who was respectfully referred to by just about everybody with whom he came into contact as *Mwalimu*, the Swahili word for teacher.

Julius Nyerere, a graduate of Kampala's one-time prestigious Makerere University, got a scholarship to attend the University of Edinburgh in 1949, a remarkable distinction at the time because he was the first Tanzanian to study at a British university.

Much to the chagrin of the British colonial authorities, Nyerere was already very much of a political factor in the old Tanganyika by the time the 'Revolutionary 1960s' arrived. He was abrasive towards the establishment, espoused a new form of African socialism which he called *Ujaama* and had the kind of chutzpah that could sway large crowds. After numerous confrontations with London's representatives in Dar es Salaam, he led his country to independence to become first prime minister, and later President of the Republic of Tanzania.

Nyerere was one of many post-war African heads of state with strong academic and emotional links to the radical British Left. Others were Kwame Nkrumah of Ghana, Milton

An arms cache recovered from a guerrilla position that had been
overrun by government forces. (Author's photo)

Obote of Uganda, and Kenneth Kaunda of Zambia. It is significant that all four chose the
Socialist path, usually through the good offices of the London School of Economics.

Political sentiments apart, Nyerere ended up embracing every revolutionary who
arrived at his door, including a good few from Angola and Mozambique.

Within a year a dozen Southern African revolutionary movements from Rhodesia,
South West Africa (Namibia today) and even a few that were not yet independent like
Nyasaland and Kenya, had set up shop along Liberation Row in Dar es Salaam. The
ultimate oxymoron, Dar es Salaam, in Arabic, means 'harbour of peace', but Tanzania now
fostered armed revolution.

Julius Nyerere made no bones about wishing to see an end to white rule in Africa. He
created an entire political and economic system to that end, first by supporting FRELIMO
– the Portuguese liberation movement in their war against the Portuguese in Mozambique
and, shortly afterwards, Angolan liberation movements. SWAPO, the South West African
(Namibian) revolutionary movement and the ANC's *Umkhonto We Sizwe (Spear of the
Nation)* soon followed.[2]

Much of the military hardware needed by these radical groups that still had some
way to go before they became fully-fledged guerrilla armies were landed at Dar es Salaam
harbour. Customarily, this matériel was moved first by road and then on the backs of
human packhorses, often hundreds of kilometers into the interior. A Soviet TM-46 anti-

tank mine, for instance, which weighs about 12 kgs, might have been hauled a thousand kilometres overland by a minor army of porters by the time it was placed in a hole in the ground in Mozambique to await the next convoy out of Tete.

With SWAPO, fighting its own war on the far side of the African continent, logistical problems would often mean journeys that might last months. Weapons would sometimes cross several frontiers, including those of Zambia and, in later stages, Mobutu's Congo.

It was not long before South African revolutionaries established a secure base for their leaders in the Tanzanian capital. Larger groups of political malcontents that had left South Africa, usually on foot, were housed in camps in the interior

With time, a revolutionary culture of its own evolved in Tanzania, together with a fairly distinct terminology. Tanzania resolutely preferred to call itself a 'Frontline State' even though the distance between Pretoria and Dar es Salaam is greater than between London and Athens. Zambia embraced the concept as well, but it was more appropriate because it bordered on Rhodesia, then in a state of war and at the receiving end of cross-border raids launched by Rhodesian security forces.

Ultimately these forerunners were joined by Mobutu Seso Seko's Zaire – as well as Congo (Brazzaville) to its immediate north with territorial interests in the oil-rich enclave of Cabinda.

While all this was taking place, there was truck between East Africa and the two most prominent revolutionary states on the West Coast, Ghana under Nkrumah and Sékou Touré's Republic of Guinea – not to be confused with today's Equatorial Guinea (formerly Spanish Guinea) or Guiné-Bissau (Portuguese Guinea).

Irrespective of nomenclature, the Tanzanian connection was one of several major issues faced by Lisbon as these expanded colonial conflicts gathered momentum.

Looking back, we're now aware that Portugal's three military insurrections in Africa resulted in a powerful groundswell of anti-colonial hostility in Portugal itself – as well as elsewhere in Europe and North America, especially among many of Lisbon's NATO allies. While Lisbon always made much about its historic and 'civilizing mission' in Africa, much of that was dismissed as the cynical propaganda of a tottering dictatorship.

As the historian and political commentator Kenneth Maxwell wrote: 'Portugal was the last European power in Africa to cling tenaciously to the panoply of formal dominion and this was no accident. For a long time Portugal very successfully disguised the nature of her presence behind a skilful amalgam of historic mythmaking, claims of multiracialism and good public relations.'

The reality, says Maxwell, was something very different. 'Economic weakness at home made intransigence in Africa inevitable. It was precisely through the exercise of [sovereignty] that Portugal was able to obtain any advantages at all from its civilizing mission. And these advantages were very considerable: cheap raw materials, large earnings from invisibles, the transfer of export earnings, gold and diamonds and protected markets for her wines and

Portuguese Air Force helicopter gunships and troopers at an
unknown location. (Author's collection)

cotton textiles.'

Vietnam meanwhile, provided Europe and America with a fertile anti-war lobby which, when circumstances permitted, was conveniently switched to Africa. Not only Portuguese Africa became targets, but Rhodesia and South Africa as well.

This approach was adopted – though much less forcefully – by the educated classes in Portugal itself. While popular stereotypes tended to depict Portugal as a stagnant backwater for almost three centuries, students, professional people, academics, the military, government officials and politicians became increasingly sensitive to the opprobrium that resulted from the reactionary policies of the Prime Minister António de Oliveira Salazar, who suffered a stroke in 1968.

Optimists on both sides of the Atlantic had hoped that under Marcello Caetano, his successor, the country would enter a more liberal phase. While some of the faces changed, the political infrastructure did not, though to be fair, much was done to bring education in line with the Metropolis. For instance, two major universities were established in the 1960s in Angola and Mozambique – the *Universidade de Luanda* and the *Universidade de Lourenco Marques* – and both offered a range of degrees from engineering to medicine.

This is all the more notable since there were then only four public universities in all of Portugal, of which two were in Lisbon.

Multiculturalism gradually took root, helped to some extent by the acceptance of the *assimilado* program which actually encouraged Africans to accept Western values in preference to tribal ones. Here, sport was a touchstone, with many Africans encouraged to vie for top international slots. Among this tiny band of sportspeople was the footballer Eusebio who was embraced by soccer players the world over.

The Brazilian political commentator Marcio Alves wrote: 'To hold on to the Empire was fundamental for Portuguese fascism. Economically, the African territories – and especially rich Angola – were so important to Portuguese capitalism that Caetano took over from Salazar on the condition that they would be defended.'

Part of the trouble was that in Portugal's African possessions, no political solution to the problem was either found or sought. If anybody stepped out of line, the only answer was the big stick ... or the gun. These people had centuries of reasonably successful African rule behind them and despite the rumblings, things continued very much as in the past.

Matters were exacerbated during later stages of this African conflict by an almost total break in communications in some areas between the security police and the Portuguese defence forces. There were several cases in Tete and Nampula where liberal Portuguese officers informed FRELIMO sympathisers of future movements by PIDE officers into the interior. They knew that such information would be passed on to the revolutionaries and made good use of.

For all this 'dissention within the ranks' PIDE had a good measure of the enemies they were up against, in all three territories. I know from practical experience that they got a lot of help from South Africa, which hosted an expatriate Portuguese community of about half a million, many of them former dissidents from the colonies.

Within the war zones, PIDE worked to a complex set of rules that involved thousands of informants that sometimes stretched all the way to rebel command headquarters in Dar es Salaam, Kinshasa, Conakry and Dakar. It was an expensive process, but it worked, as money always does in a corrupt Africa.

Much more intelligence was derived from good old fashioned sleuthing on the ground, coupled to information brought in from patrols, cross-border travellers, captives, documents taken during or after contacts as well as air and naval reconnaissance.

As John Cann tells us in his book, 'the Portuguese Army realized this critical need for effective intelligence and proceeded to build a productive network that helped its forces exploit weaknesses in the enemy.' He devotes a chapter that addresses the problems encountered with these operations in the field in selected areas and follows the solutions adopted, comparing and contrasting them to the experiences of other countries with contemporaneous counterinsurgency operations.

'These several adaptations were uniquely Portuguese and in keeping with the subdued and cost-conscious strategy,' Cann tells us.[3]

While conditions in the field in Mozambique remained uncertain until the coup, things were a lot different in Angola which had good resources backed by a settler community that numbered more than 300,000 and had been there for centuries. These people knew no other place but Angola and were prepared to fight for it.

Not so in Portuguese Guinea, where no real advance was possible for its 3,000 white settlers because of the forbidding nature of the country: most of that country was

The traditional and the modern: horses were still used extensively in certain spheres in this ongoing guerrilla struggle. (Author's collection)

pestilential swamp where the mosquitoes and bad water got you if the guerrillas didn't.

There was also little development, economic or otherwise in Portugal itself, with the result that by the time war ended, it was rated the second poorest country in Europe after Albania.

A great deal of money was squandered in Lisbon's African war efforts. At one point the government voted almost half the entire budget to the military, which, for many years during the earlier period was roughly what Israel spent on keeping its society secure. But then Lisbon did not have Uncle Sam underwriting its military tab.[4]

Yet, there are still some who maintain that although Portugal was all but destitute when the war ended, it was not economic policies that caused the collapse of its authority in Africa because it was just as poor when the insurrection started. Their argument was that the dictator Salazar was the real disaster. He had been trained as an economist, and in that he excelled. The problem was that he treated the coffers of the nation as his own, and in so doing, acted like the proverbial miser.

David Abshire and Michael Samuels in their book *Portuguese Africa – A Handbook* (Pall Mall Press, London, 1969) maintain that during the wars, the Portuguese were able to maintain their gold and foreign reserves at a fixed ratio of between 56 and 57 percent of sight responsibilities. In spite of increased expenditure on defence and the need for external borrowing, Salazar actually managed to increase Lisbon's reserves of gold and foreign exchange during the war years. Herein lay an example for South Africa, soon to be labouring under similar pressures, as the history books tell us.

The bottom line here is that as the wars in Africa progressed, the bean counters in the *metrópole* had absolutely no alternative but to cut the coat according to Portugal's tattered cloth.

It was politics, ultimately, that dealt the death blow to any aspirations the Portuguese might have had of holding on to their African possessions.

The vision among the country's ageing leaders to improve the political situation either at home or abroad, or to strengthen the military equation was blinkered. If ever there was an example of political leadership having atrophied while in power, it could be viewed in Portugal, especially since Salazar had been in power since 1933. When Caetano succeeded in 1968, the same people who supported Salazar ended up in the Caetano cabinet. There was therefore no change in form or content.

Of course, Africa was prominent in the minds of both Salazar and Caetano; and, curiously, South Africa became the focus of attention on several occasions. Salazar, it emerged after he had died, was obsessed with the threat of a Mozambique Unilateral Declaration of Independence or UDI, much like Rhodesia had declared in 1964. This later became a mania; Salazar believed that there were people in Mozambique plotting with the South Africans to overthrow the government in Lourenco Marques.

Matters weren't helped by the many South Africans who wished to invest in the Mozambican economy. Although it was permitted at first on a small scale, it was only in 1966 that any considerable foreign investment was allowed into Angola and Mozambique. By then it was too late.

Because of his UDI fears, Salazar permitted little economic development in his Portuguese possessions.

Angola was the one region where the possibilities of independence from Portugal had been mooted for decades. Had the war not arrived, there is little doubt that Angola would have followed Rhodesia's example.

Douglas Porch, in his book *The Portuguese Armed Forces and the Revolution* (Croom Helm, London, 1977) mentions an air force colonel in Angola who said:

In 1965, most of us already thought that Angola should become an independent and racially mixed country like Brazil. We saw that we could not win in the colonies. It was impossible to continue. Freedom had to come gradually because the people were not prepared for it. The military would be very useful in preparing the political solution. It was a task which we could not do in two months, but in six or seven years. We had to prepare the government and the local governments.

The army had to maintain independence, build up the armed forces and so on ...

In direct contrast, the wisdom of the day in Lisbon was twofold: first, you did not negotiate with the enemy, and especially not if they were in a position of strength, which

'Lisbon – 13999 kms' tells its own story! (Author's photo)

they were for much of the time, in Guinea and, afterwards, in Mozambique where the Portuguese was stuck with inferior leadership and a terrain that was far too big to control effectively with so few troops on the ground.

It is more than 2,000 kilometres long and almost twice the size of California; interestingly, it is roughly the same shape too.

For all that, the Portuguese Army by 1973 had about 70,000 men on the ground in Mozambique, in a country where there was a single, reasonably maintained road that stretched from north to south. Most of the rest weren't tarred, which perfectly suited FRELIMO minelayers.

The real downfall of Portuguese interests in Africa ultimately lay with the armed forces. To start with there was great dissatisfaction among members of the Portuguese military over service in Africa.

A two-year period of service in Africa was usually followed by six months at home and then another two years in the provinces. That practice had a crippling effect on morale in the war zones. There was also bad feeling between regular soldiers and conscripts, particularly within the junior and middle ranks of commissioned officers.

The MFA or Armed Forces Movement which eventually organised the coup d'état of April 1974 recognised that no political development was taking place either in the military or in the African territories. General de Spínola actually said as much in his book *Portugal*

Puma transport helicopter – French built and ideally suited for primitive African conditions – is 'talked down' at a forward Angolan base. (Author's collection)

and the Future, but more of that later.

There were also powerful radical elements at work within the regular army. Many officers were known to be communist and actually espoused the doctrine, yet they were allowed to continue to serve their country as dutiful patriots, in part because some of their senior officers were of similar minds.

Brigadier General W. (Kaas) van der Waals, the last South African military attaché in Luanda prior to the Portuguese leaving Africa has his own views on developments:[5]

The military coup in Portugal took the world, including South Africa, by surprise. To well-informed observers, however, the news was not completely unexpected. One of the general officers prominent after the coup as a member of the military junta was General Francisco da Costa Gomes. He was destined to become Portugal's second post-coup president and it was during his reign that Angola would slide into civil war in 1975. Eventually it would be left to its own fate as Portugal abandoned its responsibilities on November 11, 1975.

I worked closely with Costa Gomes after he became commander-in-chief of the armed forces in Angola in May 1970 and I found him soft-spoken, shy and a regular visitor to his troops in the field. Strange to relate, in the light of subsequent events, it

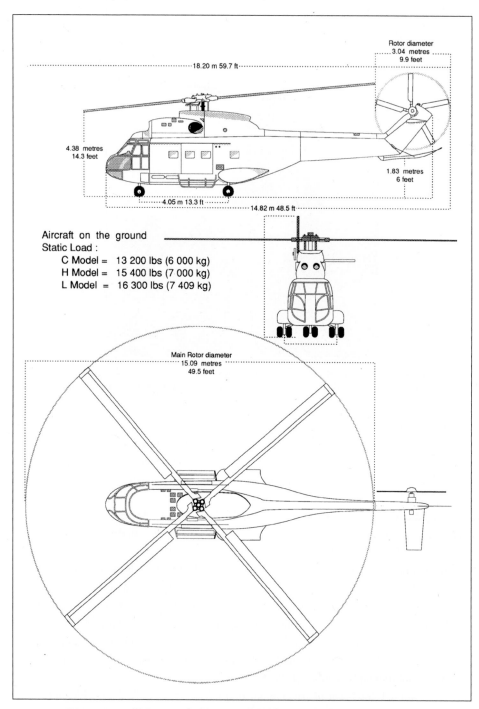

Dimensions of Aérospatiale Puma SA 330. (Graphics by Dr Richard Wood)

was he who changed significantly the military situation in Angola. He arrived at a critical time and when he left two years later the military crisis had dissipated to such an extent that optimists believed the war had been won. However, there were doubts in certain quarters concerning his sincerity and loyalty.

Shortly after Costa Gomes' appointment, a senior Portuguese officer remarked to the author that the new commander-in-chief was a communist who had been sent to Angola to prepare the ground for a handover. To some, his military successes dispelled the doubts. But having done some research of my own, I discovered that after the outbreak of hostilities in Angola in 1961, Costa Gomes had been involved in an abortive coup against the Salazar government. So doubts persisted.

Returning from Namibia a few days after the coup in April 1974, I was in contact with military intelligence in Pretoria. Two years earlier I had submitted a report forecasting the possibility of decolonisation in Angola. At the time, it was accorded little attention, but now all that material was analysed afresh.

In particular, note was taken of a letter written in March 1972 by Costa Gomes' predecessor, General Almeida Viana to a member of the Angolan Legislative Council in which he referred to a conspiracy in Portugal, after which Angola would be left to the "vicissitudes of the times".

Could the seemingly spontaneous events of the spring of 1974 have been planned two years before? There is no hard evidence to support this contention, but it is known that conservative elements of Portuguese society, including the top structure of the armed forces were very much concerned at that time about Caetano's liberalisation of colonial policy.

He was even called Portugal's de Gaulle. Something was indeed brewing.

Significantly, some Portuguese officers (as with some South Africans of similar persuasion) tended to equate their military efforts in Africa with the French in Algeria. Porch draws this analogy by stating that in Portugal, as in France, the circumstances for the military coup were provided by a long and exhausting colonial war.

There were crucial differences between the two countries. Many French soldiers believed that they were almost within striking distance of victory. They reacted against what they believed to be a betrayal by de Gaulle. Portuguese officers in contrast, felt that the country was locked in a pointless struggle to maintain a burdensome empire. Also, Portugal's colonial wars sapped the country's strength, made her appear ridiculous in the eyes of the world, and ruined the army by flooding it with half-trained conscripts whom the government attempted to promote over the heads of long-serving regulars.

As Porch maintains, the latent resentment which gradually built up to scalding point in the officer corps, was a combination of bruised national pride and wounded professional vanity, an explosive mixture of sentiments which the Portuguese military establishment shared with revolutionary soldiers in Egypt and other Third World countries.

A typical Angolan *aldeamentos*. During the Malayan Emergency these enforced settlements were called 'Protected Villages', the idea being to isolate the civilian population from guerrilla influence. It worked well enough if security was tight (as it was in the Far East). In regions controlled by the Portuguese, security was never adequately enforced, which nullified both the effort and the expense. (Author's collection)

The Portuguese experience proves that the increasing professionalism of the armed forces can hasten its entry into the political arena rather than discourage it, as American historian Samuel Huntington has argued.

Professional discontent creates shop floor militancy and the coup substitutes for the strike.

In retrospect, it is astonishing that Portugal never considered transferring families to the African colonies for these extended periods of anything up to five years. Their principal argument against such a step was the UDI bogey: a real fear that too many metropolitan Portuguese would be sent to the African colonies and then begin to think for themselves, as the Rhodesians had done.

Occasionally one found a member of a family, usually that of an officer, comfortably off and able to afford such a luxury, in one of the African capitals.

While I covered the war in Portuguese Guinea in 1971, the beautiful new wife of a young *Alfares* shared our table when her husband was in the bush. She'd been staying at the hotel for almost a year and was not dismayed by the prospect of a second year in Bissau, a dreadful tropical backwater.

The differences to what she was used to back home were immense. Unlike Luanda or Lourenco Marques, the enclave was almost totally black and, to her, quite alien. There were almost none of the pavement cafes that we knew in Mozambique; no good beaches, no recreational parks. All that lay at the edge of Bissau was the jungle and the war. The hotel which we all shared, the Grande, was a misnomer: it was a grim, rambling, stuccoed doss-house that was older than the century with no air-conditioning. Only the bar showed any animation; it was raucous by midday.

Then there was the question of money. As any soldier will tell you, he can do without women, but not his beer.

Four years in Africa was not eased by the fact that a Portuguese soldier's pay was derisory. A brigadier serving in Africa in 1971 got about US $250 a month. A private got perhaps US $ 40 and perks were few. Home leave outside the period of service was almost unheard of; and anyway, who could afford a ticket back to the Metropolis? Even if he travelled steerage on one of the many Portuguese liners serving the African colonies, time was against him since they stopped just about everywhere on both outward and homeward legs.

The pay structure was pitiful, almost Third World by comparison. No doubt this factor ultimately played a role in switching the allegiance of the armed forces.

Pay Scales in Portuguese escudos —January 1974 (with an exchange rate of about a rand, or roughly one American dollar equal to $40, where $ = Portuguese escudos):

General (4-Stars) and Admiral	$18,900
General and Vice Admiral	$17,200
Brigadier and Rear Admiral	$15,500
Colonel and Navy Captain	$13,900
Lt-Col and Navy Commander	$12,300
Major and Navy Lt.-Commander	$11,400
Captain and Navy Lieutenant	$10,400
Army Lieutenant and Navy Lieutenant j.g.	$7,300
Lieutenants and Guardo-Marinha	$6,000
2nd Lieutenant or Navy Ensign.	$4,700
Sergeant-Major (Adjutant)	$5,700
First Sergeant	$5,400
Second Sergeant	$5,000
Sub-Sergeant	$4,700
Corporal	$4,700
First Corporal	$3,400
Second Corporal	$3,300

By way of comparison, Porch observes that not long after the war started, a full colonel of an infantry regiment stationed in Portugal earned 10,200 escudos a month which would have been something like $250. A British colonel earned about double that, while a French colonel took home about 5 or 6 per cent less than his British counterpart.

Physical conditions too, especially out at the 'sharp end', were abominable. Military camps at such remote corners of the empire as N'Riquinha, Nambuangongo and Cabinda in Angola, and Zumbo, Tete, Zobue and Guro in Mozambique, or any one of the postings in Portuguese Guinea were invariably quite barbarous and unhealthy.

In some places the tribesmen actually lived under better conditions than their 'protectors', especially where they were herded together in their Malayan-style protected camps or *Aldeamentos*.

At the end of it all, there are those who maintain that for all Lisbon's problems and makeshift means to fix them, it was Portuguese Guinea that was the main cause of the decay that set in among the Portuguese armed forces. By 1972 it had become apparent to even the most sanguine supporter of Portuguese rule in Africa that the war in this grim jungle and swamp terrain on the west coast of Africa could not be won.

There were several reasons; all were pertinent. The terrain made any proper military operations not only cumbersome but often impossible. The navy was as much involved as the army, but both forces had different ideas about fighting a hidden, well-armed and aggressive enemy that was given all the arms and equipment it needed by its radical friends. To compound matters, the two arms rarely shared the kind of intelligence that might have made a difference in the outcome of scrapes in the bush with the rebels.

Moreover, unlike Angola and Mozambique, the country was almost totally undeveloped. There were almost no industries and hardly any exports.

The first question that most conscripts asked on arriving in Portuguese Guinea was: 'Why are we here?'

When I tackled one young lieutenant in a camp near Cacheu in the north of the country, he retorted with comments like 'what's all this bullshit about? This is neither my home nor my country.'

Portuguese Guinea had none of the towns, industries, diamonds, coffee or hardwoods of Angola; or any of the pleasant amenities of Mozambique. Yet, by 1961 the African colonies had actually begun to make a small profit for the metropolis. But not Portuguese Guinea.

Furthermore, the country was miniscule, barely bigger than Lesotho, and its borders constricting. Portuguese garrisons were regularly shelled or rocketed from neighbouring territories. And while the lack of space and ability to manoeuvre should have worked against the guerrilla, it also militated against the Portuguese.

There was another problem. It should have been relatively easy for the Portuguese to withdraw from Guinea. But, as apologists in Lisbon pointed out, that would have been impossible without abandoning the other two; the Domino Principle would take effect at once, they warned at a time when domino theories were being bandied about in South East Asia.

The most active Portuguese commanders constantly advocated cross-border raids to prevent attacks by insurgents who found safe havens in neighbouring territories. Permission was always refused.

Death of a Guerrilla Fighter

Guerrilla warfare has one major advantage in this nuclear age. If employed as an instrument of foreign aggression, it constitutes an 'ambiguous threat' by confusing the legal, political and even military bases for an effective international response.

Peter Paret and John W. Shy: *Guerrillas in the 1960s*

Captain João Bacar of Bissau, Portuguese Guinea – a country listed on the map of Africa today as Guiné-Bissau – was an incredibly brave man. He died brutally one quiet Sunday morning in April 1971.

Only weeks before, I'd been with him in the jungles of this remote West African country that had been at war for eight years, a Colonial struggle that pitted all the forces of a profoundly Western nation like Portugal against what was then being termed in some quarters as Moscow's Evil Empire.

This war had been a long time coming, very much a part of the gathering anti-Imperial struggle that had almost totally enveloped the continent of Africa. From passive or disobedient phases in the tradition of Mahatma Gandhi, Africa – with strong support from the Soviets and its allies – the struggle had regressed to a succession of conflicts that stretched from Algeria on the Mediterranean north, to Mozambique, another Portuguese colony on the south-east, Indian Ocean shores of the continent.

By then, Kenya's Mau Mau insurrection was already history. Rhodesia's war was just starting. Nkrumah's dream of independence for black people all over the globe – by violent means if necessary – had already taken fire. Ultimately, the Ghanaian leader declared, it would encompass the entire continent, including white-ruled South Africa. So, in the end, it did.

But this was the 1970s and Lisbon was engaged in a grim succession of wars in all three of its African mainland possessions – Angola, Mozambique and Portuguese Guinea, each one bitterly contested. An indication of the intensity weathered by Lisbon came from American academic Douglas Porch who wrote a dissertation on Portugal's military role in Africa for Stanford University Press.

Titled *The Portuguese Armed Forces and the Revolution*[1], Porch tells us that with over 150,000 men in Africa by 1970, 'the Portuguese deployment represented a troop level in proportion to the Portuguese population [that was] five times greater than that of the United States in Vietnam in the same year'.

Throughout, Lisbon's leaders – and many of their people too, let it be said – fought a hopeless rearguard action. They had neither the hardware nor the numbers to counter

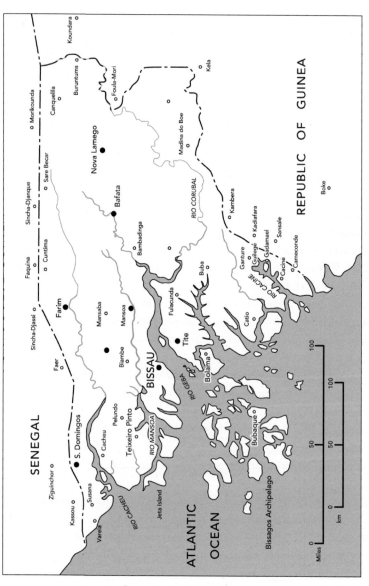

Portuguese Guinea

Jungle patrol with Bacar's troops in Guinea. (Author's photo)

groups of rebels supported and armed by Moscow and the rest of her Warsaw Pact Allies. Among these were Czechoslovakia, Cuba, North Korea, Poland, Bulgaria, East Germany as well as several radical Arab states that included Egypt, Algeria and Libya.

With her young men dying in large numbers, the powers that drove Lisbon to continue in Africa seemed to most of those who knew anything about these military struggles, as futile. There were those who regarded the ongoing conflicts as akin to some kind of improvised death wish. That, and a lot else besides, had been visited upon the Portuguese nation.

My Lusitanian friends have a name for this special kind of madness: *Loucura* they call it, a fatalism or super-optimism that, while it lasted, was also reflected in the way the Portuguese fought their African campaigns ...

João Bacar, a black man and a full captain in the Portuguese Army, was one of those who died. A brilliant tactical fighter and counter-insurgency specialist, he had been immersed in this guerrilla struggle since the beginning. He had seen it rent his tiny West African nation as no other upheaval had done since the great Malian general Mansa Musa had swept westwards, past Timbuktu, to bring the writ of this vast African empire to the verge of the great Atlantic, six centuries before.

Short, lean and as tough as Moslem Africa makes them, Captain Bacar was a remote product of this astonishingly wealthy and influential civilization which has left its mark on

Africa to this day.

He relished and vouchsafed its traditions, handed down through 30 generations, but still intact. He rallied to what he termed was the defence of the principles which had been laid down by his illustrious forefathers and which in the present era, as far as he was concerned, were being threatened by an alien and ungodly force from beyond. He told his men that the enemy was nurtured by powers which had only self-interest and quasi-Imperialist designs in mind.

Not for a moment did this commando captain – one of whose few gestures to the western society in which he lived was the small moustache he assiduously cultivated, very much like most of his other fellow officers – ever consider that this same self-interest could have been applied to the flag under which he fought. Bacar was born under that splendid green and red banner and considered himself proudly, often arrogantly, as Portuguese. Nothing else would do and he often said as much.

The Europeans from the Iberian headland, 3,500 kilometres to the north qualified that fealty by treating this black warrior as one of their sons. Their mutual empathy peaked shortly before Bacar was killed, when they rewarded him with the country's highest military honour, the Portuguese equivalent of Britain's Victoria Cross or America's Medal of Honour. The Futa-Fula captain had become one of the few.

Death holds no awe for military immortality. So it happened, early one Sunday morning that April that João Bacar made his final gesture to the people, the society in which he so implicitly believed.

A week after I had left him at Tite – while on an extended patrol in a dense jungle area in which we had spent two days scouring for the enemy – he was killed.[2] He died in an early morning skirmish with the black guerrillas of PAIGC, the West African guerrilla movement that called itself *Partido Africano para a Independência da Guiné-Bissau e Cabo Verde*.

Caught in the crossfire of a heavy enemy ambush along a stretch of jungle south of Bissau, the Colonial capital, his unit took the brunt of a well-planned and executed rocket and mortar attack. Aware that they were up against the man himself, the PAIGC guerrillas laid their trap with great care.

Three 'ballerina' anti-personnel mines – the same type known to the Americans in Indo-China at roughly the same time that all this was taking place in Africa as 'Bouncing Betty' – were placed in shallow ground across the path along which the Portuguese troops were expected. None of its vanguard noticed the nine prongs, three to each mine, bulging slightly in the red dirt.

The first soldier to cross the area would set off the explosion. The blast would also be the signal for the guerrillas to attack.

Curiously, and in keeping with the quirks of war, five of Bacar's soldiers managed to cross the kill zone without any of them triggering the prongs. The sixth followed confidently, probably satisfied that if there were mines in the path ahead, they would have been spotted or tripped by the usually eager-eyed scouts who led the way. He'd probably already stopped following in the footsteps of the man ahead of him, for the unit was on its second day of

Captain João Bacar addresses one of his men the day we all
went out on patrol together. (Author's photo)

patrol.

Number six was wrong. At the touch of his soft-soled rubber jungle boot which is
standard issue in the Portuguese Army the 'ballerina', with a dull thud, leapt upwards out
of the hollow in the earth where it had been placed the day before. It was still spinning
when it hit its shoulder-high apex and exploded downwards killing number six and badly
mauling the man behind.

Numbers eight and nine received superficial wounds in the legs and thigh and for some
minutes remained too shocked by the blast to comprehend the battle which raged viciously
around them. They lay and grimaced in the dust, barely conscious of further explosions
along the line.

Perhaps this shocked sprawl saved their lives, because two or three more soldiers were
cut down by rocket and rifle fire in the minutes which followed. One man, João Bacar, was
killed by a grenade, his own.

Bacar's reflexes were functioning almost before he heard the muffled explosion that
triggered the 'ballerina' land mine into the air about 100 metres ahead of where he marched.
He was already firing by the time the mine went off within touching distance of number six.

So were 20 more of his unit, by now crouched low in the long elephant grass on the
verge of a stretch of ragged rain forest with its dinosaur-spine of tall palms and which gave
the jungle around them a crazy trunkular effect.

Once the first ammunition clips had been exhausted, fire wavered momentarily on
both sides. Bacar didn't have to order his men to reload and keep firing their G-3s. They
were the best of Portugal's commando force in Guinea and the swarthy captain must have

been satisfied with their split-second reaction because he issued no orders throughout the action, the survivors recalled later.

For more than two minutes the shooting continued. The black Portuguese under Bacar knew the routine; exhaust a clip and hurl a grenade to back up the three bazookas that were retaliating into the adjacent jungle and then back to their G-3s again. They had done it many times before, first in training and afterwards, for real.

Mortars were out of the question at such short range and in any event, much of the action was random.

The enemy attack slackened briefly and there was uncertain movement in the jungle ahead. Still silent, Bacar palmed his second grenade and pulled out the pin. He rose abruptly to throw it. But a silent, unexpected force knocked his legs out from under him; Bacar had slipped on a patch of wet marsh clay which was not unusual in a region that has more rain in a month than parts of Europe and Africa enjoy in a year. He hit the ground hard, the grenade still in his hand.

Now the normal firing time of a Portuguese hand-grenade – a long tubular affair that looks more like a khaki can of shaving cream than a deadly instrument of war – is roughly four seconds after the pin has been pulled. When Bacar momentarily came to his senses and found himself lying there on his stomach with the grass above his head and the two nearest men only a metre away, he probably had one of those seconds left. In must have been the longest moment of his life.

The way his superiors reconstructed the attack afterwards, he might theoretically have tried to disentangle himself from his crouched position and, who knows, succeed in getting rid of the grenade. He must have been aware too, that if he did that, there was a likelihood of killing others around him. The decision was immediate: Captain João Bacar pulled the device in close to his body with both hands and dedicated his life to his beloved Prophet.

None of those around him at the time remember his last words, for they, too, were frozen in terror. One of his men, a young corporal who had joined the unit from the north shortly before, recalls seeing Bacar's lips move and reckoned afterwards that it could only have been a final call to Allah. It was ironic too, that at that critical moment, Bacar was facing the rising sun, looking east, which was the direction of his much-revered Mecca. That was when the explosion flung his body into the air, smashing it as well as the firing mechanism of the weapon. Its strap was still slung around his shoulder.

Bacar, the warrior, had finally immersed himself physically, mentally and spiritually into what the Portuguese like to refer to as 'This Christian War', even though his own divine beliefs differed radically from the deity of his Holy Roman Catholic patrons.

The news of Captain João Bacar's death swept through Portugal and her African Empire in a tide of shrouded sorrow and whispered dismay. João Bacar was dead, the people in Portuguese Guinea told one another in quiet tones, almost afraid the next man would hear the news, as if he had not already. By the next morning there wasn't a *tabanca* – a tribal village – in the country that hadn't heard the news. Drums echoing into the interior late into the night played an eerie but pivotal role in passing the message along.

Members of Captain Bacar's *Comandos Africanos* squad walking single file while
in the bush. Nobody talked or smoked in the war zone. (Author's photo)

Within the hour, the base camp at Tite from which Bacar and his men were operating
– and where I spent a lot of my time while in this tiny country – had passed on the word. A
few hours later they were setting the event in hot metal in newspapers in Lisbon, Luanda
and Lourenco Marques, complete with comment and the eulogies of a dozen men who had
lived and served with this remarkable Son of Africa.

The news was carried by the BBC shortly afterwards. Captain João Bacar, one of the
most famous veterans of Portugal's war in Guiné-Bissau had been killed in action by a
PAIGC guerrilla unit, the report read. Bacar had been a recent recipient of the coveted
Gold Order of the Tower and the Sword, Portugal's highest military award. That he had
been killed by his own grenade was inconsequential. The Futa-Fula officer was a victim of
that war, as surely as if he had been killed by a guerrilla's bullet.

Many of his countrymen only believed the news when his shrapnel-torn body was
flown back to Bissau by helicopter the next day. He had often been reported dead before,
usually by the enemy, who fanfared his death in Radio Conakry and the smaller guerrilla
station just across the frontier, *Radio Libertacao.*

In eight years they had only succeeded in wounding him four times and he had
reciprocated, always ruthlessly, by killing that many dozen of them.

It was a sombre 20-minute flight from Tite to Bissau, across swamp and river and
probably a few enemy units huddled in the daytime-protection of some of the larger

Classic shot of Captain João Bacar in the bush. The author took this photo
while out on a jungle patrol with his *Comandos Africanos* unit.

clusters of jungle. The helicopter swung low over the jungle to avoid taking enemy fire from
the surrounding bush. Not for nothing had a few foreign correspondents recently in the
country referred to this West African patchwork quilt of jungle and rice paddies as Africa's
own Vietnam.

A deep sadness pervaded Bissau's Bissalanca airport, with its rows of snub-nosed Fiat
G-91 jet fighters and vintage Harvard T-6's drawn up in echelon on the tarmac. Huge
crowds of mourners were gathered in the road beyond the security fence. The entire civilian
and military population had turned out to greet the body of the hero as it was brought into
town, his coffin draped ceremoniously with the flag of Portugal, a mantle so large it splayed
out over the back of the truck. A train of military and private trucks and cars a mile long
followed behind at walking pace.

Two outriders led the way. There was no need to clear the route; the crowds stood grim,
silent and respectful away from the road. With characteristic full-blooded Iberian emotion,
men – black and white – cried like boys when he passed.

There are not many reports of what happened across the border in the Republic of
Guinea when the news of the Portuguese captain's death came through that night. It was

The plaque that records the death of Portuguese Army Commando Captain João Bacar
is still to be seen in its original position in Bissau. The enemy hated him while he was
alive, but they also harboured a deep respect for his ability as a fighter. He was 'one
of us...a brother', they would often say afterwards. (Source Manuel Ferreira)

from this former French colony that the ambush unit had originally set out and it was in
that direction that they returned after the mission had been accomplished. Some reports
say that many of the younger guerrillas had danced in the streets of Conakry, Boké as
well as in Koundara in Guinea and Senegal's Ziguinchor to the north, for Bacar's name
had become synonymous for all that Portugal's presence in Africa represented. Now the
frightening symbol was gone and they rejoiced.

But there was also some hushed talk and a certain undefined reverence for Bacar,
particularly among some of the older guerrilla veterans.

They remembered him well, for they had often crossed swords with this seasoned
fighter. They respected both his guile and his tenacity, even if they despised the man for
what he represented. At the same time, he was still one of them: in their native idiom, a
man of the soil.

More important, his courage spoke the language often only understood by adversaries
of long standing, especially in a war that had its own code of ethics and where the fighters
were merely the pawns of other peoples' ideals.

There is a post-script to these events that is both contemporary and interesting. In 2007,
more than three decades after Bacar was killed, I was sent a message by Manuel Ferreira, a
former Military Intelligence operative and an old friend from several African conflicts. The
attachment showed the headstone of João Bacar's grave in Bissau, still undamaged in spite
of half a dozen post-independence revolutions that have rent apart this tiny community like
few others on the African continent ...

As Manuel commented, Portugal's Colonial wars went on for years, but there is still conflict in some of the former possessions, Guiné-Bissau, in particular.

A luta continua ...

13

The War in Portuguese Guinea

'Of the three theatres of operations, [Portuguese Guinea] was the most complicated and the most difficult. It was also the most important for the navy, for here its activities were vital, not only on the tactical but also on the strategic level. The reason was simple. About 80 percent of all cargo and personnel within the theatre moved on water, either by sea or through the river system ... Water transport was equally as important for the PAIGC, and for this reason the policing of river traffic by the navy was as important as its transport role ...

Captain John Cann:
Brown Waters of Africa; Portuguese Riverine Warfare 1961-1974[1]

Guerrilla conflict in and around the savage tropical mangrove country of Portuguese Guinea was like no other colonial war in Africa during the epoch that followed much of Africa achieving independence. It was the only campaign a European colonial power active in Africa actually lost. For this reason John Cann headed his chapter on Portuguese naval operations (from which the above extract is taken), 'A grim, torrid stretch of swamp and jungle'.

The Algerian War in contrast was harder, tougher and a good deal bloodier, but in the end President de Gaulle conceded that a political option was the only pragmatic solution. Independence for Algeria followed soon afterwards.

Yet, with Portuguese Guinea, it was historically significant that not a single town in this tiny West African enclave was overrun by insurgents in more than a decade of hostilities. Considering the nature of what was going on in South East Asia at the time, the largely conscript Portuguese army was never forced to abandon a single strategic position. Also, government casualties were manageable, the Portuguese Army never fled in disarray after the war ended and none of the few settlers who remained were driven into the sea after the *Partido Africano de Independência da Guinée Cabo Verde* (PAIGC) assumed the mantle of power.

In fact, things could have gone much worse had both sides not had a firm grip on their respective troops. By the time the youthful officers of the *Movimento das Forças Armadas* – the Portuguese Armed Forces Movement – had seized power in April 1974, many of those who had been active in Africa accepted that, had the war continued, conditions might very easily have gone the other way.

One young conscript was of the opinion that 'defeat hung heavily in the air' in the streets of Bissau, and in Cacine and Bafata further into the interior.

Moreover, while the fighting cadres of the PAIGC knew they had the situation in hand, the guerrilla leaders remained cautious. Amilcar Cabral had been assassinated more than a year before in Conakry, ostensibly at the hands of a dissident within the insurgent ranks who, though a trusted member of PAIGC's supreme council, was said to be in the pay of PIDE, the Portuguese secret police.

In later years other revelations came to light, including Moscow's fear that this former agricultural engineer, writer and poet – he used the *nom de guerre* of Abel Djassi in the field – might trade a closer alliance with Portugal for a more stable homeland once independence had been achieved. Like Angola's Agostinho Neto, he wasn't afraid to say as much, something that might have caused tension with the Kremlin.

Meantime, his half-brother, Luis Cabral – a sometimes-brutal adherent of the Soviet line of policy – became the leader of the Guiné-Bissau branch of the party and eventually appointed himself President of Guiné-Bissau. And while he initially followed a cautious line, promising that the rights of all citizens would be respected – including those who had supported Lisbon and fought against him – it was never to be.

A bitter civil war followed the formal handover of power to the PAIGC and conflict engulfed the country, culminating in a series of battles that lasted more than a year. It ended with the rout and death of almost all black troops that had formerly served in Portuguese Army units and though numbers will never be known, some sources maintain that almost 100,000 Guinéans were slaughtered.

It remains a curious anomaly that throughout this violent phase of settling scores, there was barely a whisper of protest from Lisbon's fledgling revolutionary government. More's the shame, because I was not only close to some of the more prominent dissidents like Vitor Alves and Otelo Saraiva de Carvalho, but I had also met quite a few of the others behind their so-called *Revolução dos Cravos*, several of them in the Alves apartment in Oeiras on Lisbon's outskirts ...

Notable about this conflict in West Africa was that it bore little similarity to other colonial struggles in Africa, or even France's seven-year campaign against the FLN in Algeria. It also differed markedly from what had been going on in the other two Lusitanian African territories and the liberation struggles that had already emerged along the northern frontiers of Rhodesia and South West Africa.

There were obviously a number of parallels with what took place in Angola. The war in Portuguese Guinea began almost overnight when small bands of well-armed and trained guerrillas crossed over from their exterior bases in Sékou Touré's Marxist Republic of Guinea in 1961, The insurgency gradually intensified until war was formally declared in January 1963 and it wasn't long before normally-placid Senegal entered the fray. In effect, the guerrillas now had safe havens in both neighbouring states.

Of all the states in West Africa during the 1960s and 1970s, the Republic of Guinea (Conakry) – formerly a French colony – might arguably have been the Soviet Union's strongest supporter. Ghana under President Nkrumah came a close second, but this political favourite of the already-radical London School of Economics overstepped the mark by fomenting revolution among his neighbours and he was soon overthrown by ambitious army officers.

For Moscow, Conakry, at that time, might have been equated to the United States military base on the Indian Ocean island of Diego Garcia, for both had great strategic value. Conakry was not only a valuable electronics monitoring station for the Soviets, it was also a refuelling stop for Soviet ships and aircraft keeping tabs both on Western shipping rounding Africa's bulge and American missile launches from Cape Canaveral on the opposite shores of the Atlantic.

I recall seeing the extent of some of it while travelling overland from South Africa to Dakar, I arrived in Conakry in January 1966, shortly before the death of former British Prime Minister Winston Churchill and stayed with a bunch of American Peace Corps Volunteers that I'd met along the way, including the scion of very famous Stateside family by the name of Vanderbilt. Thereafter I continued northwards towards the Senegalese frontier which I crossed near the small town of Koundara.

The three-day effort to cross into 'friendly territory' was lurid. With my British passport, I was regarded as an object of both interest and suspicion by an officious Guinean immigration official who forced me to return to Koundara three times in succession. My exit permit wasn't in order, he would say each time.

There was no arguing with either the man or the soldiers who backed him, even though the town was 50 kilometres from the border post: that he didn't like white people was manifest.

Fortunately, I'd made contact with another Peace Corps family who had been based in this unforgiving environment for more than a year. While their resources were sparse, they helped by offering me a roof over my head and a bed. Sadly, politics in Africa don't always make for convivial guests and I was pleased to finally say goodbye.

The delay was fortuitous in another respect. Perhaps 100 metres down the rutted track from where these two volunteers lived was a building which housed a sensitive electronic listening post manned by Soviet intelligence officials. Though my American friends weren't explicit, I soon gathered that all Portuguese Army radio broadcasts in the region to the immediate west of Koundara were being monitored from there.

They confided too, that there was regular movement in men and supplies between Koundara and Kantika, perhaps a couple of hours march from Buruntuma, Lisbon's easternmost military outpost in the beleaguered colonial enclave.

In Portuguese Guinea – a tropical spit of land fringed by numerous islands, the PAIGC took the initiative from the start, leading to the occupation of Como Island, an isolated stretch of mangrove swamp and open ground that was the site of one of the first major battles with Portuguese forces. The guerrillas resisted fierce counterattacks, including air strikes by *Forca Aerea Portuguesa* F-86 Sabres.

Initially, the PAIGC was composed of small groups of disaffected African intellectuals, many of whom had been educated at Coimbra or Lisbon universities and then granted 'most privileged' *assimilado* status prior to them returning home. It was these former students, later classified in the *Ultramar* as dissidents, that as early as the late 1950s were already urging the Portuguese to leave Africa.

A short time later these same nationalists, some of them having opted for self-imposed exile, started to issue decrees from Conakry. Portugal, they demanded, should vacate 'our Guiné-Bissau' and hand over government to the country's black population of about 600,000.

Lisbon was unmoved, which was when PAIGC encouraged the enclave's black workers to embark on a program of civil disobedience. The Portuguese reacted with force. Only after more than 50 dissident Africans had been killed by Portuguese police during a strike for higher wages at Pidjiguiti docks in Bissau on August 3, 1959 – a date subsequently commemorated by the guerrillas – did the possibility of armed conflict become a reality.[2]

The country's Africans were appalled by the deaths of their comrades and if some of the dissidents did not immediately become PAIGC members, many came to regard the movement as a hope for the future. War broke out three years later in January 1963 and went on for more than a decade. The war eventually spawned other nationalist organisations, and, as with the PAIGC, almost all of this activity was underground. Only two were to survive.

Amilcar Cabral's Conakry-based PAIGC headed the list and eventually achieved the distinction of being among the most successful black guerrilla organisations in Africa. While there were other guerrilla groups operating out of Senegal, Cabral's cadres were responsible for more than nine-tenths of all military activity in the country. He was eventually murdered by his own people in Conakry in January 1973, in circumstances that have never been fully explained. Cabral was replaced, first by Dr Vitor Monteiro, a former bank clerk in Bissau, and then by Aristides Pereira who went on to become the country's first president after Lisbon's departure.

The only other rebel movement of any consequence in the region was FLING or *Front de Lutte de l'Independence Nationale de Guiné*. Operating out of Dakar, this political and guerrilla force was comprised of at least four combined nationalist movements and regarded by the Portuguese and the West as more moderate than the communist/socialist PAIGC.

Both groups nevertheless shared a determination that the Portuguese had to be ousted, by whatever means. Their leaders approved of the violence that broke out as a result of what they called Portuguese 'intransigence'. However, as with most revolutionary groups, disputes began to emerge on questions of policy, including leadership, the timing of the takeover and the nature of the government they proposed to establish once the colonials had been expelled: while the PAIGC wanted a communist state, FLING, with strong American support, opted for ties with the West. It also indicated that it would not exclude the possibility of some kind of loose economic and cultural alliance with Portugal, similar to that between the Ivory Coast and France.

Portuguese Guinea

The Portuguese navigator Bartholomeu Diaz is as significant to early Portuguese history as Sir Francis Drake has been to Britain. In a journey that he started in 1497, Diaz discovered for Europe the elusive sea route to India. One of the replenishing stops en route on future expeditions was in Portuguese Guinea, where the navigators built a fort at Cacheu. This statue, once honoured in Bissau, was toppled after the war and shoved into a warehouse. (Author's photos)

Harsh, uncompromising and almost surreally Vietnam-like in most areas along the coast, Portuguese Guinea became Lisbon's most demanding and enervating war. It was almost lost until General António de Spínola arrived to counter guerrilla activity out of the Republic

of Guinea (Conakry). Vehicle patrols, though heavily protected, were constantly targeted in guerrilla ambushes for two reasons – first the terrain and second, because Guinea's PAIGC was the most active insurgent group in any of Lisbon's overseas provinces. (Author's photo)

General António de Spínola was always the no-nonsense 'hands-on' commander on which
he built his reputation. His career was as illustrious as his persona, having spent time as an
observer-guest of the German Army at Stalingrad. Here he addressed a group of loyal civilians,
almost all of whom were slaughtered by the guerrillas after the war ended. (Author's photo)

The Portuguese Navy played a hugely important role in the war in Guinea, with
warships supplying outlying military posts, coordinating maritime attacks and
interdicting guerrilla infiltration on the water. (Photo *Revista da Armada*)

Portuguese marines – *fuzileiros* – operating near an island known to have been used by PAIGC guerrillas. (Photo *Revista da Armada*)

The Portuguese Navy sometimes used heavy firepower against known guerrilla bases on the offshore islands south of Bissau. (Photo *Revista da Armada*)

The illustrious Captain João Bacar, who headed the country's most successful fighting unit, the *Comandos Africanos*. The author spent a week on patrol with this Special Forces group out of the small town of Tite in the interior and Captain Bacar was killed in an ambush a week later. During the course of his military career the brave Fula captain – he was of Muslim faith – was awarded the Portuguese equivalent of the Victoria Cross. Captain João Bacar is seen here wearing the decoration. (Author's photo)

One of the photos taken by the author while on patrol in
relatively open country in Portuguese Guinea.

Casual – but risky – improvised vehicle protection along a stretch of isolated road in the forests
to the south of the country. The Portuguese Army often did things differently from other
forces then active militarily in Africa and they sometimes paid the price. (Author's photo)

Portuguese Guinea – Guiné-Bissau today – is a tiny country about one-tenth smaller than Holland. Consequently many Portuguese army bases came under direct rocket or artillery fire either from Senegal (to the north) or the Republic of Guinea which surrounded the province on two sides. As a consequence, Lisbon brought in its own heavy weapons to counter these ongoing threats. (Author's collection)

A Portuguese Air Force Dornier about to land at an army base in the interior of the country. Heavy guns can be spotted in their emplacements below the left wing. (Author's photo)

The Portuguese Army in Guinea was multiracial from the start of the war and the groups moved – and fought – readily against an enemy that was both ruthless and unforgiving. (Author's photo)

One of the ambushes laid shortly before sunset by Captain Bacar's commando unit. Once down, we would remain prone until first light. (Author's photo)

Approaching Bissau – a low lying and expansive conurbation – from the sea. (Author's photo)

Portuguese marines come ashore on one of the islands from
a Navy landing craft. (Photo *Revista da Armada*)

Almost all the borders around this tiny African country were simply lines on a
map drawn by European colonial powers at a conference held in Berlin late in the
19th Century. The frontier with Senegal was no different. (Author's photo)

Sunset guard position along the waterfront at Bissau. Most guerrilla insertions took place from the sea and after dark. (Author's photo)

The war fought in Portuguese Guinea was the toughest in tropical Africa over the past century. Once away from the towns, almost all movement was on foot, and quite often through swamps or the omnipresent enervating morass. (Author's photo)

A Portuguese Navy patrol craft taking on fuel at one of the small harbours in the south of the country. (Photo *Revista da Armada*)

One of the most controversial figures in Portugal's African wars to emerge after the 1974 revolution was the author's escort officer in Portuguese Guinea – Major Otela Saraiva de Carvalho. He subsequently became a powerful advocate for anarchy and insurrection and it got so bad that he was later imprisoned by his old comrades, the leaders of the post-putsch government. (Author's photo)

Portuguese naval patrol craft in one of the river estuaries in the vicinity of Como Island. These ships worked closely with air cover in bids to locate guerrilla positions. (Photo *Revista da Armada*)

Ambush position in the jungles of Portuguese Guinea. (Author's photo)

One of the Portuguese Army camp commanders sits on top of a pile of ammunition that arrived with our convoy at a base almost within sight of the Senegalese frontier. (Author's photo)

A Portuguese marine retaliates against guerrillas who had fired on our patrol boat from the shore with a bazooka. (Author's photo)

Mortar pit at Tite camp, which came under fire while the author was visiting and which was used to retaliate against a fairly concerted guerrilla attack. (Author's photo)

Almost every town in Portuguese Guinea had a monument of sorts in the town centre, usually with old-time cannon on display. The colonial past was an omnipresent factor in the imperial mind. (Author's photo)

One of the soldiers attached to Captain João Bacar's *Comandos Africanos* with an improvised bazooka that fired French aircraft air-to-ground rockets. The Portuguese proved to be outstanding improvisers throughout the war, though it was the landmine problem that got them beat in the end. (Author's photo)

PAIGC had its own views on this matter and embraced a strong Nyerere approach. Africa – as Cabral and his lieutenants asserted – was black and despite imperialistic inroads from Europe, certainly not part of Europe. Moreover, the PAIGC was resolved to put in place a radical government along Cuban or Algerian lines, with all aspects of government – including politics, economics and military affairs, answerable to the Party alone. Cabral had always made it clear that he had learned a lot from Fidel Castro.

Despite their differences, the two revolutionary organisations – the PAIGC and FLING – continued to cooperate while opposed to a common enemy. Apart from military actions, they launched a joint propaganda campaign which drew attention to the monopolistic nature of commerce, trade and industry headed by Portuguese commercial firms.

Their principle targets were Portuguese cartels such as the *Banco Nacional Ultramarino* and Jorge de Mello's *Companhia Uniao Fabril* (CUF). Both enterprises had vast holdings in metropolitan Portugal as well as in the overseas provinces and also had powerful sway on what was happening in Portuguese Africa, mainly through family connections at the highest level of government in Lisbon.

By the early 1960s, the CUF had accumulated a series of monopolies in Portuguese Africa that stretched all the way through to the Congo and Zambia. A large proportion of the trade and exports of Angola, Mozambique and Portuguese Guinea were channelled through company books; interests included diamonds, minerals, tropical hardwoods and eventually extended to oil. No foreign or domestic interests were tolerated unless approved by the CUF.

Percentage rake-offs – to government administrators, officials issuing permits and licences and in some instances, even to military commanders in control of potentially lucrative areas to provide protection and convoys – were the norm. Obviously, there were abuses; the majority targeted at those who could least afford them: the local African people.

From the start, conflict in Portuguese Guinea was both fierce and uncompromising. Apart from its small size and forbidding terrain, many low-lying areas were impenetrable swamps or rain forest.

Also, previous lessons learnt in Angola, Malaya, Cuba, Algeria and Indo-China were put into effect by opposing forces. Conditions weren't helped by dismal communications. Things went a lot easier in the rest of the enclave, which rose slowly to a small succession of savannah plains in the interior and which allowed for better roads and regular army patrols.

One of the biggest problems facing Military Command in Bissau was getting the army to patrol a thousand or more kilometres of waterways that spread-eagled inland from the coast. Many small streams were entirely obscured from the air by the jungle; others became swamps at low tide and one had to know your way about to avoid being stranded. Quicksand was commonplace in some areas.

Here again the guerrillas had the advantage of local African help who knew these backwaters. Tribal people had been through these waterways for generations and it did not take the PAIGC long to get to plot many of the more obscure trails.

The single difference of hostilities in Guinea, compared with Angola and Mozambique, was there was little organised terror and mass slaughter. It stayed that way, but only until the colonial war had ended and all Portuguese forces had, as the saying goes, upped sticks and gone home.

Enter General António de Spínola, a man I got to know quite well in the comparatively short time I was active in the disputed enclave.

American historian Captain John (Jack) Cann, US Navy (Rtd) tells us in his book on Portuguese maritime operations in the former colonies, *Brown Waters of Africa*[3], that by late 1967 the campaign in Portuguese Guinea was not going well,

In fact, he writes, as the *primeiro tenente* Alexandre Carvalho Neto – the military assistant to Spínola – would state, 'The situation was absolutely catastrophic, on the brink of collapse. Bissau had become practically surrounded.' The President of the Republic, Admiral Américo Tomás, who visited Bissau in February 1968, returned to Lisbon to report to Salazar that 'the war was held by a thread.'

Cann continues: 'Major General (*brigadeiro*) António de Spínola confirmed this observation with an inspection visit of his own and described the situation as "desperate." He criticized *Brigadeiro* Arnaldo Schultz, the Governor-General and Commander-in-Chief, for not having an offensive aimed equally at the socio-economic and military problems and

Bacar's core group of fighters taken on a lazy Sunday afternoon at Tite military camp prior to going out on patrol. Many of these soldiers were of the Fula tribe and Muslim, which meant they didn't drink alcohol. (Source Manuel Ferrrira)

further accused the local military commanders of disguising the true state of affairs.

'Spínola, who habitually wore the traditional monocle of a cavalry officer, had a broad portfolio of experience on which to base his observations. His résumé included leading a volunteer force in the Spanish Civil War in 1938 and acting as an observer on the German eastern front opposite Leningrad in November 1941. In 1955 he was made a member of the Administrative Council of the steel concern Siderurgia Nacional, in addition to his normal military duties and thus became a beneficiary of Salazar's strategy for managing his military through such appointments.

'Military pay was poor, and to advance in pay and promotion, ambitious officers were often either removed from the immediate military environment or had their position enhanced by assigning them to lucrative and prestigious special positions. Normally these were at high levels of government or industry in both the *metrópole* and the *ultramar*, and it was these postings, promotions, and pay that Salazar controlled. Spínola thus had Salazar's ear and confidence.

At age 51 as a lieutenant colonel, he had assumed command of Cavalry Battalion 345, and later, in November 1961, departed for Luanda as part of the army reinforcement following the outbreak of violence in the north of Angola.

In this assignment, he further burnished his reputation and gained the respect and loyalty of his officers and men by leading from the front and enduring the dangers and hardships that they suffered. Likewise, he won the admiration and affection of the local population and its leaders through his pacification efforts. He travelled widely in Angola during his assignment and departed in 1964, when his tour of duty was completed, to return to Lisbon and to senior staff duty. It was while in this assignment that he undertook his survey of Guinea and on his making his report remembered Salazar saying, "It is urgent that you leave for Guinea."[4]

Spínola assumed command in May 1968 as a newly-promoted *brigadeiro* and saw his first task as one of drastically reducing PAIGC military capability and thus tilting the balance of war in favor of Portugal. He proceeded to implement an aggressive and imaginative offensive against the PAIGC, sought both a political and military victory, and as part of the political dimension, initiated a plan to win the population through a carefully orchestrated program of social and economic measures that lifted its standard of living.

Education, health, infrastructure, animal husbandry, and agricultural cultivation were improved markedly under his comprehensive blueprint, "A Better Guinea." These improvements were publicized and supported in a well-designed psychological operation to explain the changes and secure the backing of the people. The military dimension of this plan was the protection of the population from insurgent intimidation and the defeat and destruction of PAIGC armed capability. To this purpose the armed forces assumed an aggressive posture in its new modified organization that emphasized the recruiting of Africans and in its increased tempo of operations.

Spínola believed that the widespread and thorough PAIGC intimidation of the population would force him to move quickly in implementing "A Better Guinea," or, he conceded, he would irretrievably lose the battle for its loyalty.

As Cann explains, Spínola initially focused on the region's rivers, inlets and offshore islands, which he'd already accepted, served as the primary logistical lines of communication for Lisbon's enemies in Guinea. All became the focus of attention of Spínola's overall counter-insurgency programs.

In the south of Guinea, particularly, the four PAIGC supply bases across the frontier had played a pivotal role in this encroachment. During this time, the PAIGC had acquired four Soviet P-6 class fast patrol boats. These were capable 66-ton craft armed with two 25mm anti-aircraft guns and two torpedo tubes and could reach speeds in excess of 40 knots. This was in addition to an assorted collection of locally manufactured motor launches consisting of the *Arouca*, *Bandim*, *Bissau* and *Mirandela*.

Further, [Conakry] had similarly received three 75-ton *Komar* class fast patrol boats capable of speeds exceeding 40 knots. These were armed with two surface-to-surface missiles and two 25mm anti-aircraft guns. This sophisticated capability on the part of both the PAIGC and its host enabled the PAIGC to project power from Conakry to the depot of Kadigné on the island of Tristão and then to the Portuguese islands of Canefaque and Cambon.

From these islands a large fleet of canoes and modest numbers of small outboard motor boats consistently penetrated the waterways of southern Guinea largely unchallenged and effectively extended the PAIGC distribution system and consequent combat capability well into the interior. The south of Guinea was, as a consequence, thoroughly infiltrated by the PAIGC by 1969, and this dominance posed a most serious threat to Spínola's plans.

As Cann mentions, this identical situation occurred in the Mekong Delta of Vietnam during the same period when the communist forces transported foodstuffs, medical supplies, arms, ammunition, and to minimal degree, men, on its waterways.

Until the US Navy mounted a coordinated and consistent challenge, this enemy line of communication wreaked havoc with land security forces in the south of Vietnam. [Spínola always maintained that] the only solution in an undeveloped country, such as Guinea or Vietnam, where the waterways acted as the primary means for moving heavy cargos of munitions and foodstuffs, was to maintain a constant presence on the rivers to prevent this vital enemy traffic.

This had been done successfully on the Zaire against the MPLA and the UPA/FNLA with a constant naval presence and aggressive patrolling and could have been repeated on the Inxanche.

These procedures are detailed in Appendix C, which is an extract from Captain Cann's book on Portuguese maritime operations titled *Brown Waters of Africa*.

The conflict in Guinea was characterised by both sides using classical tactical actions in their efforts to make gains. On one hand, it was a textbook guerrilla war. On the other, it was a testing ground.

Many insurgent tactics were later put to good effect in Rhodesia's war and in South West Africa. Widespread use of mines was an important aspect, both anti-tank and anti-personnel.

While the nature of this war was interesting, the fortunes of the two opposing factions were even more so.

Because of Lisbon's overwhelming preoccupation with security, and consequently adverse publicity, the struggle remained in the shadows for almost the entire duration. Apart from a few Africanists who made it their business to keep themselves abreast of events, the battle in Portuguese Guinea raged for years without attracting anything like the attention it deserved.

Until Spínola arrived, things went dismally for Lisbon. While Salazar's often ill-conceived controls from abroad were at their harshest, Portuguese fortunes remained in flux. Only when he was replaced by the more liberal Prime Minister Marcello Caetano, who promised a more relaxed and open regime, did conditions improve. The ebb and flow was slight, but the advantage always seemed to be with the guerrillas.

Within a year of the first isolated FLING attacks on Susana and Verela on the north-western Senegalese border in late 1962, the Portuguese High Command was prepared to admit that the 'terrorists' controlled about 15 per cent of the country. Yet, hostilities in 1962 were only a foretaste and attacks in the north were regarded as little more than 'civilian disturbances'.

Although war was never formally declared by Lisbon, real conflict was initiated with an attack by a combined PAIGC force on Tite, Buba and Fulacunda in January 1963, which was when Cabral made his commitment formal.

Tite – from where I was eventually to set out on patrol with Captain João Bacar – was occupied at the time by a battalion of two companies under the command of a major. Buba and Fulacunda were garrisoned by one company each. In the guerrilla attack, only one Portuguese soldier was wounded at Tite, although their salvoes did manage to destroy the ammunition dump. Next day they ambushed a car travelling between Tite and Fulacunda and killed all its occupants. At the same time they attacked a section of Portuguese soldiers on patrol near a village east of Tite. In this action two Portuguese soldiers were killed.

From then on conditions deteriorated further, both for Portugal and Cabral's band of insurgents. Two years later Cabral was asserting that the area under his control had risen to 50 per cent, when, in fact, it had diminished. By 1971 PAIGC liked to say that all but the last 20 per cent of the country round the capital was theirs; simply not true, if only because I was able to travel freely throughout much of it. I had an escort as protection, always a formality with journalists.

Cabral would make his declarations at public meetings and then challenge Lisbon to prove otherwise, which he knew they wouldn't do.

He said as much when I met him at the meeting of the Organisation of African Unity in Addis Ababa in 1971. There, he told me, he only needed to take Bissau and he would have the entire country in his pocket.

The first time he made this statement was in 1965. He was still at it when he was murdered.

The Portuguese in Guinea fought a different kind of war to what was going on in Angola at roughly the same time.

Altogether there were about 4,000 black soldiers in the army, all volunteers. As one staff officer explained, this was very different from the much larger Portuguese colonies further south where some indigenes were conscripted. In addition to these African soldiers

Captain Bacar in radio comms with his base during a brief break in the bush. (Author's photo)

(that had been effectively incorporated within the 30,000-man regular army) there were another 4,000 blacks in the civilian militia groups. These were not men on active service, he explained.

> Instead, they serve a para-military role in their home areas and like our troops, have guns, mostly G-3 rifles and here and there automatic weapons, but only those who have requested them.

Additionally, he explained, there were about 6,000 local men who had been given firearms for what he termed was 'self-defence'.

For their part, the majority of Portuguese forces in the territory preferred the safety of their own camps or, if they were based there, fortified *aldeamentos* villages after dark. However, as I was able to observe during my own visit, that resulted in large areas where movement at night was unrestricted and free from control. Obviously, the guerrillas moved in as and when they saw fit to do so.

Initially, Lisbon enjoyed complete air supremacy during daylight hours and they used it to good advantage. This was to change when Russian SAM-7s drove the Portuguese Air Force out of the skies in Guinea and gave the insurgents a formidable edge. Soviet missiles first appeared in March 1973, three FAP aircraft being lost in two months. By September the PAIGC claimed to have downed 21 Portuguese war planes, which was nonsense: there weren't even a dozen aircraft in the entire country.

Foreign journalists who visited Portuguese Guinea included an American, Jim Hoagland, who eventually became the managing editor of the *Washington Post,* and the West German veterans Peter-Hannes Lehmann and Gerd Heidemann of *Stern*, one of whom was later prosecuted for trying to market bogus *Hitler Diaries.*

The consensus among us all was that there were few zones actually 'held' by the black guerrillas.

Instead, guerrilla bands embraced Mao Tse-Tung's principles on unconventional warfare, always remaining on the move, making unexpected strikes and taking actual control of few areas. It was rare that they would hold an area in the face of counterattacks. In 1971, when the rebels announced that their forces had entered the third, or 'mobile warfare' stage of this form of unconventional warfare – the equivalent of full confrontation – the statement was contradicted by the reality on the ground.

Basil Davidson's observations in 1967 concurred with those of the PAIGC, but then Davidson did not even concede that the Portuguese could fight.

The truth is that it matters little how well the Portuguese fought; they were at war in three separate and widely dispersed regions in Africa for 13 years and lost thousands of men on a defence budget in all three conflicts of less than US$450 million a year. And while they fared badly in Guinea and Mozambique, the war in Angola was all but won when it finally ended.

By the time I arrived in Portuguese Guinea in 1971, things had changed much for the better from the heady days of 1967 when General Arnaldo Schultz held precarious command. António de Spínola superceded his command soon afterwards.

Like his Guinean predecessor, and having originally distinguished himself in Angola like General Bettencourt Rodrigues in eastern Angola , Spínola was remarkably adept at achieving results in this still undecided conflict, at least until the air force lost the initiative.

One of the conditions imposed by Spínola on being offered the command in Guinea was that he should have total control of the country without direct supervision from Lisbon. He also insisted that he should be allowed to choose his own staff. Both demands were granted by the Ministry of War, which remains one of the main reasons why the war soon turned in favour of the Portuguese, be it only provisionally.

Among these was a young captain, Otelo Saraiva de Carvalho, who was to be my escort or 'minder' while I remained in Portuguese Guinea. A charming, effusive intellectual in uniform, Carvalho became prominent in Lisbon at the time of the putsch as one of the radical hardliners who demanded a full-blown communist government for the country.

After a series of bomb attacks in the early 1980s he was gaoled for anarchy and little has been heard of him since, which was a pity since he was dedicated to change.

One of the first changes insisted on by General de Spínola showed his grasp of guerrilla warfare. Following the example of Sir Gerald Templer in Malaya in 1952, he assumed total responsibility for both civilian and military organisations. This proved valuable in his attempts to come to terms with the liberation forces. He also sliced through red tape and interdepartmental hostility which, until then, had become characteristic of the Portuguese war effort in Guinea, and to a lesser extent in Angola, largely because the latter was almost self-governing.

Schulz had been both civil and military governor of the region, but his hands were tied by Lisbon's bureaucrats. Many of the plans that he tried to put into operation were thwarted. In retrospect, since he was the boss, much of the blame for tolerating interference in a rapidly deteriorating military situation must be laid at his door.

Another result of Spínola's rule was the execution of long-overdue political and economic reforms. The changes for the better came too late, but in the last analysis, Spínola stole much of the rebels' thunder, for they too promised changes and were prevented by the war from carrying them out.

The PAIGC took their country into independence with an explicitly socialist programme. Since then, after several army mutinies, the murder of several of its presidents, preceded by a civil war that lasted years, the country, in a succession of phases, lapsed into a sorry state. Bissau was a dismal backwater when I visited the place in 1971. It was bankrupt and things have hardy improved in the interim.

So much for the ideals of a forward-looking liberation army, never mind the hopes of an entire nation that were vested in an independent Republic of Guiné-Bissau.

The individual responsible for the eventual outcome of the war was always General António de Spínola, regarded by many as an ascetic and intellectual career officer. This was also the man who was to write the book that eventually altered the course of the political and military fortunes of the Portuguese in Europe and in Africa. Titled *Portugal e o Futuro* (Portugal and the Future), he expressed the idea that the only solution to Lisbon's so-called Colonial Wars was the discontinuation of the conflict.

A taciturn conservative, General de Spínola was always seen in public immaculately uniformed and, in spite of the enervating West African heat, wearing leather gloves. He was certainly of the 'old school' and unequivocally regarded as a father figure by his men. There were very few soldiers within his command that did not stand in awe of him because he was both strong on discipline and tradition, without which he said, Portugal would be nothing. Yet he wasn't averse to innovation if it made sense and could be applied without disruption.

He had other qualities at which he excelled. Few could match his ability as a thinker, tactician, historian and ultimately as a visionary. In this respect, he had a more enlightening effect on the future of Portugal than any other man in the previous century, including the dictator Salazar

I met him several times, both formally in his office and in the more relaxed environment of the local festival. Each time I returned to Bissau, I'd be ushered through by Captain, later

Major Otelo Saraiva de Carvalho at Military Headquarters in Bissau.

We got on well, even if he refused to speak English which, I gathered, he understood quite well. We'd sit down in his office and he would offer me wine or coffee and ask about my trips through Africa and the various leaders I'd met. He was intrigued by people like Nkrumah, Kaunda and Nyerere as well as the Biafran leader Ojukwu and wondered how South Africa would eventually cope with its own disaffected black millions.

It was a constant theme: whether Africa would survive intact in the years ahead. While he was sceptical because of corruption and mismanagement, he had hopes for the continent on which he had spent a large part of his career. I thought him a delightful and enlightened individual.

The last time we made contact was the day after the Portuguese Air Force plane in which I was travelling – a clapped-out old DC-6 – almost crashed into the Atlantic, something I deal with in Chapter 19.

After a string of in-air emergencies, we eventually got back safely to Bissau but because it had taken us so long to get off the ground that morning, I asked Captain Carvalho to put me on the next day's Boeing flight to Lisbon. I didn't want to wait for the old prop-job to be repaired and didn't have the funds to do it myself. Since I had a meeting scheduled with the Ghanaian foreign minister in Accra in a few days, time was of critical concern. I actually hoped that the army would pay.

Only one man in the country could make that decision, so Captain Carvalho and I went to see the General. I explained the situation and without blinking, he agreed.

I was to be given a ticket on the next day's Boeing flight to Lisbon, he told the captain.

Operation Trident – Striking at an Elusive Enemy on the Offshore Islands

One of the most important campaigns of Lisbon's war in Portuguese Guinea was the strike against fairly large groups of guerrillas on the offshore islands, of which Como was the most prominent. This extract comes from John Cann's maritime history titled *Brown Waters of Africa*: it is instructive because this joint army, navy and air force operation encapsulates many of the problems faced by the colonial authorities.

By early 1964 the border area with the Republic of Guinea and the coastal areas around Catió and Cacine had become sufficiently infected with PAIGC insurgents that a serious Portuguese challenge was long overdue. The navy in particular worried that without such action its access to Catió would be closed.[1] Accordingly a joint operation styled Operation *Tridente* would combine army, navy, and air force resources to isolate and sanitize the familiar islands of Caiar, Como, and Catunco, which were bounded by the Atlantic Ocean and the Cumbijã, Caiar, and Cobade Rivers. Caiar had been the scene of the earlier December 1962 action, which had been purely a sweep through the main island of Como and had had no lasting effect. The expanded area of operations for *Tridente* now covered nominally some 210 square kilometers of land, only 170 of which were actually usable because of the tides.

The three islands were characterized by large tracts of rice paddies with their intricate dike systems and alternated by vast areas of very dense and impenetrable grasslands and swamp forests. These latter areas provided ideal hiding places for insurgents, as troops found passage through them very difficult going. Clearly the operation had its work cut out for it, and it was to be the first such full joint operation in any of the theaters.[2] It would last for more than two months and from the naval perspective would be supported by a substantial portion of its resources in Guinea. Over time the *Vouga*, the *Nuno Tristão*, three DFEs, one LFG, three LFPs, three LPs, six LDMs, and two LDPs were committed to the operation.[3]

Como and its adjacent islands were considered important both to the insurgents and to the Portuguese command for obvious reasons. From the point of view of the insurgents it was a perfect staging point, for it was remote, and this isolation brought with it security. It could be supplied by sea from the sanctuary of the Republic of Guinea (Conakry) only about 40 kilometres distant or a few hours at most by boat, and it provided a springboard for PAIGC subversive operations further into Portuguese territory. From the Portuguese

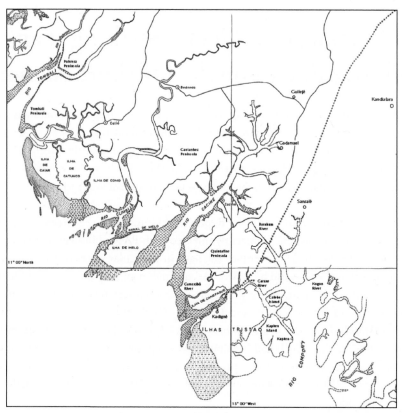

This Portuguese Navy map, adapted from Lisbon's Hydrographic Institute shows some of the coastal regions of Portuguese Guinea where many of the maritime operations against the guerrillas took place.

point of view it was perceived as a festering sore of insurgent activity and an unwelcome subversion of its population in a prime rice-growing and a very modest cattle-grazing region. The insurgents were diverting the rice crop and livestock to their own ends and establishing themselves as a relatively permanent fixture within the population. Portuguese intelligence estimated the PAIGC force on the three islands to be about 300, which number included about 15 military advisors from Guinea.[4]

The operation had five goals:

- To secure the Portuguese riverine lines of communication in the south
- To protect the population from the PAIGC subversion and intimidation
- To reinforce Portuguese administrative authority over the island
- To improve the economic well-being of the population and the area
- To inflict a grave loss of credibility and prestige to the enemy[5]

The naval concept of operations in this effort was, first, to isolate the area by securing the surrounding waterways of the Caiar, Cobade, and Cumbijã Rivers, next, to disembark and support the land forces in their sweep for enemy troops, and last, to secure the maritime and riverine lines of communication so that a permanent presence could be maintained in the area. To this end the navy established three zones to control the inland waters around the target area. Zone 1 extended from the mouth of the Caiar to the point at which it joined the Cobade, and then along the Cobade until the shallow narrows of "Canbança do Brandão." Its commander was embarked in the *Deneb*. Zone 2 extended from the "Canbança do Brandão" along the Cobade to its confluence with the Cumbijã. Its commander was embarked in the *Bellatrix*. Zone 3 extended along the Cumbijã from its confluence with the Cobade downstream to its mouth, and its commander was embarked in the *Dragão*. These zones are identified on Map 5.2. These three forces, with the aid of aerial reconnaissance in the form of an aged but capable P2V-5 *Neptune,* would prevent insurgent escape from the land forces sweeping the three islands by killing or capturing the fleeing insurgents and destroying their boats.

The operation was divided into three phases. The first began on 15 January 1964 with the landing of between 1,100 and 1,200 troops at various sites on the islands. The landings were given close air support by a single T-6 *Harvard* from the air force, and artillery provided fire from a support base in Catió some 5 to 10 miles distant, depending on where one was on the island group. As one might suspect, there was a challenge to the amphibious assault. There were a number of canoes identified by the patrolling *Neptune,* which vectored the surface craft to their locations for destruction. The *Deneb* took fire from the vicinity of 'Cambaça do Brandão' later in the evening, as it patrolled about 500 meters offshore. *Bellatrix* came to its aid, and the two of them answered the enemy's machinegun fire. A radioman was wounded, and a rubber boat and a PRC-10 radio were destroyed on the *Deneb*. Armed natives appeared opposite the village of Darsalame on the left bank of the Cumbijã and were dispersed by fire from the *Dragão*. The *Neptune* later identified a substantial group of insurgents near the village of Cametonco on the Island of Catunco about 400 meters inland from the Cumbijã riverbank. This group fired at both the *Neptune*

Aerial view of Portuguese Guinea's Corubal River mouth at low tide. (Photo *Revista da Armada*)

and later the *Dragão* before fleeing. And so it went over the several days of the first phase and into the second, with the landings encountering sporadic resistance from the insurgents and their local recruits while they tried to flee the islands in canoes or on foot or to hide in the swamp forests. The second phase occurred between 17 and 24 January and was centered in patrolling the three islands to establish a wide presence, to flush out insurgents, and to gather intelligence.

Following the landing and establishment phases, the third phase lasted from 24 January to 24 March and involved periods of intense fighting throughout the island of Como. The primary fighting occurred in the area of Uncomené near the river of the same name that separates the islands of Como and Caiar and in the Cachil swamp forest on Caiar. The insurgents suffered substantial losses in 76 killed, 15 wounded, and 9 taken prisoner, a casualty rate of around 30 percent. These numbers do not, however, consider unknown casualties from artillery fire and close air support. Captured correspondence between PAIGC leaders confirmed their besieged and desperate state and the need for reinforcements.[7] The Portuguese forces suffered 9 killed and 47 wounded in the 71-day operation, but these numbers do not reflect the toll on troops from the climate and poor diet.[8] There were 193 personnel evacuated because of sickness. The troops in the field went for 23 days on combat rations, and while they were served hot meals the other 48 days, the drinking water was very bad and should have been used only to wash clothes or to bathe. A doctor observed that in one company of 151 men, he treated 132 for sickness of one form or another.[9]

In an insurgency, taking territory is rarely critical and usually irrelevant, for the

Portuguese naval patrol craft in one of the river estuaries in the vicinity of Como Island. These ships worked closely with air cover in bids to locate guerrilla positions. (Photo *Revista da Armada*)

struggle is over the loyalty of the population. Operation *Tridente* was a Pyrrhic victory in this sense; however, it did assert Portuguese sovereignty over an area where its presence had long ceased to be felt and disrupted enemy operations by denying the PAIGC a logistic base. While a contingent of army troops remained in Cachil as a caretaker force following the operation, it was eventually removed as not being worth the cost of policing the terrain. Indeed, it also tended to be an object of curiosity for the insurgents, as it was isolated from its support and seen as the proverbial "sitting duck."[10] Small numbers of insurgents consequently moved into the vacuum left by the departing Portuguese troops, and naval craft entering and leaving the Cumbijá River tended to give the islands a wide berth. In the end, none of the original goals of the operation were fully realized. General Arnaldo Schultz, the Commander-in-Chief of the Armed Forces in Guinea, was having limited results treating the insurgency with a conventional solution. As if to underscore the shortcomings of *Tridente*, Amílcar Cabral held his famous Cassacá Congress during February 1964 at his base near the settlement of that same name on the Quitafine Peninsula, which extends south of Cacine. Its purpose was to reorganize the PAIGC war effort and consolidate the independent commanders into a national army to be called the FARP (*Forças Armadas Revolucionárias do Povo* or Revolutionary Armed Forces of the People).

The numbers of both local inhabitants and insurgents remained small in the Como Island region, as it subsequently lost its importance to the latter as an area of local support and a refuge in their operations. Alpoim Calvão confirmed this when he returned to Como five years later in Operation *Torpedo* with DFE 7 and found only weak resistance.[11] The

Some of the *fuzileiros* – Portuguese Marines – who took part in actions along the Cacheu River onboard a patrol in the south of the country. This region was uncomfortably close to the Republic of Guinea. (Photo *Revista da Armada*)

PAIGC moved progressively northward onto the peninsulas of Quitafine and Cantanhez adjacent to the Portuguese Guinea border and proceeded to isolate the local market towns of Catió and Bedanda.[12] The ports of these besieged towns, however, remained the secure link to Bissau via the waterways. These moves positioned the PAIGC advantageously to subvert the interior of the Portuguese colony, as its lines of communication from its Guinean sanctuary through these two peninsulas became increasingly safe from Portuguese interdiction. For the Portuguese, this proved to be one of the grand operations that from time to time punctuated what might have been an otherwise sound and patient strategy of counterinsurgency in Africa. This type of large conventional manoeuvre seemed to hold a fatal attraction for local commanders, as it appeared to be a means to end the war quickly. In fact it was just the reverse. It inevitably fell short, for while many arms were generally found, insurgents captured or killed, and bases destroyed, the enemy tended to melt into the terrain or into the local population. The operation could not be concealed because of its large scale, and other areas of Portuguese Guinea were denuded of troops to support it, a situation that left the population elsewhere vulnerable. It was not a sound counterinsurgency operation and invariably yielded disappointing results at great expense. The constant pressure of small patrols as part of a *tâche d'huile*-style strategy, for instance, was far more effective in its low-key, low-cost approach.[13]

The Air Combat Information Group (acig.org) provide valuable information on many of

Portuguese *fuzileiros* operation in incredibly difficult jungle and mangrove
swamp terrain in a bid to get to grips with the guerrillas. There was little like
this in the other two African territories. (Photo *Revista da Armada*)

these operations, including Operation Trident. During the course of that campaign, it tells
us, the Portuguese Air Force (FAP) flew 851 combat sorties. Some of these are listed as
follows:

- F-86Fs: 73
- T-6:   141
- Do.27:   180
- Auster: 46
- Alouette III: 323
- PV-2 Neptune: 16
- C-47/Dakota: 2

ACIG also says that in October 1964, following powerful pressure from Washington,
the FAP was forced to pull out all the Sabre jet fighters it had stationed at Bissalanca. The
Americans complained – with a certain justification – that Lisbon was endangering NATO
defences of the European Atlantic coast 'due to the deployment of F-86s to Africa, and
their use in counter-insurgency operations'.

Curiously, ACIG reminds us that:

... the USA did not complain about the deployment of Sabre jet aircraft to Angola,
but the presence of these fighters [in the war in Portuguese Guinea] was obviously
disturbing for one reason or the other.

The Portuguese experienced similar problems with deployment of their P2V-5

Bellatrix class patrol boat *Formalhaut* (P367) at speed on the Congo River in Northern Angola. Its rubber boats are alongside. Apart from land operations in all three of the overseas territories, huge swathes of ocean, river and lake also had to be covered. In Mozambique, which included many offshore islands as well as Lake Malawi in the interior, this was a distance of more than 2,000 miles. (Photo *Revista da Armada*)

Neptunes. These were originally obtained to replace their aging fleet of PV-2 Harpoons as maritime patrol and anti-submarine aircraft. Due to US pressure, they could not be permanently deployed in Africa, and were based in Portugal. Nevertheless, small detachments were sent to Portuguese Guinea and Angola as necessary.

One of best known such deployments was Operation "Resgate", undertaken in December 1965, when two Neptunes had been forward-deployed at Sal (Cape Verde) and were sent to Bissau's Bissalanca Airport loaded with 350kg bombs.

After delivering a highly successful attack against PAIGC positions, both planes had to return to the Montijo air force base in Portugal, again due to adverse US reaction.

Lieutenant Jimenez, a Futa-Fula like Bacar, sat opposite me and didn't have much to say. But he was friendly, smiling and nodding each time our eyes met.

'A good fighter, that Jimenez,' one of the other officers acknowledged when he heard I was to go out with him on patrol in the morning.

'He is unconventional in his tactics as he is in his dress. He prefers a light-collared woollen astrakhan to a cap and you'll never see him without his AK. That gun is his Excalibur; he took it from a man in the jungle after he had killed him with his knife.'

The other black officer present in the group was a huge friendly hulk of a man, *Alferes* Tomaz who, though only recently commissioned, had come through a number of scrapes. Tomaz had been recommended for a decoration after a particularly weird attack in which one of his men was wounded and dazed by an enemy RPG-2 rocket. Instead of lying low and waiting for a medic or for the enemy to withdraw, the injured soldier staggered, shell shocked and aimless through the trees with bullets popping all around him. Unbidden, Tomaz had left the safety of his own position, sprinted through the jungle towards the man, picked him up like a bag of string beans and returned him to his own group.

Tomaz was of Sierra Leonean stock. Of that much the youthful officer was aware, but he confided, had no idea how his parents had come to Portuguese Guinea or why they'd done so. 'It certainly wasn't for money,' was his comment.

Tomaz spoke good English and knew some Freetown Creole which his father had taught him. At the same time, this hulking black officer was proudly Portuguese, and like Bacar, willing to fight to uphold that identity which he considered sacrosanct for reasons of his own. It was an unrealistic and, some would say, unwise dedication which few Europeans or independent Africans understood, but, as I was discover for myself, the same irrefutable quality that caused so many black men to fight valiantly for the British in Malaya, with French troops against General Vo Nguyen Giap in French Indo-China and, more recently, with white South Africans in their own border wars.

Also notable was the fact that at that time there were many more black soldiers in the uniforms of Rhodesian security forces than whites, all of them actively combating African ZAPU-ZANU insurgents in the Zambezi Valley.

In sheer size and physical strength, young Tomaz was probably bigger than Jimenez and Bacar together. He had the power, they'd joke, to lift them both – and perhaps another like them – and carry all three to the edge of the base. They hadn't tried it yet, Jimenez quipped in good English, because he reckoned it would have been too darned uncomfortable.

Tomaz was known among his friends as the 'gentle giant', though he was considered 'frivolous' by some of the senior men in the mess.

'It's his youth ... he does crazy things at times,' said the Colonel.

Tomaz was only 21 and, as young as he was, he was regarded by his colleagues as a master of the art of practical jokes. He'd once even offered his commanding officer an exploding cigar. He got a week in the cooler for that stunt and had some of his pay docked but it didn't affect his rank. He was too valuable a combatant, somebody at headquarters had argued.

Although a Moslem ('but not a good son of the Prophet', he'd argue), he didn't hide the fact that he enjoyed his liquor. In contrast to Bacar and Jimenez, both of whom abstained, *Alfares* Tomaz drank just about anything handed to him.

In the words of some of the men who shared the mess, Tomaz was 'quite a guy'. Those who served under him, even some troops who were considerably older, held him in deep respect, for in the short time he'd been commissioned, he'd already proved himself a leader of men.

I'd arrived at Tite in the long-disputed Quinara region after returning to Bissau with an officer who'd introduced himself as Captain Alcada. I was offered another aide, but refused his services, at least for the time being. I thought I had an adequate grip on the war, I told Lieutenant Colonel Lemos Pires, my liaison officer in Bissau. If he had no objections, I'd prefer to make my own way about the country.

All I asked for was transport and surprisingly, he agreed, though obviously I'd be passed from one military unit to another and radio messages would take care of the details. The units I'd be visiting obviously needed to know about this hack by the time I arrived.

In part, my gesture was self-serving. With another man as part of my retinue, I couldn't cadge lifts on the occasional chopper as easily as if I were alone. The same with small fixed-winged planes like the Dorniers. I had to constantly be on the move and singly, I felt, was the obvious way of doing it. There would always be somebody waiting for me at whatever destination I chose and clearly, I'd have to tell headquarters where I was heading each time.

Captain Bacar was waiting for me at Bissalanca Airport the morning I was lifted to Tite by helicopter. The captain had come across the river to greet me. I'd specifically asked to meet the man who was already more than a legend beyond the borders of his own country.

The Fula officer didn't have much to say on the way over but he kept his eyes on the jungle below as we sped south. This is 'my' area he explained through his interpreter as he did so. At one point he thought he'd spotted movement in a thick clump of palms about 15 kilometres from our destination and ordered the pilot to turn around and make a closer inspection at tree-top level. Bacar was right.

Tiny figures scattered in all directions as we shot past, barely a metre above a ragged row of tall palms which surrounded a nearby paddy. We circled a few more times while the pilot gave directions on the radio. Bacar identified the clump on a large-scale map which the pilot handed to him and passed on a row of digits to base. The first T-6s could be seen approaching the site before we moved on.

At Tite, the regional headquarters, and after Portugal's Colonial war, the scene of huge battles between competing liberation groups that left thousands dead, it was business from the start. Two Daimler armoured cars greeted us on the runway and our little party was taken past some pretty formidable defences to the mess.

Colonel Lopes had about 500 men under his command. His was an important zone in the middle of Balanta country and they were often in contact with what he termed 'hostile forces'. The Balantas – there were about 20,000 of them, – were a cautious lot; neither for the enemy nor against.

The position was best summed up by the officer who spoke to Jim Hoagland of the *Washington Post* who covered the war shortly before I did; he was speaking about Balanta country.

'There are villages where we go in the day and receive a very good welcome. At night, the terrorists receive a very good welcome, too.'

According to the Portuguese, the men of the Balanta tribe were a gregarious, generous lot. They were good workers, good drinkers and good fighters with whichever side they chose to embrace. It was not surprising therefore that many PAIGC members were from this tribe, which was also scattered north of the Geba River.

There were also a good many Balantas in the Portuguese army. As a people they enjoyed life and showed it. When they threw a party it went on hard, sometimes for more than a day.

The Balantas had some peculiar customs. Every man, woman and child in the community were animists. They worshiped Ira, their god of fate.

Essentially, the nucleus of their belief was that worn old maxim: what will be, will be; it was Ira that decided which way the cookie crumbled. It was up to the individual to appease his god in his own way in his or her day-to-day considerations and this was done by making regular offerings of rice or palm wine in a succession of tiny shrines in every Balanta *tabanca*.

It was interesting to observe that the authorities – the majority Roman Catholic – rarely attempted to tamper with these tenets. Since most indigenous ritual fringed on voodoo or black magic – called ju ju throughout much of West Africa, with rites conducted by the local Balanta witchdoctor who charges a small fee for his services – it had long been evident that there were Balantas among the slaves who were shipped westwards from Africa two or three centuries ago. It is to be expected therefore that some of the customs observed in Haiti, Jamaica and elsewhere in the Caribbean and Brazil, suggested Balanta overtones, even today.

Full-scale Balanta ceremonies are held at all stages, from birth, early childhood up to puberty and the circumcision stage. Boys as well as girls were circumcised at a certain age, usually about seven or eight, and that tradition continues.

The operation on young boys is simple enough and is usually performed by the resident medicine man with the help of a piece of broken glass, a razor blade or a jagged jam tin lid. It becomes a lot more complicated with the girls.

The procedure – today the subject of a United Nations campaign to eradicate practices that are universally regarded as both inhuman and nefarious practice (except in much of primitive Africa) – is to 'surgically' remove the clitoris, almost always without an anaesthetic. In later life this is supposed to preclude coitus during intercourse which, Balanta men believe, results in their women remaining more faithful to them than would otherwise be the case.

It's all nonsense, of course. It was curious that the Portuguese in their part of Guinea were divided as to its purpose. There had been debates about the debilitating effects such

A Portuguese soldier gives instruction on the handling of weapons. As with the army, the rifle was the standard G-3, manufactured in Portugal under licence from Heckler and Koch by Fabrica de Braço de Prata as the FMP m/961. (Author's photo)

abuse would have in later life, for the long-term effects as we now know, are serious. In Nigeria's Calabar area, the suicide rate among those who have had a clitoridectomy have been the highest in the nation for a while now.

For the rest of it, the Balanta community appeared to live and work willingly enough under government control. At Tite they were administered by a rather obese, self-important district commissioner who ran local affairs from his office in the base. He struck me as distinctly pachydermic, in both senses.

He, in turn, was aided by tribal leaders, most of whom were based on the nearby *aldeamentos* or *tabancas,* the former being the bringing together of rural communities under one command. The idea was to avoid the guerrillas enjoying the support of unprotected communities in the bush.

Tite had formerly been a regional capital and was still an important agricultural area with rice paddies stretching away in all directions. Coming in from Bissau by air, we spotted paddies just about everywhere.

I should have arrived the week before, I was told. The previous weekend had been the annual crop festival known locally as the *Quesunde,* the most important of all Balanta feasts. Because of the war there had been no *Quesunde* for seven years and the Colonel was proud that he'd been able to create a small chink in the enemy's grip.

It hadn't been all one-sided. PAIGC command in the area had served notice on tribal elders that they would sanction no festivities while the Portuguese ruled. Countering this move, General Spínola, the supreme commander in Bissau took the initiative and ordered Tite and other encampments to go ahead anyway. Consequently, the first *Quesunde* festival for a long time went off like a charm.

A lot of it had to do with the annual crop that had been the best for some years and also that things seemed to be improving all round, even the outcome of the war. Consequently, the message came through that there was no time like the present for a little frivolity. The guerrillas retaliated by warning that anyone taking part in the festival would be killed.

The feast went ahead in any event, during the full moon phase. Something like 15,000 Balanta men and women kicked up their heels for three days and nights and significantly, the colonel said, there were no insurgent antics.

Immediately afterwards, during my visit to the camp they hit Tite. That was the attack I'd experienced.

The onslaught graphically illustrated a remark made to me by one of the officers at Tite, Major Art Valente. He spoke excellent English and served on and off as an interpreter for much of my stay in a region which stretched from the Atlantic to Fulacunda and Buba further east.

For every action made by the Portuguese, he said, the enemy reacted. If Spínola endorsed a fiesta, PAIGC demonstrated its disapproval by hurling shells at the camp. If Spínola happened to visit a region outside the capital, the guerrillas would retaliate, if only to make it known that they disapproved and were still active militarily.

Spínola did, in fact, visit Tite while I was in the country. It was the last event I covered before returning to Lisbon; in the presence of thousands of local tribesmen, with the general handing out certificates and medals to local civic dignitaries who had stood fast with Portugal during difficult times. The guerrilla ambush in which Bacar was killed followed shortly afterwards.

'It's really a point of honour as far as those bastards are concerned; they counter our every move,' Major Valente explained.

'And if they haven't the manpower available just then, they'll send for reinforcements and do it later.'

PAIGC attempts to stymie events at Tite reflected only one aspect of the kind of clandestine operations conducted by insurgent forces in this Portuguese colony. At the same time, it barely concealed the more salient characteristics of guerrilla strategy: that apart from the military effort, there were also economic and political considerations that involved a huge measure of intimidation of the locals.

If someone was believed to be colluding with the government, at whatever level – attending a government clinic, visiting a relative in a military camp or perhaps paying a government tax – a brief Comintern-type show trial would be held in the village and that person would be executed. Kafka would have immediately recognised the pattern had he been able to visit the place.

Unarmed civilians had long been a focus of PAIGC attrition. So had public services, lines of communication, transport, commerce, industry and agriculture – the warp and woof of everyday life in Portuguese Guinea and, to a lesser extent, in Angola and Mozambique.

Such operations as the rebels conducted against the hated colonials were directed – it was repeatedly claimed in their communiqués – to attain greater freedom of action with regard to the real objective – the destruction of the fabric of the nation.

By then these same arguments were being bandied about in other guerrilla struggles in South East Asia, Indonesia, Tanzania, and later in southern Africa, almost as if they had emanated from a single source, which they probably had, though clearly, Beijing by then had almost as much influence in some of these Third World conflicts as Moscow.

The guerrilla strategy in Portuguese Guinea was neither offensive nor defensive: it was principally evasive.

For example in areas where government control was relatively weak, the insurgents would go onto the offensive. But that rarely happened. It was more a case of seeking out a soft underbelly, which wasn't difficult in a country so grossly undeveloped.

Elsewhere, evasion remained the keynote of PAIGC military strategy.

16

Jungle Patrol in Portuguese Guinea

... by 1966, Guinea already had 18 militia companies, and the authorities were requesting funds to create more, although still acknowledging the risks involved in having to deal with a volume of people armed, equipped and trained ...

João Paulo Borges Coelho:

African Troops in the Portuguese Colonial Army, 1961-1974:
Angola, Guinea-Bissau and Mozambique; Eduardo Mondlane University, Maputo.

The patrol on which I was to go with Bacar and his men would take me close to the proposed camp site at Bissassema (not to be confused with Bissau's Bissalanca Airport), which was actually an extension of Tite's operational area. We would circle the zone and hope to achieve a contact, which is basically what counter-insurgency is about.

Also, we'd been told in the final briefing that ambushes would be set as and when necessary. Bacar would be guided by his local trackers or scouts who accompanied every patrol, mostly Balanta natives from an area immediately around Tite.

I was warned by Lieutenant Jimenez that we'd be out for two days, possibly three; his men were fit and this was what they did; they'd consequently be moving fast. Earlier he'd quizzed me about my ability to keep up because the schedule he'd planned was unrelenting. He cautioned too, that this was a serious business: our adversaries were equally tough and fit, perhaps even more so because they didn't have the comfort of a local base to return to once they'd 'walked their beat'.

We'd rest possibly once every four hours he reckoned, but once on track, it was all systems go for as long as it took. Also, we'd sleep in the wild and haul our food with us.

'If things start to happen and it looks promising, we're going to go for it, even if it takes an extra day or two.' Then he posed the obvious: did I still want to go?

I nodded, well aware that he didn't need a 'passenger', which was when he said something about bringing in a chopper to haul me out of the bush if things got really bad or if I was hurt ...

I told him not to worry: I was more than eager and had been doing my 400 metres in the pool each day in recent months. Still, he was worried and as a concession, I'd be allowed two additional litre cans of water as opposed to the single water bottle issued to the rest of the squad. They'd be refilled from streams along the way, which, for me, meant taking along a supply of water-purifying tablets. The rest of the group had been drinking unfiltered water all their lives and each time I filled my bottles and popped the pills the procedure was viewed with quiet amusement by the rest of the team. Give them their due, they never said a word.

It was clear that I faced a stiff challenge. Because of the heat, I was going through two pints of water before breakfast. It was worse in the jungle where conditions could be stifling. I'd sometimes find myself dehydrated after only an hour's march. More to the point, this operation would be more testing than anything I'd tackled so far – including a Kilimanjaro climb.

Still, I was young and possibly a little overenthusiastic. And while everything pointed towards the impossible, I wasn't going to let up, especially since I might never get the opportunity again.

Much of the country we'd be passing through would be heavily overgrown terrain, some of it triple-canopied and interspersed by swampland or rice paddies. While there were paths galore, we'd avoid them if possible because of mines. Since I'd managed under similar conditions in Biafra. Angola and Mozambique, I felt confident.

Each member of the 30-man patrol was handed his rations the evening before we left. This so-called rat-pack[1] consisted of a large box that weighed perhaps two kilos and contained a tin of sardines, two small cans of sausages, chocolate milk in a carton together with a number of tubes containing a fruit concentrate, marmalade and butter. Bread was issued separately, just before we pulled out, which was when each man was handed two loaves, according to the camp doctor, 'more than enough for the time you'll be out'.

The rations were expected to last a soldier two days. The package was standard issue and used throughout Portugal's African wars.

Saturday morning – the day we were scheduled to depart – came and went without the unit pulling out. It was a bind, but we'd have to hold over for another 24 hours, the colonel explained. A patrol already out in the bush had made a tenuous contact with something and was in an encircling move. Since there was the possibility of an ambush later, some of the squad were made ready for a heli-airlift: they'd be deployed in a stop-gap role.

The unit already out there was having a particularly hard time. They'd been moving at the double for many hours at a stretch and their food had run out, but the colonel said his men were accustomed to hardship. 'This is how we normally operate, the good with the bad,' were his words.

We left the camp in a long file before dawn on Sunday morning.

Tite lay silent and unprovoked against a dark jungle screen that crept up on all sides. Occasionally a figure moved in the darkness as we passed and once or twice we could hear the guards as they shuffled at their posts. Nothing was clearly visible for the moon had long since faded.

Bacar took point from the start. He said little, except that I should stay near Lieutenant Jimenez who, for the first leg, would be my guide or more appropriately, my mentor. In the end, young Jimenez was with me for the entire patrol; it was manifest that I was his responsibility.

The two of us pulled aside to let the column pass and took up our positions towards

Prominent African dignitaries gathered at an official function on the outskirts of Bissau to hear General Spínola's latest pronouncements. Many of these elders have been decorated for their loyalty by Lisbon. After independence, the guerrillas who came to power murdered everyone who had ties, or even suspected of having links to the old order (Author's photo)

the rear. Tough, disciplined men shuffled past, their austere faces unsmiling, more because they were still heavy with sleep than because of what lay ahead. Only Tomaz, a young junior officer barely out of his teens could manage any humour at this ungodly hour; the hulking youngster loped past as if he were off to Sunday school.

'Hi,' he croaked cheerfully with a flash of white teeth. I don't know how he did it because he'd led the liquor stakes in the mess the night before. Tomaz patted his kit bag before hurrying forward with the rest:

'I'll have something for you here later,' he grinned. 'I've got a small *garrafa* of wine for our supper ... '

The early morning was cool, but because of the humidity, it started to get uncomfortable within 10 or 15 minutes of leaving base.

The men in the patrol carried a strange assortment of weapons. Of the 30-odd black soldiers – I was the only white among them – more than half were armed with a new weapon that I'd not previously spotted in any of Portugal's wars in Africa. This was a rifle grenade about 25 centimetres long and which protruded from the tips of their rifle barrels. Its business end was oblong and distended around the middle, like a badly swollen finger that had been caught in a door.

It was deadly, I was assured by Jimenez. Known as the Instalaza, it was of Spanish design and manufacture and had an effective range of about 400 metres. The anti-tank version could knock out an APC or an armoured car, but in Portuguese Guinea it was used mainly in an anti-personnel role.

The colonel had explained earlier that the Instalaza was a small weapon which gave the infantryman a bit of muscle. If the unit came under attack, a dozen men using this kind of retaliation would be enough 'to send the enemy scurrying', he reckoned. They'd had remarkable success so far, he stated. Not only was it handier than the bulkier Chinese-supplied RPG-2 rocket in everyday use by the insurgents, but it was lighter and more portable.

Another piece of hardware in our ranks was a recoilless rifle adaptation which had been designed and built by Portuguese engineers around the 37mm Matra aircraft rocket. Special firing tubes with dozens of ventilation holes had been built to make an improvised bazooka. Its firing pin was activated by a small portable battery fixed to the barrel, which made it look like an elongated kitchen utensil rather than a sophisticated device of war. The warhead was French and like the Instalaza, packed an even more destructive AP punch.

Each 'operator' in the squad who carried the device had about a dozen rockets that he hauled about in special sleeves slung about his body. The two men on either side of him shared the load and carried some of the warheads. The downside was that if any of these projectiles took a hit, there would be quite a few more hurt among those nearest the initial casualty.

There were three mortars included in our patrol, one each fore and aft and another towards the middle of the column where I eventually marched. Again, the two soldiers on either side of the tube had more of these bombs strapped to their belts which would sway to and fro. If not covered in swabs of sacking, the mortars would sometimes connect loudly with protruding bits of metal or their rifle butts.

Each member of the patrol was armed with two or three grenades, like GIs fighting elsewhere, customarily suspended from their uniform lapels or protruding from their top pockets. Grenade belts were provided, but the men preferred it this way. It made for easier access in an emergency, one of them told me.

It took about an hour for the dawn to clear. By then we were well away from the camp, moving west at a steady pace. We would reach a position well to the south of Bissassema and then turn north, Bacar had explained before we departed. After that, he'd told his troops in the pre-departure briefing, we'd double back on our tracks again.

Only when the first rays of the sun lifted over the horizon did the troops perk up a little: they had been silent until then. Light-hearted banter was tossed about in desultory Portuguese undertones and it didn't amuse their captain: the order had been strict silence all the way.

They kept at it while still in open country, moving from one rice paddy to another, but went quiet as soon as the first stretch of jungle loomed up. This, Jimenez whispered, was

PAIGC country: from here on in we were on our own.

Bacar worked to a plan based on previous experience. Whenever the patrol approached an area where an ambush might be possible, he would detach some of his men and send them forward independently. Some of the heavier stuff would be brought forward to give fire support. Others would go round the flanks.

Two or three times before, Bacar told me, he'd found that an enemy ambush group had withdrawn in the face of this encircling action. In truth, the tactic was only possible in open country where easy movement was possible. In some parts it was impossible to leave the track we were on because we were moving alongside heavy undergrowth on both sides of the bush, which sometimes tended to envelop the squad.

At other times the black commando officer would move his men carefully a kilometre or two down a jungle grove and then quickly double back. Once he deliberately flanked a huge patch of palms and bush, working his troops through an open paddy field, but out of any effective close-quarter contact range.

'We're waiting for them to present themselves,' he told me later when we stopped for a break. 'PAIGC uses the Maoist principle of tactical retreat. They strike only when they're certain of being able to knock us hard; then they pull back. This way we hope to draw them into making contact or perhaps making a mistake,' he reckoned

He called the tactic 'tantalizing' the enemy. In doing this, his men took chances, but everything was pretty well calculated.

Part of the problem facing Bacar and other Portuguese officers in this war was that the enemy rarely stood and fought. They'd hit and run, strike at a camp and melt away to avoid retaliation. It was a system, of course: feint, strike, retreat or play possum in the tall grass or possibly come in from behind.

'The guys are keen, you can see that, but we don't always get the chance to exchange blows, all good classical guerrilla stuff.' Often they preferred to lay mines or booby traps; 'then having caused us some damage, they'll strike while we're waiting for an evacuation.'

At base earlier, I'd been shown a set of PAIGC directives that had been captured. These warned that serious contact with government forces was to be avoided. As one of the Portuguese officers explained, Cabral and his deputies had been trained in the tradition of Mao and Giap: guile, stealth and better to live and fight another day.

We made our first long stop at noon for a meal. Some of the men ate in small groups between the trees while others stood guard out of sight in the jungle beyond. Afterwards the procedure was reversed.

When everyone was done we left, but I noticed immediately that our patrol had noticeably thinned. Following pre-arranged instructions, about a third of our group had disappeared into the jungle and set up an ambush position along the track by which we'd arrived.

'We're under no misconceptions that the enemy doesn't know we're here … they've been conscious of that from the start … their own intelligence system and it works well,' was Bacar's laconic comment when I asked him. Though he spoke no English, his translator was

Casualties are tended by medics after an ambush in the Guinean countryside. Helicopters would have been brought in to airlift the worst of the wounded to hospital in Bissau (Photo *Revista da Armada*)

an educated man and managed easily with the sometimes-difficult diction.

Bacar explained that the idea was to move from one area to another, sometimes across open country and paddies. More often than not the guerrillas were able to observe the column as it moved. 'Once we're actually spotted, they'll try to keep tabs on everything we do, day, night, every minute ... if they can manage that and, of course, if our movements allow it.

'When they are about, they're likely to do something. Then we act. That's why I have left some of the men behind. If they come in – slam! We'd have them, and of course we can follow up because we're in radio contact. Or we call in air support, which they don't have. That's it, in theory, anyway,' Jimenez explained.

We'd taken a short break about mid-morning and Bacar had sent off some of his men to check a booby-trap position. We'd been moving at a fast pace all the while and must have covered at least 15 kilometres by then, over some fairly difficult terrain that included paddies half-filled with water.

There had been a few aircraft passing across our line of vision for some of the time, followed by concentrated strafing and rocketing towards the south-east. The targets, towards Buba and Fulacunda, were visual, Bacar reckoned...another patrol must have had a contact. Or been ambushed.

Though our column must have been clearly visible by Portuguese Air Force pilots operating in the area, we were secure: our position was constantly being relayed to base and, in turn, passed along to Bissau. Prior to emerging from any area that was foliaged, he'd radio in.

During several trips across the country while in Portuguese Guinea, I often spotted patrols out in the bush and at first it amazed me that the operations centre could keep track of so many fragmentary groups in the field. But the tracking systems employed by headquarters were old hat and efficient by then, even if the Portuguese Army and PAIGC guerrillas wore a similar kind of camouflage.

Still, accidents happened. More than once there had been men in the field that came under 'friendly fire'. Usually it was the air force that was responsible and then only because procedures weren't properly followed. But then that, too, is modern-day warfare.

In Bacar's words, the column's radio was the next best thing after his rat-pack. He made contact with Tite each hour on the hour, his radio operator always close on his heels. The man lugged a bulky American-built 'Man-Pak' transmitter which, he said, could reach Bissau if necessary.

There had never been a patrol where he hadn't called for air strikes in the past, especially if he saw a guerrilla group slipping away before his unit was able to close, but it required a reasonable amount of precision strikes on the part of the aviators as his men were never far behind. The fact that a Bacar patrol had yet to be hit by 'friendly fire' spoke volumes for this commando officer's direction, especially since there were times when his men were sometimes perhaps a hundred metres behind the guerrillas while on the chase.

Bacar also liked to keep in ready radio contact with the extremities of his patrol. This could be difficult because the column was sometimes spread out over more than a kilometre. The officers used hand-sets, something that I hadn't seen Lisbon's fighters doing in Mozambique.

'They're handy when the other people are about,' Bacar said, for once stating the obvious.

Thanks to the sets, orders were given quietly and competently, for sound travels far in this humid climate. Instructions were first relayed by radio and then passed on down the line from man to man in whispers.

There was rarely need for more.

It was noon before we made contact with the patrol that was waiting to be relieved.

We met up with them as planned along an overgrown ridge of high ground that I'd observed from a distance earlier in the day. The feature was notable, because Portuguese Guinea must be the flattest country in Africa, without a single mountain, or anything even resembling one.

Bacar had deliberately avoided taking the shortest route on the off-chance that guerrillas lurking nearby might have been aware of the other group and have possibly set an ambush.

The patrol which had preceded us into the jungle was led by two native Guineans, Lieutenant Alphonse and a young *Alferes*, like Tomaz, who called himself Manuel. Both men were dressed like we were, with one curious difference: they wore gleaming black monkey-skins over their heads, like large shiny bouffants that made them look more animal than man when glimpsed from a distance.

The element of camouflage was obvious, but it must have been hell wearing those contraptions in that heat. For these officers there was more to the skin headdresses. Monkey skins have significant tribal overtones in Africa, part of it sexual because simians are prolific breeders and therefore potent. After the lion and the leopard, the skins of certain anthropoids hold a distinct mystical charm for some coastal tribes in West Africa. There are those who believe they're the re-incarnation of departed souls and are to be accorded reverence whenever encountered in the forest. In certain regions of the Niger Delta, Liberia and Congo, monkeys are only killed for food, or to provide the chief or an Oba with a badge of office. In Guinea the ritual has similar connotations.

The troops with whom we made contact, were bushed. They had been out on their own for three days and were tired and hungry. They'd not had a single contact, though it'd been close. Lieutenant Alphonse didn't elaborate. Because their stay had been longer than expected, Bacar had brought along a few supplies which was handed over with little ceremony.

Like our own unit there were no white faces among them and they were surprised to see mine.

Words of parting were cursory. A raised hand, hardly a salute. Then they were gone, very much as we'd arrived, melting silently away into the jungle. They were keen to get back to their families, Bacar said.

We passed several villages during the course of our trek. A few were abandoned, though there were those that thrived and were typical of *tabancas* throughout West Africa. The majority would comprise a medley of children, goats, chickens and a skeletal hound or three. Occasionally there would be a monkey or a parrot at the end of a rope.

There'd always be women pounding corn or millet somewhere near the verge of the settlement, usually within sight of the roadway or track. If there was trouble, they'd be the first to sound a warning. The villages were domestic and fairly secure, reflecting a deceptive laid-back approach which had settled on this land wracked by almost a decade of war.

Jimenez and Tomaz took few chances in some of the remoter areas where loyalties followed the traditional jungle law of not having to take a chance if you don't have to. Whenever we approached a *tabanca* that might not be familiar to the men, they'd go ahead after leaving a detachment on the fringe for cover. It was the same pattern as before, since there had been PAIGC reception committees in the past.

Only after friendly contact had been made did we pass through. It was no secret that the enemy covered this ground as often as the Portuguese did – sometimes many times more – because their secure bases lay across the border. The civilians that we encountered had long ago accepted the philosophy of extending a hand of friendship to all newcomers,

Portuguese troops on patrol in thick bush country. (Photo *Revista da Armada*)

which was fundamental if you were going to survive in a region where political differences could be terminal.

Once we stopped at a *tabanca* fairly near Bissassema. It was late afternoon and we would eat there before going on for the night. The village was evidently used by both forces as they welcomed us with a courtesy that was friendly but guarded. Bacar accepted the gesture in good faith. It was an uneasy symbiosis but a pragmatic one in the fluctuating fortunes of war.

These people, Bacar felt, would eventually choose for themselves on which side their allegiance lay. If things continued as they were, he said, it wouldn't be with the PAIGC.

The patrol mixed easily with the local tribesmen and their families. They were accepted with amity; some even shared their food as they probably would with the next PAIGC patrol that might arrive out of the dark. Our intrusion lasted barely an hour; Bacar handed over some money for the effort and we went on our way.

Apart from trying to improve relations between the government in Bissau and the ordinary folk 'out there', Bacar always insisted that his men always be cordial with the peasants. Any kind of intimidation or heavy-handedness was unacceptable. So was fraternizing with the women, which he always held, might be somebody else's wife. Now and again some intimacy would take place, as it always does in Africa, though in this regard

Bacar, faithful to the Quran to the end, followed stringent personal dictates.

On how the enemy operated, the black commando officer was specific. The PAIGC, he said, followed Mao and Giap's theory on how relations with the civilians were conducted. A rebel directorate had declared early in the war that PAIGC forces were to be concerned with establishing and maintaining good relations with all country people, whatever their political affiliations. PAIGC policy was based solely upon the identity of their aims, or so it was declared.

The people, said Amilcar Cabral, the rebel leader who had a penchant for echoing the words of his hero, the great Chinese leader, 'were to the army what water is to fish'. He'd included this maxim in the PAIGC code of honour, which, like the Viet Cong, took the form of an oath.

It declared that 'in contact with the people, each comrade would follow three recommendations: to help the people, to respect the people and to defend the people'.

'You see we have to fight fire with fire and the terrorist is pretty subtle at times,' the black Portuguese officer remarked as we marched away through a large grove a short distance from the last *tabanca*.

The village stop was the first time I'd been able to refill my water bottle that day. The locals provided fresh water from a pump set in the ground; as much as we liked, they said. The troops could drink it as it came; I filtered mine, an agonizing 30-minute wait since I'd finished my original two cans a while before.

We set our ambush for the night shortly after leaving the *tabanca*. Bacar marched us due south alongside, but not on a well-used track for about an hour. He then abruptly left the route and doubled back towards the village we'd just left, keeping to the cover of the bush. If the enemy was to follow us to the settlement that night, we'd have them.

We could hear village activity in the distance as we approached again on our turnabout. They too were preparing to settle in for the night. There was music, laughter, conversation. Someone banged a gong in the distance, another called on a bugle-like instrument which I had seen earlier and which was fashioned from the horn of an antelope; a single discordant note which carried deep into the dark. I was to hear it afterwards in Bissau, a sound that couldn't be mistaken for anything else once you'd heard it the first time.

There were more noises somewhere to the left of us. In the far distance the women of another *tabanca* were singing. This was Africa talking – melodious and harmonious in some regards, guttural and bizarre in others, but generally not unpleasing. These were simple, human sounds signifying age-old settlement in the bush.

It's the same primitive discordant symphony one sometimes hears in Kenya, or Zululand, or Togo or even the Congo in places. They speak different languages, all these people, but on hearing sounds dissipated by distance and the irregular countryside, we could have been in any one of them.

Bacar carefully spread his men out a short distance off the track. We were about a kilometre from the village, with the troops on a small rise and roughly equidistant from each other. Riflemen were spaced between some of the others handling heavier weapons. Behind them were the rocket carriers and bazookas. At the two extremes the light machine-gunners were positioned, their muzzles trained in a wide arc that covered all the points of the compass.

Behind, he placed his mortars. They were positioned in a clearing just beyond some low trees over which they would fire if the need arose. The men worked out the elevation of the mortars while Bacar directed elsewhere. But they also needed their backs covered and several pairs were detached from the main group for that purpose.

It was an ideal site for an ambush. To cover an eventuality, the Fula officer sent two more men into the jungle behind us to cover the distant rear. They disappeared into the bush where they would lie up secreted for the rest of the night with only a small hand-held radio to make contact with their commander if things started to happen.

Bacar didn't have to explain the need for silence. It was to be absolute, he'd told me earlier and applied as much to me as to them.

No talking! No smoking either ...

The men settled down silently in groups, first the one lot, then another, leaving about a third of the patrol awake at any one time while some of the officers moved silently between their charges.

Only Allah could help the man who snored, never mind anybody caught sleeping on his watch. Bacar had his own brand of punishment for this offence and it was ruthless.

It was a long wait till dawn. Ants, mosquitoes as big as houseflies and other jungle insects were resolute, with the crawlies particularly fierce, especially since we lay on bare ground with no netting. There was no question of using any kind of lotion or cream: the enemy would smell it before the mosquitoes did.

Nobody thought of spiders or snakes, or even scorpions – of which I'd been told there were a lot – or if they did, they kept it to themselves, as I did. They were there, to be sure, but it's different when you're with a large group of men; it's usually the other man who will get bit ...

Earlier in the evening, before everybody had properly settled in, Tomaz had approached and produced his elixir and it was like magic. We each drank a little wine that night and had a couple more sips after it got light in the morning. I'd never handled wine for breakfast before and it made a change, especially since I'd hardly slept. It was a good substitute for coffee under the circumstances but I'd have preferred water. Again, mine was long gone.

The night was uneventful and I found it difficult to stay alert, even though we had the moon for company for more than half the time. Occasionally there'd be a rustle in the night to our left or the right and one of the men would start. There were few other distractions.

All weapons were already cocked; any metallic click can be heard over hundreds of metres by a trained ear and it was an effective measure. Bacar had imparted his basics well.

Shortly before midnight we heard a muffled explosion somewhere not too far to the south. It came as a dull thump in the dark and Jimenez who was dozing alongside me looked up but said nothing. I knew what was going through his mind. Someone had probably put his foot on a mine somewhere in the bush.

One of ours? Or theirs?

Capitao Bacar's circuitous jungle safari followed a set pattern. The entire route had been detailed between him and the colonel before we left camp and they'd taken a while to settle the route, Bacar's boss wanting the men to go in one direction and Bacar in another. The black officer must have made good tactical sense, because he ended up winning the day.

The route had to be established for two reasons. The first was to advise air force command at Bissalanca so the men wouldn't be rocketed while out patrolling. Second came mines – Portuguese landmines this time that had been set along some of the routes we would traverse. Quite a few tracks had already been mined or booby-trapped by government forces.

Two could play at that game, Bacar reasoned when he explained. To avoid injury to the civilian population, tribal leaders were ordered to keep their people within the bounds of the territory they normally frequented. They knew the paths that led to the watering points or to the next village and so did his people. Beyond those limits their safety could not be guaranteed was the warning. Obviously, the Portuguese Army also had to observe these strictures. Shortly before I arrived at Tite a soldier had his leg blown off trying to return to camp along a route which had been mined by Colonel Lopes' men. It was a vicious cycle.

We left our positions in the jungle at the first hint of a false dawn. Like an effulgent curtain, the glow crept slowly over our position, diffused and evocatively beautiful. One moment Africa is jet black and then, within minutes, trees suddenly appear 100 metres away, as if through a London smog. The men were up and on the move even before many of the birds had stirred. Like phantoms we slipped silently onto the track and were on our way again.

It came as a surprise to us all to learn a little later that morning that a PAIGC unit had set up an ambush only a short march from us on the same track. But Bacar said nothing to me, nor did Jimenez; not then, anyway. Apparently, shortly after we'd left our ambush site, our trackers found the evidence.

The unit had been large – two bi-groups – about 60 men in all, the scouts had estimated. Had contact been made it would have been tough. Like Bacar they'd used an L-shaped position from which to attack. It might have been the luck of the draw that we stopped where we did for the night. Or perhaps it was the PAIGC on whom the lady smiled, for this was the same bunch of guerrillas that ambushed Bacar seven days later.

I was to return to this country quite a few times in the decades that followed. Twice I went in to make television documentaries of the country whose representatives now sit at the United Nations with the name tag Guiné-Bissau before them. It's been an extremely difficult transition because the country has teetered from one violent insurrection to another with tens of thousands of people killed.

The lovely old town of Bissau is a macabre shadow of what it was when Lisbon was still around, its buildings battered or imploded as factions battled in the downtown areas for control. Many of the old historical structures have been purposefully defaced, some five centuries old.

I wandered about the interior with my film crew for weeks, though not to Tite. That, some of the locals told me, had become one of the biggest 'killing fields' in Africa, with the rebels initially ranged against the same black troops who had once fought for the Portuguese until they were all wiped out.

One source said that in the end, anybody even vaguely linked to *Comandos Africanos* had been slaughtered. So were their families. There was no word of young officers like Tomaz or Jimenez or even the Monkey-skin-clad Lieutenants Alphonse or the rest. Memories die hard in Africa.

I also went north to Bigene, where the early Portuguese navigators landed on this stretch of coast six centuries before

The old fort still stands, today a repository of some of the old colonial relics that couldn't find a home elsewhere. Many of the bronze statues were lodged there, behind two-metre-thick granite walls, including one of Vasco da Gama, the first man to round the Cape on the sea route to India. By now, with metal prices hitting the rafters, they've probably been melted down and sold as scrap.

Half a kilometre away, along the narrow estuary that leads into the sparse interior, there was one of the original gunboats used by the Portuguese Navy in the closing stages of this Colonial war. Lying high and dry on the beach, the craft had been stripped, its aluminium plates long ago oxidised all the way through in places.

They were proud little fighting craft in their day and had been handed over intact to the new regime. Within a year, they'd been beached and left for scrap. Their engines were sold to a passing Chinese fishing boat.

17

Portuguese Guinea-Bissau's North and East

If you concentrate exclusively on victory, with no thought for the after effect, you may be too exhausted to profit by the peace, while it is almost certain that the peace will be a bad one containing the germs of another war. This is a lesson supported by abundant experience.

> Sir Basil Liddell Hart's famous prediction about hostilities in Europe. Made in 1941, it was equally relevant to Lisbon's former colonies after they achieved sovereignty in the mid- 1970s: all three experienced lengthy civil wars or insurrections.

The rewards of guerrilla warfare can be problematic. For two days I'd trundled about the southern jungles of Portuguese Guinea with João Bacar's commandos looking for insurgents and found nothing. A week later I was taken on a waterborne patrol in a Zodiac by a squad of marines and came under fire.

We'd been on the water perhaps ten minutes when a fusillade of shots echoed across the water. The guerrillas kept firing until we were out of sight and our little convoy of rubber ducks were ordered to stop around the next bend. The marines – there were three of them armed with a G-3 and two LMGs –retaliated, as did the men on the two boats that followed and while the exchange must have lasted a minute or two, both sides scored a lemon.

For good measure a soldier on one of the boats had even fired his bazooka. None of us could be sure what he was aiming at because the bush along the river bank was about as dense as it gets in this region. In places it stretched out into the water for metres. Clearly, it had been as difficult for us as for our attackers.

Our inflatables had been moving at speed when the shooting started. Instead of slowing down to allow for better accuracy, all three boats gunned their engines towards the opposite bank, creating a three-foot-wide foaming wake behind us. Meanwhile, the men furiously retaliated.

Tenente (Lieutenant) Tony Verela, commander of the marine camp of naval *Fuzileiros* at Bigene in the north – a region where the war was considered at its most intense – earlier told us that a good speed on water was our best defence. After a short while the lieutenant gave the signal for the boats to move on.

We would never know whether any damage had been inflicted. We'd suffered no casualties and nor, in all probability, had they.

The man at the prow checked his weapon, tried the action a few times, inserted a new belt of ammunition which hung draped, macho-style over his left shoulder and took his place again as we sped westwards.

Verela said his men were often fired upon, which was why they travelled in convoys of three, sometimes four boats at a time. Because they liked to move at speed, often in excess of 60 or 70 kph they were rarely hit, though obviously not for want of trying.

While the Zodiacs were regarded as easy meat by the enemy, they rarely fired on the larger navy gunboats which patrolled the upper reaches of the Cacheu River. These former US Navy river patrol craft, similar to those used in Vietnam, were armed with batteries of 40 mm rockets which intimidated even those using them.

Verela was sceptical about the firepower of the PAIGC. He had operated on the river for almost two years and although he'd made contact with the enemy often enough, only two of his complement of 200 marines had been killed while working the river.

Land operations were different; some of his men had become casualties in ambushes and from landmines. Still, he averred, Cabral's men had been given many opportunities but they rarely took the initiative. First shots, he reckoned, would usually be reasonably accurate: the enemy had time to aim. After that, their placement became erratic, almost as if the guerrillas closed their eyes and fired at random. And it was almost always on full auto.

Had his assailants been anything like the Vietcong, he suggested, Portuguese losses would have been much more severe.

'Some of these people were fairly well-trained ... they would probably do OK in any man's army ... but the majority seem to lack that additional something that turns a successful attack into a rout.' His men were using rubber ducks, he stressed: 'if I was at the other end, I'd aim at the boats and not the men ... at some stage or other I'd have them helpless in the water ... '

The lieutenant was the first to admit that the Portuguese troops were sometimes as lackadaisical as the enemy. For that reason, he reckoned, the opposing forces should have done a lot better.

He continued: 'If you consider that this war has been on the go for 10 years [by the time I got there] and that during that time the PAIGC has never once succeeded in overrunning one of our camps, you might understand what I'm getting at. Often some of the outlying positions are manned by perhaps as few as eight or a dozen men. There have been times when they sometimes come at us in their hundreds.

'We have abandoned camps of our own volition – Beli, in the east Cacocoa, and Sanchonha – all camps that we've considered too remote or impractical to effectively maintain. But when we move on, it's a planned, predetermined effort. We are never driven out...'

Verela challenged the PAIGC to name a single Portuguese position overrun by their guerrillas.

There were four marine bases in Portuguese Guinea similar to the one at Bigene. Another was at Buba on the river of the same name near Tite, with two more along the coast. Most of their operations were at night, with priority given to intercepting enemy pirogues that tried to cross waterways with supplies and men for the war zones.

Of all the men under his command, Verela explained, about 60 were operational at any one time, some on the river and more on land patrols in adjacent areas. His men were all professional soldiers, trained almost to Special Forces level and obviously a lot more competent than the average foot soldier from Europe. Each was skilled in counter-insurgency warfare and in the broader context, he liked to consider them Metropolitan versions of Bacar's black commandos.

Certainly, he commented, his unit had been every bit as successful as the *Comandos Africanos*. Over the past four months, only one of his men had been wounded, compared with 10 insurgents killed in confirmed body counts.

'There were definitely more, but we didn't find the bodies because we don't always go into the bush and search, he said. In any event, it's enemy policy that the wounded and dead be taken from the scene of a battle to avoid giving our people any kind of satisfaction. During this period there had also been two guerrillas captured, as well as a bunch of PAIGC sympathisers, mostly civilians who had been ferrying war supplies. All had come from Senegal.

Lieutenant Verela operated a basic search-and-destroy system on his river patrols. The boats went out in pairs in the late afternoon and towards sunset in the broader reaches, the engines would be cut and the boats either rowed or allowed to drift out on the current. The region was tidal for about 80 kilometres inland and the men made liberal use of the ebb and flow.

It was after dark that most of the material for the guerrilla war effort was usually ferried across the water. They would lie in wait in their pirogues in a thicket until a river patrol had passed and then they'd scoot across and hope that they were not spotted. They would sometimes do the same during daylight hours, but then there was always the possibility of being spotted from the air.

Lieutenant Verela was a veritable fount of anecdotes about the war, almost as if he'd been collecting them for a book of his own. Some were humorous, other quite tragic. He made no secret of the fact that he abhorred the war. Once after a few drinks, he admitted that it was all pretty pointless, though he refused to explain why.

Verela told me of an interesting anecdote involving General António de Spínola. He said it provided an insight to the man's character, which was invariably authoritarian and quite often inordinately severe on his own men. In contrast, he could be quite avuncular where the enemy was concerned, especially when personal contact was made.

Verela was in one of two helicopters that were taking the general and his party on a tour of the southern regions. While on these flights the pilots would try to spot for anything related to guerrilla activity. They were crossing some paddies just north of the Corubal River when they saw a man running hard along one of the dry irrigation canals; his light-coloured camouflage uniform was distinctly Czech and the man had the usual AK with its distinctive red Bakelite butt.

To the surprise of staff officers accompanying him, the general ordered his helicopter to put down near the man, who, by then had taken refuge under an overhang. The helicopter duly landed and everybody sprang towards the insurgent who was taken into custody without a shot having been fired.

With the other chopper hovering overhead the general ordered that the man be brought before him. At gunpoint, the guerrilla was marched forward to the general, who by now had also disembarked.

In front of this astonished little gathering of soldiers and airmen, the black guerrilla was asked a few questions and then sternly upbraided. The general told the guerrilla to get his act together and not make a fool of himself by fighting to usurp law and order. Instead, he should try to do something constructive with his life. He addressed the guerrilla like a schoolmaster who had caught a student stealing fruit.

The terrified captive could only nod. When he'd finished, the general asked the insurgent whether he'd understood anything of what he'd said. The insurgent replied in good Portuguese that he had. He then actually thanked General de Spínola for his advice.

'Well then,' said Spínola, 'get yourself out of that circus dress and report to the nearest *aldeamentos*. You have my word that you will be well received.' With that the general climbed back into his helicopter and the party flew off.

Later that day it was Verela who told de Spínola that a radio message had been received from Bafata, headquarters of the Central region where the contact had been made that a young rebel soldier had presented himself to a camp in the south.

Like other guerrillas who defected, he was first interrogated and then allowed to return to a village of his choice, this time within the ambit of Portuguese authority.

Life at the marine barracks at Bigene might have been boring, but it was not unpleasant. The river regions were cooler than the dry interior of the north and east.

The encroaching sea and surrounding jungles provided their own diversions, including fishing for marlin and shark or perhaps duck hunting during off-hour periods. The record marlin taken at the base, a day's river journey inland from the Atlantic, was landed the previous month. It was landed by a young medical orderly, who had spent most of his savings at the only sports shop in Bissau, and tipped the scales at over 300 kilos. It took him two hours to land and during this time his line had only snagged once among the mangroves. He was assisted by one of the Zodiacs to untangle it. Portuguese military bases up and down the river ate fish for days afterwards.

Barely a day went by without one of the boats heading back to base without something for the pot. The day after our little escapade, I went out again and three ducks were shot about a kilometre from the base, picked off on the wing with army service rifles: the marines were all fairly crack shots.

Portuguese troops put members of a local voluntary militia through
their paces in a training session. (Author's photo)

Occasionally they bagged a crocodile for no other purpose than to rid the region of
these pests that had claimed many lives in the past, particularly among local children who
swam in the murky waters.

The Portuguese officer said he was certain some of the victims were taken by sharks,
which were fairly common upstream. These fatalities were usually put down to crocs,
especially since bull sharks were a feature of these tropical waters and this species is an
acknowledged man-eater and in some regions, sometimes ventured hundreds of miles
upstream. That said, the troops were never encouraged to swim in the river.

The mess at the marine base was in an old house that lay half way between the river and
the airstrip. About a dozen officers were billeted there and the atmosphere was casual and
hardly complicated by the rigours of living among their troops, as was the case with so many
other camps in the country.

The walls were decorated by the latest full-colour *Playboy* foldouts and other objects of
interest. On the door of the mess was something I hadn't seen elsewhere in any of Portugal's
African wars: a large poster that laid out the United Nations Declaration of Human Rights.
Point-for-point, it was in Portuguese. A photo of the manacled legs of a black man adorned
its top, a sombre touch as we sipped our beers on the veranda.

'That photo helps to keep things in perspective in this often terrible struggle,' Verela
told me.

Another poster, this time on the drab, dusty wall of one of the small shops at Sare Bacar offered a simple message: *Juntos Venceremos;* 'Together we will win.' It was the government's catchphrase, not the guerrillas.

Below the large inscription, a black hand clasped that of a white. An arid mile away, fringed by the stumps of grey-trunked baobabs and misshapen thorn bushes lay the border with the Republic of Senegal. A new metalled highway ended abruptly at a chain that stretched across the road.

'Beyond is the enemy,' remarked a bald-headed, aquiline-featured Portuguese who had earlier introduced himself as Captain Manuel Medina Matos, also from Lourenco Marques. He was one of the surprising number of Mozambicans I was to meet on the west coast.

Tough and wiry and dressed in a set of faded green cammos which looked like they'd been through all of Portugal's wars, he said there was a brace of enemy machine-guns a few hundred metres into Senegalese territory which ran parallel to the frontier.

His intelligence network had informed him of the positions. They had also disclosed that the guns were placed in a defensive deployment 'just in case our troops decide to wander too far into Senghor's country'. He was referring to Léopold Senghor, the much-revered president of the country to the north.

Meantime, I'd barely arrived when the wind arrived in gusts from the south. With a wicked glint in his eye, the captain pulled out a box of matches and set alight a few tufts of grass. He explained that the fire would carry all the way through into Senegal territory and help to clear the bush. It might even force the machine-gunners to evacuate their posts, he suggested with a chuckle.

'We often play this game with each other. When the wind comes the other way, they try and set us on fire. They almost succeeded once. Which was why we cleared the area around the camp for a couple of hundred metres.'

Camp Sare Bacar, about a kilometre from the village, was not like most other military concentrations I visited. It was hexagon-shaped, about 90 metres to a side and with observation posts at three of the points nearest the border.

Not a single tree sheltered the almost 200 men who were based at this desolate spot. Nor was there a blade of grass to poke its way through the loose red soil which seemed to creep in everywhere as the light wind churned our steps into dust. The muck would follow our jeep in thick vermilion layers three metres high. Sare Bacar might have been the loneliest outpost in Europe's most enduring African empire.

Captain Matos explained that he and his men had been there a year and they had another nine months to go. 'Nine more fucking months in this shit hole' were his words.

During their 21-month sojourn at Sare Bacar the officers – but not the men – were allowed to visit Bissau every six months for a few day's break. In a way, he said, the African draftees were the lucky ones. Had these troops not been posted overseas their period of conscription would have been extended by another year. All the same, it must have been an austere existence for those young men from Europe where traditions were centuries old, the family was always on call and social life usually centred on the town *barra*.

The isolation in Guinea hardly helped morale and curiously, conditions were only exacerbated by the monthly PAIGC attack. From the safety of foreign soil, the guerrillas would hurl 122mm rockets and the occasional mortar across the border and one of the upshots would be the arrival of more troops and helicopters and officers from the general staff to inspect the damage.

Even among the officers, some of them accountants and lawyers or engineers, all fresh out of university and thrown together in the farrago of army life, it could only have been extremely difficult at times. Though they had each other for company and most read a lot, there were no diversions apart from going on patrols. And occasionally, tall and quite beautiful Mandingo girls who would amble across the frontier after dark.

What about the mines, I asked. There were plenty laid, one of the officers retorted. He explained that the women knew the drill and which paths to take. When I suggested that if that were so, then so did the enemy, to which there was no comment.

Because there were so few alternatives, many of the young officers and NCOs – more by circumstance than choice – voluntarily honed their skills. Many had become accomplished killers. With time, they had come to understand the bush around them almost as well as their own locally-born scouts.

Some had earned reputations for themselves in the enclave and beyond and quite a few had prices on their heads in Conakry and Dakar. To these men, it was a 'badge of honour. The fact that their efforts were recognised by the PAIGC, was ample achievement and they relished their notoriety.

Even so, it was a dreary, dreadful existence, for the opportunity for actual combat was a rare event. It was that same boredom that prompted so many of these men to volunteer for service in the commandos, Lisbon's crack anti-insurgency units that were always stationed where the fighting was heaviest. Even if they didn't make the grade, they would do the selection course and that in itself was a diversion. At least it took them away from hell holes like Sare Bacar.

One and all, the men thought highly of the *Comandos Africanos*.

They had seen Bacar's men in action a few months previously when his group had been stationed at Farim, to the south, where the authorities were building a road. Speaking about the black fighters, the bald-headed captain maintained that Portugal should be thankful that they were there.

'We have seen them in action,' he said, 'and they can smell a man's tobacco breath at a hundred metres. If they see a footprint in the sand, they can tell us whether it was one of ours or enemy, how long it's been since the person left it and whether he was carrying a load..

'They would follow a group for two days, whistle like birds when there was an alarm and make the bush sounds of a dozen animals along the entire length of the patrol ... they read the language of the jungle like you and I read a newspaper.'

Captain Matos was responsible for an area of roughly 300 square kilometres that stretched for much of the distance along the Senegalese frontier. It wasn't a lot of ground that he had to cover but much of the terrain was flat and featureless and it was easy for the guerrillas simply to walk across the unmarked frontier at night. And if pursued, they could just as easily slip back into Senegal again. Essentially the same situation applied to the other two-thirds of the country that fringed on Sékou Touré's Republic of Guinea.

Apart from the 165-man garrison, commanded by Captain Matos, he had two African civilian militia groups under his command. The men were divided into four combat groups, of which two were out on patrol at any given time. The other two either rested or handled guard duties.

The nature of guerrilla attacks on the camp were both fragmented and diverse. These ranged from anti-personnel mines laid on the main road – or on tracks that might be used by patrols – to 120 mm Chinese rockets and mortars fired from six or eight kilometres away, always well within Senegalese territory.

Matos commented: 'Their aim is putrid ... but then we know that ... they can see the tops of our buildings from five kilometres away in this kind of country and they haven't yet put a shell down our chimney ... if we had a chimney ... and that in a decade of war...'

He reckoned the calibre of the guerrillas in the north were inferior to those of General Nino who operated along the Guinea-Conakry frontier. They were neither as disciplined nor as single-minded. More to the point, he suggested, they hardly ever took the initiative. A close-up attack with bazookas and rifles, for instance, was unknown. Guerrillas operating in the north preferred to fire at long distance or lay booby traps along bush paths in the hope that someone would get their legs blown off.

For all that, he needed to keep his men on their toes because things could change overnight. The local insurgent group might get a more disciplined, more determined commander. In fact, after I'd left, that seemed to have happened because some frontal assaults had taken place on Sare Bacar and there had been some serious casualties. There were also mass attacks on Cameconde, Gadamael, Farim, Bambadinca in the central region and Cuntima, all taking place in the latter half of 1972.

It was the same further west at Cuntima, just south of Faquina, another guerrilla base in Senegal. To me the only difference between the two camps was in the number of vultures flying around Cuntima and the dozens of scraggly bush paths leading into the wilderness in all directions. At least that was the impression I got from the air. Like Sare Bacar, Cuntima lay barely a kilometre from the Senegalese frontier.

Like Tite, this was also Balanta country, though a feature of the place was the presence of local Felupe tribesmen who did not tolerate an insurgent presence.

The Felupe – spread out in villages along the length of the Senegalese border – had been armed by the Portuguese and weren't shy to use their weapons. And if ammunition ran short, they'd revert to their primitive bows and arrows.

Those officers who had contact with groups of Felupe elders reckoned there was good reason for this. There was a real fear among the Felupe that should the authorities lose control, the PAIGC would deprive them of Portuguese medical facilities.

There were many tribal people in southern Senegal who resented the guerrilla presence,

A pair of Portuguese *fuzileiros* – in a marine rubber duck – do a scouting run
at speed along the heavily foliaged Cacheu River. (Author's photo)

because in the past, they too had made liberal use of Lisbon's welfare aid, which included
visits by doctors and free medicines.

I was taken by road from the north to Bafata, the second largest city in Portuguese Guinea,
but in reality, little bigger than a provincial town. The journey quickly became soporific
along a tarred highway that seemed to go on forever. Several times I thought our driver
would nod off, which was why the officer kept prodding him to keep him alert. Eventually
he called a halt and took the wheel himself, which was when I could relax.

Our jeep travelled ahead of a Unimog looking more like an armoury than an escort
vehicle.

The region had once been bitterly contested, my aide told me. But since the road had
been properly surfaced, the enemy seemed to have lost the initiative, mainly because the
guerrillas' main means of inflicting damage – mines – had been eradicated.

Nevertheless, the Portuguese could take no chances, and it was only when we reached
Contubael, about halfway between the border and Bafata, that our escort left us. We
travelled alone into the inchoate dusk.

Bafata was a quiet town situated on a row of hills overlooking the river. It was cleaner
and quieter than Bissau and the climate hardly a fraction as intemperate, although it lay
near the headwaters of the same river that finally wends its way murkily past the capital.

We arrived shortly before dinner, which was held with great ceremony in the officers' mess, a low bungalow near the middle of town. It was to be a special occasion in honour of the visiting journalist, I'd been warned earlier. Which meant still more whisky ...

Later I was taken to a Mandingo ceremony that was being held a short distance out of town, beyond the airstrip. A group of youths and maidens had recently been circumcised and this was to be their 'coming-out' ceremony after having been in isolation, in the Biblical (or Koranic) sense for 40 days. The period obviously had a strong religious significance which went way back in tribal lore.

I sensed that the ritual was every bit as serious as a pontifical mass, although the final night was given over to a frenzy of festivity and palm-wine drinking which, I was told by one of the local doctors who was interested in African traditions and customs, would go on until morning.

We went to the village in one of the army station wagons and it was only after we'd left the lights of Bafata behind us that I realised that not one of the men was armed. The only precaution they took against a possible attack was to remove their shoulder tabs so as not to be recognisable as officers.

A cluster of primitive buildings suddenly loomed up in the dark. We could hear the drums a long way off but there were no lights; only a low smoky fire around which the novitiates danced. There were about two dozen boys and girls and they were all naked and covered in a dull dusty white paint which, in the shadowy light, made them look like so many *pierrots* out of a French pantomime act. Their ages ranged from about eight to 18.

Now that the necessary rituals had been performed, the medical officer assured me, these youngsters would be ready to take their place in society as adults.

Interestingly, there was nothing lascivious about these young people mixing together unashamedly in the nude. The traditions of centuries had instilled in them the gravity of a tribal custom on which all future male-female relations would be based and in which their children, in turn, would eventually take part.

We were warmly welcomed by the villagers after they had recognised our doctor guide, who was clearly a regular visitor. They did not resent our intrusion as I expected they might, for it is not often that the white man is allowed to enter the esoteric domain of tribal custom. We were offered the choice of palm wine or soured goat milk mixed with fresh blood taken from a cow that had been sacrificed earlier that evening. We opted for the wine and left about an hour later as silently as we had arrived.

For a long while the dull throb of drums followed us down the long track back to town; it was atavistic but appealing.

'This is all part of that irresistible urge which has brought generations of explorers and settlers back to Africa,' said the lieutenant doctor as we drove towards Bafata.

The mysterious lure is a powerful one and is probably one of the reasons why there are today still five or six million white people living and working in what some hacks still like to call the Dark Continent.

I spent two days at Nova Lamego, eastern stronghold of General de Spínola's forces in Portuguese Guinea. Like the others, the road from Bafata was tarred throughout. Here, for the first time, I saw signs of normal habitation along the way, in a region that the insurgents often claim as 'liberated'.

Civilian cars heading in both directions constantly passed us. Some were loaded with sacks of produce, others with passengers. A few trucks rolled by, each carrying an assortment of animals – cattle, goats, chickens and one with a huge sow billowing with fat and securely strapped between four poles on the carrier.

The countryside on both sides of the road was well-cultivated, dotted every so often by small thatched villages, each with a wide matting fence that surrounded the living quarters and to keep prowlers at bay.

We reached Nova Lamego at noon, and here, for the first time, I was to be the guest of a civilian, the regional administrator, which was several steps up from a *Chefe de Posto*. Until now I had mixed solely with the army and air force and although I had come into contact with some of the civilian functionaries, such as the one at Tite, these muftied functionaries had caught my interest.

At first glance, the role of these officials among the African people seemed superfluous, for the army appeared to have everything under control. After all, I asked one of the officers, was General de Spínola not the civilian and the military governor of the enclave?

Dr. Aguinaldo Spencer Salomao, a tall bushy man had spent 23 years – most of his adult life – in the enclave's civil service. He'd been educated at Canterbury and was a confirmed Anglophile. His father was apparently an admirer of Churchill, thus his middle name. For a while during the last war it was said, the old man had worked for SOE in Lisbon.

If the lugubrious *Chefe de Posto* at Tite had been a disappointment, Aguinaldo Salomao was a breath of vitality in the otherwise hidebound realm of Portuguese officialdom in Guinea. A dignified, cultured man, his pleasant double-storied home near the centre of town bore the mark of its master. His books in English, French and Portuguese ranged over just about every subject, from animal husbandry (which fell within his province) to the works of Henri Bataille and Sartre's plays.

His record library was vast. He preferred Vivaldi to Schoenberg, but he was eclectic enough to be able to haul out a Beatles' recording. He liked some of the group's earlier work, he admitted.

The administrator was also interested in astronomy and the clear tropical night skies in the region offered many opportunities to pursue this bent, though he could only afford a small reflector telescope. From others I gathered he was a mathematician of some repute, though he denied this.

Dr Salomao was responsible for the welfare of almost 100,000 people in his region, or about a fifth of the entire population. Among these were more than 10,000 Mandingos and 72,000 Fula, as well as a range of sub-tribes, each with its own traditions, foibles and idiosyncrasies which had to be taken into account whenever he made a decision.

His town, Nova Lamego, had a population of about 3,000 of whom roughly 100 were from the Metropolis.

The administrator told me that did not encourage white traders to enter the area and his reasons were simple: 'These people come here to trade with the locals. They do not have the welfare of the country at heart. They're often unscrupulous in their dealings with these simple-minded tribesmen.'

He deplored those who went to Africa to profit from what was essentially tribal ignorance, because the locals were mostly unsophisticated folk who didn't have the advantage of education. Also, they tended to take the white man at his word, which was usually where the abuse started.

Most traders exploited these people and then left again to settle comfortably in Europe, said Dr Salomao.

He felt that few contributed anything of value, either socially, intellectually or culturally, and that within societies that had nurtured themselves and their families for decades.

At Bambadinca, Lt. Colonel João Monteiro, head of Battalion 2917 (motto: *Bravos e Sempre Leais*) was headquartered. The campsite lay on one of the few rivers in the interior and there was none of the humidity of the soggy coastal region.

The base controlled an area that included the confluence of the Geba and Corubal rivers, another part of the country that had seen much bitter fighting in the pre-1968 period.

The last attack occurred exactly a year before I arrived; an infiltration group had spearheaded northwards across the border from Kadiafara in a bid to cut and mine the Bafata road and the guerrillas had hit Bambadinca one evening from across the river. They then withdrew to a pre-determined position to wait out the following day before joining up with two other groups. This combined force was then expected to hit at other positions during the foray.

Then something went wrong. A scouting party from the attack group ran into one of Colonel Monteiro's patrols and was captured intact, without a shot being fired. One of the men was a senior PAIGC officer. The four men were taken back to Bambadinca by helicopter, where the officer was given the choice of either telling all or accept the consequences. It was a no-win situation and the rebel was smart enough to comply.

Which was how General António de Spínola had the entire guerrilla battle plan in his hands later the same morning ...

18

Bissau – Portugal's Wartime Capital in West Africa

Because of its size, Bissau, capital of Portuguese Guinea, can hardly be called a city. But it is, because it has a cathedral, and in its day, one or two hotels regarded as 'smart' but which would have been rated Three Star in Europe. Things have changed a lot since the Portuguese left the country 40 years ago. I have been back since – several times – and found that very little functions in this rather primitive conurbation where a succession of army mutinies and civil wars have taken a toll. Indeed, Guiné-Bissau has been ravaged by violence on a far more destructive scale than anything the Europeans might have visited upon this sad, emerging African nation.

Since Guiné-Bissau's independence in 1975, there have been half-a-dozen coups, tens of thousands of people killed and entire stretches of this expansive city destroyed. It does not help that Bissau was originally built on a mangrove swamp and that without some measure of human control, nature has taken its course and reclaimed much of the lower ground that adjoins the ocean front.

Why anybody would have chosen this low-lying, thoroughly inhospitable and fever-ranged stretch of coast for a settlement in the first place is puzzling. There were other, far more friendly spots up and down the coast where Lisbon's early navigators could seek shelter, but then, as the saying goes, history tends to create its own puzzles, in much the same way, more than five centuries ago, present-day Cape Town would have been the best halfway refreshment station along the entire African coast. It took the Dutch another 200 years to recognize that much.

Though Lisbon withdrew both its troops and its authority when it handed the country to its new black leaders – much as they just had in Angola and Mozambique – the locals still like to blame the Portuguese for their travails. They probably always will, because that's the way that things happen when there is a colonial tradition involved.

When I first visited Bissau in the early 1970s, about 40,000 people regarded the city as home. That was about double the number at the start of colonial hostilities in 1963. Even so, this island settlement – it is separated from the mainland by a shallow canal – remained a modest, listless place. In its heyday, it was typical of some of the Portuguese conurbations we found a generation or two ago in some of the remoter regions of Lisbon's African empire.

With its central cathedral dominating the scene for miles around, pavement cafes, plump, dark-haired Iberian wives waving at one another from balconies and the ever-

In this photo, used earlier with his book, General António de Spínola addresses a public meeting on the outskirts of Bissau. He was the force that motivated changes that hastened the army coup d'état in Lisbon in April 1974. He was replaced as overall commander in Portuguese Guinea shortly before the war ended by General Bettencourt Rodrigues, who had shown remarkable success against the guerrillas in Eastern Angola. (Author's photo)

smiling bootblacks who pestered you long after you'd paid your single escudo and had your shoes polished with much ceremony and banter to a mirror-like glaze, it could easily be compared with Luso in Eastern Angola near the Zambian frontier or possibly the city of Tete which lies on the great Zambezi River in Mozambique.

As a freelance military correspondent for, among others, Britain's Jane's Information Group, London's *Daily Express,* the Argus Africa News Service, (and the BBC, until they fired me), all these places were my domain. While these were difficult times and I went down with malaria and half-a-dozen other tropical diseases including typhus – I enjoyed covering the African beat.

Portuguese Guinea was different though: it was always a tough call, even getting in and out of the country. We've already seen what happened to me when I tried to leave the first time in a Portuguese DC-6 loaded with war wounded …

Such was one of the joys of visiting the capital of Portuguese Guinea. Although I was there a while, I never did get acclimatized in an environment where the humidity in Bissau was as intense as it might have been within the jungle walls that surrounded it.

In its day, it might have been an appealing kind of place, though like Freetown, Libreville, Calabar, Lagos, Abidjan and Accra further down the coast, the early settlers suffering appalling losses from 'the fever'. Heaven only knows why the early navigators settled on making Bissau – in its early days little more than some houses adjoining a swamp – one of their major settlements along the African coast. Even with its quaint, rambling waterfront and a setting that was different to anything in either Angola or Mozambique, nothing could have compensated for that terrible climate.

As someone was heard to comment while I was there, Bissau, while not Colonial Portugal at its best, was nevertheless home to thousands of émigrés from the Metropolis.

On the west coast of Africa, the city that Bissau then most closely resembled might have been Bathurst – Banjul today – somnolent capital of the former British colony of Gambia, about 100 miles up the coast. The same brand of enervating heat pervades the sticky atmosphere, which greets you like a steaming, clammy face-wrap the moment you step off the plane.

There is the same lethargy about the townspeople. They amble about their business, dragging one foot reluctantly after the other, often preferring to rest a few moments in the shade before again crossing the street. Or they spend hours talking aimlessly about yesterday's weather, which is the same as today's and almost certainly tomorrow's. Only then might they get down to the grit of business, such as it is in these parts.

Graham Greene admirably captured that ambience in his novel *The Honorary Consul,* even though that plot was set in the French-speaking colony of Dahomey, or what we refer to today as Benin. Greene got it right because he spent part of World War II in Freetown working for British Intelligence and Sierra Leone is perhaps an hour's flying time further down the coast.

There are other similarities with his African milieu. Here and there among Bissau's multi-coloured crowds one could pick out traces of the same Creole and pidgin English that is spoken in Banjul and sometimes echoed in the towns and countryside of Liberia or Sierra Leone. Also, there was movement between Gambia and Portuguese Guinea, limited to about one boat a week outside the rainy season, usually through Cacheu in the north on the Senegalese border.

Even in the architectural layout, the two are similar. Bissau's waterfront is spread-eagled across the lower or 'downtown' region. Strange picturesque hotels, looking more like mysterious mansions out of a novel set in the Carolinas, are stuck away behind clusters of mangrove and bougainvillea on what little higher ground there is on this rehabilitated marsh which Africa has gradually won back from the sea with the help of the annual silt flood from the interior.

The roads too, all lead to one central square somewhere near the docks. This layout appears to be the norm in West Africa, for one finds it too in Accra, Bathurst and Dakar. They call it the colonial touch and it is regarded as a legacy of some long-forgotten regiment of town planners in Paris and London, few of whom had ever seen Africa, much less lived there.

As far as Bissau's African community was concerned, it was in the vicinity of Pidjiguiti docks where most things happened. Actually, they still do.

Here, near the always-bustling, raucous market, the town was once a rush of movement and activity from first to last light with black and white faces outnumbered by the tawny complexions of mulatto traders and fishermen that crowded ashore through a succession of well-guarded harbour gates. Photography in this area, the scene of a brutal 1959 massacre, was forbidden when Lisbon ruled. Though I'd been warned about the restriction beforehand I thought it a pity because the area was one of the most colourful anywhere along this stretch of coast.

Here the mammies could be seen trading in a thousand items of everyday use; corn, cloth, flour, stinking dried fish which turns brown in the sun and regarded as a West African gourmet's delight, birds' eggs, rusty tins of canned milk, vegetables and fuel and cooking oils in battered old paraffin tins. Inevitably, there was also palm wine, the universal drink of choice among the natives of West Africa. In Bissau in the old days it came in a variety of bottles, flasks and casks, some of which look as if they'd survived a century of use.

Palm wine is a potent drink which starts to get lethal the longer it is left in the sun. Add some real hooch to it and it'll knock the unsuspecting imbiber flat after the second round, even though locals drink it by the pint, usually starting with the first meal of the day.

Bissau's other market area, closer to town, combined a succession of tiny kiosks with the local fresh meat, fish and vegetable store. Because of the heat and the lack of refrigeration, the wise like to shop early. Here too, Fula and Hausa traders from the north matched wits with townsfolk selling everything from a pair of shoes to a witchdoctor's potion which would exorcise a wandering spirit in a *tabanca*.

What was not generally known – even to some of the Portuguese living there, was that

Bacar's *Comandos Africanos* were armed with a variety of weapons when they
went out on patrol. Apart from standard GPMGs, some of the troops were issued
with RPG-2 rocket launchers and grenades – forerunners of the ubiquitous
RPG-7. One of these can be seen on the extreme left. (Author's photo)

this place had a few secrets of its own. In this large shaded building with half a dozen exits
and entrances, one could buy genuine Ashanti gold dust as well as nuggets and diamonds
brought across overland from Ghana and Sierra Leone. All were smuggled into the country,
only who-knows-how if you consider that this land was totally surrounded by its enemies.

The gold and silver filigree work some of the craftspeople displayed here behind glass-
covered cabinets and trays was intricate and sometimes reflected superb craftsmanship. A
lot of it was reminiscent of similar items which were once on sale in Zanzibar before Beijing
helped drive out many of the traditional Arab gold and silversmiths.

And for those who want them, there were ebony carvings such as one today finds at
every airport along the west coast of Africa. The bulk of it is petty and stereotyped, but the
wood has been well worked and sometimes it's possible to find a good piece at a reasonable
price if you're interested in that sort of thing. So too was the odd chunk of carved ivory,
though Bissau then boasted nothing as outstanding as the works of art one sees today in
Abidjan, or further east in the markets of Douala and Yaoundé in the Cameroon Republic.

The bartering was always a constant jumble of noise and dialects, interspersed here and
there by the colloquial Portuguese of young Metropolitan housewives – mostly espoused to
local traders – who arrived to do the morning shopping. Military wives, in contrast, rarely
went to the market themselves; few of the women who came out to Africa to be with their

men in uniform had less than two servants.

Another sound, sometimes an echo, which one picked up clearly when walking through the downtown area was the unmistakable cry of the Koran being chanted in Arabic by some faraway Imam. The high-pitched, ascetic voice always came over in fits and starts as one of Cairo's broadcasting stations or Radio Algiers faded and then picked up again. The lips of the devout didn't miss a verse as they followed the chants in silent, abstract mimes.

The presence of Islam was distinct. It is even more so today, now that Lisbon's influence has been whittled away to perhaps the use of a common language and some of the dishes that will always remain popular. One felt at the time that the Muslim presence was perhaps a little incongruous in this staunchly Catholic land, but then the Portuguese have almost always been more tolerant of others' beliefs than their European neighbours.

Lisbon's hierarchy was trying to learn to live with other people's creeds when Spain's Inquisition was at its worst.

A stone's throw from the harbour remains the original old fort built centuries ago by the descendents of the legendary globe-trotting navigators. The building, dilapidated today and scarred by half a dozen coups and attempted army mutinies remains a legacy of that period when Lisbon's kings finally decided to 'pacify' this coast in a bid to capture a portion of the meandering Sahara trade from the north.

They settled here; on the Rio Fresco, near present-day Dakar; at Mitombo further south and at a number of points along the coast between Ghana and Nigeria. Their principal base along the entire seaboard was Arguim Island off Mauritania which became an entrépot for the slave trade and which only lapsed into insignificance with the rise of transatlantic trade.

Granite-walled, low-lying and speckled with cannon running the gamut of 500 years of Portuguese ordnance, this was General António de Spínola's military headquarters while the war raged in the interior. He rarely used it, preferring to work at the more stately governor's residence.

I recall being told that the general would regularly join his staff officers shortly after seven each evening for a run-through of the day's events in the castle's map-lined conference room.

In spite of this activity – rumbustiously chaotic early in the day and easing off to a steady hum after a lunch when most of the population bedded down to a three-hour siesta – one couldn't help sensing that there was an undefined tension in the streets of Bissau. It was neither easily defined, or fathomed at first. In a way, it was almost as if something was about to happen.

Bissau's people, though no different from those of any other African city, were strained, a little more tense and tired than one would have expected at this fulcrum of Portugal's military might on the west coast.

Bathurst, in contrast, was also lethargic in the heat of day but that city has its own brand of vibrancy. The Gambian capital can be a pulsating, very-much-alive African centre where most people long ago learnt to laugh as the world goes by. Gambians have even mastered that subtle British technique of being able to chuckle at their own inadequacies, as Nigerians were able to do before their war.

These are a happy, carefree people imbued with a lighthearted grace and dignity not often seen elsewhere in a West Africa preoccupied with corruption, trade deficits and the occasional military putsch.

The people of Bissau in contrast, were sombre and serious for much of their day. There were few wisecracks as one walked between the rows of huge, spreading mango trees which lined Avenida 5 de Outubro or the majestic Avenida da Republica closer to the main business centre.

Here, between yellowing, moss-covered old structures which reflect more than their share of 19th Century colonial charm, the people rarely smiled as they passed a stranger. Rather, you were accorded a cursory glance as you passed or when your eyes briefly met.

To be fair though, Portuguese Guinea had not yet lapsed into the hopeless melancholy I found throughout most of the Republic of Guinea further south. Even then it was clear that Sékou Touré's brand of 'Scientific Socialism' – his instant panacea for all the ills of Africa (like Nkrumah's equally-crazy *Consciencism* and Nyerere's *Ujamaa* programs) – had been tough on the ordinary man.

It was certainly a lot harder than the way of life instituted by the oft-times ruthless though usually avuncular Lusitanians.

Though the people of Bissau were subdued – some said detached – they liked to emerge once the sun disappeared in a flurry of colours over the Atlantic beyond. Then, hundreds of dark-skinned white-collar workers and brown-uniformed messengers gathered round their favourite cafes and bars just as they still do in Lisbon and Oporto and quaff a few for the road.

Among this mass of civilians there were always the soldiers in their khaki-green camouflage uniforms and rubber army boots. The men, out on an evening's furlough, moved about mostly on foot, usually in pairs, traipsing from one bar to another in search of the off-beat. They mixed easily with the locals and their women. Being a small town, most of the people travelled about the city on bicycles, scooters or on the troop-carrier bus which plied regularly each hour between town and some distant barrack on the Bissalanca Airport road. Here and there army jeeps scurried about on official business, rarely stopping at intersections and often moving at speed in built-up areas and sometimes causing horrendous accidents.

To many of these people the phrase 'road discipline' was just that: a phrase. Curiously, even today it is still something which one sees so often in the Metropolis, and may be one of the reasons why Portugal, while the wars went on, was losing almost as many men in road accidents she did in her African conflicts.

The jeeps with right-hand drive steering columns immediately caught the eye. They look out of place in streets full of cars travelling on the right, continental fashion, with their drivers sitting on the far side of the vehicle. It was only afterwards, when my questions

Two of the patrol boats used in inshore patrol work by the Portuguese Navy – they were given to Lisbon on a lend-lease basis by the Americans – were permanently stationed at Cacheu. When the author returned to Cacheu decades later while making a TV documentary, he found that only the hulks remained, pulled up high on the beach. Everything else had been stripped. (Author's photo)

had been pointedly ignored that I realized South Africa, like Britain, still observed the British code. Closer inspection revealed that many of these army utility cars still had their bilingual South African instruction panels alongside the speedometer detailing gear changes in relation to speed, the one in Afrikaans and the other in English and not a word in-between of Portuguese.

Traffic in Bissau was not always hectic. The first sight which greeted my arrival after I'd landed was a military cortege crawling towards the centre city area from the airport. The body of a dead Portuguese marine had been brought in by helicopter that morning.

He'd been killed during a night action near Buba, I was told, and would be buried later that day. Corpses are rarely left longer than a day in the stifling heat before being interred. As with Bacar, who followed the same route almost a month later, his plain wooden coffin was draped with a green and red Portuguese flag as the 20-vehicle convoy barely moved down the long, straight tarred road into Bissau.

A few curious spectators, Fula and Mandingo traders, mammies and a host of children watched the scene as it passed. They'd witnessed the spectacle often enough before for they barely spared the cortege a glance as they continued with their endless business harangues under the tall pepper trees that lined the airport road.

For their part, the solid, sober faces of the Portuguese soldiers who formed the guard of honour did the necessary. They too seemed to have grown accustomed to their role, but in their stiff uniforms and heavy webbing that almost seemed to date from the First World War, the duty must have been constricting.

The troops looked aggressive. One of their number had been killed, by a black enemy no less, and here were black people all about them, even within their own ranks. So were many of these people who had lived and died within earshot of the barracks and who depended on these foreign soldiers for succour and protection.

To the observer, like myself, who came to see the war for himself, one could only speculate what passed through the minds of those who stood and watched.

Approaching Bissau from the air was invariably a different kind of experience. I did the trip often, for General Spínola was easy on the use of military aircraft by visiting foreign journalists.

Flying in from the Cape Verde Islands, the coast loomed up stark on a hazy African horizon ahead. A dozen tiny ribbons of rivers snaked crazily through the low-lying swampland approaches and the pattern was almost uniform, broken sporadically by the squares and triangles of a hundred rice paddies spread out between the mangroves. They were like angular, heavily-lined corduroy sheets.

The water below, even 20 miles out to sea was a dirty, muddy brown, like the kind of turbulence you see at anchorages along the Texan or Louisiana coasts. It's the same when approaching the estuaries of the Congo and Niger rivers further down the coast.

Only occasionally was the rhythm broken by the dark-stained sail of a *nhominca,* the Portuguese-type fishing boat which is in everyday use along this seaboard as far north as Mauritania. Centuries ago local fishermen in Senegal, Gambia, Guinea and Sierra Leone adopted the protruding keel design, which tourists today are more likely to associate with Estoril than Africa.

Bissau, when viewed from the air was a bit larger than expected and semicircular in shape. Again the resemblance to Bathurst – or Banjul – was striking, both places lying on a promontory that faced open water. This was probably one of the reasons why a Soviet-built Antonov transport plane, bearing the colours of the Guinea Air Force landed at Bissau in 1971.

The stocky freighter had lost its way on a flight between Labe and Conakry in the Republic of Guinea and mistook Bissalanca for Bathurst. The crew was still being held in Bissau when I was there, though Spínola did try to exchange them for some of his own prisoners-of-war captured by the PAIGC. President Toure rejected the offer.

Coming in to land in Portuguese Guinea one couldn't help but notice that all roads leading outwards from Bissau's cathedral doubled back again on reaching the outskirts of town, almost as if, nudged by the nearby jungle, they swung in again of their own accord. The uniformity was broken at irregular intervals by a row or two of barracks and workshops, each distinctive with their rows of open ground between twin barbed-wire fences.

Machine-gun turrets marked the corners of these defences that in typical military fashion were drab. From where we flew, they resembled circular blobs on a more-than-detailed architect's plan.

Bissalanca Airport, half-a-dozen miles on the road north out of Bissau is an impressive affair set across an otherwise uninteresting, flat countryside. Alongside the heavy tarmac fortifications stood rows of squat artillery pieces with their muzzles covered in canvas behind raised gun pits. Their jobs, clearly, was to protect up about 30 military aircraft, all in various stages of readiness for the morning operations. We'd arrived early after an 18-hour flight from Lisbon. It was a long haul.

About 10 Alouette helicopters and the same number of Fiat G-91 jets were concentrated at the far end of the runway, distant from what one officer referred to as 'the prying eyes of civilians who pass through en route to Europe and beyond'.

The Harvards and Dorniers – there were more of them – were parked close to the terminal building, their engine cowlings reflecting bright day-glo orange that reflected in the early morning sun. The gaudiness, I was told, had something to do with identification and spotting in the event of one of the planes being forced down. On its own pad nearby stood one of Bissau's two Nord Atlas transports, the same air freighters we'd used to gad about in Angola. These NATO-type planes looked impressive in their wavy green and brown camouflage paint and were used for daily supply runs into the interior.

An unusual aircraft stood on its own in a bunker near the fringe of the airport cluster. This one was a jet but with a long, low-slung silhouette that contrasted readily with the stocky fighters around it. Incredibly, it was one of Britain's World War II Gloster Meteor fighters. On its fuselage, as if someone tried to add a rider to a riddle, was painted, in large black capitals: ENTERPRISE FILMS.

No photographs of this plane or of the Antonov were allowed 'for security reasons' whatever they were. But it was perhaps inevitable that I'd snap them eventually as virtually all my movements into the interior were through Bissalanca Airport.

The story regarding the Meteor goes like this: During the Biafran War the rebel leader Colonel Ojukwu paid for two jet aircraft from a very well-known international arms salesman. The fighters were to replace the French Vantour bombers that he'd intended using against Federal lines and which were destroyed on the ground outside Uli Airport by Nigerian Air Force MiGs before they were ever put into use.

Meantime, both Meteors were flown out of Britain illegally and once in international air space, they headed down the West African coastline for Nigeria.

The designers of the Meteor series – a remarkable aircraft and well ahead of its time which first flew in 1943 – had never intended the plane to be used in long-range operations. Halfway to Africa, one of the surreptitiously-acquired aircraft developed engine trouble and had to be ditched into the sea. The other landed at Bissau and, like the Antonov, remained neglected and soon became dilapidated and unserviceable. For the rest of the war, the two aircraft were more than an embarrassment to a Portuguese Government that only wished to forget that Biafra had ever existed.

Tackled on the subject of the jets during my visit, General Spínola refused to be drawn. As far as he was concerned, the aircraft had made an emergency landing and that was that. It was not his concern where the plane had come from or where it might have been headed.

Pro government militia members cock-a-hoop in front of the camera. (Author's photo)

The pilot, he maintained, had been repatriated shortly after he had landed and nobody had ever claimed the jet.

Enterprise Films was the cover organization in Britain which handled the sale, ostensibly for use in a long-forgotten film on the Battle for Europe. Legal action had since been taken by the British Government against the individuals responsible for the sale, eventually convicted on the grounds that they'd not declared the true purpose of the venture: in effect the charge was arms smuggling and the offence a military one, newspapers concluded at the time.

There was only one place for the few visitors who came to this corner of Africa to stay and that was the Grande Hotel, a rambling, stuccoed building edging well onto Avenida 5 de Outubro in the centre city area.

Mango trees rose up in a flourish of viridescence and sheltered the building on all sides, giving the structure a deceptively cool appearance. In reality it was as hot on the broad covered porch as out on the sidewalk, but then there were seats and long cool drinks prepared by African workers in starched white ice-cream suits and that was what we paid for. The real problem was that air conditioning – as you and I know it today – hadn't yet been properly introduced in any of these outlying colonies.

Although Bissau boasted about half a dozen hotels, it was 'not done' to stay anywhere but at the Grande: it was reserved for officers and the likes of hacks like me. Other ranks used the Hotel Avenida, the Miramar or the Intercontinental, regarded by most of inferior standard, though I could see little difference because I used them all at one stage or another.

Like much else in the Portuguese African colonies, a lot of it had to do with status and perception: the two went hand-in-glove and had little to do with reality, except that one paid more at the one place than the other. The food at Avenida was streets ahead of the Grande because the owner went down to the docks early every day and waited for the fishing boats to return from their overnight forays with some of the best game fish catches on the west coast of Africa.

And *lagosta* – lobster – lots and lots of these crustaceans at perhaps a dollar a throw ...

Talking about the Grande Hotel, the major who'd collected me at the airport and deposited my bags and baggage at the front entrance of my new hotel, made the point while I rented a room at the place that 'we don't go there and they don't come here'. He'd pick me up later, he called over his shoulder as he headed back to the fort.

I walked slowly up the stairs towards reception. The hotel had all the trappings of pseudo-sophistication which I'd half expected as a result of a conversation with someone on the aircraft. There were a number of well-dressed women wandering aimlessly about waiting for their uniformed husbands. All were military wives, done up to the gills, though it was still early in the day. How different to modern-day British and French wives who'd rather wander about the tropics in a pair of shorts or a slip than suffer the agonies of tight-fitting corsets and garters.

But that's the Portuguese, in those days still half a century behind the rest when it came to the little things of life.

A couple of well-groomed poodles lopped lazily past towards their regular pitch, in the shadow of some giant ferns which hung over the balcony. There, I subsequently observed, they spent most of the day gasping for breath in heat which came wallowing almost in waves from the road below. They were decorative, I suppose, and added a measure of status to the place in a *gauche* sort of way.

Yes, said the maitre, he'd been informed of my arrival after I'd been left standing alongside the bar for 15 minutes. But since then other things had happened, he added. I'd have to sleep in one of the store-rooms.

'Same rate' he affirmed without looking me in the eyes. I accepted. What else? This *patron* had recently bought the hotel, I learnt later. Like others of his ilk in Portugal's African provinces, he was out to make his money and head straight back to the Metropolis.

For my five dollars a day, all meals included, the fare wasn't at all bad. I shared a table – surrounded almost entirely by military personnel – with two West German correspondents from *Der Spiegel*. Drinks in the bar were cheap, with scotch going for about 15 cents a large tot. The food was OK considering the climate; most vegetables were flown in from Europe three times a week.

Prices in Bissau, I found, were a lot cheaper than either Luanda or Lourenco Marques. General Spínola has deliberately kept taxes and import duties low in order to stimulate trade and keep the cost of living down for those who had little. He'd also hoped to make life in the territory more attractive financially than it was in high-inflation Dakar or Conakry, the capitals of the two neighbouring countries that so powerfully opposed him in his war.

In this he succeeded. If the full gambit of tourism were allowed, Bissau would probably have become one of the hippie paradises of the world: at that stage it was comparatively easy to exist on less than a couple of dollars a day, which might have included a primitive roof over one's head and a moderate amount of wine with meals. The rest of such a lifestyle would have encompassed living at the African level, but then American and European unconventional youth regarded such things as fashionable in those faraway days.

There was no segregation among the races as it was then known in Southern Africa, or even the economic discrimination of Kenya, the Ivory Coast or Kinshasa, which, like the 'Deep South' weighed heavily in favour of whites.

The lesson for Southern Africa – and probably Rhodesia too – was obvious. General Spínola regarded it as a tactical priority to keep most of the essentials of life within easy reach of the black people under his control. Because just about every African in Portuguese Guinea earned a good deal less than his European counterparts, it was Spínola's view that the black man would be the worst affected by any inflationary spiral were he not to protect him from inflation where it affected the prices of essentials such as bread, meat and transport. That way, he reckoned, with some of the political considerations he had in mind, he'd ultimately win the hearts and minds of all.

He was right, of course. But looking back today you can't help thinking that he'd missed the point and that it was the old argument of too little, too late. And anyway, the revolutionaries who were trying to usurp his authority were offering a lot more than he could ever give.

They were promising the people – the *povo,* in the language of these West African guerrillas – an entire country.

19

PAIGC – Portuguese Guinea's Liberation Organisation

A few, using intellect, are a match for hordes of heavily armed automatons.

Lawrence of Arabia

One of the tragic political disasters of modern-day Africa must be the way in which Guiné-Bissau, having bravely won its freedom on the battlefield, managed to self-destruct a few short years after gaining independence.

With his brother Luis, Amílcar Cabral founded the Party in 1956, a political grouping that was to follow strong Socialist principles. Originally advocated was total independence from Lisbon of both the Cape Verde Islands and Portuguese Guinea and the instrument was to be the African Party for the Independence of Guinea and Cape Verde (PAIGC). These were times of great promise.

Sadly, it was this same Party that eventually destroyed the cohesion that brought this tiny nation into being, with dissident Party members also responsible for assassinating their founding leader, Amilcar Cabral. The Party finally eventually led the nation into a series of bitter civil wars and it was these fierce struggles that tore the fabric of Guiné-Bissau society apart as Portugal's military chiefs could never have dreamt of doing.

If fighting was intense during the course of a Liberation War that cost both sides an ocean of blood – and certainly more so than in Angola and Mozambique – then the fratricidal battles that followed Lisbon's departure were both mindless and gory. As might have been expected, the troubles ultimately led to a split of the Cape Verde/Guiné-Bissau alliance, with both nations heading off on their own.

Cape Verde, a string of islands off the coast of West Africa was fortunate in making the right choice because it emerged as a stable and progressive multi-party quasi-democracy.

I visited the islands several times in subsequent years and made a film there. Though apprehensive at first, I was amazed at its tranquility and the fact that it had not yet been overrun by American tourists. Praia, the capital is a pristine little backwater with low-cost, good quality hotels and where very little has changed from the time that Lisbon ruled. It is a fishing and underwater paradise still waiting to be explored.

Not so the mainland component of the original alliance. The ink on Guiné-Bissau's Freedom Charter was hardly dry before the country spiraled into violence. The worst of the bloodshed in the post-independent phase took place in the late 1970s and 1980s, much of it in the vicinity of Tite, that same military base from where I set out on patrol with João

Bacar. These battles often went on for weeks and it mattered little that they received scant attention abroad, largely because the international community was preoccupied with other matters, like the downfall of the Soviet Union at the time.

What we do know is that the fighting was so ferocious that the area was eventually dubbed 'The Killing Grounds'. When I visited Bissau 20 years later, those few people who were prepared to talk, spoke in awe about the period.

None of this should ever have been allowed to happen. At its prime, the PAIGC led the field in running and maintaining a strong, independently-minded Freedom Army. It was not only streets ahead of anything else in Africa but compared favourably with some of the better-known liberation groups in the Middle East and Central America

Cabral's troops were both well-trained and disciplined, often more so than their historical foes. The Party got all the cash and hardware it needed from the Eastern Bloc, so there was never any shortage of funds, even though huge amounts of money were stolen by Party functionaries and secreted in overseas bank accounts. It was in Portuguese Guinea that General António de Spínola had to accept that the ultimate solution had to be a political and not a military one. He said as much in his book *Portugal and the Future*.

Much of the social, political and military infrastructure created by the PAIGC was exemplary. Cabral's was the first liberation group to introduce SAM-7 MANPADS into the fray, shooting down several Portuguese Air Force planes.

And while the majority of the rebel units operating in Angola and Mozambique had only rudimentary medical facilities to treat their wounded, the PAIGC ran a string of clinics in the two neighbouring states. Large military hospitals were established at Ziguinchor and Dakar in Senegal and another in Conakry, in the Republic of Guinea.

The PAIGC took the lead in disseminating party propaganda. There was an illustrated monthly bulletin entitled *Libertação Unidade e Luta,* published in Portuguese together with *Caderno Escolar*, a primary reader published in Peking. With a variety of other simple publications, the message was simple: the revolution had come to stay.

PAIGC leaders liked to echo what Mao wrote in the 1930s; that every major guerrilla unit should have a printing press and mimeograph stone ... and also paper on which to print propaganda leaflets and notices.

Meanwhile, the PAIGCs *Radio Libertacao* was established and made daily broadcasts in Portuguese to the war zones in the north. One prominent source reported that while the station was mobile and its sites were supposed to be secret, everybody was aware that it was in Guinea. It went on for the duration issuing a steady stream of cryptic coded messages, apart from the usual anti-Portuguese diatribes.

While the PAIGC effectively rallied the support of the majority of the people – its campaigns, at peak, ranged over about 90 percent of the country – there were other political groups at work.

FLING, the acronym for *Front de Lutte de l'Indépendence Nationale de Guinée* – as

The guerrillas that opposed Lisbon's presence in Portuguese Guinea were aggressive, imaginative and tenacious. They also received solid Soviet support. (Author's collection)

indicated by language – was headquartered in Dakar, capital of Francophone Senegal and was comprised of at least four breakaway liberation groups. The oldest and largest of these was MLG *(Movimento de Libertacao da Guine)* formed in 1960 by a veteran anti-Portuguese campaigner, Francois (Francis) Mendy Kankoila, a Manjaco exile who lived most of his adult life under the patronage of Léopold Senghor. Mendy was known in Africa by his middle name.

Other groups included in this coalition were the FLG *(Frente de Libertacao da Guine),* the UPG *(Uniao das Populacoes da Guine)* founded by Henry Labery and the URGP *(Union des Ressortissants de la Guinée Portuguaise)* and led by Benjamin Pinto-Bull, brother of Jaime who was killed in the 1970 helicopter crash.

It is noteworthy that the brothers Benjamin and Jaime, long at political loggerheads, were the sons of an Englishman who had married a local African girl. Both had been well educated and were easily assimilated into Bissau's upper-crust Portuguese society and both went to the top in their respective spheres of influence; Benjamin as highly respected in his newly-adopted capital as Jaime was in Bissau and Lisbon.

Benjamin, in fact, never abandoned his dream of an independent Guinea which would retain close economic links with Lisbon, and this always made him suspect among some of the more radical elements within the movement. It was known that he visited Lisbon in June 1963, and held discussions on the practicalities of this subject.

While it operated in the field, FLING drew most of its support from alienated Fulas,

Manjacos, Mandingos and the Papeis. There were also some Balantas, though this tribe tended towards Conakry for reasons of their own.

FLING, like the PAIGC, was partly hamstrung by the inability to establish forward bases in the arid north. There were a number of mobile camps between Farim and Mansao but nothing permanent; for this reason there was a steady two-way traffic across the border.

Territorial bases, FLING always maintained, quoting Guevara, were of great importance before any attempt was made to regularize operations. The guerrillas needed secure training and rest areas, supply dumps and hospitals, but like General Nino's troops in the south, they had to continue falling back across the border into Senegal for an effective back-up and opportunity of respite.

It was the task of Portuguese Army border commanders, like those at Sare Bacar and Cuntima to try to destroy these movements.

PAIGC guerrilla forces operating in Portuguese Guinea were split between three distinct operational zones or regions – the north, the south and the east.

At the time of my visit, Mamadou Djiassi headed the forces in the North. His colleague of long standing, Osvaldo Maximo Vieira was is in charge of the east, while one of the most illustrious figures to emerge from the continuing battle, João Bernardino Vieira – also known among his own men and the Portuguese authorities as *O Nino* or General Nino – was active in the south, where the fighting was at its fiercest.

General Nino had been in action against the Portuguese since the beginning, and at that stage he was still in his early thirties. The Portuguese claimed that he'd once been a stretcher bearer in their army.

His tactics and deployment always marked him as a brilliant strategist in the traditional guerrilla mould and was known for his aggressive penetration which incorporated the methods of Mao and Guevara. Nino never favoured the principle of tactical retreat and as a leader of men, he quickly acquired a reputation for ruthlessness. He was known to have executed some of his soldiers for not obeying commands or for sleeping while on sentry duty.

Nino also had the distinction of being one of the first of the young revolutionaries who answered Cabral's call to arms. Together with six others, including his blood-relation Osvaldo, he was sent to Communist China for training in insurgency warfare. Nino spent eight months at the Nanking Military Academy in 1961.

Cabral told of an interesting anecdote in one of his interviews. Shortly after returning to Portuguese Guinea, this short, well-built, proverbially pitch-black fighter with a deceptively young face was seized by the Portuguese. At the time, Cabral explained, Nino was one of the agents of his mobilization organisation and Party chief in the Cobucare zone, which extended southwards from Tite and Bolama to Catió. A disaffected member of Cabral's organisation had denounced him.

Nino spent days in custody and was questioned at length about his activities, but

Portuguese marines on patrol in Guinea waters. (Author's photo)

government officials simply could not believe that somebody so young could be a hard-core rebel. In any event, it was decided to send him to Bissau and let PIDE, the notorious Portuguese secret police deal with him.

The same evening Nino passed on a message through a sympathiser in the local police barracks that he was being held and that he was about to be sent to Bissau. Within hours a group of insurgents broke into the police station and released him.

Cabral claimed he still had the padlock of the jail where Nino was kept when I interviewed him in Addis Ababa in 1971.

Each of the PAIGC's three military regions or fronts was subdivided into sectors, controlled by a sector leader who was answerable to the regional commander personally. From time to time the regional and sector commanders met with the leader and his senior aides to discuss problems, past mistakes and future tactics.

Prior to the entry of General de Spínola into the fray, such meetings were held within the Portuguese enclave, but eventually the 'Supreme Command' was forced southwards into 'neutral' Guinea (Conakry) territory.

For the purpose of military operations, sectors were again divided into groups of guerrilla infantry, also known as bi-groups. These were the men who did the actual fighting. About 38 men strong, each bi-group usually has its own political commissar in attendance and were fully self-contained when operational.

The men were mostly armed with AKs and a few heavier weapons, bazookas, machine guns and RPG-2 rocket-carriers for support. While anti-personnel and anti-vehicle (AT) mines were supplementary, there was actually not that much difference between a bi-group's firepower and that of the average Portuguese Army patrol.

The political organisation of the PAIGC was a little less complicated. The Party was headquartered in Conakry, with Cabral, until he was murdered in January 1973, at the top of the pyramid with the title of secretary general and commander-in-chief.

After Cabral's death, Dr Vitor Monteiro, a former bank clerk, was appointed to the post. In turn, he was replaced by Aristides Pereira.

Ranged below this hierarchy was a 20-man elected body known as the Political Secretariat, and from these members a Council of War of seven members was elected. Among those at one stage was the secretary general, Amilcar Cabral's brother Luis, three military regional commanders and two others. In their hands were entrusted the full scope and ramifications of the 10-year guerrilla struggle.

Acting in conjunction with the Political Secretariat was the Central Committee which was composed of 65 members, in turn, subdivided into five departments or ministries:

- The Commission of Control, whose principal task, like an Ombudsman, was to monitor the work done by every facet of the Party machine
- The Commission of Security; otherwise known as PAIGC's own KGB/GRU. Most of its members were trained by East Europeans
- The Commission of Foreign Relations, responsible inter alia for propaganda, and (according to Lisbon sources) not adverse to a little espionage when the occasion warranted it
- The Commission for National Reconstruction; the smallest of the five departments and while the war went on, waiting hopefully for the day that Lisbon would withdraw her troops; and finally,
- The Commission of Organisation and Orientation responsible for the day to day problems within the party, in the broadest sense

Beyond the borders of the Portuguese enclave, the PAIGC operated a number of institutions which served the comrades. In Conakry, the movement ran a secondary school for Portuguese Guineans.

According to an American authority on the war, Professor William Zartman, both the University of Dakar and the 'Workers' University' in Conakry were open to them.

Beyond Africa, numerous members of the PAIGC received military and other training in communist states including China. Throughout, the Party showed little interest or inclination in developing comparable opportunities in Western countries, although admittedly little was offered prior to independence.

While still in office, Cabral often complained of a 'lack of interest' in his war among the more prominent Western nations. He recalled sending a young university graduate, Miss Maria Luz de Andrade, to London and Paris for aid. In both capitals the officials she met were evasive. When she asked the British Red Cross for medical assistance she was

One of the weapons supplied to PAIGC guerrillas was this BM-21 multiple rocket launcher, nicknamed Grad in Russian (it means 'hail'). Because the Portuguese Army rarely retaliated across the frontier - except in November 1970, when they raided Conakry in Operation *Mar Verde* to free and bring back prisoners of war – these vehicles would be driven to the border after dark to hurl clusters of 122mm rockets at pre-selected targets. (Author's collection)

referred to the Portuguese Red Cross in Lisbon.

Cabral experienced similar detachment when he visited London under the assumed name of Abel Djassi in 1960. He canvassed members of the British Labour Party for assistance in his struggle but achieved little. It was the same when he returned in 1962, this time under his own name.

Cabral afterwards told Basil Davidson: 'Why should we be surprised? After all, Portugal is Britain's ally!'

Another venture undertaken by the PAIGC was the establishment in the middle-1960s of an economic bartering system within Portuguese Guinea known as 'People's Shops'. The system was run on the lines of buying rice and other crops at prices slightly higher than those offered by the Portuguese, or bartering goods for such everyday items such as soap, sugar, salt, cloth or tobacco. This way, it was maintained, the revolutionaries were depriving Lisbon of additional revenue. The crops were then removed across the border into the Republic of Guinea.

Biafra operated a similar system during its civil war. Odumegwu Ojukwu's rebel government would buy whatever cocoa beans were available and shipped them out of the beleaguered state by air.

In principle, the idea was sound, but the PAIGC system made little headway for two reasons. The first was the intensification of the war after General de Spínola took over command – which made even the movement of troops hauling only their own hardware difficult.

The second factor that worked against the system of barter was the steadily deteriorating economic situation in Toure's Socialist Republic of Guinea, which, in turn, affected the buying power of the guerrillas as many had to use the almost worthless Guinea franc.

While medical services improved markedly as hostilities progressed, things were primitive at the start. Rags and crushed palm fronds were used for dressings and drugs, medications that included anesthetics were a rare luxury. Russia soon stepped in and trained more than 100 nurses at Soviet hospitals. Similarly, Czechoslovakia provided drugs, clinical equipment and on-the-spot field training.

Cabral had distinct views about the military struggle. He told a correspondent of the Cuban revolutionary magazine *Tricontinental* during the 1969 Khartoum Conference of Solidarity with Freedom Fighters in the Portuguese Colonies and Southern Africa, that the PAIGC maintained a basic structure under colonialism.

'Throughout, the land remained co-operative property of the village, of the community ... a very important characteristic of our peasant, who was not directly exploited by the coloniser but was exploited through trade, through the differences between the prices and the real value of the products.'

Cabral made it clear that his struggle was different from similar guerrilla wars at present being waged in Africa. There was no inflexible settler community to speak of, no nationalistic chauvinism among a white community which had found a new identity in Africa and was determined to hold on to it to the exclusion of all else, and no real exploitation of the masses as was often contended by other PAIGC spokesmen when presenting their case abroad.

Portuguese Guinea, he maintained, was consequently in a class on its own. 'The nature of the guerrilla conflict and the organisation conducting that struggle bears little comparison, for instance with FRELIMO or the MPLA, two other liberation movements in Portuguese Africa'. He said.

Amilcar Cabral epitomised the nature of his movement. A small, ascetic-looking man with a burnished complexion in his early fifties, he had the piercing eyes that characterised so many of the more prominent African leaders. His bold chin was set off by a thin ring of salt-and-pepper beard.

Even in camouflage uniform, which he donned when he occasionally crossed the border and ventured into enemy territory, his dress was tidy. He reflected the bearing of a senior staff officer, although in reality, his military training had been fragmentary.

When I met him for the first time in Addis Ababa during the 1971 Summit of African Heads of State, he was strolling casually through the press centre prior to the start of the third day's session. His grey suit of Continental cut contrasted readily with the more conservative styles of a few of the delegates around him and the plain-clothed Ethiopian security officer who followed him around the building. This man was there more for his

Portuguese *fuzileiros* coming ashore after an operation in
adjacent islands. (Photo *Revista da Armada*)

own safety, I gathered later, than for any insurrection he may have contemplated while in
Haile Selassie's capital.

His manner was informal when I stepped forward and introduced myself. Only a
month before I had been with Bacar in the jungles of Portuguese Guinea searching for his
men. I told him so and he was genuinely interested. He translated what I had said for the
benefit of one of his aides, who was also present. Cabral spoke fluent Portuguese and fair
English.

'We must talk,' he said. 'There is obviously much that we could tell each other.' Not for
a moment did the easy affable smile leave his lips. After ten minutes he excused himself in
order to enter the debating chamber in Africa Hall.

My immediate impression was that his personality exuded forcefulness and authority.
It blended with an undeniable old world charm that one so rarely encounters among the
African or American dignitaries one meets these days. An American might have described
him as Mister Nice Guy.

In the words of a Scandinavian colleague who was with me at the time, Amilcar Cabral
was very much of a 'complete individual – unquestionably a leader of men'.

'If he and the Portuguese could come to terms,' the journalist suggested, 'Cabral could
easily lead his nation to maturity and probably make a success of it.' I could only agree. It
all boiled down to ideals; Cabral was too far to the left and the Portuguese way out on the
right. Neither was willing to compromise.

And yet, I wrote at the time, the PAIGC without Cabral would, relatively speaking, be like a United States without its First Citizen, an emasculated force of some consequence but without the direction to which it had become accustomed.

In the words of another PAIGC delegate at the same OAU summit: 'Cabral *is* the PAIGC and the PAIGC *is* Cabral.'

Amilcar Lopes Cabral was born at Bafata, as we have seen, one of the larger centres of the enclave, well into the interior. His parents were of Cape Verde stock and of mixed blood, which is one of the reasons why his complexion was tawny rather than the jet black of so many of his fellow party members, including Nino.

From the start young Amilcar distinguished himself at school. He was always at or near the top of his class. This prompted the local authorities to take more than a passing interest in this brilliant young *mestico* who showed promise in just about everything he did.

Assimilado status followed as a matter of course; Cabral became one of 11 who were politically assimilated into the ruling establishment in the country. Which was why, shortly after the end of Europe's war, he was awarded a scholarship to the *Instituto Superior de Agronomia,* a technical university in Lisbon where, in 1950, he graduated with honours as an agronomist, or what the Portuguese call an 'Agricultural Engineer'.

Political awareness must have come early, for already in 1948, Cabral the student was exchanging views at the subsequently-banned *Casa dos Estudantes do Imperio* with such men as Agostinho Neto, who was to become head of the Angolan Liberation movement MPLA, and Mário Pinto de Andrade, a poet of renown. Pinto had studied in Frankfurt and Paris and, according to Portuguese sources, was recruited by the radical Portuguese underground and French communist parties.

Shortly after heading back to West Africa, Cabral made his first serious political gesture by forming an African political movement of his own. It was known as MING – the Movement for the Independence of Guinea. Meanwhile, he was employed by the Government Agronomical Office at Bissau. His work during this period (1952/1954) entailed travelling throughout Portuguese Guinea to make contact with the inhabitants at all levels which allowed him contact with all levels of society.

Cabral's approach was always sympathetic. Local peasants confided in him, while the more outspoken demanded that he help them right their wrongs, which, at the hands of the Portuguese authorities of that period were many.

Quietly, systematically and with great diligence, he built up a list of reliable supporters. The more militant among them were told to bide their time. They were assured that forces were in the making to bring power to the black man. The pattern was not unlike that followed by many of the young political aspirants in other West African colonies of the time.

Cabral made his mark during this period. Long after the war started, many Portuguese and local blacks still remembered him as an energetic young official who would do as much work in a day as most Portuguese managed in three.

One of the agricultural reports drawn up by Cabral at the time, recommending certain measures which should be taken to improve conditions in the interior, was adopted by the governor and was still in force when the war ended.

At the same time, his revolutionary talk did not go unnoticed.

Gradually reports filtered through to Bissau that the young Cabral was a revolutionary. However, he was well liked and invariably the rumours were scotched because it was believed Cabral was an ambitious, hardworking fellow who was eager to make his way to the top and this was his way of doing it.

The idea of political maturity among the indigenes was so remote at that stage, even in more developed states such as Kenya and the Gold Coast – soon to become Ghana – as to make revolution unthinkable in most official white African circles. But matters came to a head early in 1954 and Cabral was given the choice of ending his activities or leaving the country.

Cabral took the latter option and returned to Lisbon.

A competent man in Portugal is rarely without work for long and he was soon offered several positions in Angola. There he joined his old political soul-mate Agostinho Neto, and in 1956 became a founder member of the MPLA.

Cabral meanwhile kept close ties with Bissau. He had established the embryo of a revolutionary movement and obviously it was important to keep it active.

The formation of the MPLA was the impetus he needed to set a train of events in his own country moving and in September the same year Cabral again took the lead and formed the Central Committee of the PAIGC. Apart from Cabral himself, there were five others present at that first clandestine meeting in Bissau.

He spent the next three years establishing the political structure which eventually brought the movement to maturity. Speaking to an American journalist, David Andelmann of the *New York Times*, about the period, Cabral explained the systems employed at the time:

'We decided initially to try peaceful coercion as a means of obtaining independence. The Portuguese use of massive force to crush a dockworkers' strike in Bissau was decisive in prompting our movement to change its tactics.

'In the beginning we thought it would be possible to fight in the towns, using the example of the experiences in other countries. But it was a mistake. We tried strikes and demonstrations but after the massacre at Pidjiguiti docks in Bissau, we realised this would not work. The Portuguese used force of arms. There was no choice; we must do the same.'

What happened at Pidjiguiti in 1959 finally convinced Cabral that he must leave the country, create a guerrilla organisation and then return to concentrate on armed insurrection.

On a September evening, barely a month after the killing at Pidjiguiti, Cabral, on a brief

In the latter stages of the war, villages formed their own anti-guerrilla protection units and were issued with firearms by the government for protection. Some serious battles were fought with PAIGC cadres over time. (Author's photo)

visit home, met with his fellow leaders and declared for total war against the Portuguese 'by whatever means possible'. He then bade farewell to his family and crossed the border into the Republic of Guinea where President Sékou Touré – himself barely independent of French rule for a year – offered him a base from which to operate his tiny guerrilla army.

From there, the PAIGC went underground. The movement had already been assured help from another quarter. During his period of self-imposed exile Cabral had visited Prague and Moscow and had been promised unlimited military and material aid should he be able to get the movement firmly established.

The early years were difficult. Men and women had to be trained in both insurgency and administration and as Portuguese Guinea could only boast 14 university graduates in 1960, human resources were distinctly lacking. Many of his cadres first had to learn to read and write.

A steady stream of recruits sped southwards to Conakry to undergo training – usually for periods of between one and three months. All came under Cabral's personal guidance.

The leader travelled extensively. Apart from visiting Communist Bloc states, he attended a variety of meetings in African capitals and abroad. It was during this period that he visited Britain.

He had meantime spent a few years in exile in Rabat, Morocco, with his white wife (an acknowledged communist) and their four children. It is interesting that all three leaders of revolutionary movements that opposed Lisbon's influence in Africa – Cabral, Angola's Agostinho Neto and Eduardo Mondlane of Mozambique, were married to white women. Janet Mondlane, was an American national whom I met during a visit to Dar es Salaam and I discovered an enlightened individual who was also a passionate revolutionary. Like Cabral, her husband was also assassinated.

The record is not a good one: three brilliant anti-Portuguese African leaders and only one of the three – Agostinho Neto – was to survive and see the handovers.

Much of Cabral's own training during this period came from the Russians. A mentor at the time was the Soviet Ambassador in Conakry, Daniel Semonovitch Solod, an acknowledged authority on guerrilla warfare and infiltration. Both Cabral and Andrade are known to have had close contact with this man and other members of his diplomatic staff.

Cabral also acknowledges that 1961 was the year he first became acquainted with the works of Mao. Looking at the subsequent struggle and tactics of the PAIGC, the influence of this Chinese leader has penetrated to all levels of the movement, from the secretary-general downwards was seminal.

Arguably, the man known simply as Nino, or O Nino, is regarded by some military specialists as among the most brilliant guerrilla leaders Africa produced in the last century. Only afterwards did he start to call himself a general. Yet, this was the same João Bernadino Viera Nino who had been arrested by the Portuguese and freed by his own troops on the evening prior to being handed over to PIDE, the Portuguese secret police.

In my subsequent visit to Bissau long after the war, I was able to meet with him, by then President of Guiné-Bissau. I was invited to the presidential residence in Bissau, offered drinks and we spent an hour together. I gave him a copy of the book I'd written some years before on his war, even if some of my comments about his counterparts were unflattering.[1]

I found a man who was quiet-spoken and unassuming. Had I bumped into him in the local supermarket, I wouldn't have recognised him.

What later emerged was that Nino had from an early age made a serious study of the teachings of Ché Guevara. It was his view that only with the application of strict discipline could any guerrilla force meet the extraordinary physical and emotional demands placed upon them by this type of irregular warfare.

The biggest drawback in applying this system, he would always say, lay in effective command. If results were not forthcoming from the leaders, these selfsame irregulars laid themselves open and vulnerable to psychological attack. General de Spínola was of a similar mind, which was why he, in turn was so successful in turning the war around

Lisbon's High Command admitted for a long time that Nino's bold, penetrating tactics produce good dividends. Should he have been killed or replaced by a lesser man, they reckoned, the entire southern front might have collapsed, in much the same way as FRELIMO's Northern Mozambique areas of penetration around Nyassa and Cabo Delgado was limited by tactics employed by General Kaúlza de Arriaga, though not nearly as effectively as de Spínola's efforts.

Amilcar Cabral was astute enough to recognise the need to maintain the status quo, but then he was also aware that Nino, like himself, was ambitious. There had been personality clashes in the past which could eventually result in a crisis if more tangible gains were not made in other sectors where lesser men were in charge.

As we're now aware, Nino wanted everything. In the end, after Cabral had been assassinated, he went on to achieve his objective and became the supreme leader.

Meantime, this was Africa and there were reports that linked him to Cabral's death. But the man was a competent organiser who understood the implications of using disinformation to good advantage – either his own or that of the enemy – and the rumours were never substantiated.

One that did surface at the time indicated that every member of the party responsible for Cabral's murder was eventually brought before a kangaroo court, found guilty and shot. That included a plotter, fearful that he might be next and who tried to defect to Lisbon. But he'd left it too long...

Nino was eclectic in his studies; Ché, Mao, Giap and the rest were all on the shelves of his living room. He became a friend of Castro and many of Africa's leaders. He encouraged his men to read military history and to apply lessons learnt elsewhere to their own struggles.

20

The Aviation Component in Portugal's Colonial Wars

Unlike France, which bolstered its own aircraft industry after World War II, the Portuguese had to rely on American aircraft for counter-insurgency operations. Portugal had 125 F-84G Thunderjets and 65 North American F-86F Sabres when the revolution started and many were deployed in Africa to counter the guerrillas.

After my session in the wilds with Captain João Bacar, I was scheduled to depart from Bissalanca Airport in one of those lumbering old four-engine Portuguese Air Force DC-6s that would take us from Bissau to the Cape Verde Islands. From there, we'd go on to Spanish territory in the Canaries before touching down in Lisbon. It was a lengthy series of hops in those days if you weren't on a commercial jet.

We were loaded, as they say, to the gunwales. That meant that all passengers and their baggage were weighed not once, but twice. The idea was that the engineer would then be able to accurately compute his maximum take-off weight. In Bissau's overbearing heat, there could be no mistake: the plane needed a certain runway length to get off the ground and Bissalanca wasn't the biggest airport in Africa.

Part of the problem, somebody said, involved the number of war-wounded onboard. There were about 20 or so, some of whom who were critical. At least one wasn't expected to survive the trip.

We left Portuguese Guinea late that morning and even then it took what seemed an age to get off the ground. To this observer, there was a 30-second phase when I wasn't sure that we'd clear a bunch of palms that stood firm at the far end of the runway. We made it, and finally the DC-6 was up and away. Minutes later we were over the open sea which changed colour from a dirty, ochre-brown to almost incandescent hues of tropical blue. Roughly about then, I propped my head up against the bulkhead and fell asleep.

Since every farewell in Portugal is an event, such things can sometimes be pretty headily celebrated. It is the same almost throughout the Iberian Peninsula and I consequently didn't have too much sleep the night before. All I knew was that I'd certainly been plied with brandy, 20-year-old Constantinho, no less. Consequently, it must have been an hour or two before a set of jarring vibrations caused me to open my eyes. To my horror, the aircraft was shuddering.

The first thing that caught my eye was that one of the two propellers immediately outside my window had stopped turning. We were at twenty-something thousand feet

Ground crews in the process of 'bombing up' one of the F-86 Sabre jets
that were operationally deployed in Portuguese Guinea until pressure from
Washington forced them to be withdrawn. (Photo *Revista da Armada*)

and there it was, hanging motionless in the air. A string of instructions followed over the
intercom, none of it explicit, but delivered in a high-pitched voice that suggested that it
emanated from somebody as disturbed as I was. It was the pilot and frankly, I understood
none of it.

Clearly, we had a problem. The soldiers seated around me were distinctly uneasy, and
since I was the only foreigner onboard and in their minds, a 'world traveller', they looked to
me for advice. I had none to give, because not only had this kind of thing never happened
to me before, but I was just as terrified as they were. I did my best not to show it, stiff upper-
lip and all that.

By then one or two of them had made their way forward to the cockpit, for all the good
that was likely to do.

Turning towards my window again, my heart sank still further. Huge plumes of white
smoke were emerging from out under the wing. My immediate reaction was that we were
on fire!

We were not. The flight crew was dumping fuel, which was standard procedure even
then, only I didn't know it. Aviation fuel tends to vaporize at altitude and when the cocks
are opened, huge swathes of steam-like vapour emerge. It must have looked fairly impressive
from sea level, and since we were over one of the major sea lanes between Europe and Africa,
there must have been quite a few reports transmitted by radio of an aircraft on fire. Trouble
was, there was more to come.

Portuguese Air Force F-86s on the flightline. These jets were withdrawn from Africa because of pressure from Washington and replaced by Italian Fiat G-91 jets, but never deployed in Angola.

Moments later the plane's right wing dipped and as we banked sharply towards the African coast, somebody muttered something about another engine having started to splutter. What a predicament!

I was also aware – since you could hardly miss the implications – that with all the sick and dying onboard, any prospect of ditching in the open sea would have meant more blood being spilled. And in these open, tropical waters, it was axiomatic that there were sharks galore, something I knew quite a lot about since I'd just recently published my first underwater book.

Though a plenitude of instructions constantly poured out of the intercom, I finally got someone to tell me exactly what was taking place.

We were heading back towards the coast, one of the nurses onboard explained. No, she said, we weren't headed for Portuguese Guinea, because we might not get that far. As it was, we were losing altitude. Rather we'd set course for Dakar, in Senegal, which was still about 15 or 20 minutes away. I didn't have to tell her that Senegal was one of several African states then technically at war with Lisbon. A string of Maydays had gone out and Dakar knew we were coming, she happily reported.

As we got within sight of Goreé Island, the pilot turned sharply right and instead of landing, our aircraft headed down the coast. As he explained later, we were close enough to get into Dakar Airport, but why risk the diplomatic brouhaha that would almost certainly follow should a Portuguese military aircraft be forced to put down in enemy territory?

'So, after that, once we got over Banjul in the Gambia, I just kept going – still further

The Fiat G-91 was a versatile combat aircraft. An Italian jet fighter, it was the winner of the NATO competition in 1953 as standard equipment for Allied air forces and Portugal took 40. The first G-91s arrived in Bissau in 1966 and served with Esquadra 121 Tigres. Two were shot down by Soviet SAM-7 (Strela-2) ground to air missile in 1973 and two more some months later by conventional ground fire. (Author's collection)

south. We kept at it until we reached Bissau.'

It was close, pretty damn close, he reckoned, 'but we made it back safely', were his words.

It was a dreadful experience, hopefully never to be repeated. Not eager to climb onboard the DC-6 the next day, which, I was assured, would have been repaired, I was able to cajole General de Spínola into getting me onboard one of the bi-weekly TAP Boeing flights to the Metropolis, which he did with a smile.

His government paid for the ticket as well.

What was clear from the beginning of the war was that the Portuguese would have to fight their wars very differently to what other nations had done. For a start, it was the age of the whirly-bird, but Lisbon was never able to afford the kind of helicopter support that the Americans enjoyed in Vietnam.

Alouette IIs were superceded by the more sophisticated Alouette IIIs and used in all three conflict zones, but like the majority of indigent folk, Lisbon's military commanders thought long and hard before deploying these valuable assets. No matter what the purpose, a chopper would need a very good reason to be committed to a specific operation.

The Portuguese Air Force was equipped with a range of obsolete World War II aircraft which, under stress, did what was required of them in difficult African conditions. The PV-2 Lockheed Ventura – also known as the Harpoon bomber – was one of these planes, seen here on the airstrip at N'Riquinha in Eastern Angola. (Author's photo)

Though some Aerospatiale Pumas were eventually deployed to Africa, their numbers were also restricted, in large part because a dozen new Pumas had barely arrived in Lisbon from France before the anti-war Portuguese underground destroyed them all in a spectacular night raid that stunned the nation.

In larger operations, Special Force units such as the *Caçadores-Paraquedistas* – literally 'Hunter-Paratroops' – would be taken in by the gunships referred to in the lingo as *Lobo Mau* or, more appropriately, 'heli-cannons'. Though fitted with all-purpose GPMGs in the earlier stages, the Alouettes eventually came equipped with 20mm cannons, mounted – as with both the Rhodesian and South African air forces – on the port side.

These special units were customarily based on groups of 25 men and under 'normal' circumstances, a clutch of helicopters would each uplift five paratroops at a time.

On the offensive side, the Portuguese Air Force took a while to make effective use of their gunships. When these helicopters first arrived in Africa, some unit commanders would try to squeeze six men on board, even though this remarkably resilient little gunship was designed for a maximum two plus four. French technicians attached to the Portuguese armed forces warned that excess weight could result in the gearbox being stripped, so numbers were afterwards reduced. It was a recurring problem, Acting Captain Ron Reid-Daly discovered while serving as an advisor to the Portuguese Army in Mozambique.

Mostly, these Special Forces would be dropped from Nord-Atlas transporters. The rest

Luanda's main international airport doubled as the country's major air force base.
There was a constant flow of planes passing through. (Author's collection)

of the Portuguese Army deployed in such raids – usually called a *golpe de mao* (a hand blow) – were taken forward to positions from which a strike could be made by truck or they went in on foot.

But even that was sometimes difficult when there were casualties and vast distances over hostile terrain had to be covered.

When the revolution started in Angola in 1961, the *Forca Aerea Portuguesa* (Portuguese Air Force, or FAP) had almost 400 aircraft and more than 22,000 personnel on its books.

There were roughly 150 military aircraft deployed in the three 'Overseas Provinces', including North American T-6 Harvards, Lockheed PV2 Harpoons, and Lockheed Neptunes (bought from the Royal Netherlands Navy) as well as the more modern Republic F-84 Thunderjets and North American F-86F Sabres. The transport air arm included the Noratlas-2501, Douglas C-47s and C-54/DC-6s as well Boeing 707 transports. More modest aircraft included Austers and the German Dornier Do-27s.

For counter-insurgency purposes, the T-6s Harvards were the workhorses, armed as they were with machine-gun pods and light bombs. In spite of their relatively low speed, these plucky little snub-noses proved to be useful in providing back-up at critical moments and while travelling about Angola and Portuguese Guinea, I would often see them returning from sorties in pairs and the pilots would wave as they drew level.

Considering the duration of the war – 13 years in all – and the number of contacts registered annually, relatively few planes were lost in action. Even more remarkable was the fact that initially, the only strike capability came from the T-6s: jet fighter/ground-support aircraft only arrived later.

Like the French, the Portuguese were initially obliged to turn to Second World War aircraft in their search for any kind of effective counter-insurgency potential. There were plenty of aircraft out there in the 1950s and 1960s, including lots with limited hours on their clocks. Among the most user-friendly were Lockheed PV-2 light patrol bombers – designated Harpoons by NATO, many of which had originally done anti-submarine work in the North Atlantic.

With several variations – depending on application – the basic PV-2 had five .50-calibre machine guns mounted forward: customarily three in the undernose and two above, though placement could be varied. Up to a ton-and-a-half of bombs could be loaded internally, with possibly six or eight 122mm HVAR rockets on the wings.

Napalm soon became a feature of many of the raids into the interior – first in Angola, and afterwards in Portuguese Guinea and Mozambique, though when I raised the issue at official briefings, nobody knew what I was talking about. So much for truth being the first casualty of war ...

Tracking rebel groups from the air in some of the most difficult jungle terrain in the world was a serious issue for the Portuguese. While government forces obviously enjoyed some success, especially among groups cornered in isolated patches of bush, Lisbon was aware that even though Washington had deployed squadrons of B-52s – and routinely pounded Viet Cong and North Vietnamese infiltration routes (like the Ho Chi Minh Trail) – this kind of interdiction had had no real effect. In South East Asia there would be damage, of course, and the flow of arms would be temporarily interrupted, but then everything would go forward as before after the holes had been filled.

Something similar applied to Africa, though with significant differences. First, the Portuguese Air Force was a lightweight when it came to delivering tonnage, as we've seen with the PV-2s. More important, much of the terrain in which the war was being fought was in a region that had always been sparsely populated. That meant there were hundreds of paths that were neither mapped nor identified, by either side. That also suggested that there were no set or detailed infiltration routes in or out of the Congo. And no matter how many bombs were dropped, nobody ever bothered to fill the holes.

The Portuguese Air Force eventually managed to partially solve the bomb-load problem by acquiring surplus B-26 'Invaders', quite a few of them on a 'nudge-nudge' basis from the Americans who would not demand end-user certificates. They would usually look the other way when the Invaders were flown out of holding bases in Arizona and elsewhere by Portuguese nationals.

The initial acquisition of these COIN-type Invaders was clandestinely handled by international arms salesmen in Europe, largely because sales of B-26s tended to raise eyebrows. The bombers had already been linked to a variety of illegal operations in Central

The French-built Aérospatiale SA330 Puma helicopter. Portugal emerged as an early export customer for this machine, ordering 12 in 1969. Many of these were sabotaged by anti-war elements at the Tancos Air Base in March 1971, shortly before they were to have been sent to do war duty in Angola. (Author's collection)

and South America (including the Bay of Pigs debacle) Vietnam, Laos, as well as the Congo, where they were flown by Cuban émigrés living in Miami.

There were still more problems before they could be taken into active service in Africa because all were past their prime. The aircraft were acquired at a time when the B-26 fleet worldwide had been grounded following a series of wing-spar failures, though this impediment did not apply to newly-remanufactured OnMark B-26K 'Counter-Invaders', then finding favour in South East Asia.

The Portuguese Air Force went ahead anyway and with the kind of improvisation for which this nation became known, they took these ageing bombers in hand and solved most of the problems.

Once the B-26s arrived in Europe, the air force central maintenance facility, OGMA Aviation Services was waiting for them. Their technicians set to work correcting flaws, strengthening spars, fitting armaments and making other modifications. For instance, rear cockpit canopies were replaced with metal fairings and extra fuel tanks installed for long-range operations.

Also, a number of B-26C models were converted for strafing use in ground-support roles that eventually proved successful. In a sense, these were modest European forerunners of what was already referred to in Vietnam as 'Puff the Magic Dragon'. C-47 Dakotas were also deployed in this role, but on a more limited basis when overwhelming suppressing fire was required for a specific operation.

For all that, the air force always had a limited role in interdicting insurgent presence, especially in regions with heavy forest cover. Aircraft played a valuable role, but when push became shove, it was men on the ground that achieved the most results. Those who have experienced this kind of warfare know that a single large tree can easily hide six or eight soldiers from prying eyes from above.

It was the same during South Africa's Border War in what was eventually to become Namibia. The country was arid and sparse, but even there the guerrillas were able to make good use of what little cover the bush offered. Most times, when detected, the insurgents were in open areas and on the move and most of this spotting was by helicopter aircrews.

Areas of aviation responsibility were divided up between Portugal and the African colonies, with *Primeira Regiao Aerea* (1st Air Region) in Lisbon, *Secunda RA* in Luanda and *Terceira RA* in Lourenco Marques. Additionally, there were several transit airports, known as *Aeródromo de Transito* on Sal in the Cape Verde Islands and another on Sao Tomé, in the Atlantic Ocean to the south of Nigeria.

Forward airfields, *Aeródromo de Manobras* (AMs), we're informed in an excellent report published by the Air Combat Information Group (ACIG) and compiled by Tom Cooper and Pedro Alvin,[1] were strategically placed in all the African colonies. Cabo Verde, at Sal Island, is known to have been AT.1 until 1975, while in Portuguese Guinea, there were at least six AMs (at least three with paved runways), at Aldeia Formosa, Bafatá, Bubaque, Cufar, Nova Lamego, and Tite. Each airfield was guarded by a squadron of the *Policia Aérea* – FAP military police.

Every large settlement throughout Portuguese Africa had at least one air strip that could handle light planes. Further afield, in Angola and Mozambique, almost all larger centres ended up with fairly sophisticated flight facilities. Cities like Angola's Lobito, Lubango, Nova Lisboa, Luso and Henrique de Carvalho and Mozambique's Beira, Nampula, Nacala and Tete were capable of taking the full range of passenger planes, including jets.

Maintenance facilities were restricted to the regional capitals, with modest secondary repair units at a few outlying airports. Unlike Rhodesia and South Africa, if a plane crashed in the distant interior, it wouldn't be hauled back for repair unless this was feasible. Roads in Angola and Mozambique often made this impossible.

It happened, of course, but most times the wreck would be stripped of anything useable and left where it had come to rest.

As hostilities progressed, the role of the Portuguese Air Force was continually upgraded to provide additional firepower. F-84G Thunderjets were deployed in Angola and Mozambique, F-86F Sabres in Portuguese Guinea and, at a later stage, Italian-designed Fiat G-91s in Guinea and Mozambique (but not in Angola).

The veteran United States Air Force Texan T-6 – also known as the Harvard – was another aircraft of World War II vintage which saw a lot of action in all three theatres of African military activity. During World War II it was used to train American, British and Commonwealth pilots and continued in that role in the South African Air Force for many years afterwards. These two were operational in Eastern Angola when they were snapped by the author.

The Aeritalia G-91 (nicknamed 'Gina') was an Italian fighter intended to serve as standard equipment for NATO air forces in the 1960s. Though a first class operational aircraft, it was eventually adopted by only three countries – the Italian Air Force, West Germany's Luftwaffe, and the Portuguese Air Force, but enjoyed a long service life that extended over 35 years.

In Africa, the G-91 replaced Lisbon's F-86 Sabres, which were withdrawn following US protests over the use of these aircraft that had originally been supplied for NATO defensive purposes, though interestingly, the F-84 was to continue flying operationally for some time, probably because Washington believed them to be obsolete.

Portuguese G-91s continued providing tactical support to ground forces until Lisbon's withdrawal from Africa in 1975 and were finally phased out in the Portuguese Air Force in 1993 and Italy in 1995.

It is interesting that Italian planes were involved in several African wars. Italy supplied the South African Air Force with more than a hundred Macchi 326-MBs jet fighters under a contract that included a squadron or two of underpowered single-engine reconnaissance/spotters.

Robert Craig Johnson tells us that Portugal had more than 100 Thunderjets and something like 65 F-86F Sabres when the rebellions ignited, but that it could not afford to buy additional combat aircraft purely for use in the colonies.[2]

'The F-84Gs were the first to go to Africa [with] two squadrons at Air Base 2, in Ota, transferred to Air Base 9 in Luanda, Angola. They remained there for the next 16 years. Detachments occasionally operated in Mozambique, and when the Thunderjets stood down in 1974, they were the last operational examples of their type in the world.

'F-86F Sabres were sent to Guinea-Bissau in 1961. Eight aircraft – as Detachment 52, operated out of Bissalanca Air Base at Bissau [having flown] 577 sorties, using bombs, napalm, and Matra and HVAR rockets', says Johnson. Though he doesn't say so, the Portuguese, as with the Americans in Vietnam were not averse to using defoliants to achieve certain strategic aims.

Portugal remained secretive about losses throughout the war, he adds, 'but ... they were relatively light. A Sabre fighter was destroyed when it overran the runway during an emergency landing, and [another] was shot down by ground fire in 1963 (the pilot ejected and was rescued)'.

It is worth mentioning that in February, 1973, a decade later and with the war in full swing, a FAP G-91 jet fighter was shot down by a SAM missile. The pilot, Almeida Brito, was killed and it was only after two more were lost that the Portuguese began to follow the South African example and started flying at tree-top level. It was then too that the FAP opted for olive green anti-radiation paint and limited the size of their national insignia on the fuselages.

During my visits to Angola and Portuguese Guinea I would see the Fiats lined up on the runways, but was always steered clear of them 'for reasons of security'. There was no comment on their role, or what weapons they might have onboard.

The decision to withdraw the Sabres from Portuguese Guinea left the Portuguese without any fighter jets in Bissalanca for as long as it took Lisbon to establish connections with its European NATO partners and find replacements. Both Germany and Italy acceded to initial requests and sold some ex-*Luftwaffe* Fiat G.9 reconnaissance fighters to Portugal on condition that they would be used only on Portuguese soil.

Once the Fiats were delivered, the FAP deployed them in all three African *metrópole-províncias ultramarinas*, having declared that the possessions were national territory.

The G-91 – a modest-sized aircraft that was able to operate under Third World conditions, which might mean a landing on a road or on dusty strips – probably had the most lasting effect in this series of counter-insurgency campaigns. In Portuguese Guinea they saw service with 121 Squadron (*Tigres*) and in Mozambique, with 502 Squadron (*Jaguares*) and 702 Squadron (*Escorpiões*). The jets were similarly deployed in Angola, operating out of Luanda's Craveiro Lopes International Airport where they provided a pretty good account of both their versatility and fire power.

Armed with a variety of weapons, they came with four .50-calibre machine-guns instead of the usual 30-mm DEFA cannon which the Germans mounted. It is indicative that their need in Guinea was so urgent that when they first arrived in Africa their *Luftwaffe*

Another aviation asset of French origin that was extensively utilised in Portugal's African wars was the Nord Noratlas. Initially a dozen were bought from France and deployed to Africa and later, another 19 were acquired from West Germany's *Luftwaffe*. They served with *Esquadra 32* at Tancos, *Esquadra 92* at Luanda, *Esquadra 102*, Beira and at Bissalanca in Portuguese Guinea where, from 1969 to 1974, they formed the mainstay of *Esquadra 123*.

markings could still be seen on their fuselages.

In Mozambique, where the Portuguese had complete air dominance, the G-91s subsequently flew numerous reconnaissance roles with K-20 camera-pods mounted up-front. In the process, a large part of this East African country on the Indian Ocean was mapped.

Not so in Portuguese Guinea, where the fighting was too fierce to allow for anything diversionary.

Nobody in Lisbon was under any illusion that the air force would be able to operate unchallenged forever. In 1973 the strategic emphasis switched overnight once the PAIGC were provided with Soviet-supplied SAM-7 MANPADS. In March 1973, three FAP aircraft were lost in two months and by September the PAIGC claimed to have downed 21 Portuguese war planes, which was pushing the propaganda envelope because Lisbon never suffered such losses.

To quote Cooper and Alvin in their ACIG report, the disappearance of the air force from the skies as a consequence of repeated missile strikes was a heavy blow for the morale of the Portuguese Army troops.

'These [troops] now knew they would get no helicopter support for casualty-evacuation, nor for gunfire support, and also the appeasing sound of the Fiats flying CAS-sorties would not be heard overhead. Moreover, the Portuguese morale was in decline after the departure of General de Spínola in 1972. These negative developments finally enabled [the guerrillas] to attack and capture Guiledje, an important military base commanding supply routes.'

To their credit, documents have subsequently come to light that the PAIGC had several opportunities to shoot down civilian aircraft, but did not do so because of the fear of adverse publicity. Not so Rhodesia's Joshua Nkomo's guerrillas, who targeted two Rhodesian Viscounts in succession after they had taken off from Kariba. Scores of passengers were killed, including several passengers and crew that actually survived the crashes and were summarily shot by the terrorists.

Then there were conflicting reports about the military wing of the PAIGC having formed its own air force that included MiG-17s, ostensibly flown by East-European pilots and based in Conakry. There were said to have been five MiG-17s and two MiG-15s delivered. The truth was that these were all Nigerian Air Force jets, supposed to be flown by Nigerian pilots and had recently seen a lot of action in the Biafran War where they were flown by South African and British mercenary pilots.

The Portuguese took these new threats seriously enough to install a battery of Crotale anti-aircraft missiles at Bissalanca Airport. This French system was the same as the Cactus missile which South Africa funded through development and production.

Shortly before the Lisbon coup, Portugal was already talking to France about buying a squadron of Dassault Mirage III interceptors, similar to those acquired by South Africa. Had the war continued, these would have been stationed in Portuguese Guinea.

In Angola, South Africa entered the war on the Portuguese side soon after Jonas Savimbi's UNITA joined the war in 1966. Aware that Lisbon's forces were already fully extended, Pretoria made the decision to send in South African Air Force helicopters a year later and 1 Air Component was established at Rundu in the Caprivi in May, 1968. The first helicopters deployed in cross-border operations were Alouette IIIs, followed by the larger Aerospatiale Pumas for trooping and supply airlifts.

Also involved in these operations were tandem-seated Bosboks, mainly in reconnaissance roles and the South African-built Kudu. Cessna 185s were used mainly in Sky-Shout roles.

Throughout Portugal's African campaigns transport remained the single biggest bugbear. It had been a problem even before that, since 1930s-vintage, triple-engine, former *Luftwaffe Junkers*-52s comprised about half the FAP transport fleet as late as the 1960s, with the other half being Douglas 'Dakota' C-47s, or what the grunts in Vietnam got to term the 'Gooney Bird'. Some of these aircraft in FAP livery dated back to the Second World War.

ACIG tells us that by 1971, the FAP operated 18 Dakotas, obtained from very different sources. Four were in Angola (though only two were operational), ten in Mozambique (four operational), and two with 123 Squadron in Portuguese Guinea (reinforced by one more by the time hostilities ended in 1974). 'While their main task was transportation, they were also used for reconnaissance, instruction, search and rescue, and medical evacuation, while a single example was deployed as a make-shift bomber [out of Bissau]'.

The Douglas DC-3, seen here at a remote air strip in Northern Angola played an invaluable intermediary transport role with Portuguese forces in Africa (Author's photo)

The war soon made the need for a more advanced and expanded air transport capability essential. Lisbon started by assembling whatever DC-6 airliners it could acquire, the same plane that almost ditched into the sea after I'd left Bissalanca Airport the first time. Efforts were also made to buy more Boeing 707s, which Washington vetoed because they were to be used by the military

Finally, Lisbon obtained 30-plus twin-boom Nord-Atlas (Noratlas) freighters, with 18 coming direct from West Germany with their original markings which, ironically, included elephant decals on the fuselage.

The Noratlas-2501, with an eventual production of more than 400 planes, had an interesting pedigree. It initially gained fame when squadrons of these transporters dropped French paras and supplies during the 1956 Suez Crisis.

The Israeli Air Force (IAF) originally purchased three 2501s in 1956, and they performed so well that three more followed in 1959. And then another 16 were ordered, timed for involvement in the Six Day War. One report states that several were used on long-range strikes to drop bombs on Egyptian targets. Still more were converted for maritime reconnaissance work. It was a Noratlas-2501 that was responsible for the deaths of 31 American naval personnel and 171 wounded, when the USS *Liberty* was wrongly identified as an Arab warship patrolling the Mediterranean.

During my own sojourns about Africa, I relied almost solely on this transport aircraft to get to some of the more remote destinations. One flew me to Eastern Angola, another to Cabinda and back. A Noratlas was used on our initial flight over the Dembos when supply drops were made on bush camps in the jungle.

It was not always a smooth transition, because getting back was always a problem. We were promised flights to get us around Angola and Mozambique which never materialised. Or perhaps took three or four days in doing so. For example, once I'd finished my stint with Captain Vitor Alves in N'Riquinha, I was told that a plane would arrive to take me to Serpa Pinto. One day's wait became three and finally, on the fifth day, it was an Auster that popped out of nowhere.

Obviously Lisbon devoted a lot of effort in trying to acquire cheap, reliable and easily serviceable transport aircraft and initially there was an urgent need for a smaller, sturdy all-purpose utility transport that would not have a role in counter-insurgency operations. It needed to be dual purpose since it would also be used in liaison work, which, in such vast regions, was essential.

The Portuguese Air Force already had a number of Douglas C-47s, but this reliable old veteran was often too large for remoter air strips. Efforts were made to obtain the Canadian-built De Havilland Otter, but American opposition made that impossible, which meant that Lisbon had to look inwards, towards Europe and once more France came to the rescue.

Following the end of the Algerian War, there were suddenly large numbers of Broussard short-take-off-and-landing (STOL) aircraft available that although past retirement age, were cheap and functional. Their most serious shortcoming was weight limitation and after several accidents said to be because of overloading and other factors, the Portuguese Air Force settled for the German-built Dornier Do-27. With a slightly smaller engine than the Broussard, it lifted an equivalent payload of between six and eight troops and crew.

More than 100 of these remarkably reliable little planes were eventually required and Robert Craig Johnson tells us that many were Do-27As that had originally served with the West German Luftwaffe. All these sported a strengthened, wide-track undercarriage, extra fuel tanks, and underwing hard points which allowed the aircraft to serve in a Forward Air Control role with smoke-marker rockets or close-support, with 18-round pods of 37-mm Matra SNEB rockets under each wing. These were the same rockets – adapted as bazookas for ground use – which Captain João Bacar's men used when I went on patrol with them from Tite.

Johnson: 'The Dorniers proved popular and highly successful in use, though losses were comparatively heavy. [While] vulnerable to ground fire, the rocket-armed Do-27Ks were useful close-support aircraft ... but they were in increasingly short supply (11 were lost in action).

'A number of Dorniers were fitted with fuselage racks for two 50-kg bombs and used in action, but the modification does not appear to have been successful enough for general adoption. [One of these planes] was given an experimental door mounting for a 1,200 round-per-minute MG-42 machine-gun and successfully tested, using a circling, gunship-style flight path. Though this would have been the easiest way of arming them, it was not accepted for service use. In any case, the Do-27's days as a viable combat aircraft were clearly numbered by the late 1960's. Light aircraft could not survive in the face of the increasingly common 12.7mm machine gun fire.'

Cloete Breytenbach took this classic shot of a Dornier spotter plane on
the air strip at Nambuangongo in Angola's *Dembos* region.

A final word about the French-built Alouette helicopter, without which Portugal's wars in
Africa would have ended much sooner.

It is of interest that helicopters as an extension of the military fighting arm only came
into its own not that many years before, something I deal with in some detail in my book
The Chopper Boys: Helicopter Warfare in Africa.[3]

While the British initially formed the Far East Casualty Air Evacuation Flight in
Malaya with three Westland S-51 Dragonfly choppers in 1950 – an unsuccessful venture,
as it transpired – it was the French in Algeria that first strapped men onto litters on either
side of the fuselage to deliver support fire in the mountains behind the Mediterranean. It
was primitive for what it was supposed to achieve, but it worked.

From then the French worked vigorously towards the implementation of the helicopter
gunship as we know it today and some of the early Alouette IIs were delivered to the
Portuguese.

Like the South Africans and the Rhodesians in their bush war before them, the
Aerospatiale SA-316 Alouette III was arguably the most successful counter-insurgency
machine ever built outside the United States. Lightweight, underpowered and with
comparatively low speed, these tiny choppers could take a remarkable amount of
punishment from triple-A ground fire and still manage to return to base, sometimes with
their tail booms or a rotor hanging by a thread.

Although almost half a century old, there are still Alouettes operational in both
military and civilian sectors in scores of countries around the globe, which might be
expected since there were almost 1,500 units built by the time production ended in 1979
(apart from another 500 in India and Romania under license).

It is interesting that one of the first Alouette IIIs to come off the production line landed

Once Lisbon decided to withdraw its troops from Africa, many of the aircraft
that had played solid roles in these bush wars were shoved to the fringes
of some airports in the interior and abandoned. (Author's photo)

and took off in July 1960 with seven people onboard and reached an altitude just short of 5,000 metres in the French Alps near Mont Blanc.

Apropos Portugal's relationship with the United States, this was an issue that constantly came into question, especially since Lisbon was perceived to be at war in a part of the world where Washington was eager to cultivate friends and influence governments. Yet many of the aircraft fighting the rebels had American origins. Altogether Lisbon fielded ten different types of aircraft of United States manufacture.

This reliance placed Lisbon in a prickly position vis-à-vis its principal ally. The aircraft had been supplied under American military aid programs on the clear understanding that they would be dedicated to NATO for the defense of Europe.

When it became manifest that the Portuguese High Command was diverting some of its aircraft to the three African territories, Portugal was in breach of contract in American eyes. The US Government consequently blocked spares and replacements and protested volubly in the United Nations and other international forums, apart from putting Lisbon under direct diplomatic pressure.

There were two consequences, both of significant international interest. The first was that Lisbon increasingly turned to Europe – and specifically to France and Germany for its aviation needs. Second, a lot of other countries took note that if you bought American hardware and your actions displeased Washington, sanctions or restrictions could result.

This was a lesson not lost on many Third World nations, particularly in Asia and the Middle East. The prospect of having your military assets circumscribed by some functionary in the US State Department has often caused countries to look to alternative sources of supply. For this reason alone, the Soviet Union and, today Russia, scored heavily in making sales, always at the expense of the Americans.

This is an unenviable situation and sadly, it persists to this day.

PART III: THE WAR CONTINUES

It is almost a truism to say that the colonisation of the African continent would have been impossible without local collaboration. The stereotyped picture of immensely superior European forces defeating small, fragile and unarticulated African resistances rarely corresponds to the historical truth. Much closer to reality is the picture of European officials able to foster and manage internal contradictions, attracting African forces into their orbit to make them fight other African forces in order to install and preserve the colonial order.

African Troops in the Portuguese Colonial Army, 1961-1974: Angola, Guinea-Bissau and Mozambique; João Paulo Borges Coelho; Eduardo Mondlane University, Maputo, Mozambique, 2002 [Extract from *Portuguese Studies Review*, 10 (1) (2002), pp.129-50].

PART III: THE WAR CONTINUES

21

Land at the End of the Earth

Finally, on the dusty landing strip at N'Riquinha and two days' travel by road from Luso in the extreme south-east corner of Angola, I found a signboard that pointed north. It read: 'Lisbon 13,999 km.' In fact, it was more like half that distance.

At N'Riquinha, arguably the most distant camp in the Portuguese colonies, even Luanda seemed remote. As the crow flies, this isolated military base – almost within sight of the Zambian frontier – was actually closer to Mozambique on the Indian Ocean than to the Angolan capital.

We'd travelled eastwards by air and passed through the diamond centre of Henrique de Carvalho (Saurimo today) and touched down for lunch at the Luso rail junction near the Congolese frontier. The last leg was in a German-supplied Unimog. In the process we covered more than 2,000 kilometres.

As a tiny trading post established many years before, N'Riquinha – while originally only a tiny tribal village – had become a vital link in the chain of Portuguese military command in Angola. It was commanded by a young army professional, Captain Vitor Manuel Rodrigues Alves, who bore a striking resemblance to the South African cardiac pioneer Professor Chris Barnard.

'Most people who come to the camp for the first time think I am his twin', the captain chuckled, which was the way this cheerful, friendly individual did things.

The area under his command – roughly more than 30,000 square kilometres, or the size of Switzerland – was bounded on the east by Zambia and to the south by the Caprivi Strip and Okavango River. It was the duty of Captain Alves to garrison certain villages in his area; keep them stocked up with supplies that arrived irregularly by road, rotate relief forces at regular intervals, or sometimes – because of the rains – irregularly and, hopefully, keep insurgents in check. It was an impossible task because there was no borderline fence, or anything else that told you that you might have crossed from one country to another. Eastern Angola was an ocean of sand.

In a sense, Captain Vitor Alves was guardian, mentor and protector to everybody within his fief, including hundreds of African refugees who returned to Angola after having been shanghaied by the rebels. It was these pathetic souls who, desperate to get to their original bush villages, had subsequently escaped and landed on the captain's doorstep.

On average, his men fought perhaps one action a week, some half-hearted contacts where a few shots might be exchanged, after which both sides would withdraw. There was nothing reminiscent of the intensity of what was then going on in Vietnam: essentially it

341

wasn't that kind of war.

At other times, some of the convoys heading in his direction might be ambushed, which was when things got serious and casualties would result. Inevitably, in this kind of primitive campaign, landmines took a toll.

Captain Alves had a company of 165 men and five officers under his command and in spite of distances and an obvious lack of manpower (as well as inadequate firepower because he had no artillery) he seemed to manage.

'Sometimes we stretch things a little fine' he told me in good English, for he was an educated man. It was not always easy, the captain declared with disarming candour.

Behind the mask of charm and congeniality, Captain Vitor Alves was also a man of cold logic and efficiency. His bearing was strictly military, but not ostentatiously so. Among those under his command, his disposition was one of easy informality, but there was no mistaking his authority.

He would ask one of his men to do something rather than order him. Similarly, he would put his arm across the shoulders of one of the young lieutenants as they spoke about a patrol that had just returned from the bush, or discussed the best tactics to rout a new group of guerrillas that had entered the area. You could see he cared about what happened and such gestures were appreciated down the ranks. When he gave an order he expected it to be carried out. Conversely, he could be uncompromising with those who took advantage of his affability.

The captain had personally trained all the men in his company at their home base in Portugal. They had headed out to Africa together four months before and there wasn't a man in the unit who didn't know and appreciate their *capitao*. One sensed that they had a healthy respect for him, which was quietly reciprocated.

Most actions since they had got to N'Riquinha had been fairly low key – Captain Alves had lost one man with three wounded, one seriously. The unit's tally of guerrillas killed, wounded and captured was impressive; it numbered scores, but that trend also demonstrated shortcomings in insurgent training and discipline. Many of the guerrillas in Angola's eastern region had been shanghaied, which made them unwilling participants in a conflict in which they had no real interest.

The officer talked well of his men: 'I'd like to say that these are my sons, but of course they are not ... though you do get the message. To each I must be a father, judge, disciplinarian and confidant. I must take them all back with me to their homes in the *metrópole* at the end of the two years because I am responsible for their welfare. The unpleasant part is that I have to answer if something goes wrong'.

When there were problems, he told me, he would write to their families, wives or sweethearts because like it or not, he was their official and unofficial go-between.

Cold beer in hand, we sat on the porch of the little shack that he called home and watched the sun disappear over the arid scrubland as he spoke. We could just as easily have been on safari in Maasai Mara, many hours' jet flight to the north.

Although only a lowly captain and an academic at heart, Captain Vitor Alves displayed some unusual qualities.

He was married to Theresa, the daughter of a Portuguese admiral, which made him and his family de facto members of the one of the most exclusive aristocratic establishments in Europe. His own background was distinctly upper class and as I spoke to him that memorable night, I recall a well-furnished intellect who could quote Proust or Sartre as easily as Ché. He had been in the army for 11 of his 33 years. Part of his African military career had been served in Mozambique and, while abroad, Theresa looked after their children and studied at Lisbon University.

Metropolitan by birth and bearing, the captain spoke four languages fluently; English, Portuguese, French and German. He also believed that his roots in Africa went deep and liked to think of himself as someone who had adopted the continent as his own... 'an adopted son of Africa', he would remonstrate.

'I have drunk of the waters of this continent ... it runs in my veins. I do not think I could live anywhere else for very long', he would say.

He was unequivocally free of bias and believed all men, black and white, were equal. He said so, unabashedly, even in the presence of the occasional South African Army or Air Force officer who would make their way to his camp for an off-the-record pow-wow in the bush about what the 'other side' were doing. By then Pretoria was well aware that there was trouble coming, having already experienced the ramifications of insurgency in South West Africa, a guerrilla war that was eventually to last 21 years.

Writing nearly ten years after the event on the nature of the MFA revolution in Lisbon, the American military writer Douglas Porch makes some interesting comments on Alves as a young officer. It was Porch's view that the political leanings of a handful of MFA elite went back long before the war and this guerrilla struggle.

Like Nassar, Sadat and Gadaffi, some Portuguese left-wing officers (including Alves) had been conspicuous as cadets. His classmates at the Military Academy noticed that he had been politically active even then. One of his associates, a naval lieutenant, had even slept with a copy of a book entitled *Lenin* under his pillow and with time, had managed to convert one or two close friends to their revolutionary views. But most of those with whom the more radically inclined associated remained unaffected by any such entreaties.

It would have been interesting to hear what Theresa's family with its strong naval traditions would have said about the left-wing views of this recalcitrant son-in-law.

The N'Riquinha posting must have suited Alves' temperament, for in spite of his excellent counter-insurgency track record, much of his time was spent on rehabilitating civilian refugees who crossed the border from Zambia.

A significant part of his day was spent trying to rehabilitate civilian refugees that had returned to Angola from Zambia and, by all accounts, it was an immense task. By his own admission, it was made that much tougher because he had so little of the wherewithal

In a bid to keep the rail link between the Angolan port of Lobito and the copper mines in Katanga open, a variety of anti-insurgency options were tried, including this improvised armoured mobile fire base. None were successful. The railway service remained inoperable for decades during and after the colonial war. (Author's collection)

The guerrillas had their own means of using the rail link to their advantage. While this picture was taken after the colonial struggle had ended, it does illustrate one of the ways in which the war was being fought. (Author's collection)

required to adequately manage the flow: newcomers were arriving at an average of about 20 a day, and that tally was increasing by the time I arrived.

Most of these poor souls had appeared out of the bush at remote camps in the interior and asked to be allowed to live at the 'Big Town', as N'Riquinha was known among the natives. The post had a population of nearly 1,000, which made it the largest concentration of people for several hundred kilometres.

Refugees arrived at the camp, literally with what they had on their backs. Few had extra clothes and certainly no blankets; many of them wore only loin-cloths. More often than not, they didn't have a cooking pot between them. Without cover, cold nights cut deep, which meant that the weaker ones suffered from colds or worse. All had to be fed and the sick separated from the healthy.

Each family was allotted a small stretch of land alongside the main camp where they were allowed to build a hut. It was all makeshift, the idea being to allow them to eventually return to their original villages and, in the process, if they could grow something to help with food, so much the better. He supplied seed and that money came from his own pocket.

'When you see some of these poor people arriving here, ordinary tribal folks who have lived in terror for two years and probably hardly ever known whether they would ever see another sunrise, then only do you realize the cost of this war in human terms', he said as he beckoned towards a truckload of people who'd reached the base shortly before.

'We give them what we have. We feed them and, if we can, we try to clothe them. I have some clothes and blankets—all new, good stuff captured from the terrorists. At the present rate we might soon have enough for everyone, because only yesterday some of my men uncovered a cache: blankets, boots and shirts, all stashed at a hide-out south of here and that has turned out to be quite valuable.' The group of refugees hung about almost listlessly on a patch of open ground adjacent to the base, a pathetic, emaciated little gathering, with the youngest clutching wide-eyed at their mothers' breasts.

All the children in the group suffered from malnutrition, he'd observed; they were tribal Camaxis, he said, a river people who lived on both sides of the Zambian border.

Here and there new arrivals would spot an old friend or acquaintance among those already settled and almost furtively greetings would be exchanged in the traditional way. That involved them clapping their hands and then energetically shaking hands six or eight times. The process would be repeated for a minute or two, after which everyone would squat down on their haunches and exchange gossip.

Later that morning the elders called at the mess to express their thanks. One of the men was so old and skeletal he had to be supported by a two young men. Unashamedly tears ran down their faces; they had come home, they told the captain.

'They have found their little niche in the sun here—it's all they want. Now they will build a hut. When that's done I'll give them some land where they can grow a crop and within a couple of months most will have put on a kilo or two in weight.'

It was – and still is – a sad reality of conflict in Africa – that those who suffer the most, almost always have nothing to do with the war.

The camp at N'Riquinha was astonishingly self-sufficient. It grew its own vegetables and the captain had his own modest herds of cattle, pigs and goats, all of which helped to supplement the community's diet, isolated as it was from the rest of the country, he explained, though he had no need to. Most supplies arrived by road and the columns often only reached them once a month, having usually detonated the requisite number of mines along the way.

His one 'secret weapon', as the captain liked to call it, was to send his sharp-shooting company sergeant-major into the bush a couple of times a week to bag some venison.

I was to do that myself before I left N'Riquinha. At the instigation of the captain, I went into the bush with two escorts and using an antiquated World War I Mauser with iron sights, I managed to down an eland with a single shot. The biggest of Africa's edible game, it is called 'mountain of meat' by the locals and I was pleased to be able to feed everybody at the base for a day or two. The rifle I used was an original 8mm K-98 with an integral box magazine. It was all but antique, but in immaculate condition: in its day it was rated the best bolt action rifle of all time.

The medical side at N'Riquinha base camp worried the captain the most. Many of the new arrivals required treatment because just about everybody suffered from malaria or tick bite fever or had open sores, usually as a result of insect bites that had gone septic. Many of the younger kids suffered from kwashiorkor, the ultimate infantile debilitator.

I could also see that quite a few of the refugees had lesions caused by a skin disease that attacked the area around the groin and buttocks and made walking painful. It was exceptionally contagious, but the clinic had experimented and appeared to have developed a lotion that helped.

In charge of matters medical at N'Riquinha was Dr. Manuel Carlos Guerra, who had already spent two years in Africa on conscription, having been forced to temporarily give up a lucrative practice in Oporto. He'd volunteered to stay on and help and had been posted to N'Riquinha, as 'punishment', from another camp near Luanda.

'They wouldn't provide me with the research facilities I required, so I kicked up hell', the doctor quietly explained, though he was clearly perplexed at his predicament.

There were three major maladies that affected the children; trachoma (an eye disease), skin and bone diseases caused by lack of vitamins over an extended period, and, of course, the dreaded kwashiorkor, though in his view, it was relatively easy to treat. In the four months at N'Riquinha, he had saved the sight of five children by reversing the effects of trachoma and was treating dozens more in the camp for this ailment, which he suggested was rife throughout Black Africa.

'These are the ones I see ... think of all the others out there that have no help ... ' It seemed hopeless, but the medical man was upbeat about the future. With the right input, he reckoned, this thing could eventually be turned around.

The captain disclosed that Dr. Guerra had only recently returned to N'Riquinha after two weeks in hospital. A parasite had lodged in the doctor's genitals and deciding that he couldn't afford the time to be sent back to be treated in Luanda, he operated on himself. Trouble was, he passed out half-way through his self-imposed surgery and had to be evacuated by plane the next day.

But he was fine now, he said. There were no after effects, he added, after which he smiled broadly through the gauze windows of his clinic and turned towards the morning sick parade. About 150 people waited patiently in the hot sun in front of the squat little bush hospital while the young doctor fussed about some of the newcomers.

Captain Alves disclosed that the doctor had done a considerable amount of research on tropical diseases since he'd arrived at the camp. In fact, he was dedicated enough to sometimes work through the night. The area contained a wealth of possibilities for research work, he reckoned, and he was certain that South African doctors would ultimately learn a lot of which might be of benefit to the subcontinent.

N'Riquinha had its own school and, as in other sectors, there were NCOs and a young *Alferes* teaching the refugee children the three Rs, all in Portuguese. While many of the younger set had never heard the language before, some were already using it among themselves as they played between the barracks.

More from my notes

Water, Alves said, 'is a great problem in this country.' There was little rain. Though the Cuando River ran powerfully almost all year round only a few miles away, getting there involved security issues, so the Captain had to devise other methods.

A detachment of men spent most of the day at hand-pumps in a bid to provide enough water for the garrison and civilians. A water-bowser had been promised by headquarters and a new electric pump would soon be installed, but that would take time. Once he'd achieved that much, he reckoned, everybody would have enough water for irrigation. The idea was eventually to teach the villagers to grow cash crops for profit.

'It helps them and it helps me if they make a bit of cash. They can't live on charity forever', he maintained.

This enthusiastic young army captain reckoned that if he could make the area economically viable (he believed he might be able to do so in a year), it would be an additional defence against insurgency. 'These people will then be anxious to protect their livelihoods against the kind of idle promises the rebels are making,' was how he viewed the issue.

Soon he hoped to be able to grant a concession to one of the villagers to start a store, as a few of the villagers already owned small herds of cattle. Some were collecting skins to barter.

The garrison at N'Riquinha had a routine all its own. Apart from routine patrols which were essential and the water fatigue, there were few regular duties in the camp.

Some of the younger Africans were being taught to cook, others carpentry and several to assist as medical orderlies. One bright young fellow from Barotseland had asked the commandant to be taught hairdressing. He was now being trained as a barber's assistant. Three others were learning elementary mechanics in the motor pool.

Monday was the biggest day of the week, which was when the weekly flight arrived from Luso with mail and supplies. That also meant time put aside for taking things easy.

The officers carried the tradition a stage further by wearing civilian clothes.

'It is their Sunday', the captain commented. 'It's also when one soldier from each platoon has dinner with us; our way of keeping in touch with what is happening out in the general quarters.'

An interesting group at N'Riquinha were the Bushmen. These tiny San people had lived for thousands of years in the Kalahari Desert, further towards the south, and were also found in many parts of southern Angola. Their community at the base numbered about 20.

'They've suffered badly ... the enemy ... . they're often hunted like wild animals. I hire them for what they've always been best at ... trackers and hunters ... they pay the price'.

Although these remnants of a Stone Age culture had assimilated a few Western customs – they liked their liquor and the white man's tobacco – they had lost none of their age-old talent for tracking. In sandy wastes, they could pick up trails that was often three or four days old.

'My Bushmen here can smell the presence of humans, sometimes from a kilometre away and tell me whether they're black or white ... quite remarkable when you think about it.' More than once they had flushed a group of insurgents out of a thicket, *Alféres* Manuel 'Zapata' Martins admitted, adding that he had two Bushmen in his group: he called them 'the little people', who always marched alongside him while on patrol.

'Zapata' was 22, a professional soldier who had been in the army for four years. Of Jewish extraction, his parents had arrived in Portugal from Spain during the Civil War.

At Serpa Pinto, further west, I was later to meet the famed Bushman anti-terrorist leader 'Satan', who was reputed to have killed more of the enemy than any other black man in Angola. 'Satan' was a deadly shot with his favourite rifle, another old KAR-98. Reputedly, he could pick off the enemy at 500 metres, without the advantage of telescopic sights

The grey-haired old man was surprisingly agile for his 65 years. He earned his name as a result of the ritual to which he subjected all his victims. As soon as he had killed a man, he would slit his chest open and cut out the heart. Only then would he be satisfied that the man was dead. 'Satan' smiled approvingly while his story was related with the help of an interpreter, another Bushman.

There were not many Portuguese who had been able to master the 'click' language of these ancient people, even though I was to discover that Lisbon's protégés were fairly adept at picking up African dialects.

The Bushmen at N'Riquinha all wore the uniform of the Portuguese Army. Their boots were their pride, though it noticeably cut their pace and they often looked uncomfortable in them. They would persist and stand smartly to attention at sunset when the Portuguese flag was ceremoniously hauled down.

This mark of respect was also observed by many villagers as the bugler sounded 'Retreat'.

Portuguese troops moving stealthily through open country in Central
Angola after a landmine had been triggered. (Author's collection)

Captain Alves explained that the war in his area differed quite markedly from similar
campaigns being fought near Luso. The fighting was more tenuous and over a wider front,
he explained, since the enemy were not intent on making contact with Portuguese units so
close to the frontier, where he was based. Their orders were to infiltrate through Sector CC
to the west and join their comrades in taking the war to the hated colonial enemy.

'They come through here from staging areas in Zambia. Most times they're well armed
and stocked, many of them struggling with heavy loads for the interior.' He reckoned that
the situation might almost be equated to Sector D north of Luanda, though without the
jungle. 'This hinterland is far more exposed and they have to get across it; it is our job to
stop them', he added.

When contact was made with insurgents, he said, it was not simply a matter of trailing
them through the bush and trying to force them to make a stand. Retaliatory stands were
a given, so were ambushes. Yet, if terrain allowed, the Portuguese would try to leap-frog
ahead and set up ambushes of their own. Ideally, he'd liked a couple of choppers to be able
to move his forces ahead of the fleeing enemy.

Captain Alves had tried a number of tactics in the time he and his men had been at
N'Riquinha, a few of which had been reasonably successful. In his first month he and a
large squad had trailed a group for more than a month. The unit was eventually responsible
for the death and capture of an entire MPLA group.

'That was my 40 days in this wasteland ... it was tough, often disheartening and in the
end, nasty. But it was stamina and perseverance that did it for us and in conjunction with

two units that were brought in as things started to develop, we ended up killing 31 and capturing a dozen.' It was on that operation that the he lost a man, while a sergeant had been badly wounded in the leg and gut.

The captain maintained that black soldiers in the Portuguese army were capable of surviving far more serious wounds than most Europeans. In a training exercise in the Dembos, shortly before his unit had been posted to N'Riquinha, one of his African corporals had been wounded. He'd been shot by a large-calibre rifle, or what hunters like to call an elephant gun. The blast had done terrible damage to his rib cage but quite remarkably, hadn't penetrated any of his vital organs.

'His entire chest was cleaved open ... obviously a shocking mess and our medical orderly was ill while treating him. When we got him back to base the priest offered Last Sacraments before he was taken out by helicopter. The man survived though, and while it has taken time, he'll be back here within a month or two.

The captain stressed that this remarkable natural resilience was one of the reasons why the insurgents had been successful.

'They might not always have the initiative to hold on when we're coming at them with Unimogs, though they manage that often enough because some of these people are extremely fit, but they have far better chances of surviving wounds than our own people. Where they have more serious problems is in their primitive medical procedures.'

Fresh cow pats were sometimes used to cover the wound and it was no surprise that infection took an awful toll, usually preceded by tetanus.

Captain Vitor Alves had returned from a long chase through south-east Angola a few days before we arrived at N'Riquinha. He had rushed to help 'Zapata' follow a band of infiltrators for something like 250 kilometres along the Zambian frontier. The *Alferes* had managed to relieve the terrorists of their civilian charges and Captain Alves continued the chase.

'We were out for three weeks after Zapata had come back here with the civilians. They would try the occasional half-hearted ambush and then rush off again, obviously eager to shake us off rather than do anything confrontational. They'd never allow us meaningful contact.

'So I tried something that had worked once before. Altogether, there were about 80 men in the patrol, which was a lot, but then some enemy units were 300-strong. So when we reached a large abandoned *kimbo* on the Luiana River, I split my group. I picked 18 of my best men and sent the rest back to base ... made it look like we'd abandoned the chase.

'We spent the first night in the deserted village and though the routine was that half the men stood guard while the others slept, I doubt whether anybody got any shut-eye. It was an eerie experience alongside the river, with hippos grunting and foraging in the tall reeds almost on top of us. Every time one of these beasts moved close, the guards would get a fright, but they couldn't warn them off by firing their rifles.'

It was another day and a half before the enemy showed up, Captain Alves explained. He was prepared to wait three days and his patience was rewarded because the insurgents appeared on the third evening.

'It was difficult, far more so than any other place I've waited in ambush. I knew they were somewhere in the vicinity, which meant that we couldn't speak or even smoke ... the atmosphere was really tense. A single spot of light in the dark would have revealed everything.

'Suddenly there were a bunch of them approaching the village. There was a clearing about 200 metres across from the *kimbo* and they waited and watched for about 20 or 30 minutes before they decided that things looked safe. They stopped a second time about 100 yards from our position and by now we were more than ready for them.

'I could see that all was not well during the second halt. They were in the middle of the clearing but their leader, or someone in at the head of the pack sensed something wrong. That made them all uneasy. But they were well spread out, all were armed and a handful whispering to each other, probably weighing up the odds.

'It was the kind of thing they constantly did ... the only way in this desolate land where nothing is certain.

'That was when I decided that the best action would be to take them on immediately ... I was worried that they'd withdraw. In any event, they were standing there in the moonlight totally exposed with my boys awaiting the order. I had already planned for this kind of attack.

'The best shot in the company was *next* to me—my NCO sharpshooter. My arrangement with him was that if the rebels stopped a distance from the camp, on my command he'd try to pick off as many as he could. That would also be the signal for the others to get busy. And that's exactly what happened.

'The sergeant killed three men with his first three shots even before the group knew what was happening. By this time everyone was firing and the chase was on'

Captain Alves said the action lasted only a minute or two and all twelve guerrillas were killed within about 100 metres of where the first shots were fired. Among the dead they later identified a well-known MPLA group leader who called himself 'General' Kulunga.

My visit to N'Riquinha was far too short. To do justice to the experience, I needed to spend a month there, possibly two and go out on more patrols, shoot another eland or two and speak to some of the captured rebels, who, having entered from Zambia, quite often spoke good English.

One issue about which Vitor Alves commented was the relatively poor standards set by the average insurgent, and in particular, that their training never appeared to amount to much. He'd gone on record on the matter in an interview with the Portuguese weekly magazine *Expresso* on September 20, 1975.

By the time he'd arrived in Eastern Angola, the enemy had suffered many losses, Alves told the interviewer. Most recruits were thrown into the fray barely having been prepared for the complex intricacies of guerrilla warfare that had evolved over the years. Also, they were not to know that they faced the intransigence and dedication of the many Angolan settlers, whose resistance had eventually caused the entire Eastern Front to collapse, for no other reason than that their instructors never told them. The official line back in Lusaka was that all the whites in Angola were paper tigers and that the struggle was a pushover.

Many of Lisbon's successes in Angola were due to inroads made by several well-trained black regiments such as the *Flechas* (Arrows), and the *Comandos Africanos*, both of who established a pattern for subsequent elite South African units such as 32 Battalion. Interestingly, most *Flechas* had originally deserted from the guerrilla fighters and, in turn, were then organized into efficient Special Forces units.

Their strength lay in the fact that they had intimate knowledge of the country in which they were operating. Also, they were familiar with the locals, because so many of them were from the region and spoke the language. More important, they had come to appreciate what was expected of them and understood both the tactics and the psyche of their old comrades in the bush. Generous bounties for the numbers of insurgents killed provided additional motivation and basically, it all made good sense.

Even though the mainly white officered *Flechas* were to instil a new dimension to these largely unconventional hostilities and I had originally intended going back to cover them, the struggle ended before I was able to do so.

For his part, Vitor Alves was reluctant to take things further when we met in Lisbon; he was under severe pressure in trying to help run his country, he told me. This former army officer eventually ended up as a representative of Portugal in the European Parliament in Strasburg.

There was a remarkable twist to Captain Vitor Alves' story which only emerged years later.

After my trip to N'Riquinha I returned to South Africa and made a formal approach to the Portuguese Embassy in Pretoria to have Captain Alves and, by now, my old friend Captain Ricardo Alcada from the Dembos, visit South Africa and speak to groups of university students about this war, then in its eighth year.

One of these public meetings was held at Witwatersrand University, and while most of the students present were white, they were forthrightly hostile towards what some termed 'these two Portuguese Fascists.'

In full dress uniform, Captain Alves addressed the crowd in the University Great Hall and it took him perhaps 10 minutes of reasoned debate to swing just about everybody around to his way of thinking, in part because he told them that things simply couldn't go on that way indefinitely in Portuguese Africa. He also made a strong case for the full implementation of the United Nations Human Rights Charter throughout Portuguese Africa, at which point the students cheered. Captain Alcada was next and his approach was a good deal more hard-line, detailing the role of the Soviets in the struggle.

When they'd finished, both officers answered questions for about an hour and left the podium to an ovation.

Subsequently, I'd stay over with the Alves family in their delightful little apartment at Oeiras whenever I visited Lisbon. It didn't take me long to discover that Ché Guevara occupied a prominent place in the life of this youthful Portuguese Army captain.

On April 25, 1974, Alves – by now a fully-fledged major in the regular forces and once more on home soil – became a member of a triumvirate that included Otello Saraiva de Carvalho (who had been my escorting officer in Portuguese Guinea) and Vasco Lourenco. These three, with several others, became the nucleus of the Coordinating Committee of the Armed forces Movement responsible for the putsch that topped the civilian Lisbon Government. The Portuguese Armed Forces were now in effective control.

In a relatively short few years Vitor Alves had transmogrified into the ultimate revolutionary, or, more likely, he had probably always been one, though he never allowed his radical views to colour our friendship.

Yet Alves, the political malcontent was a very different man from Alves the counter-insurgency specialist officer in the field, or the Alves who came from Angola to South Africa to visit me after I had launched my first book on guerrilla warfare.

We were to see each other quite often in the years before that momentous day in April 1974. On one visit, I spent a week there while waiting to enter Portuguese Guinea.

Several times, returning to the apartment quite late, I was surprised to find him in deep discussion with groups of fellow officers. I paid little attention at the time because I knew he was on a staff course and probably engaged on some project or other. That was early 1971. The rest, as we now know, is on record.

Eastern Angola

'In that job [Angola] I sat on a sub-committee of the Nation Security Council [in Washington], so I was like a chief of staff, with the GS-18s (like 3-star generals), Henry Kissinger, Bill Colby (the CIA director) and the CIA, making important decisions. My job was to put it all together and make it happen and run it, an interesting place from which to watch a covert action being done....'

John Stockwell, former CIA station chief in the Congo on his clandestine role in the post-colonial Angolan conflict. These ruminations became the subject of his book, *In Search of Enemies*, one of the best of the subsequent epoch.[1]

I t took a while, but following my visits to Cabinda and the Dembos, my peregrinations through Angola – to which I returned often enough over a period of years – finally led me to the eastern half of this astonishingly vast country. America had its Wild West: Angola's was disparagingly termed by some as the 'Wild East'.

To the majority of Lusitanians, it was always known as *Terras do Fim do Mundo* – Land at the End of the Earth.

Bigger than Texas, as dry as the Mojave in places and sparsely populated, it is still today a most exquisite mopani and baobab country. It is also the same wilderness that the British missionary explorer Dr David Livingstone wrote about while he lived in Luanda. He loved its open plains and meandering rivers and a countryside populated then by more wild animals that it is possible to imagine today. A dozen species of antelope would sometimes come into view, their numbers almost Serengeti-like, stretching across the tropical savannah. Elephants were counted in their thousands, though these days the visitor is fortunate to see a handful. Their predecessors were all shot for their ivory.

The almost monotonous table-top flatness of the region is integral, as are the sandy wastes which make the construction of proper roads almost impossible. It meant that while war raged, you avoided landmines by using any one of perhaps a dozen tracks that headed roughly in the same direction you were going.

Frontiers with Zambia and the Congo fuse somewhere in the remote reaches of the bush and even today, decades after that war ended, there are still no real lines of demarcation. Looking back, this might be expected when you consider that in 1885, more than a century and a quarter ago, the neighbouring Congolese state was established not as a country, but as the personal fief of Belgium's King Leopold II.

This can be an extremely harsh region. The sun beats down brutally almost all the year round, though when the rains arrive, they do so with an almost-monsoon fury and the

African plains are sometimes turned into inland seas where only a pirogue will do. At night, during the cool season, the mercury drops sharply after sunset.

What sets Eastern Angola apart from the rest of the country is its aridity in the dry season and its sand, which, like the Sahara, seems to go on forever. There is barely a rock or a boulder in the entire region. As one wag commented, after a week spent in this kind of desolation, that if he and the others with him were to run out of ammunition, there weren't even any rocks to hurl.

It is much worse when the wind blows. A deluge of miniscule particles – often as fine as baking powder – can work their way into your eyes, your mouth and clog your nose. The white dust is debilitating, acutely so, and will penetrate everywhere. When it goes on long enough, it sometimes messes up machinery and can end the working life of a perfectly adequate vehicle, never mind cameras, electronic devices and firearms.

Layer after layer, this soft white stuff goes down unimpeded for 50 metres, sometimes double that before it hits bedrock. That often means scant vegetation and roads that only four-wheel-drive vehicles are able to navigate, not always with confidence. If ever a place deserves the appellation 'Raw Africa', this is it and not much has changed. Contrasts in this rigorous terrain are always severe and even today, only the hardiest in animals and man survive.

Yet, as desolate and disconcerting as it was to those unaccustomed to some of the realities of Africa, all that could sometimes quickly change. After the rains this veritable desert would bloom, transmogrified from sand pit to a flurry of shrubs and plants that can top half a metre in a week. Among the side effects, while the war went on, this was also the signal for the insurgents to become more active: the new foliage would give them the cover they sought.

It was much the same further towards the south, where the Kavango River formed a kind of natural boundary with the Caprivi Strip – the *Zipfel*, as the Germans liked to call it – and while Lisbon's troops were around, it was still under South African domination.

A narrow wedge of land that is sometimes barely 20 kilometres wide, its only discerning feature was, in Afrikaans, *Oom Willie se Pad* or, to the rest of us, Uncle Willy's Road. This almost-featureless, straight-as-an-arrow 'highway' that was never fully tarred until after the war ended, became a prime insurgent target for enemy minelayers: it stretched all the way to where the three adjacent Southern African nations – Namibia, Botswana and Zimbabwe – conjoined in the middle of the Zambezi River.

Roughly 500 kilometres long, it was originally ceded by Queen Victoria to the German people towards the end of her reign, the idea being to give Kaiser Bill, her favourite grandson, access to the great Zambezi River and the Indian Ocean. He was never allowed to see this dream become a reality because the Great War interceded and South West Africa became a League of Nations – and thereafter – a United Nations Mandate.

Part of the original, flawed treaty meant hiving off Kilimanjaro – Africa's tallest mountain (then lying within Kenyan boundaries, which was British) – to become a part of German Tanganyika. It was only one of many territorial wrangles of the time and why the frontiers of Africa are in such turmoil today.

In the mid-1960s, Agostinho Neto's MPLA, having helped start the war in the jungles north of Luanda, went on to initiate hostilities in these distant reaches in the east of the country, thus creating what the guerrillas liked to call their 'Second Front'. Neto came to be backed by rebels who were loyal to a comparative latecomer, Dr Jonas Savimbi, but that didn't last, in part because the Maoist Ovimbundu tribal leader had aspirations of his own for a movement which he called UNITA or Union for the Total Independence of Angola.

Things deteriorated and eventually Savimbi became Neto's harshest critic. That pleased the South Africans because the 'domestic' feud took pressure off their own forces, just then engaged with SWAPO, the guerrilla force aspiring to create mayhem in South West Africa. In fact, starting just before Angolan independence in 1975, Pretoria was to give Savimbi much of the war matériel he eventually came to use against the MPLA, almost all of it captured in a succession of annual battles with FAPLA, the military wing of the MPLA guerrilla movement. Some details of this war can be found in various earlier books by this author, including *War Stories by Al Venter and Friends*.[1]

Such shenanigans are typical of Africa's contradictions: always something new ...

Nor was Eastern Angola a relatively simple side-show compared to what was going on elsewhere in the country, the *Dembos* north of Luanda, especially. The area in dispute in Eastern Angola during the late 1960s and early 1970s was almost three times the size of England. It stayed that way for decades, with rebel forces entering Angola from Dr Kenneth Kaunda's Zambia and afterwards, a civil war that eventually enveloped the entire country.

In a bid to counter insurgent gains during Lisbon's struggle to maintain its hegemony, High Command in Luanda established a new military region which it called Sector ZIL (*Zona de Intervencao Leste*). This was headquartered at Luso, a rambling Portuguese settlement that straddled the rail link between the Atlantic and the copper mines of Katanga.

I went there by air from Luanda, on board one of the rickety Portuguese Air Force Noratlas transport aircraft and it took us two days. There was plenty of 'off-time' along the way, because the Portuguese Air Force rarely took their planes up after dark. That, coupled to interminable lunches that could last three or four hours, made for a fairly long haul to the eastern half of the country, but then that was how Lisbon did things. And since I was invariably seated at the head of the table – the usual 'honoured guest syndrome' – I did not complain.

Eastern Angola has always been regarded by the Portuguese as not only remote, but, as it was phrased by one officer at military headquarters in Luanda, 'virtually uninhabitable for any civilised being.'

There are few hills or mountains to break the monotony of the countryside. The east is not unlike much of the country in Rhodesia and Mozambique where other insurgents were then also active.

General José Manuel Bettencourt Rodrigues – on the right - was responsible for turning the war around in Eastern Angola during its latter stages. His tactics were so successful that the Portuguese settler community believed they had all but won the war. (Photo Richard McIntosh)

In Eastern Angola, Lisbon always maintained while the war went on, the insurgent presence was precarious. Nonetheless, Neto's guerrillas were able to maintain a steady pressure on the Portuguese civil and military authorities and once Savimbi entered the equation, the military threat became more pronounced. That said, there was never any likelihood of the enemy gaining the momentum required to give them any kind of advantage: the region was simply too vast and there were Special Forces like the *Flechas* active, controlled by remarkably successful counter-insurgency specialists like Óscar Cardoso. And, of course, the South Africans helped where they could (See South African helicopter operations in South Angola in support of Portuguese Forces in Appendix B).

'They have been particularly successful in one direction' a government intelligence officer disclosed. 'They have managed to divert attention from the war in northern Angola.' The MPLA, he continued, had been able to stretch Portuguese resources to cope with the new war. The new threat was not formidable, but more of an inconvenience and the Portuguese were confident they could cope with it were the region three times as big. It was a remarkable claim at the time, because, as I'd discovered by now, optimism was hardly a trait of the Lusitanian character while in Africa.

Few officers I spoke to, however, did not register some concern at this escalation of what had previously been a limited campaign.

Since the start of the war in the east, MPLA attacks from Zambia had moved steadily inland through the under-populated hinterland. In some areas the guerrillas moved quicker than others, depending on the extent of Portuguese control. Two years after the first attack, there had been onslaughts on places as far afield as Luso, Cuito-Cuanavale and Serpa Pinto, many hundreds of kilometres from the Zambian and Katangese frontiers.

The MPLA campaign in eastern Angola was both consistent and well-co-ordinated. Also, the training these insurgents received was good and their weapons, centred on the AK-47 and the RPG-2 – as well as TM-46 landmines – were of the best available in the Communist Bloc. Portuguese losses in the area consequently, though not yet as high as in the Dembos, were rising steadily.

The Portuguese military command at Luso gave two reasons for the increased attacks in the east. One was the immense flow of communist arms into Zambia and Tanzania since early 1967. The other was the augural hand of Red China.

The Chinese influence in Zambia has grown steadily since 1967, they said, and it was only discovered that this was partly Savimbi's influence because he was probably the biggest fan of Mao on the African continent. Always inauspicious in its movements and activities in host countries, Beijing played a prominent part in also guiding the destiny of the MPLA.

The intelligence officer said they had considerable information to prove that Chinese tacticians and training officers were behind a good deal of enemy strategy.

'This assistance ranges from training, all the way through to logistics, propaganda and the planning of attacks on specific targets', he declared. He was careful to point out that although MPLA was communist-orientated, the majority of the Freedom Fighters were not. They were simply receiving aid from the most available source and making the best use of it. There were few hardened Marxists within the African command, not yet, anyway.

There was the odd exception. The principles of Marx and Lenin are alien to Africa, he continued. An African might embrace communism superficially, but this was not a lasting creed. To them, that kind of radical policy meant, quite simply, revolution. He added that Africa had had centuries of wars and revolution and that all the people asked for now was an end to bloodshed, tyranny and uncertainty.

He went on: 'The average man in Africa wants a place in the sun for himself and his family. He wants to be sure that next week he will still be eating regularly, that his children can go to school and, once in a while, perhaps, he can let his hair down. He asks for little more.' The officer that addressed me had grown up among the black people of Angola. He believed he knew them better than most.

The authorities in Luanda were emphatic that although MPLA might be receiving aid from Red Chinese sources, the Chinese in Zambia never entered Angola to fight with the insurgents.

'We have seen them from time to time across the frontier through binoculars— in fact we have taken pictures of them with telephoto lenses. Their high-buttoned jackets and cloth caps give them away every time', another officer said.

I then asked about what was termed in scuttlebutt reports within the ranks as the 'Chinese woman'. I had been told about her by some of the men in the east and afterwards, heard about her from different sources, but the Luanda top brass were adamant that she did not exist. She is a myth, they insisted. Yet, in parts of eastern Angola this Asian woman had almost become a legend. She was said to be leading a fanatical group of insurgents who had already inflicted heavy casualties on the Portuguese forces. It was difficult to separate fact from rumour.

Known simply as 'Chinese woman', insurgents who had been captured and questioned on the subject claimed that she had a charmed life. Like the men she commanded – about 50 of them – she led a Spartan existence, living under similar conditions to the soldiers and sharing their food. In battle she would often expose herself in the most dangerous positions. As far as was known, though about 30 years old, she was not married. Another report that did the rounds was that she might have received part of her training in Guinea, further up the West African coastline.

Looking back years later, one has to accept that the story might have been a myth. At the same time, it was too widespread and detailed not to contain an element of truth.

The first time I heard the story was from a young infantry lieutenant, Antonio da Silva, who had spent 18 months following guerrilla bands in the east. His path had often crossed that of the mysterious female, he reckoned. Antonio was a serious individual and conflict in the bush was his métier. He had joined the army as a professional and he was not the kind of person who would easily fabricate a story.

According to Antonio, the woman had spent a year in Zambia before coming to Angola. She always operated near the frontier of what has formerly been Northern Rhodesia, and would slip across the border if things became too uncertain in Angola. He said that he had first made contact with the woman's guerrilla group towards the middle of 1967: she had been operating in an area about 200 kilometres south-east of Luso. Her main sphere of operations until then had been in the Cazombo region, the Angolan panhandle that juts eastwards between Zambia and Katanga. I let him take up the story.

'After days in the bush following numerous trails, we found nothing. I decided to split my company into groups of 40 men each. The four sections would then move eastwards in a fan-like formation.

'Many of the trails we followed resulted in lemons. This was apparently part of her plan to shake off anyone following her group. At a point in the bush she would send three parties from the main group off into the bush in different directions and they would march through the bush for two or three hours, turn around and retrace their steps. You can imagine the quandary one is faced when you come to a place and there are four different trails leading off in all directions. It took the men at least half a day to find out which one did not lead into a dead-end.'

At other times, Tony explained, she would suddenly leave the main track. Her group would break a fresh path into the bush either to the right or the left and cover up their traces very carefully with leaves and dead brushwood.

'She was expert at the art of camouflage. She must have learnt her trade in Asia somewhere', was his view.

Tony and his men followed the band for 11 days. Every fifth day fresh supplies of food would be brought to his group by helicopter, guided in by radio. He was not happy with this arrangement because it pin-pointed his position to enemy groups lurking nearby, but he had to keep his men fed and water was also a problem because it was the dry season.

'Then, one of my African trackers found a trail leading off the main track. It was remarkable that he discovered it at all: he'd stopped to relieve himself and saw that the ground alongside the track had recently been disturbed.'

Tony and his men followed the new track for two more days. Often the path would merge with the other, cutting across and leading out in an obvious attempt to shake off pursuers. But by now the youthful lieutenant had an idea of the general pattern.

'The trail was exceptionally well-laid. It must have taken a great deal of time and trouble but it was very effective. Only someone who had grown up in this area would have spotted it in the first place, as those people were meticulous with their camouflage.'

On the 13th day, Tony's group suddenly came upon a village in the bush. It was obviously a large one as they could hear considerable movement a few hundred metres ahead. In the distance someone was calling movements to what sounded like a physical training class.

'We moved forward stealthily, having already sent two scouts ahead. They came back with news that there were two sentries immediately ahead of us and about six or eight others stationed at various points around the camp. It was a tough call for the Portuguese officer because he had not been able to assess the strength of the force and realised that he could easily be led into an ambush.

Unlike Sector D and Cabinda, the bush in that area was sparse. A man could be seen moving between the trees 20 or 30 metres away. Also, there were no natural obstacles behind which he and his men could approach the camp.

'So we had to creep forward on our stomachs; the entire bunch. We killed the two men with knives—more by luck than design—they had been dozing in the sun, which was when I sent some of the men to the right and left in order to make a narrow three-pronged attack. We couldn't spread out too much or we would almost certainly have been sighted by the sentries. I ordered the men to attack immediately we were spotted us and the alarm sounded.

'About ten minutes later one of the terrorist sentries detected some movement and got up to investigate. We were still about 100 metres from the camp, which was when he fired a succession of shots in the air. It was a warning signal directed at the camp. We then went on the attack, at the double.

'We killed four and captured another two out of a group that could easily have been 200 strong. Had they been aware of our numbers, they would probably have stood their ground, but they didn't and melted away into the countryside, as they had probably been trained to do. The moment the alarm sounded, about 20 of them took up well-protected positions in the camp and held us off while the bulk of the insurgents escaped. Only after the last man had fled did they withdraw.

Without the helicopter providing ground support and more often than not, top cover, Portugal's wars in Africa would have ended with guerrilla victories long before they did. (Author's collection)

'But even then, we could hardly rush in blindly—there might have been others waiting and, of course, we had to watch for booby traps'.

Tony said that the camp had been a training unit—one of the first found on Angolan soil. Documents hauled back to base by helicopters brought in afterwards by radio indicated that the men had been receiving instruction in languages, the handling of arms, political theory and physical training.

'The Chinese are great ones for keeping themselves fit. They believe in making everyone spend an hour or two a day doing physical jerks, especially when on campaign and usually before breakfast.' It was the same in Malaya, he said.

Perhaps the most interesting discovery during the subsequent follow-up operation was another camp about 400 metres further into the bush. The second installation, also makeshift, had been the insurgents' sleeping-quarters. When the people in the barracks heard the first shots, they also disappeared into the bush.

The whole organizational structure indicated that someone with considerable experience in guerrilla warfare was in command: everything had been planned beforehand. Also, it was clear that the possibility of an attack by the Portuguese Army, or helicopter gunships, had been rehearsed. Even the women and children in the barracks area were able to get away undetected. Not a single weapon was left behind.

It was later ascertained that this could have been the base camp of the 'Chinese woman' and her guerrillas while she operated in the area. One of the captives admitted this after several were captured in subsequent follow-up operations and tortured by PIDE, the Portuguese secret police.

By far the most popular method of attack in eastern Angola – as in other sectors – was the road ambush, and the reasons were basic.

The revolutionaries were aware that many of the military posts strung out in this vast area had to be regularly supplied, much as American military camps in Afghanistan are today. There were also a number of camps along the Zambian frontier that maintained small airstrips. Fuel supplies had to be delivered at intervals to keep reserves at safe levels.

Travel in the east, as in Sector D and Cabinda, was a gruelling process and often slow. There were few roads and even today, the region doesn't feature many all-weather throughways. Once the truck left the main routes between the bigger towns in the region, the army was forced to negotiate sandy tracks that had never been worked by a road-grader.

Convoys travelling along these *pistes* often made their own way along the flat terrain and it was rare to travel more than a dozen clicks without digging one of the vehicles out of the sand. A three-ton Unimog vehicle that had gone into the soft gravel up to its axles could take a dozen soldiers two or three hours of hard graft to extricate—especially if it was loaded with 44-gallon drums of fuel.

The insurgents showed a predilection for striking at heavily-loaded convoys which, because of the sparse terrain, could never be adequately protected. They would pick off one vehicle at any time, sometimes two and then disappear. Most times they would choose a sandy spot between the trees and set up their positions, the approach road primed by an anti-tank mine like a Soviet TM-46. As the trucks passed and mine detonated they would blast off with machine-gun and mortar fire for a couple of minutes and disappear.

Obviously, the enemy –and Portuguese Army – could never be certain which of the tracks they would be using in their approach. Convoy leaders often preferred to follow the hard-baked pans and river-beds which seamed across much of eastern Angola and then the mines would come into play.

The rainy season in Eastern Angola lasts several months and, for the rest of the year, nature provides these solid clay beds as a form of road-link between towns. Baked hard by the sun and dead straight in places, these routes were sometimes better than the more solid gravel strips in other parts of the country.

A road could follow a dry watercourse for as much as 50 or 100 kilometres at a stretch.

Shortly after we arrived at Luso, a convoy arrived from the south. There were about 15 trucks in all, half of them army vehicles. Many were splattered with bullet holes and shrapnel splinters.

The convoy had left Cangamba, a few hundred kilometres to the south four days before. On their second day out, shortly after dawn, they had been attacked by a large MPLA group while travelling along one of these dry river-beds. The action had lasted unusually long, this time about 40 minutes, in part because the enemy dominated the bit of high ground there was in that area. There had been Portuguese casualties but there were few traces that any enemy had been killed. After the guerrillas had withdrawn some helicopters were brought in and the Portuguese were able to survey the scene. They found traces of blood in several places, but no dead. Interestingly, the insurgents left few of their used shells behind.

The ambush was a solid, professional job, said the captain who'd travelled with the convoy. They had obviously planned the whole thing beforehand and deployed five machine-guns – thought to be PKMs, because somebody thought he had spotted a box magazine – together with a single 82mm mortar. Had they added anything in the 12.7mm range in the attack, said the captain, it might have been a very different story, 'but then, it is difficult to haul heavy equipment across sandy country, even if the Zambian border is relatively close,' he added.

The enemy had spaced their men to good effect prior to the attack. They had done such a good job of it, in fact, that the Portuguese troops had been pinned down for much of the firefight. 'They basically had us where they wanted us', the captain stated through an interpreter.

He explained that they had camped the previous night on the verge of the hard clay of the river-bed. He knew the area fairly well—he had already taken half a dozen convoys along the same route, but that was the first big contact in which he had engaged the enemy.

Luso at the time of my visit was a fairly expansive place of about 5,000 people. It reminded me of one of the many small towns in the American Mid-West. In Angola it played a pivotal communications role because it was one of the main centres for the rail link that ran from the port city of Lobito all the way across the country to Katanga in the Congo with its enormously wealthy copper resources.

In the town itself, just about everything centred on the cathedral opposite the main square and mayor's parlour. Roads lead off neatly into well laid-out suburbs and then halted abruptly at the encroaching bush. It had its own market, a radio station, two newspapers, a couple of cinemas, a large hotel that had been commandeered by the army and a number of smaller pensions that attracted the occasional scribe like myself.

From Luso railway station, a train left every day for Nova Lisboa, Angola's second city towards the western interior (Huambo today). It took two full days to cover the distance—travelling only during daylight hours. Further east, more than 300 kilometres distant, was Villa Teixeira de Sousa, another medium sized conurbation that lay almost adjacent to the Congolese border.

'We do not travel at night—the terrorists sabotage the line too often', one of the officials commented. 'If you are in a hurry, why don't you fly? Everyone flies these days.' The official was curious about my movements.

A note would probably appear on the desk of the local PIDE inspector within the hour advising him of the bearded foreigner who had been asking questions about train movements. The official consulted a colleague as I walked away. He was obviously another of those single-minded Portuguese who believed the security of the nation rested solely on his shoulders and who sensed an agent provocateur behind every bush.

I had experienced it during a previous visit to Angola, when I'd traversed the country overland from north to south in the mid-1960s. At Lobito and also at Novo Redondo on the coast – this was much earlier in the conflict that was gathering a momentum of its own – I had been arrested by the security police and kept in custody until I was able to prove I was a bona fide tourist.

'It's the war, *Senor*—it makes everyone suspicious', the young *Alferes* said apologetically later that morning as we drove to military headquarters.

The headquarters building at Luso, a high-walled structure of Moorish design, was guarded by a military policeman with a Sten. He clicked his heels smartly as we passed through the barricaded gate.

A number of Portuguese marines were leaving just as we got there, and in answer to my question, the *Alferes* explained that there was a fairly large contingent of marines in Sector ZIL. They were used in the swampland bordering on Zambia's Barotse Province. The guerrillas like to use the unchartered channels in the swamp to infiltrate large quantities of arms, equipment and men into Angola. 'Some of the largest insurgent bases were believed to be in that swamp and our marines hunt these groups in rubber boats,' he explained.

Heading the Portuguese war effort in the east from Luso was Colonel de Souza, a short stocky man and a veteran of the Portuguese brigade that fought with Franco's forces in the Spanish civil war.

After we'd been led into the building, I was to discover that the walls of his office were lined with scores of firearms and other weapons that had been captured over the past two years. The majority were antique blunderbusses, but there were also a few Israeli Uzzis, Russian Degtyiarev machine-guns and World War II Lugers. In other rooms the officers had arrayed an assortment of bows, arrows, hatchets, feather head-dresses and primitive home-made firearms captured from the enemy. Indeed, the Luso military headquarters was a veritable armoury of insurgent firepower: 'A museum of terrorist armour,' the balding colonel joked.

Later we were to see more of what had been taken during military operations. These included Chinese hand-grenades, Russian carbines, West German Solingen steel commando knives, American bazookas and fragmentation bombs, Belgian and French pistols, Cuban and Egyptian boots as well as the distinctive mustard-coloured Czech camouflage uniforms. Curiously, there was also some Rhodesian camouflage jackets and pants as well as South African canned foods and medical supplies. There was even a packet of Australian dried fruit. The officer quipped something about the cosmopolitan nature of the war.

The matériel from Southern Africa, he said, had been imported by Zambia and distributed among several enemy units. With the help of the South African authorities they had managed to trace batch numbers of some of the drugs supplied by Johannesburg pharmaceutical firms: these had originally been ordered and paid for by the Zambian government.

The biggest problem faced by Colonel de Sousa and his staff in Angola's eastern regions was one of communications. The conversation centred on sand, as well as the kind of problems that might evolve as a consequence.

'It is impossible to build roads on this kind of foundation. We do, of course, have some good roads, but it's a huge task keeping them serviceable.'

Most of the garrisons in the interior were kept in touch with the outside world by aircraft, but even that was a difficult task, too few planes and in the rainy season storms and high winds that could rip smaller aircraft out of the sky. The Portuguese keep boats handy to reach many of the outlying areas— particularly in the swampland and obviously, helicopters were also used.

It was a supreme exercise in logistics, he added, as we discussed the war over a map spread out on his desk.

What became apparent during that visit was that the Portuguese Army seemed to have won a few notable victories in the months before I arrived. In various battles, they had killed three enemy 'generals' in the first quarter of 1968. One of them, Jose Carvaho, known as 'Wenda' among his men, was a nephew of Neto and was second-in-command of MPLA's Zambian-based 'garrison'. He had been shot at Caripande, in the Cazombo region.

In the same month a UNITA 'general', Calacala, was killed near Luso. He had been leading a modest force that had been intent on attacking the town when he was surprised by a bunch of Portuguese commandos. He walked right into them and they were all killed. Unless ordered otherwise, the commandos were not known to take prisoners during or after their actions ...

A third 'general', who went by the name of Sangue do Povo died near Lucusse, on the road to Gago Coutinho. That was an area constantly under enemy attack.

'So you see, we are not doing too badly against their "group leaders" as these people like to call themselves', the officer said proudly.

He pulled out a detailed map of the Barotse and north-western provinces of Zambia. 'Now I will show you exactly where our friends are operating from. You can work out for yourself how good our intelligence boys have been', he chuckled, obviously pleased with himself. His aide, Major Simões pointed at two towns in western Zambia that had been ringed with a pencil mark: Balovale in the north-west province and Sikongo further south, in Barotseland proper.

'These are the two command headquarters of the MPLA. Balovale is responsible for terrorist activity towards Luso and the north and the other co-ordinates activities in the south', he said. Two more names had been underlined with a blue marker pen: Chavuma, just south of the Cazombo region, and Shangombo in the far south-western corner of the

Bush patrols were often casual affairs in Mozambique, reflecting a serious lack of combat readiness: the guerrillas were able to smell tobacco smoke from a kilometre away. Also, the kind of obligatory silence imposed on foot patrols in Angola and Portuguese Guinea were not observed on the watch of General Kaúlza de Arriaga in the disputed East African territory. (Author's collection)

territory. His finger moved to a town called Yuka. 'This is an MPLA field hospital.'

Recently, he said, there had been more activity in Barotse province. The Zambian government were building two air-strips at the swampland village of Siluwe.

'We are not quite certain yet why they'd want an airstrip on our border, considering that the area is so remote and of no economic or political significance to the country ... Kaunda talks about protection against our bombing raids, but it does indeed indicate that aircraft may play a role in future terrorist tactics, as it already does in Guinea (with Russian and East German help). Let's hope Zambians will fly the planes and not their British or Canadian instructors—we would hate to shoot up innocent expatriates'.

I asked about the rail link. Though it linked Zambia through the Katangese Copper Belt, it remained one of President Kaunda's major links with the outside world. Yet, he stressed, Zambian-based terrorists were still sabotaging it.

The major went on to explain that attacks on the line averaged about one a month. The insurgents would pry loose sections of the track or remove fish-plates. Only once had explosives been used, though after my visit the line was blown up quite regularly.

It was quite an extraordinary state of affairs, Major Simões maintained. President

that the action of war, as such, could and did happen at any time. The men were consequently subjected to fatigues that sometimes start at two in the morning and could last for two days, most times without sleep.

While under training there were no weekends. After a couple of weeks of hardship, the men might be given a day off, but even then they were not actually told they had time off, so they never really knew what was waiting to happen to them. They simply did nothing and waited for orders.

The routine varied constantly. They were sometimes required to spend a week in the jungle on their own, or swim ten kilometres across one of the lagoons along the coast. Additionally, the men were taught the finer points of marksmanship as well as unarmed combat. 'They must be able to kill efficiently and silently with a knife,' said Lt da Silva. He went on: 'If, during a course, a man wavers, even momentarily, he is taken off the programme. There are many other volunteers within the ranks of the armed forces who are anxious to join this elite corps.'

An important aspect of the course apparently was psychological indoctrination, though some critics of the Lisbon regime called it brainwashing.

Microphones throughout the camp beamed out slogans and doctrines at irregular intervals during the day and night. The messages, he explained, made the men aware of their physical capabilities, the task before them, the enemy, the threat that faced the motherland and, as one commando instructor succinctly put it, 'their duty to Christ and country'.

Commando instructors took great pains to keep abreast with the latest in enemy tactics, methods and equipment, landmines and their deployment especially. Officers who returned to Luanda from the various fronts on leave or duty were usually debriefed at the specialist training camp about what was going on 'at the front'.

Also, said the lieutenant, their instructors regularly went into battle with them in order to study conditions at first hand. The training programmes that follow were re-orientated according to what they had learned from these on-the-job sessions in the bush.

Mozambique: Conflict along
the Indian Ocean

*What has to be achieved is that people themselves discover the need for armed struggle.
As for guns, those you can always find ...*

Nguyen Van Tien; *Notre Strategie de la Guerrilla* 'Partisans'
Paris, January/February 1968

One of the developments that immediately preceded the succession of African rebellions that Lisbon faced in the early 1960s was the need to prepare for a conflict that most observers believed was imminent.

Former United States Navy Captain John Cann, with several published titles to his credit, remains at the forefront in chronicling Portugal's African campaigns and he makes the point in his book *Counterinsurgency in Africa: The Portuguese Way of War 1961-1974*, that Lisbon took a number of initiatives in preparing for conflict and in formulating the basis of doctrine for that eventuality.

'The first occurred in 1953 when Lisbon's Institute of Higher Military Studies (IAEM) conducted an eight week course for 53 officers, known as the *Curso de Estado-Maior de Pequenas Unidades*, or Staff Course for Small Units ... '

Designed to prepare officers for staff functions at battalion or regimental levels, it had its roots in the composite experience of officers who had primarily attended United States Army schools or visited American military units in Germany. Subsequently Lisbon sent five officers to the Intelligence Centre of the British Army at Maresfield Park Camp, Uckfield, Sussex to attend courses at its School of Military Intelligence. 'These courses contained a strong component of subversive warfare ... the British were heavily influenced by their experiences in Malaya, Kenya and Cyprus,' Cann tells us.

He makes the point that while these courses were not especially designed for subversive warfare, such as was to be experienced shortly in all three African territories, they did prove to be important after the first attacks had taken place in Angola in 1961, and subsequently in Portuguese Guinea and Mozambique.

Obviously, when the first squads of guerrillas crossed the Ruvuma River from Tanzania into Northern Mozambique, some of this expertise came into play, as did the experiences of veteran Portuguese Army combatants who had already seen action in Angola. Many Portuguese soldiers, at all levels, had already been 'blooded' in that African campaign that was to last 13 years.

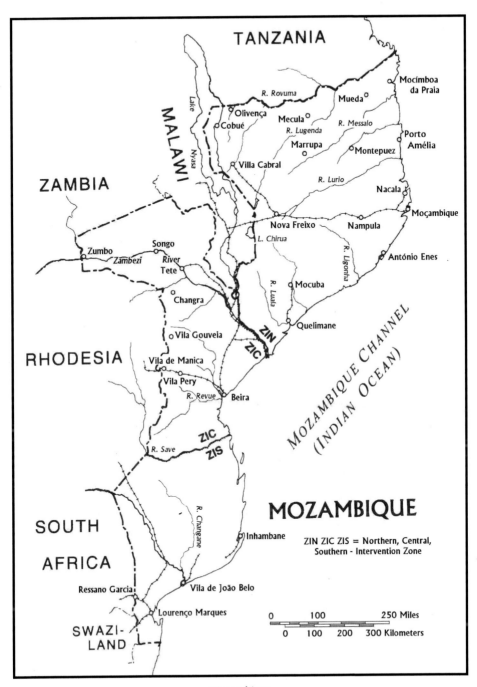

Mozambique

Captain Cann continues: 'With comparatively few resources and no army trained in this type of fighting initially, Portugal had to improvise. While it anticipated employing the standard type of counterinsurgency operational practices, it also sought innovations that were able to utilise the unique terrain and demographic characteristics in each of its three theatres.

'The concept might be borrowed from others and modified so extensively as to be nearly unique, or it might be purely Lusitanian.'

This noted American authority in Portugal's three conflicts lists some of the broader challenges and solutions that characterised the Portuguese wars of counterinsurgency:

- The complete reorientation of the entire Portuguese armed force from a conventional force to one for counterinsurgency, thus focussing this resource on a single campaign
- The realignment in recruiting for this force to the indigenous colonial manpower pool to a degree not seen in modern times, thus allowing the colonies to shoulder a substantial portion of this burden
- The shift to small-unit tactics and associated training based on experience in the wars, thus matching Portugal's force with that of the insurgents and keeping the tempo of fighting low and cost-effective
- The implementation of an economic and social development programme that raised the standard of living of Portuguese Africans and, in doing so, largely preempted insurgent arguments and raised the ability of the colonies to shoulder part of the war burden
- The extensive psychological operations that rationalised the Portuguese presence in Africa to the population.

For all this, Lisbon was faced with an enormous task to counter a series of revolutions that had taken root in its African possessions. As Cann says, there were eventually '27,000 insurgents spread over the three theatres ... and it was a problem for Portugal in that it was difficult to prevent their entry, and, once across the border, equally difficult to locate them. Their ability to cross long, unpatrolled borders in the remote areas of Africa and to make contact with the population remained a dangerous threat. In no other modern insurgency was there such a multiplicity of national movements across such a wide front in three [separate regions].'[1]

Cann provides us with a variety of comparative statistics which underscore the problems faced by Lisbon.

'Britain's security forces at the height of the 1948-1960 Malayan emergency[2] numbered 300,000 police and British as well as locally recruited troops in 1952: they were faced by Chinese communist guerrillas numbering 8,000, giving a numerical superiority of 37.5 to 1. In Kenya from 1952 to 1960, British security forces numbering 56,000 faced 12,000 Mau Mau terrorists: a ratio of 4.6 to 1. In Cyprus from 1955 to 1959, British security forces of 24,911 faced 1,000 EOKA guerrillas: a ratio of 25 to 1. The nearly 400,000 French troops in Algeria faced 8,000 FLN guerrillas at the close of 1956: a ratio of 50 to 1 ... while the

We found some remarkable contrasts in the Angolan war, ancient traditions
sometimes working comfortably with modern innovations. The horses could
go where armoured cars could not. (Photo Richard McIntosh)

United States in its Vietnam experience held a ratio of 4 to 1 prior to 1964, escalating to
8.71 to 1 four years later.

> Portuguese security forces of about 149,000 faced 27,000 guerrillas at the close of
> the war in 1974, giving nominal superiority of almost 6 to 1, although this ratio was
> increased somewhat through local militias ... few contemporary insurgencies went
> against such odds ... [3]

The guerrilla war in Mozambique was launched into Cabo Delgado Province from Tanzania
in September 1964. Conflict was to debilitate that country from the start.

Central government authority in Lourenço Marques (Maputo today) – more than
2,000 kilometres south of the Tanzanian frontier – was both weakened and encumbered
with an insurgency that seemed to have no end. It was exactly that mind-set the FRELIMO
High Command in Dar es Salaam intended to impart to the majority, part of a game plan
for ultimate victory advocated by this heavily Marxist organisation.

Simply put, maintained Eduardo Mondlane, FRELIMO's early leader, 'there will be
no end to the military struggle until Lisbon has been ousted and a black government takes
over power in Mozambique'.

The first 250 FELIMO guerrillas to enter Mozambique were trained in Algeria, as were the first 300 MPLA insurgents from Angola. Having inaugurated the insurgency with a foray into northern Mozambique, and soon thereafter, into Niassa – this corridor from the north became the fulcrum of disputed authority. It was not long before regions around Tete, further to the south on the Zambezi River came into sharp focus as hostilities progressed, though the bulk of that support came from Zambia. It stayed that way for almost a decade.

Forewarned by uprisings in Angola and Guinea, Portugal bolstered its military strength in the East African colony to 16,000 men, though initially it had only five serviceable aircraft. By 1973 the troop tally had grown to about 70 000, while the air force comprised a dozen Italian-supplied Fiat G-91s, 15 US-built Harvard T-6s, 14 Alouette helicopters and a single pair of Puma transports. Additionally, there were five Nordatlas 2501s as well as seven C-47s Dakotas, hardly inspiring for a country as big as France and Germany together.

Somehow, the Portuguese seemed to manage, in part because the insurgents didn't have a single aircraft between them. They made up for it by deploying 12.7mm and 14.5mm heavy machine-guns, a feat difficult to emulate in Eastern Angola because of the sand and lack of proper roads.

It was hardly easy going in the kind of inhospitable, quasi-jungle of Northern Mozambique where the rebels faced similar problems: as in Vietnam with the Vietcong, the insurgents had to stick to the bush. That problem persisted until the end of the war and meant that just about everything needed for the guerrilla war effort had to be physically manhandled from Tanzania across a couple of thousand kilometres of a still-undeveloped Africa.

The Portuguese Air Force played a significant role in keeping things on the boil, but they didn't go unscathed either. There were many FAP aircraft hit by ground fire – as well as by the occasional SAM-7 missile – but this East African colony suffered relatively few losses compared to what was then taking place in Guinea.

On one occasion, a Dakota DC-3 that was ferrying foreign military attaches and senior members of the Portuguese military command around the country took a hit from a SAM-7 missile in one of its two engines. The crippled plane managed to land safely.

Interestingly, the same happened a few years later when a Dakota, carrying most of the South African general staff, was struck towards the rear by a MANPAD.

It is worth mentioning that when the author moved through parts of Northern Mozambique in November 2011, news reports emerged of the wreck of a Portuguese Air Force Alouette helicopter having been found in the Zambezi Valley, not far from Tete. It had originally disappeared during a routine sortie almost 40 years before, and by all accounts, had not been plundered. Everybody on board must have been killed outright because their remains – only bones were recovered – all lay in or around their downed machine.

Looking back, the general consensus among military historians today is that without Tanzania, the war in Mozambique would almost certainly never have happened.

One can go further and say that with the level of colonial exploitation going on in

One of the American-donated landing craft, complete with heavy gun ahead of the wheelhouse used for patrol purposes by the navy in local waters in 1968. (Photo *Revista da Armada*)

Lisbon's colonies– and in this regard the Portuguese were ruthless – there would almost certainly have been some kind of an uprising, as there had been many before, but always ruthlessly dealt with. This time though, with the infusion of modern weapons and Soviet support, the guerrillas needed a secure external base. With President Julius Nyerere at the helm in Tanzania, they got it. Consequently, almost all the military supplies used in the early days of conflict throughout Southern Africa – and that included Rhodesia, Eastern Angola and northern South West Africa – were channelled into the various theatres of military activity through the port of Dar es Salaam.

It is also true that *Mwalimu* Julius Nyerere – 'traditional espouser of peace and maker of war', as he was described by one of his critics – was powerfully under influence of both Moscow and Beijing. In says a lot that Nyerere never disabused his allies.

Insurgents would take delivery of their war cargoes in the Tanzanian capital and head south. Some of the matériel would go by road to Zambia (and then on to Rhodesia, or some of it into Eastern Angola) but the bulk was intended for what was once known as Portuguese East Africa. Having unloaded the trucks, porters would make their way, surreptitiously and usually at night, across the Ruvuma River, which forms Mozambique's northern boundary with Tanzania. Some of this hardware would be used against the Portuguese Army on the Mueda Plateau, the Cabo Delgado region and further into the interior towards Lake Malawi; the rest would wend its way south towards the Zambezi.

This was a trek that could sometimes take months. The insurgents, while helped by local tribal folk, who, in turn, also lent a hand as carriers or were press-ganged, had to carry everything they needed with them on their backs. It was never an easy task, because natural obstacles and great rivers apart, the Mozambique countryside with its tsetse and other endemic insect-borne diseases is a harsh adversary. Moreover, it is land that has never favoured either the mule or the pack horse.

Later, once Kenneth Kaunda's Zambia had entered the fray, logistic lines were eased. But even then, the Portuguese had only marginally developed Mozambique's interior and roads and other communication infrastructures remained sparse.

In their book, *Armed Forces and Modern Counter Insurgency*, Ian Beckett and John Pimlott make the point that the size of FRELIMO units steadily increased as the movement approached a maximum strength of perhaps 8,000 guerrillas by 1967/8 ... [4]

'FRELIMO did succeed in closing many sisal plantations along the northern frontier, but had been mostly contained by the time General Kaúlza de Arriaga – who had become the Portuguese ground force commander in May, 1969, undertook a large-scale offensive. That was the controversial 'Operation Gordian knot' that took place in the dry season of 1970.'

The campaign lasted seven months and involved some 10,000 troops. In that period, de Arriaga claimed 650 guerrillas killed and almost 2,000 captured for the loss of only 132 of his men. He also claimed to have destroyed 61 insurgent bases and 165 camps, while 40 tons of ammunition were taken in the first two months alone. In retrospect, we now know that de Arriaga's claims were inflated, astonishingly so.

Unlike his counterparts, the illustrious Brigadier – later general – José Manuel Bethencourt Rodrigues in Angola and General António de Spínola in Portuguese Guinea, the man could almost have been regarded as an amateur.

Becket and Pimlott: 'The coordination of heliborne assault after initial artillery and air bombardment, followed by mine clearance and consolidation on foot undoubtedly severely damaged FRELIMO's infrastructure in the north. But in the manner of such large scale operations, it did not totally destroy the guerrilla capacity for infiltration, which Arriaga's critics maintained his predecessors had achieved at much less cost and effort. Further operations were thus required in the north such as 'Operation Garotte' and 'Operation Apia' during 1971.'

The problem with 'Operation Gordian Knot' and similar operations, is that in military jargon when a counter-revolutionary campaign becomes spectacular (and they were spectacular, since they involved nearly every man in the security forces who could carry a gun, including office staff, cooks and bearers), the writing is on the wall.

Yet, when the Ruvuma and Tete regions were visited by the South African vice-consul in Luanda, Colonel (later General) 'Kaas' van der Waals, he didn't think the war was going too badly for the Portuguese. He was soon made aware of the fact that, as a result of heavy insurgent attacks in Tete Province, it was Rhodesia that was taking the brunt of these insurgencies because of the inability of the Portuguese upper ranks to cope with the situation in their own backyard.

As he recounts, they had tried their best to clear FRELIMO out of the region around Tete (and which included the Cahora Bassa Dam), but they were unsuccessful. By then

The consequences of mine damage were catastrophic. Apart from an horrific
explosion generated by almost 10 kgs of high explosive, temperatures generated
by the blast were about 3,000° Celsius. (Author's collection, from Angola)

Rhodesia's 'Operation Hurricane' had been launched into the adjacent Mount Darwin area
of Rhodesia by the Zimbabwe African National Liberation Army (ZANLA), the military
wing of Robert Mugabe's Zimbabwe African National Union (ZANU). As a consequence,
Tete – a not immodest town straddling the Zambezi – became the guerrilla cauldron, from
which the conflict was ultimately extended outwards.

In 1967, the war also progressed from the northern precincts of Makonde country
towards Niassa and areas further south, but guerrilla hostilities never extended anywhere
south of the road that linked Vila Pery (Chimoio today) and Beira. Throughout, Tete and
its nearby dam construction program on the Zambezi – which was never sabotaged or
breached while war lasted – remained the focus of both adversaries.

Colonel Ron Reid-Daly, former founder-commander of the Selous Scouts in the Rhodesian
War, was then an acting captain with the Rhodesian Light Infantry. He was also the first
Rhodesian officer to be attached to Portuguese forces. Others involved, including some
Rhodesian SAS specialists like Darrell Watt, were also seconded from time to time. Some
of them were also sent on short tours of duty with the Portuguese Army in Angola.

Their comments about the way in which the Portuguese were fighting their war in
Mozambique (and, ultimately, why they eventually lost) are instructive.

From Reid-Daly's experience with the British SAS in Malaya (he told me he must have done something right there, because he was awarded an MBE for his efforts), it soon became apparent to his superiors in Salisbury that the Portuguese brass in Mozambique had no basic understanding of the nature of guerrilla warfare. They were certainly far behind anything that the British had experienced in Borneo, Malaya or even Kenya during the Mau Mau emergency. That was surprising, says Reid-Daly, because many Portuguese Army commanders had already seen good service in Angola and Guinea, yet almost none of them had benefited from the original IAEM counter insurgency course at Lisbon's Institute of Higher Military Studies.

The counter insurgency pattern was the same each time. Some intelligence of insurgent activity would arrive and the local garrison commander would spend days getting together a force of several hundred men. They in turn, would embark on a massive cross-country sweep, often 500 men strong.

'The Portuguese Army would never act immediately on a tip-off, with the result that when an operation was eventually launched – perhaps a day later – the birds had invariably flown,' Reid-Daly recounted after spending lengthy periods with Portuguese forces.

He goes on: 'During bush operations, everything in their path would be destroyed; livestock slaughtered, crops and villages burnt, the local people rounded up for questioning and anyone acting in a suspicious manner arrested and hauled back to base. Tribesmen who attempted to escape this treatment were regarded as "fleeing terrorists", and shot. The death would then be formally listed as a "terrorist kill".

'If they managed to escape into the bush, well and good; there was no question of sending in a follow-up force. By nightfall the unit would be back at base, everybody congratulating themselves on a job well done. Naturally, any one of the local people who had experienced one of these Portuguese "search and destroy" missions was by then a firm supporter of FRELIMO; the business of "hearts and minds" came only much later. In that way many neutral tribesmen soon became not only FRELIMO sympathizers, but ended up joining the guerrillas and being sent out of the country for more advanced training.'

Although Colonel Reid-Daly was considered by his peers to be critical of the Portuguese war effort in Africa, and specifically what was going on in Mozambique at the time, his views were largely empirically-based. As he told this author, 'I was there. I saw it for myself. I went to war with these people, so I was in a good position to assess the insurgent threat as it developed as well as the people who were doing the defending, the Portuguese fighting man. I was impressed with neither.'

He had his own views about Lisbon's *aldeamentos* program of resettling rural communities in organized camps, something that was already in full swing in all three African provinces and which he had experienced at first hand in Malaya as 'new' or 'fortified' villages. As in South East Asia, large sections of the civilian population was moved *en bloc* into areas where they would be under Portuguese control and, in theory, out of reach of the insurgents. The justification for this policy was ostensibly that it denied the guerrillas the ability to wage war because there "would be no popular indigenous support and no food,

In Mozambique, old-time cavalry proved a useful adjunct to counter-insurgency measures – horses could often go where man and machine could not. (Author's collection)

which was supposed to be essential for survival in the bush.

'In reality, although a million people, roughly 15 per cent of the population in Mozambique were resettled, it failed utterly.' Beckett makes the point that food grown in the *Aldeamentos* went straight to the guerrillas.

For all that, the bulk of the war – apart from what was going on in Tete Province – was, as we have seen, confined largely to the north of Mozambique. Lourenco Marques, the capital – Maputo today, with its tourists and bright lights and from where almost all of us journalists operated, might have been in another African country.

In actual combat conditions, the South Africans and the Rhodesians found the Portuguese military in Mozambique both clumsy and inept, which was in marked contrast to the far more efficient campaign then being fought by the Portuguese in Angola.

There were notable exceptions, like Óscar Cardoso who established *Flecha* counter-insurgency units, but generally, army patrols in Mozambique were too large, too loud and too nervous of the bush and the enemy to be able to do anything constructive. Indeed, some units would go to great lengths to avoid contact with the guerrillas. As Reid-Daily pointed out, something like 30 or 40 men at a time would go into the jungle, and this when his own people had become accustomed to four-man 'sticks' that were achieving excellent results.

Most of the Portuguese Army failures, the Rhodesians believed, resulted from a distinct lack of regular professional troops at the 'sharp end,' and the fact that most of these boys from the metropolis neither understood Africa nor wished to be in what they referred to as 'this dreadful tropical hell hole'. Their letters home were full of such comments and worse.

Even more disconcerting, as hostilities in the Mozambique war continued, the traditional trust between officers and the men under them deteriorated. In a sense, it could almost have been a repeat of the Vietnamese syndrome, though as far as is known, there was never anything as dramatic as 'fragging'.

There were many reasons for this imbroglio and Ron Reid-Daly lists several: For a start, he points out, radio communications in Mozambique were poor, which was probably one reason why the troops in the field tended to work in large numbers. 'They were terrified of being overrun, which, he suggests might be expected of such unprofessional soldiers.

'Also, their radio sets were unwieldy American instruments designed rather for vehicles than the backs of soldiers in the bush: quite a number dated from the Korean War period. As a result, communications with base was a long and complicated business. At one main base the Portuguese were using large antiquated German sets from World War II.

'Then there was the Portuguese soldier himself, reasonably well trained and probably quite enthusiastic to start with, but totally lacking in motivation after a few months in the bush. Though there were exceptions, the enlisted man was regarded as street trash by his officers and treated according. And though Lisbon claimed that medical facilities were exemplary, practical examples proved otherwise.' But more about battlefield casualties later.

The truth was that almost throughout the Portuguese Army in Mozambique (as opposed to conditions in Angola where success on the ground was more apparent), both officers and men simply could not wait for their tour of duty to end, which would allow them to go home. Most came to despise the African bush and the primitive conditions under which they were obliged to operate.

Many of Reid-Daly's observations are insightful. During all the operations in which the Rhodesians took part in the Tete Panhandle, he recalls, the Portuguese were found to be completely base-bound. They fought much as the Americans had in Vietnam.

The upper command was happy to let the insurgents control the bush, while the government held onto the towns, communications links as well as strong points. Reid-Daly said that in Tete, when he first propounded the concept of long-range patrols that might last anything from four to six weeks and be supplied by air, the idea was regarded by the upper command as preposterous. At that time, the Portuguese Army would never countenance anything beyond three days, spending the dark hours in camp, if at all possible.

The Rhodesians, it will be recalled, already regarded as masters of counter-insurgency warfare, always emphasized the need to dominate the bush by night as well as by day. And while most Portuguese officers might have agreed with him in principle, they very rarely did anything about it.

Ground level view of the enormous Cahora Bassa dam which was to develop into one of the largest hydro-electric projects in the Southern Hemisphere. It is still operating successfully. (Author's photo)

The ability of FRELIMO to move freely at night was clearly illustrated by the number of mines, both anti-tank and anti-personnel, that they were able to lay, almost at will. This freedom extended all the way from the Ruvuma to Tete.

During one morning's clearing operation in the Mueda area, Portuguese sappers cleared 189 landmines along an 11 kilometre track, about a third of them Soviet TM-46s. The rest were anti-personnel (AP) mines. I was to see some of this for myself in the brief, three-day safari I completed from Tete to the Malawi border in 1971 where roughly 50 were laid along the route we traversed.

There were other problems, recalls Reid-Daly. Physically, the Rhodesians regarded the average Portuguese conscript as 'a poor physical specimen'. They couldn't march any distance without frequent rests. Most of these young men had come from poor backgrounds, and although they were put through their first physical training session on the day they joined the army in Portugal, they were many that were barely fit or strong enough to meet the rigorous demands of their officers. Again, there were exceptions.

One of their worst faults on the march was that the column was both noisy and straggling. Instead of maintaining silence, they talked loudly among themselves which, even FRELIMO knew, was one of the first principles of counter-insurgency warfare. After dark, when an ambush had been set up, Portuguese soldiers would cough and fidget, Reid-Daly recollects from his own experiences in the bush with these people.

'It was as if they were warning the enemy to keep clear, so that they would not be compelled to fight. Clearly, this was an impossible situation ... '

On the other hand, some of the *Flechas,* parachute and black commando regiments were excellent operators. Most were superior to FRELIMO, and many of the kills in Mozambique were attributable to them and to the air force.

While most operational plans were carefully prepared by the brigade staff, Reid-Daly discovered that they seldom allowed the battalion commander scope for flexibility or even a modicum of personal initiative. It all had to be done 'according to the book'. There was even a marked reluctance to change plans in spite of fresh information having been brought in as the operation progressed.

A sorry example of this was the failure to capitalize on the discovery – towards the end of 1967 by one of the helicopters during an operation in the mountains near Cahora Bassa – of a large insurgent camp about 500 metres across. It was only a day later that an infantry attack got underway: the Portuguese officer responsible wasn't prepared to change either the original plan or the sequence of events that he and his colleagues had mapped out earlier.

Reid-Daly was with them when this happened. He insisted that they scrape together another body of men and try for a vertical envelopment. 'That would have been possible because there were eight Alouettes available,' Reid-Daly remembers. 'The operation eventually got off the ground several days later, and it produced a lemon ... '

Reid-Daly believed that the Portuguese soldiers with whom he came into contact on these operations were, considering the nature of hostilities, not adequately equipped. Apart from the standard G-3 rifle of 7.62mm NATO calibre, there were no illumination flares, no claymores and none of the elementary means of protection employed as a matter of course by most armies of the world. Also, the average grunt from Europe simply had no idea of how to use a smoke grenade or even how to call up a helicopter in the event of a casualty evacuation. 'I had to teach them how to use small mirrors to attract the attention of aircraft – and many other little quirks that most bush fighters take for granted in remote or isolated areas.

Whereas the Rhodesians maintained excellent liaison between pilots and ground forces in their own war, that situation was never allowed to happen in Mozambique and no one took any real steps to improve the situation: they just were not talking to each other, he said. It was the same real or imagined superiority syndrome that I'd observed at close quarters in Angola's Sector D, though clearly, things were going a lot better there than in Mozambique.

Another device taught by the Rhodesians and eventually taken up in the East African colony was to set up radio relay stations on hills, which also served as observation posts. Rhodesian officers posted to Mozambique began to take some of the elementary equipment lacking and which attracted great interest. Reid-Daly even ran a course showing his

Mozambique

The Zambezi Valley from the air, taken while the author travelled by small plane from Tete (not to be confused with Tite in former Portuguese Guinea) to the air force base near Cahora Bassa. The great river can be seen in the distance and below, exclusively guerrilla country.

Wherever we went in the Mozambique interior, we would encounter army vehicles ferrying troops. But because the country is one of the largest along the east coast of Africa, there was never enough military manpower to counter the insurgent threat. (Author's photo)

When a vehicle hit a mine, there were invariably casualties, which was when the air force would be tasked with uplifting casualties and flying them to the nearest hospital. In this stretch of the "Hell Run" – from the Zambezi to Mwanza, on the Malawi border - it would have been the clinic at Tete. (Author's photo)

The most pressing problem that faced the military in Mozambique was landmines, both anti-tank and anti-personnel. There were more casualties suffered by the men on the ground from these weapons than in all the ambushes and bush strikes together. Though Lisbon tried, it could never effectively counter the threat of bombs that had been secreted on tracks and public roads by the guerrillas - as the South Africans were able to do in their own Bush wars in South West Africa and Angola in later years. The mine exposed here is a Soviet TM-46. (Author's collection)

Like Angola, the Portuguese province on Africa's east coast followed the economic traditions of the Metropolis. Like Angola too, it had its own carbon-copy version of the ubiquitous escudo and both were directly linked to the Portuguese money market in Europe.

The great bridge across the Zambezi River at Tete. Though not clearly visible, the
army did sling some observation 'turrets' directly under the bridge spans to prevent

guerrillas from sabotaging the structure. All convoys headed north gathered together on the north bank of the river at first light. (Author's photo)

Having just come under attack from a group of insurgents, this patrol took to digging themselves a temporary defensive position on the bush road along which they had been travelling.

Road convoys in Mozambique followed identical patterns to road convoys in Portuguese Guinea and the more rugged and overgrown regions of Northern Angola. (Author's photo)

On one of the author's trips along the "Hell Run" - from Tete to the Malawi border - he moved about in this Land Rover, having taken up a position near the rear of the column (so that if there were any mines in the road ahead, somebody else's wheels would detonate them). As can be seen, the vehicles were well spaced out, sometimes over a kilometre or more and we could easily have come under attack if there were no military vehicles nearby. We never did, but two of the trucks detonated land anti-personnel mines. (Author's photo)

But when a vehicle does trip a mine, such as this military transporter which detonated a Soviet anti-tank TM-46, the vehicle is invariably a write-off and many of the troops onboard would either have been killed or wounded. (Author's collection)

At the core of the war in Mozambique was the giant Cahora Bassa hydro-electric scheme, which involved building one of the biggest dams in the Southern Hemisphere. When completed, the wall towered up 170 metres or 50 metres taller than the dam wall built at Kariba. Funded largely by European investors, it began to fill just as the war ended in 1974 and its powerhouse comprised five 415 MW turbines that today power industry on the faraway South African Highveld. The second view of the dam shows early stages of construction, with the winding road leading down the side of the Cahora Bassa Gorge to the Zambezi River. (Author's photos)

There were lighthouses all the way up and down the Mozambique coast that continued to function normally throughout the war. They were never attacked by the rebels. This one stands on Bazaruto Island and still sends out its rays after dark, though it has since been automated. (Author's photo)

Early Portuguese colonial settlers in Northern Mozambique who settled on Ibo Island built the Fort of São João in the 18th Century and it still stands. For a century the nearby town was a prominent slave port along the East African coast and at one stage, became the second most important in the region after historic Mozambique Island further towards the south. During the more recent war Fort São João, because it was so remote, was used to house political prisoners. (Author's photo)

While many of the colonial memorials in Portuguese Guinea – Guiné-Bissau today – have been defaced, destroyed or removed, most of the old colonial monuments in what was once Lourenço Marques – Maputo today – still stand. The bronze plaque commemorates an important historical event of more than a century ago. (Author's photos)

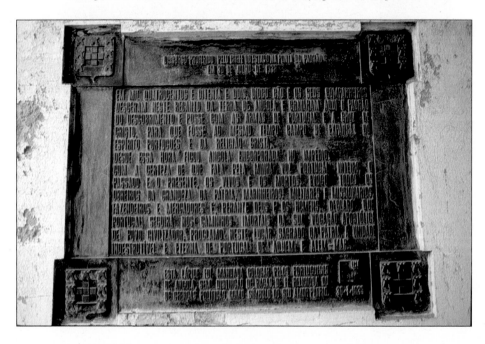

While Beira and Lourenço Marques might have been spared guerrilla hostilities, fighting remained intense in a vast region in the south-west of the country for some distance eastwards along the Zambezi River. Intelligence would arrive at military headquarters about an insurgent group operating in a specific area and as a matter of course, some of the villages would be attacked, usually with top cover provided by Portuguese Air Force Alouette helicopter gunships. (Author's collection)

Visitors to Maputo – who remember the Lourenço Marques of old – will discover that though the majority of Mozambique's leaders today are ethnic African, not an awful lot else has changed in the interim. Maputo is a much more expensive city than it was before but the delightful old Polana Hotel, a landmark in the city since 1922, is still one of the better hotels on the east coast of Africa. Down the coast a few kilometres, the Cloub Navale maintains its own traditions for the international yachting community, just as it did when the Portuguese strode tall along these shores. (Author's photos)

Unlike Angola where a large proportion of the wildlife has been seriously poached, it was Mozambique's antelope and other animals that quite often kept the guerrillas alive when supplies failed to arrive from Tanzania or Zambia. With a coastline that stretches almost 2,500 kilometres it would have taken a dozen wars like the one launched by FRELIMO to destroy the country's natural infrastructure. (Author's photos)

Curiously, much of the country's coastal regions remained unscathed by the war. The tiny harbour-town of Vilanculos south of Beira (shown here) never came under attack by the guerrillas, although that changed drastically after independence once the Renamo rebel group (funded by Rhodesia and South Africa) got into full swing. (Author's photo)

Hostilities in Mozambique did not end with the departure of Lisbon's troops. By the time the war ended in 1974, a dissident group of combatants, weary of FRELIMO's Marxist proclivities (and with solid Rhodesian and South African military support) launched a guerrilla war of their own which went on for 17 years of intense fighting in which tens of thousands more people died. This shot, taken by former British Television producer Tim Lambon, shows some of the rebel fighters in a bush camp near the Malawi border.

The *Mercurio*, one of the Portuguese Navy gunships successfully transported overland through Mozambique's extremely difficult interior to Lake Malawi. It was moved on a South African Army tank transport. (Photo *Revista da Armada*)

counterparts how to make a simple Claymore mine from a ploughshare.

He and other Rhodesian officers explained to them the principle of a stopper group and its role in a frontal attack. They needed to work hard at it, for the Portuguese choice of positions was almost always bad; they rarely planned escape routes. In fact, said Reid-Daly, they were simply not trained for the kind of bush warfare which, by then, had become second nature to many of us Rhodesian as well as South African units.

For instance, the very idea of taking a prisoner live immediately after a skirmish was frowned upon. Although not all FRELIMO captives were shot, there were some who would argue that they ought to have been. It depended largely on the attitude of the officer in charge at the time. On more than one occasion Reid-Daly stepped in; in his view it took a long time for the Portuguese Army to understand the need for interrogation and the importance of military intelligence.

PIDE, the secret police, was constantly calling for prisoners, and that frequently resulted in friction and occasionally, an exchange of words. Soldiers in the field were supposed to take insurgents alive if and when they could, but few bothered. Under today's conditions, many of the officers responsible for these transgressions would have been accused of crimes against humanity, especially since every one of them was familiar with the Geneva Convention.

As the war progressed, relations between the Portuguese Army and PIDE's security officers deteriorated markedly.

The Rhodesians noted that Portuguese military vehicles, the West German Unimog and the French-built Berliet – both of which formed the mainstay of communications in the bush – were excellent, as was their maintenance. Like their uniforms, of which the troops were issued two per tour of duty, it was all they had and they took the trouble to service them. But they did not do the same for their weapons.

Perhaps because the G-3 was virtually proof against stoppage, few Portuguese soldiers bothered to clean their guns, either before or after a contact or spell in the bush. They would smile among themselves at Rhodesian officers who took great care of their firearms at all times. One young captain told Reid-Daly that the last place he had seen a man actually cleaning his rifle every day when not ordered to do so was in Goa, the Portuguese colony on the Indian sub-continent. That happened after he'd been captured by Indian troops when they liberated the enclave.

Morale among Portuguese forces was seriously affected by the lack of facilities for the evacuation of casualties. That was due mainly to the shortage of operational helicopters. Also, while most of the camps had medical officers, most were conscript students who had only the bare essentials available for their needs.

A man injured by a land mine would usually have to be moved to an airstrip, where a small plane could be brought in. Depending on where the incident took place – often in remote areas – that could take an entire day and in the tropics a serious torso wound can result in septicaemia setting in if not treated within six or seven hours. The result was that because of delays, many Portuguese soldiers died of their wounds.

The Rhodesian officers found it curious that the Portuguese in Mozambique never went out of their way in a bid to encourage the kind of reconnaissance patrols that had resulted in serious losses among their own insurgents. They would seldom reconnoitre a position beforehand or use aerial photos for intelligence purposes after a known FRELIMO camp had been pinpointed. Instead, they would deploy their Special Forces in an operation with little or no primary reconnaissance, very much a hit or miss affair.

Reid-Daly spent time with one of the *Flecha* units. He became a close friend of Colonel Óscar Cardoso, who was brought from Angola to establish the *Flecha* concept in Mozambique. Unlike so many of his fellows, Cardoso proved to be an excellent soldier and tactician and, as Reid-Dale once commented, very much in the tradition of the Rhodesian fighting man. But then Cardoso had been born in Africa: he relished life in the bush and understood its people.

While the *Flechas* worked in smaller groups, they initially lacked scouting ability. Captured insurgents, turncoats and local recruits provided some of it, the latter because they were paid bounties. At the same time, the training of these *Grupos Especiais* was hard and discipline draconian. A petty misdemeanour would often be treated as a serious offence. But the *Flechas* also made excellent soldiers. Their ability to shoot straight with a rifle was

Fast Portuguese Navy patrol along the eastern shores of Lake Malawi. (Juhan Kuus photo)

unmatched even in the Rhodesian army; they either got one- or two-inch groups at 50 metres or they were thrashed by their officers.

They considered a 40-kilometre patrol between sunrise and sunset as normal, in spite of the difficult mountainous and jungle terrain. Some Rhodesian SAS men who worked with them were amazed at their ability to keep going and there were many times when they themselves were hard-pressed to keep up. They were also required to be exemplary in their actions; they would cross a river or other obstacle by first sending tactically across two sections: they would scout the area ahead and only then would the rest of the group be sent through.

Interestingly, they had only one break for a smoke the entire day in the bush, a respite that most soldiers regard as their right. As Reid-Daly noted, they were among the first to observe that under the right conditions, the waft of cigarette smoke could sometimes travel miles and alert the enemy of their presence.

Other Special Force units also used by the Portuguese Armed Forces in Mozambique included:

- Special Groups (*Grupos Especiais*): units similar to the ones used in Angola
- Paratrooper Special Groups (*Grupos Especiais Pára-Quedistas*): units of volunteer black soldiers that had paratrooper training
- Combat Tracking Special Groups (*Grupos Especiais de Pisteiros de Combate*): special units trained in tracking
- *Flechas*: a unit similar to the one employed and trained by Colonel Oscar

Cardoso in Angola

The Rhodesians achieved some good successes in Mozambique, but they never persuaded the Portuguese to effectively follow-up tracks after a contact. Some Rhodesian officers managed to teach a few of the units how to run a proper operations room and to set up an efficient Joint Operations Command, but once they had returned to their own units, everything went back to 'normal'.

For all that, some of Lisbon's officers were receptive and Portuguese Army trackers gradually began to play a solid role in countering terrorism, and here members of the Rhodesian SAS played an important role. Unfortunately, in the long term, there were basically too many Portuguese and too few Rhodesians to have any real effect on the outcome of this protracted military campaign that lasted almost twice as long as the Americans were in Vietnam.

Colonel Reid-Daly made many other observations about Mozambique before he died in 2011. He told of how the Portuguese would often refuse outright to go into the bush unless a large force had been mustered, and then only with additional helicopter support. The result was that FRELIMO units were able to snipe at Portuguese patrols almost with impunity. They knew that the European troops would rarely detach men from their columns and go after them.

To the conscript army, capturing a FRELIMO camp was the pinnacle of success, even though it might have been abandoned days before because the rebels had somehow gained foreknowledge of the attack or they could hear the Portuguese Army coming. Holding ground, said Reid-Daly, was the ultimate achievement, even if they abandoned that ground an hour later.

Reid-Daly recommended on his return to Salisbury that Rhodesian Light Infantry units should be allowed to work with the Portuguese, not so much for political reasons, but rather to demonstrate what ordinary young soldiers were capable of achieving when properly led and trained. He was aware too that the presence of Special Forces like the SAS might have been regarded by the Portuguese command as an attempt by the Rhodesians to 'show them up', with consequent bad feeling.

In the opinion of most Rhodesian and South African soldiers who came into contact with the Portuguese, the quality most needed was initiative. As it was, it was lacking, almost across the board. Occasionally a brilliant officer would be encountered – a professional soldier who knew his oats, was familiar with the enemy, the ground which they were contesting, and capable of inspiring his men to better results. But they were a rare breed.

Discipline generally, was not what it should have been in wartime, and it has been well said that an army usually reflects its national character. In the final phase of these hostilities most conscripts were able to ignore indirect commands and get away with it.

Though Mozambique was able to field only a nominal number of French-built Alouette helicopters, many of them gunships, they performed a vital role for the duration of the war. (Author's collection)

Thus, the average Portuguese soldier, while respectful to their officers, except during the final phase of the conflict when the entire army was pulled back to the Metropolis after the army mutiny, was sloppy in both dress and bearing and slack in military operations. I would observe them in the streets of Luanda and Lourenco Marques, many of the soldiers not bothering to properly secure their boot laces.

Often a battalion commander would be of the best type imaginable, but he would lack good professional officers to support him. Senior commanders usually had a handful of regular officers supplemented by many more *milicianos,* the title accorded temporary officers from universities, the majority of whom had not the slightest interest in fighting some remote war in Africa ... .

There were other problems. A battalion colonel would often have senior visitors from Nampula, Beira or Lourenco Marques. These would be brigadiers and generals, breathing down his neck in his own operations room, often countermanding the orders he had just given. Four or five would sit about and veto the next phase. At other times they would change his entire operational plan, to the extent that he might not even have needed to be in the room.

Such a scene, witnessed twice by Reid-Daly, was not a rare event; it happened often enough in all theatres in Mozambique. Certainly it would never have been tolerated in Portuguese Guinea under General António de Spínola or to the same extent in Angola, where the conflict was much more professionally handled.

In Mozambique, one sensed, the high command had lost control. As military correspondents, we were all aware when visiting the colony that de Arriaga (or the 'Pink Panther' as his men called him) was frequently accused of employing too many subordinates who had failed elsewhere. He was recalled in July 1973, but by then the damage was done.

Mozambique, from the beginning of the campaign, was never imbued with the same kind of determination displayed in Angola or during the later stages in de Spínola's Portuguese Guinea, the fundamental belief that this was a war that could be won. Even to the end, let it be said, it was never lost; but there was no will to win it either.

Because it began later in this East African territory fringing great swathes of the Indian Ocean, and most intelligent Portuguese knew that Mozambique was their third African war and that the homeland had become over-extended, this campaign lacked the necessary impetus for any effective or lasting counter-insurgency measures. In a word, just about everything was done spasmodically.

As Beckett says, the Portuguese had growing problems in Mozambique by 1974 – the last year of the actual war – but nothing serious enough to warrant defeat. We must therefore look elsewhere for the failure to consolidate Lisbon's position along the Ruvuma River to take advantage of the serious splits that were developing within the FRELIMO hierarchy.

Like Colonel Reid-Daly, Porch spoke of deteriorating morale among regular cadres. This was manifested in the steady desertion rate in Portugal itself. Nor were matters helped by the country's dictator, Salazar, who, like Hitler before him, ignored the advice of his generals. He was warned repeatedly against fighting on more than one front and by the time the end came, his forces were over-extended in three different regions of Africa. To give him his due, there was not that much he could do about it.

The antiquated Portuguese war machine had been beefed-up by trebling its strength from 60,000 men in 1960 to 210,000 almost 20 years later. And Caetano, who succeeded the ailing Salazar, admitted when he was in exile in Brazil, that 'we had no organization capable of directing the army in operations.'

Most of the Portuguese defence structure was haphazard and piecemeal, which, as Porch declared, meant that the army was 'ill-equipped to cope with a long war.'[5]

24

Casualties of War

Two weapons today threaten freedom in our world. One – the 100 megaton hydrogen
bomb – requires vast resources of technology, effort and money. The other – a nail
and a piece of wood buried in the sand is deceptively simple – the weapon of a peasant.
Lieutenant-Colonel T N Greene, US Marine Corps:
The Guerrilla and How to Fight Him

As in any war, including those in Portuguese Africa, there are two issues of paramount
interest to the average soldier. The first is news from home, which is why the mail
needs to get through, no matter what.

The second is no less personal, and it involves his personal well-being. Should he be
wounded during an action or caught in a landmine blast, he needs to be assured that he
will get the kind of attention that will enable him to survive. Israel's Defence Force has this
down to a fine art. During routine cross-border forays into South Lebanon when the IDF
still held onto the Exclusion Zone – that inappropriately-termed stretch of real estate in
South Lebanon that adjoined the Israeli border – it was estimated that if it took a helicopter
more than three or four minutes to reach a casualty, somebody wasn't doing his or her job.

Western or Coalition forces east of Suez are equally efficient. Casualties are sometimes
lifted from the scene within minutes of an IED having been detonated alongside one of the
main roads leading into Baghdad, because there are always helicopters hovering somewhere
in the vicinity.

The South Africans tried to emulate that example, but with such huge distances to
cover in Pretoria's Border Wars, minutes would sometimes become hours. Essentially it
all depended on where an incident took place in relation to one of the helicopter bases
along the Angolan Border. Close to Oshakati or Rundu further to the east, and it could be
minutes. Across the frontier into enemy-held territory – and depending on whether it was
day or night – it often took much longer.

The same equation applies to Coalition Forces in Afghanistan, a large country with a
limited number of air bases. For all that, if a wounded man can be saved in the Hindu Kush
or along open ground leading into Kandahar, he usually is.

How different in Portugal's African wars, though not always because there were willing
hands available to help. Those few scribes who were able to put a foot inside some of the
military hospitals in Portugal's African domains were in for a surprise, especially if they

Ground crew rush a casualty to waiting ambulance at Bissau Airport. (*Revista da Armada*)

were outside the mainstream.

While conditions in the largest military medical establishments in places like Luanda, Bissau, Beira, Nova Lisboa (Huambo today), and Lourenco Marques (Maputo) were exemplary, it wasn't lost on some of the critics that these were the showpieces of Lisbon's wartime effort. All *major* medical installations in the overseas provinces were kept in good order, but the problem was that the same could not be said for the rest.

My personal observations were limited to what went on outside the capitals of Portuguese Guinea and Mozambique, the latter especially, and my cachet in the East African territory was a South African aid group that were gathering funds for medical supplies for Portuguese troops. Fund-raising efforts in South Africa were remarkably successful, to the extent that there was a constant flow of medicines and drugs going to the three Portuguese provinces from all major centres down south.

Larger items included ambulances, every one of them appropriately emblazoned with the name and logo of the fund-raising organisation as well as x-ray machines and other items of medical hardware, much of it delivered overland and often to much fanfare.

Because of my South African connections, I was able to get into some of these medical establishments at a time when they were very much off limits to the Fourth Estate. What

Colleagues of a soldier wounded in a guerrilla attack place the victim, strapped to a litter, onto the rear seat of an Air Force helicopter. (*Revista da Armada*)

I discovered was disturbing. While all the cities had adequate medical supplies, there were critical shortages in the interior that included items as mundane as bed linen and gurneys. Worse, nobody appeared to have any interest in rectifying matters: it was always 'somebody else' who was said to be in charge of such matters.

Nor were these incidents isolated: in fact, anything but! I visited several military hospitals in the interior and it was much of the same each time.

Conditions at Tete Military Hospital, for instance, were appalling. While there weren't an inordinate number of troops on the injured list, we were shocked at the condition of some of them. Also, hygiene standards were well below par.

Though it would have been difficult to specifically lay blame for these inadequacies, because I wasn't around long enough to do an investigative study, my initial observations with regard to modern medical methodology, sanitation and equipment coupled to inattentive or simply disinterested medical staff were sobering.

In one of my reports I described conditions – witnessed at the time by Michael Knipe of the *London Times* – as barbarous. An American observer who accompanied one of my groups as far as Tete equated conditions at the local military hospital as 'symptomatic of another epoch, probably pre-World War I'. We would emerge aghast from some of these establishments and talk about the experience afterwards in whispers. Worse, there didn't appear to be anybody in charge willing to rectify matters, yet we were dealing with medical personnel, doctors included, the majority of whom had been educated and trained in

Wounded are gathered together to await extraction from a remote bush area by helicopter. Significantly, the insurgents had no such facilities. (*Revista da Armada*)

Europe.

While there were exceptions, especially in the bigger centres, much of what we were able to view from up close made the American TV series M.A.S.H. look like the Mayo Clinic by comparison.

There was a consensus among us all, that if one of us had the misfortune to take a hit or be injured by a landmine, the others were to get that individual out of Mozambique as quickly as possible. Money was to be the last consideration, we told each other. We even agreed to pool resources and bring in a charter flight from Salisbury if there was no other way. The last thing needed was to end up as a patient in one of those wards ...

In almost the entire country the troops were exposed to malaria. At the time, the same situation held for Rhodesia. Yet the two countries might have been on separate continents. In spite of quinine, malaria took a steady toll in the Portuguese Armed Forces throughout the Zambezi Valley, with deaths, proportionate to the number of serving troops, many times higher than in neighbouring Rhodesia.

Similarly, many Portuguese soldiers went down with hepatitis, again because of abysmal hygiene in the cooking places and latrines.

Israeli studies of the disease among their own units in the field discovered fairly early on that one of the principle causes of hepatitis was fat residue in kitchen dishes. This was information available in medical journals all over the world, but somehow, nobody in Portugal seemed to have noticed, especially since Portugal is a progressive Western nation.

Portuguese troops fighting in the three overseas territories often faced an experienced, well-trained and adequately-armed enemy. Once blooded in action, some of these combatants proved to be crack fighters, in large part because most had been trained abroad and often gave as good as they got when it came to exchanging fire with Lisbon's people. (Author's photo)

The hepatitis concept was immediately squashed by some of the Portuguese doctors I spoke to. Jaundice, they argued, was everywhere. In any event, this was Africa and there were flies everywhere. One got the impression that fresh ideas were a closed door and that nobody seemed to care. In some camps in the interior there were even inadequate supplies of fresh water.

Portuguese Guinea, it seemed, offered a more efficient medical quotient to those serving there, in part, one suspected, because the commanding general took a personal interest. Unannounced and most times unheralded, General António de Spínola – always the stickler for the right thing – would arrive at hospitals or clinics under his command. There he'd spend an hour or two, not only talking to those in charge but doing the rounds of the wards, the kitchens, emergency rooms and the rest. He'd spend time talking to the wounded, always interested in trying to right wrongs.

If he found something amiss, God help the offending party. While he or she wouldn't be put on the next plane home – there were too many Portuguese servicemen praying for that option, that individual would be charged and likely as not, placed on extra duties. If there was a second offence, it might even be the brig. In that enervating climate – coupled to short rations and possibly no mosquito nets – this kind of punishment could be harsh. But, as we all know, fear tends to engender efficiency and it didn't happen that often.

Portuguese troops assess the situation after an ambush in Mozambique. (*Revista da Armada*)

It was while covering the war along this stretch of the West African coast that I met a Portuguese Army nurse, Natércia de Conceição Pais, a rather delightful young lady of 26, who, with a dozen others, served under General de Spínola's command in the minuscule West African enclave. One and all, the troops loved her and would refer to her fondly as 'Our Angel of Mercy'. It was over the top of course, but you got the message.

Conceição Pais' group was part of a rather unique female parachute corps attached to the Portuguese Air Force. While it rarely happened, the idea was that she or another of her colleagues would be dropped by parachute into a beleaguered camp in the interior to tend to the wounded, but then only if things became desperate. Her main role, while I was there, was hauling some of the worst casualties out of the bush, usually by chopper.

Nurse Pais had her own reasons for joining the Army. She was young, attractive, charmingly ebullient and erudite enough in English for us to get along fine. By her own admission, she'd never been seriously in love, though that didn't prevent her from getting about three or four marriage proposals a week, which might have been expected in Portuguese Guinea since single women were at a premium in all these tropical conflicts.

'Why did I join?' She was evasive at first. Then it came out.

'I had a brother in the army and he came home with some terrible stories about the war, especially here, in Portuguese Guinea. One of his friends had been badly wounded on the outskirts of Bissau. They did their best for him, but it wasn't enough. The last word he spoke

The majority of injuries in all three theatres of military activity
came from landmines. (Author's photo)

before he died – he was just 18 – was "Mama".'

She hesitated to gather her thoughts before she went on.

'That's when I thought that I might be able to do something. I'd been working as a doctor's receptionist, so I had something of a medical background.' That was four years before, and after training and having been dispatched to Africa, she was glad it had happened.

'And the war?' I asked. 'Doesn't the futility of it all depress you?' It was a loaded question and she knew it.

'Yes, but we'll win in the end, you know.' She was deadly serious.

Nurse Pais wasn't a member of any select group of propagandists hauled out of the cupboard to impress this transient military correspondent. We'd met by accident, on a flight from Bigene in the north to Teixeiro Pinto, the colony's second largest town. Onboard the chopper was a man who was almost stung to death by bees. He'd survived only because somebody had a few antihistamine tablets that he'd kept for his own allergies.

The patient had taken more than a hundred stings and his face and arms were grotesquely swollen and almost indigo in places from subcutaneous bleeding. The African bee can do that when they're disturbed.

Two Portuguese Paranurses assess the situation prior to an
operation in Portuguese Guinea. (*Revista da Armada*)

It was while I was transiting Mozambique that I was given the opportunity to spend several
hours at the military hospital at Tete. It was February 1973 and the Portuguese, always
meticulous with their records, will be able to check this event, one of the most horrendous
I'd experienced in any man's war.

Having been left to wander about the wards on our own, we discovered a soldier alone
in a ward with terrible leg and abdominal wounds. 'Landmine' he said, his face contorted
by pain. The stench in the ward was something else: it hit us like a foul wet rag when we
entered the building.

The boy – he was not yet a man – was perhaps eighteen years old and obviously in
terrible distress. His pain must have been awful because he blacked out twice in the 20
minutes or so that we were there. Even to this inexperienced observer it was obvious that
gangrene had set in, more than adequately amplified by the stench, which is symptomatic.

I was with a group of South Africans at the time, some of them nurses, and we said as
much to the Portuguese doctor who accompanied us. He dismissed our suggestions with a
shrug. We nevertheless persisted because it was obvious that something had to be done and
this was clearly some mother's son, never mind that he'd been serving in the Portuguese
Army.

A Portuguese Army Special Forces squad together with their
wounded after an action. (*Revista da Armada*)

On pulling back the bedclothes, we could see that part of the youngster's upper thigh that had not been wrapped in bandages had turned an evil shade of green.

Clearly embarrassed, steps were taken by the hospital authorities, but we were never to discover what treatment he eventually received because we weren't allowed near the ward again. My sentiments at the time were something in line with a pox on the homes of the medical personnel who were responsible and who frankly couldn't care a damn. It would have been very different had it been their sons lying there ...

Interestingly, there were other Portuguese present, including some junior doctors and orderlies who shared the experience, but it wouldn't have been worth a nickel for them to have countermanded a senior medical officer.

One sensed that such things had a seriously debilitating effect on morale. More to the point, it would be interesting, 35 years later, to establish who exactly was in charge at the time. More to the point, did the gangrenous young man come out of that horrific experience alive?

By comparison with other African colonial wars, Portugal did not suffer excessively severe casualties during her 13-year campaign in Guinea, Angola and Mozambique. Official figures from the book *Africa: A Vitoria Traida,* published in Lisbon by Intervencao soon after the coup, show that from May 1963 to May 1974 Portugal lost altogether 3,265 men killed in action in all three theatres of war, with something like another 5,000 who died of other causes, many of them on the roads.

As one publication phrased it afterwards, ' ... in 13 years of war, we lost 8,863 soldiers... *que deus vos tenha em paz, bravos soldados ...*'

This bears little resemblance to the 2,000 men that France lost every year in Algeria over an extended time-frame of seven years; or less than the thousand South Africans killed in over 21 years of combat on Angola's frontiers.

The number of driving deaths among the Portuguese was not surprising, since the average Lusitanian at the wheel takes more risks on the road in a week than most Americans or British do in a year. Some of us hacks long ago decided that, on the face it, the Portuguese seemed imbued with some kind of death wish, which was why they drove the way they did. And as for covering their wars, I was always of the mind that I was far more likely to die in some kind of traffic disaster than from enemy action.

This was the same *loucura* that I spoke of earlier, a fatalism or super optimism that was also reflected in the way they fought their wars.

That said, there was none of the regimentation or militarism of the Germanic races, but some Portuguese soldiers, more often than not did what they had to and would emerge from these frays as unusually valiant fighters. I was to see this for myself while I accompanied their forces over several years in all three of Lisbon's overseas territories.

The following casualty figures were provided by official Portuguese sources some years after the war ended:

Description	Theatres of Operations (a)			Across all three Theatres of Operations		
	Guinea	Angola	Mozambique	Total	Daily average (b)	Daily average per thousand (c)
Killed in action	1,084	1,142	1,039	3,265	0.80	0.0075 (d)
Died from other causes	791	1,529	755	3,075	0.76	0.0070
Total dead	1,875	2,671	1,794	6,340	1.55	0.014
Wounded in action	6,161	4,472	2,245	12,878	3.16	0.030 (d)
Accident casualties	2,167	6,595	6,279	15,041	3.69	0.034
Total wounded and accidents	8,328	11,067	8,524	27,919	6.86	0.064
Disabled (e)	-	-	-	3,835	0.94	0.0088

(a)   Date ranges are Guinea from 1 May 1963, Angola from 1 May 1961 and Mozambique from 1 November 1964, all terminating on 1 May 1974.

(b)   The following were used as the bases of calculation – Portuguese Guinea, 4,016 days; 4,746 in Angola; 3,647 in Mozambique; an average was thus 4,076 days.

(c)   From 1961 to 1973, the total number of troops in the three theatres of operations reached 1,392,230, which corresponded to an annual average of 107,095. The indices for this annual average and for the average duration of the war were calculated on 4,076 days.

(d)   According to Field Manual 101-10-1 (1072 of the United States Army and based on relevant figures for the Second World War in Europe) the indices corresponded to a theatre of operations in classical non-nuclear warfare. If these figures are applied to the total number of troops deployed throughout the duration of the war in the Portuguese overseas territories on a daily basis, it would be equal to 61,112 killed in battle, 240,083 wounded in battle with 707,154 casualties through accidents or sickness. The Second World War lasted for seven years, while Portugal's colonial wars went on for almost double that.

(e)   The number of medically-processed Portuguese Army cases of combat and service accidents up to July 31, 1974.

Figures relating to the Portuguese Navy and the Portuguese Air Force were unobtainable.

As Colonel Ron Reid-Daly told me, the Portuguese and the Rhodesians were fighting on both sides of the Zambezi, so it was the same kind of unforgiving terrain. Conditions could be exacting, he admits, in summer months especially, when you had additional issues like malaria and the tsetse fly to deal with.

The incident described by the man who was to become the founder-commander of the Selous Scouts, one of the best tracking units in any man's army, took place in November 1967. At the time he was serving as Training Officer in the 1st Battalion, Rhodesian Light Infantry, his first post as a commissioned officer. Occasionally he was required to deputise for commando commanders who were on leave, or on a course at the School of Infantry.[1]

During their absence Reid-Daly would take over their commandos on border control operations and it was during one of these stints that he had an unusual experience which, had things turned out otherwise, might have resulted in catastrophic consequences. The program was centered on bush survival, something about which this officer was outspokenly critical when it came to his allies, the Portuguese Army.

Colonel Reid-Daly takes up the story:

It was already well into summer when I was ordered to command the Battalion's Support Group for a six-week border stint at the northernmost corner of the country where Rhodesia, Zambia and Mozambique shared common borders at the junction of the Luangwa and the Zambezi rivers. A temporary military base large enough to house a company or even an RLI commando had been built behind a police post known as Kanyemba, which was a pleasant place set in picturesque surroundings on the bank of the Zambezi.

Whoever sited the post obviously had the natural beauty of the place in mind but very little else. Tactically, in event of an attack, it was a potential death-trap, which we all knew would happen at some time or another because this was quite an important infiltration region.

Things were rough in the bush: troop deployments were carried out by vehicles along atrocious bush tracks, or by boat skimming up the Zambezi River. The Mpata Gorge which formed my north-western limit was considered uncrossable because the Zambezi stormed through almost all year round, its passage constricted by the ravine. Further downstream, below this obstacle, the river spreads out again, slowing down the flow in the process.

The width of the Zambezi River in this region is considerable, almost a mile in places and the Rhodesian military, taking cognizance of the lack of any kind of watermanship among the insurgents, considered it unlikely that they would come through there.

I went up to this point by boat, landed and looked around, not at all impressed with what I saw. The promontory was littered with piles of junk from the rubbish pits of previous patrols that had been dug up by wild animals. We could see that there had been fires lit all over the place, which told me that some of these units had been casual in their observation duties, at night especially. They'd used fires either to keep warm, or more likely, to keep prowling animals at bay.

I didn't see much point in travelling up the Zambezi River in full view of the Zambian side to take up what should have been a clandestine observation post.

So, on my return to base, I studied the 1:50 000 scale map pinned to the wall of the operations room while looking for a land route to what we referred to as the 'The Gates', our name for the gorge. There were no properly surveyed maps of this part of the Zambezi valley at the time and the men on the ground had to make do with sheets of paper covered with a military grid system.

I now understand why the previous commanders had used boats to position their patrols there; but I was determined to find a way to insert a patrol without the whole of Zambia – and of course, the enemy – being aware of it.

A careful study of the map showed that the nearest accurate jump-off point for the patrol to enter the area was the western corner of a bush airstrip which lay southeast from The Gates and served Kanyemba. I worked out a compass bearing to the top of a high range of hills known as Kapsuku. If the patrol's map-reading was accurate, they'd find themselves at the headwaters of the Euguta River; all they had to do was follow the river down through the hills to the Zambezi.

The total length of the patrol was 17 map kilometres, a distance which should easily be covered in a long daylight march, or about 12 hours. However, taking account of the fact that this was the hottest period of the year with temperatures around noon running at something like 90 degrees Fahrenheit (roughly 32 degrees Celsius), it was not going to be an easy march. In addition each man was carrying a load, the lightest of which clocked in at almost 30 kgs. All these factors, coupled with the kind of terrain that included steep gradients, made me accept that the patrol might have to sleep out one night and reach The Gates only the following morning.

Orders were issued for the task ahead. At dawn the patrol debussed at the airstrip

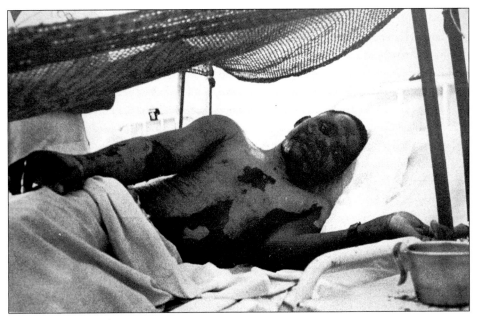

A Portuguese soldier recuperates at a military hospital in Mozambique after
having been targeted by a phosphorus grenade. (Author's photo)

in preparation for an early start so that as much ground as possible could be covered in
the relatively cooler part of the day. I checked the patrol commander's compass bearing
and pointed out a clearly visible gap in the mountains that formed the headwaters of
the river which would lead him to The Gates.

The patrol set off and I returned to my operations room to monitor other counter-
insurgency units deployed on the valley floor.

We worked to fixed routines, which required patrols to adhere to a strict radio
schedule. They would call their control station (headquarters) at 0700 hours, noon
and then again at 1600 hours and provide us with routine sitreps or situation reports.

I heard nothing from this particular group throughout the day and by last light,
I was starting to feel a bit uneasy. Failure to observe radio scheds did occasionally
happen, so I left it at that for the time being, aware that there were many reasons
which could affect communications. These might range from mechanical failure to
a faulty radio or possibly screening by mountains. Still, I had a nagging feeling that
all was not well. Before getting my head down, I advised Brigade Headquarters that I
might need a helicopter for a casualty evacuation the next day.

The following morning's 0700 radio sched still showed no sign of the patrol. I
summoned the boat crew and proceeded upriver, stopping along the banks of the
Zambezi in a bid to reach the patrol by radio. It just so happened that one of our
Canberra bombers on a cross-country map-reading exercise passed overhead. I called
him up, gave him the approximate map coordinates and asked him if he could deviate

slightly from his course and give The Gates patrol a radio call. He returned a few minutes later to report nothing heard or seen of the patrol.

It was now 1200 and I knew that we had something serious on our hands. I returned to Kanyemba base, called up Brigade Headquarters and requested the immediate use of a helicopter. But that was easier said than done because in those early days of border control, we had the same kind of problems that the Portuguese faced. Getting a chopper was a major exercise and Heaven only help the field commander who called for one only to discover that there was no emergency.

Flying time to Kanyemba by helicopter was about three hours and as arranged, an Alouette arrived at 1500 hours. I gave the pilot a quick briefing while his technician refuelled and loaded onboard as many water bags as could be found in the camp. Then, together with my medic, we headed off into the bush to try to locate these chaps.

We reached the location that the patrol should have passed through and though we circled for a while, there was no sign of the squad. The pilot then headed over the next range of hills.

Suddenly he cursed and then banked sharply. Something had caught his eye, and then I spotted it. It was an astonishing sight: there was a bunch of men running around in the bush below, all of them stark naked.

We landed and they came running. We actually had to fight them off as they desperately tried to get at the water bags.

Although it was late in the afternoon, the sun still radiated an intense heat, as it always does in the Zambezi Valley. There were many patches of forest in the area, but in November, few of them have leaves and the parched soldiers had no almost shade to shield them from the sun.

It was obvious that this patrol had reached its limit of endurance. Had we not pitched up that afternoon, I'm pretty certain that we'd have several dead by morning.

I flew the soldiers back to camp in relays, where, on touching down, they rushed to the showers, where they'd stand or lie down under the cold flow of water. At the same time, being youngsters, it was astonishing to see how quickly they managed to recover, their mouths wide open, taking in as much as they could.

In the debrief which followed it appeared they had missed the gap. But instead of pushing on north towards the great river, they'd wasted valuable time trying to find the Euguta River to follow down to The Gates. Climbing up and down steep hills with the sun beating down had exhausted them all. Even worse, the exercise generated thirst.

What had happened was they made good time on the first day out and had their map-reading been more precise, they would probably have reached the Zambezi River that evening, thus achieving the objective. Instead, an element of panic apparently crept in when some of the men thought they were lost. It became more serious when they found they had no comms with base.

Had I taken them in hand before, I'd have been able to tell them that anxiety and fear often make a man sweat profusely. All this, plus some heavy physical toil while the patrol crossgrained exceptionally difficult terrain in their bid to find the river soon exhausted their two standard water-bottles. Dehydration set in rapidly.

I asked them why they had taken off their clothes and their reply was interesting. They found that dehydration had made their skins become paper dry and they simply couldn't stand their clothes rubbing against their skin. The only obvious relief was to take everything off, which they did. Some, in desperation, even tried to drink their own urine, disguising the taste by mixing coffee powder with it.

I noticed that the younger soldiers had been the worst affected. It was clear that the older men had a tougher mental outlook and were much better able to cope with the stress. It was a good lesson and we took it to heart because we'd only just begun to teach bushcraft in the Rhodesian Army and this particular group had not had any of it.

When we flew to recover the group, we passed over an astonishing range of wild animals. In fact. a herd of elephants together with a large herd of impala: all were in clear sight of the patrol. Had the men been properly trained, their water problems would have been over: the average impala provides about two litres of water from its stomach and an elephant holds on average, 36 litres.

Later, during 1973, when the bush war began in earnest. I was given the task of raising and training a special multiracial unit, the Selous Scouts. Bush survival and tracking formed an important part of the operational training of these men because it gave them tremendous self-confidence in their abilities to survive and live comfortably in the African bush. Indeed, once put through their paces, they found nothing unusual in carrying out long-range, two-man reconnaissance patrols over distances, sometimes, of hundreds of kilometres.

These two-man patrols, comprising a black and a white soldier, would be dropped by parachute (high altitude, low opening), often 200 kilometres from the Rhodesian border in hostile country, and operate behind the lines for up to six weeks at a time. It was a tribute to their training that they never ran into problems from a bush survival point of view ...

As Colonel Ron Reid-Daly was to comment in later years, the Portuguese Army knew none of this. Nor was anybody in either Lourenco Marques or Beira interested enough to learn, even though the offer was repeatedly made – both by himself and other Rhodesian Army officers who spent time in the bush with their allies from Europe – that they were willing to pass on this vital experience.

Had they done so, he ventured, an awful lot more lives might have been saved.

The author made contact with Portuguese *Furriel Enfermeira Pára-Quedista* (Sergeant Para-Nurse) Maria Natércia Conceição Pais Neves (above) while working in the Guinea enclave and accompanied her on one of her 'medevac' extractions. This involved a young conscript who had been almost stung to death by bees (top of next page). While helicopters such as the Alouette were constantly on standby for this kind of evacuation, most of the casualties were taken out by fixed-wing Dorniers fitted with litters. In Portuguese Guinea there was always a good chance of survival once a helicopter reached a victim (bottom) because flying time to Bissau was measured in minutes rather than hours (as was the case in the vastly bigger Angola). The Paranurses were a tight-knit group (bottom of following page) and though very rarely required to drop into action by parachute, they were trained for that role. (Photos by author and *Revista da Armada*)

25

Last Word

War makes rattling good history, but peace is poor reading.

Thomas Hardy (1840-1928)

The message was clear. The story was told of a British and French officer who met in wartime Algiers shortly after Rommel's panzer divisions had been routed by the Allied Armies.

The British officer asked the Frenchman why his government had not considered bringing troops from French Indo-China (present day Vietnam) into the war as they had done with so-called 'native levies' from French Equatorial Africa. Many of these black troops had distinguished themselves in action against Hitler's army. For their part, the British had been using Kenyan, Nigerian and Ghanaian troops in the Burma campaign against the Japanese and the English felt that the same could be done with the Vietnamese.

'No,' answered the Frenchman. 'The Vietnamese are hardly good enough to use as stretcher bearers, never mind tested in battle.' Less than a decade later France was to suffer horrific losses in a dozen battles at the hands of these same Vietnamese people.

Of these, Giap's victory at Dien Bien Phu has gone down in history.

This Vietnamese guerrilla specialist made the point at the time (echoed afterwards by Guiné-Bissau's General Nino) that a guerrilla army does not need the most modern weapons to fight a war.

In another document taken from a PAIGC insurgent, it was stated that when Giap started his military campaign against the French he was using 16 different types of rifles, including some of Tsarist vintage. Quite a few had been wrested from Japanese occupiers during the Second World War. The message in this document said it all: Use what you have and use it well ... with fortitude you will win in the end.

And while we might be aware of what took place in the past, there is some conjecture about what might happen in the future, for as sure as night follows day, there will be many more conflicts on the African continent. Some of these will involve oil – Nigeria, almost certainly Angola again, Gabon, the Cameroons, Equatorial Guinea – while others will involve precious minerals and commodities. In the Congo the fighting has already started, as it has, partly over oil in the Sudan.

More disconcerting, the majority of these conflicts waiting to happen are likely to involve at least one or more of the Major Powers.

Which also leads to something more pertinent: can Asian conditions be effectively applied to Africa? This issue remains open to conjecture, though, on the face of it, it can, for

While the Portuguese were still fighting, UNITA was hardly as effective as it later became. To many of these youths, the war was a game, deadly nonetheless, but still not taken too seriously. That all changed once they started to counter Cuban-bolstered MPLA forces. (Author's collection)

.conflict in all its ramifications is exactly that. In these struggles there is always a victor and a loser, be it in Africa, the Middle East or in Asia.

Portugal's General António de Spínola could not have been more precise when he declared shortly before he finally stepped down, that the West had not paid due attention to the clever corollary of Clausewitz's definition of war: 'If war is the continuation of politics, using other means, politics is also the continuation of war through other means.'

He went on to say that against these realities "the West established NATO with its heavy divisions and rockets. But it is clear we can only win a war with weapons like, or adapted to those of the enemy. As regards [any] great offensive, we must realize, however much it shocks us, that we can only overcome the 'revolution of the masses' *through* the 'revolution of the masses'."

Speaking in the 1970s, his comments are as relevant today as they were then, especially since al-Qaeda has inherited the mantle of the contemporary international revolutionary.

De Spínola went on: 'It shocks us because the West is locked up within an irresponsible conservatism and does not enjoy sufficient breadth of view and flexibility to conceive the anti-reactionary counter-offensive, the only weapon that can effectively defend the values of Western civilization.

Faced with such different concepts, the Western strategy is, of necessity, outdated, as the history of the last few years has abundantly demonstrated.

'We must develop and oppose an effective counter-revolution to face the revolution, thus combating ideas with ideas. Otherwise the West, stagnating and restricted to its classic concepts, will die, stifled by the so-called "world revolution of the common people" that has gained such youthful support.

'We must thus go out and meet the ordinary folk and young people and carry out, within our own culture, the revolution which, if not performed by us, will inevitably be brought about, but within a different culture.'

In some respects, the conflict in Angola might be likened to Britain's 12-year campaign against communist-backed insurgents in Malaya. This African campaign was largely the same kind of hit-and-run affair with the insurgents rarely willing to make a stand. They would strike swiftly and silently and then melt away; here one moment, gone the next.

What went on in the jungles of Malaya made a tremendous impact on the West at the time. It was as closely studied at West Point as by Portuguese military strategists as well as the Rhodesians and South Africans who were later faced with similar problems, in large part because that campaign was one of the few modern insurgent wars in which a victory was achieved by conventional forces over Maoist-style guerrillas.

In terms of balance of power employed in both guerrilla wars, the numbers were different, though not substantially so. In Malaya, government forces numbered about 175,000, ranged against something like 10,000 CTs, or Communist Terrorists as they were designated by London. In Angola the comparative figures were about 60,000 Portuguese and between 7,000 and 10,000 insurgents.

Also notable was the fact that war was never formally declared in Malaya. Rather, the troubles were termed an emergency, in large part because insurance premiums in the City would have gone through the roof had full hostilities been officially acknowledged.

The nature of what went on in Malaya at the time is instructive, especially since there has been a resurgence of irregular conflicts in recent years that include semi-conventional insurgencies in places like Nigeria, Colombia, Darfur, Chad and the Philippines.

The Malayan Communists, it should be remembered, had been allies of the British in the struggle against Japan. But at the same time they were preparing to continue the struggle against 'British Imperialism' after the war. The perception among the majority in that faraway peninsula was that it would be a comparatively easy task since Malaya after the war was in a mess.

Against a background of food shortages, labour unrest and a police force demoralized and corrupted after collaboration with the Japanese, a variety of political groups squabbled over whether the country should amalgamate with Indonesia and how power should be distributed between the Malays, the Chinese and the Indians. For its part, Britain seemed intent on preserving Malaya as an imperialist stronghold, though violent Malayan opposition ultimately forced her to replace a proposed Malayan Union (to be ruled by a

With the Portuguese out of the country, Angola's media took on a decidedly Marxist slant, as shown by this Lisbon newspaper which, after the revolution, was reprinted and distributed in Luanda. (Author's photo)

British governor), by a Malayan Federation in which the traditional rulers preserved their powers, very much as was already the case in Northern Nigeria with what was termed 'indirect rule'.

It seemed an ideal revolutionary situation, and there were a variety of other reasons for choosing the end of World War II to launch the guerrilla war.

'Moderate' policies of subversion had failed, Mao's successes were becoming apparent, and the power of communism was growing throughout South-East Asia. Add Britain's withdrawal from Palestine the previous year and London, as with France in Indo China, came across as a vulnerable imperial power.

The communists declared war in June 1948 and from then on, terrorism became part of daily life for all Malayans. Chinese and European estate-owners were murdered, rubber workers frightened into co-operation, estates, mines and factories burned and rubber trees slashed.

With the arms caches stored up during the war with Japan coupled to plenty of experience of jungle life in adverse conditions, the communists aimed to set up 'liberated areas' as demanded by Maoist strategy. They hoped to create so much chaos that Britain would be forced to concede defeat and leave the field clear for the establishment of what the dissidents were already referring to as a so-called 'People's Democracy'.

At first everything seemed on their side. The terrorists – initially known as bandits – organized hit-and-run raids from camps hidden in the jungle, well screened from the air, with sentries out to a kilometre and escape routes all worked out in advance. They controlled a corps of underground sympathizers in the countryside numbering tens of thousands.

For its part, the Min Yuen guaranteed the supply of money, food, intelligence and medicine.

In response to this assault, rubber estates, tin mines, police stations and isolated homes became armed camps surrounded by high wire fences, lit at night by searchlights. Planters and miners slept with revolvers under their pillows, with grenades on nearby tables. They moved about in heavy vehicles converted into armoured trucks, complete with escorts.

No stretch of road could be guaranteed safe from ambush, and railway travellers had to contend with derailment as a permanent hazard along isolated sections of track.

It is remarkable how similar the situation was to Angola after the first attacks took place in the north-east in 1961.

Initial communist successes in Malaya did not give a true indication of their position. They were largely a result of the slow response by the British caused by the death of the High Commissioner, Sir Edward Gent, in an air crash over London soon after he had declared the Emergency. His successor, Sir Henry Gurney, was not appointed until September, and the real military response did not get under way until General Sir Harold Briggs, a veteran of the Western Desert and Burma, arrived to direct operations in March, 1950.

It was only then that the severe disadvantages under which the communists were operating began to emerge. There was no rush among local folk to suddenly join the Malayan Races' Liberation Army. Even the two-and-a-half million Chinese in the country showed little interest in making the tough discipline and harsh life of the mainly Chinese guerrillas something that they would like to embrace.

Insurgent strength never rose much above 10,000 and the Malayan guerrillas never had significant help from either Russia or China. Throughout the 1950s these weaknesses became more and more obvious until the insurgency threat dissolved.

There was one significant reason for their ultimate failure, the first being that there was no initial realization that to terrorize those British who remained behind – coupled to their economic organizations – brought untold hardship to the workers and peasants. According to the teachings of Mao, these were the same people whose hearts and minds they should have won.

Instead of ensuring overall sympathy, the most they obtained from towns and villages was a grudging and often fearful level of co-operation. Their plans of establishing 'liberated areas' went by the board when estate-owners failed to flee. In fact the expatriates running Malaya's rubber estates and plantations, having survived a Japanese conflict, were hardly likely to succumb to pressure from a bunch of locals with guns. Instead, they rapidly set about building up their own defence forces and their workers remained remarkably loyal unless terrorized.

At the same time, the war that evolved was a painfully slow progress. This can be judged by one of the operations launched by the British against the communist terrorists and detailed in one of the most illuminating publications on insurgency warfare during

The author was in Angola during the transition to revolutionary rule. He headed
to Nova Lisboa, soon to be renamed Huambo, and joined *Chipa Esquadrao*, a rebel
group that was later to form the core of 32 Battalion in the South African Army. With
South African forces advancing from the south, he headed home with a group of
refugees travelling in convoy, when this picture was taken. (Author's photo)

that period. It was written by an American officer servicing with the US Marines and was
titled *The Guerrilla and How to Fight Him*.[1]

Much of that work deals with 'Operation Nassau', which began in December, 1954
and ended nine months later. It took place largely in the South Swamp of Kuala Langat
that covered an area of roughly 200 square kilometers; dense, triple-canopied jungle with
trees reaching up to 50 metres where visibility on the ground was limited to perhaps thirty
metres.

After several assassinations, a British battalion was assigned to the area. Food control
was achieved through a system of rationing, convoys, gate checks and searches. By the time
that full operations had been launched, all available British assets were brought to bear and
included artillery and mortars. Royal Air Force planes began harassing attacks in South
Swamp.

Originally, the plan was to bomb and shell the swamp day and night, the idea being
that the insurgents would be driven out into ambushes. Instead, the terrorists were well
prepared to stay in hiding indefinitely. Food parties would occasionally emerge, but the
civil population was too terrified to report them. Consequently plans were modified and

harassing attacks were limited to the dark hours. Meantime, ambushes continued and patrolling inside the swamp was intensified.

Operations of this nature continued for three months without results.

Finally in late March, after days of waiting, an ambush party succeeded in killing two in a group of eight terrorists. Thus it was that the first two red pins that signified confirmed kills appeared on the operations map. Local morale was given a minor boost.

Another month passed before it was learned that terrorists were making a contact inside the swamp. One platoon established an ambush; a single rebel appeared and was killed.

May passed without a contact, but in June, a chance meeting by a patrol accounted for one killed and one captured. A few days later, after four fruitless days, a platoon en route to camp accounted for two more. The third most important guerrilla leader in the area promptly surrendered. Under interrogation he was to report that British food control was so effective that one of his men had been murdered in a quarrel over food.

By early July, two additional companies were assigned to the area and patrols and aerial attacks were intensified. Three terrorists surrendered, one of whom led a patrol to his leader's camp. As a consequence four insurgents, including their leader were killed.

Other patrols accounted for four more and by the end of July, only 23 terrorists remained in the swamp with no food or communications with the outside world...

This essentially was the nature of operations: 60,000 artillery shells, 30,000 rounds of mortar ammunition as well as 2,000 aircraft bombs for only 35 terrorists killed or captured. Each enemy represented 1,500 man-days of patrolling or waiting in ambushes, a hardly impressive tally for all that effort and expenditure.

It seems absurd at the time that so much effort should have been expended to eliminate only 35 insurgents. Yet, as in Mozambique, the tally – though measured in terms of a couple here, one there and perhaps five somewhere else grew steadily over the years, for such is the nature of the modern guerrilla struggle, even today.

It is worth noting that at the start of the Malayan emergency, the rebels had fewer than 5,000 men under arms. Three years later this figure doubled and they were actively supported in the field by nearly 50,000 civilians, mostly locally resident Chinese.

In contrast, government forces at the start totalled about 21,000, giving it a rough ratio of five-to-one. This ratio was steadily improved with the expansion of the police force, British troops brought in from abroad and the Commonwealth, as well as the enlargement of the Home Guard. Their numbers at the height of the campaign were something in excess of 300,000, of whom the police and the army comprised about 60,000 and 30,000 respectively.

It is interesting that in later years the trend in Vietnam was exactly the reverse. Initially, according to Sir Robert Thompson one of the foremost authorities on unconventional warfare in the 20th Century, the ratio in favour of the Saigon government was 50 to one.

By 1963, in spite of some expansion of the government force and the formation of a full-time hamlet militia, the ratio had fallen to under 25 to one as a result of the armed Vietcong units having increased their strength to nearly 25,000.

The favourable ratio continued to drop in favour of the Vietcong until, at the beginning of 1965 when it came to about 10 to one. It fell still further until American combat troops arrived but, even then, the tally never regained its original numerical advantage. Thus, says Sir Robert, the morale of the civilian population is of vital importance to the success of any counter-insurgency venture.

He remarked as follows:

A loss of morale in the civilian population is likely to occur quicker than in the government forces, where there is greater discipline. This particularly applies to the regular troops, who though they may become discouraged and less aggressive, will still remain capable of putting up a stiff fight if attacked or if attacking under favourable conditions.

The many abortive operations, however, in which they will have taken part begin to take their toll, and the confidence of the troops in those directing the war effort is not improved by information blurbs issued by the government claiming victories which in many instances the troops themselves know to be false.'

'A more dangerous loss of morale will occur in the police and other local territorial forces of a para-military nature which will have borne the brunt of the insurgents' advance into the populated areas. They will have suffered heavy casualties and a loss of weapons on an increasingly large scale; recruiting difficulties will have caused units to be greatly under strength; officer material will almost certainly be poor and inexperienced.

In Malaya, one of the vital aspects of the emergency was the ability of government forces to recover weapons from the Min Yuen. According to Sir Robert, successes in this regard contributed greatly to the eventual defeat of the insurgents.

There are parallels too with Mozambique and the Algerian campaign, which, by the spring of 1956 had almost a quarter of a million French regulars and conscripts in the field. At peak the *Armée de Liberation Nationale* (ALN) – the military wing of the FLN – grew to about 120,000 fighters, though this dipped to about a third of that figure at ceasefire.

From the start, Arab rebels in Algeria sought succour abroad. Algeria's independent neighbours, Morocco and Tunisia, permitted the operation of ALN training establishments for Algerian recruits.

Again the 'strategic hamlet' concept was implemented (*Aldeamentos* in the Portuguese regions and protected villages or kampongs in Malaya), with the French relocating almost two million civilians between 1955 and 1961.

In the civil war period, the town of Cuito Cuanavale was to become the focal point of Angolan and Cuban ground and air forces in the south of the country. (Photo Brigadier-General van der Waals)

Coupled to this was a massive programme of psychological warfare and indoctrination of the masses, though with a hostile European settler element (*pieds noire*) – who were as strongly opposed to the Arab nationalists as they were to any possibility of French withdrawal – winning hearts and minds at indigent levels was made even more difficult for Paris.

It is the measure of foreign involvement that interests us here. Although Algeria's Arab neighbours were unequivocal in their support for the revolution, France never impinged on the territorial integrity of her former colonies, who themselves had only been independent a few years.

During its seven-and-a-half year duration, the war in Algeria moved from urban to rural areas with the rebels countering French moves in the hinterland at all points with an offensive strategy of insurgent attacks on the cities and towns.

Bombs and sniper attacks were a daily occurrence and thousands of lives were lost. The official total has been conservatively estimated at about 20,000 in Algeria and another 3,000 in metropolitan France. Of these the French settler secret army (OAS) accounted for a sizeable number.

In his assessment of the war *Guerilla Struggle in Africa*, Kenneth Grundy made the assessment:

In every sense the FLN-ALN independence fighters can be regarded as an ID-type guerrilla movement. The goal was clearly independence on a national scale and the appeal was consistently national in scope. Although the first base of the revolt was the Aures mountains and the key wilayas throughout the war were the Aures and Kabylie – both drawing their strength from Berber speakers – the movement aspired to transcend sectional, linguistic and tribal interests.

Moreover, the movement succeeded in these goals. The guerrilla strategy and techniques employed by the FLN-ALN movement were modern ... they never lost sight of their ultimate political end, and of the obvious linkage between popular support, external aid and assistance [coupled to] long-range strategic planning.

In the planning and conduct of the war, Algerian military leaders were inspired by the classic texts on guerrilla warfare. They borrowed ideas and techniques from Mao, the Yugoslav partisans, and the Viet Minh, and creatively applied them to significantly altered Algerian conditions.

It was for three reasons – flexibility, creativity and success – that later African guerrilla movements anxiously turned to the Algerians for inspiration, advice and assistance,' Grundy maintained.

For its part, Lisbon had no qualms about calling a shovel a spade. The Portuguese were fighting three major wars on six or eight different fronts, though there were few in the Metropolis prepared to go on record as to exactly how many insurgents they were up against. Most Portuguese staff officers to whom I spoke conceded privately that there could be a lot more. Possibly even double the number put out in routine pronouncements, I heard more than once.

As one of Portugal's most illustrious – and successful – tacticians declared: 'Angola is too vast for its size not to have been one of the most serious considerations, if not *the* most serious. 'Hang it, you could lose a guerrilla army in the Dembos'. My old friend, General José Bethencourt Rodrigues was correct, because the immensity of the issue could be gauged from the fact that Angola is almost ten times the size of the original Malaya.

That said, numbers provide only part of the answer, dramatically illustrated by the fact that Arab guerrillas under Colonel TE Lawrence in 1918 were a relatively small force of Arab troublemakers. At no time did Lawrence have more than 3,000 of these desert people under his command and they were able to tie down large numbers of Turkish soldiers. He was instrumental in immobilizing a Turkish force numbering more than 50,000 at a critical period towards the end of World War I.

From a logistics point of view, all these issues eventually came into play. Remote army posts in the interiors of Angola, Malaya (and the Saudi Peninsula in World War I) – and subsequently with the Rhodesians and the South Africans and the French in Algeria – had to be supplied and at regular intervals. Letters from home and medical supplies had to get through. More important still, casualties needed to be evacuated and all these obligations

After the colonial war against Lisbon's forces had ended, much of the country was laid waste by the warring factions. This was the bank in the town of Ongiva, in the south. (Author's photo)

created some horrific difficulties.

There was, however, one big difference between the Malayan campaign and what went on in Angola. The Portuguese were able to control some of the food supplies of the enemy, as did the British in South East Asia, which was not the case with the Rhodesians. South of the great Zambezi River, the African bush supplied most of what the insurgents needed, as it had always done for the people who lived there.

The rice of the Vietcong and Min Yuen was the manioc or cassava root of the MPLA and FNLA.

Another aspect of both wars and one that has a direct effect on the outcome of any guerrilla struggle was the need for friendly relations with the civilian population.

Strategists in Luanda pointed out that government forces in Malaya were successful both militarily and politically. The British beat the terrorists at their own game and though it took time and lives, they ultimately won the bulk of the population to their side. This, the Portuguese reckoned, was what they were trying to do in Angola, Mozambique as well as Portuguese Guinea.

They were confident they could counter the irregulars on their own turf. At the same time, they did not want to make the same mistake that France did in Algeria by ignoring the needs of the civilian population. 'This will not happen in Angola', said General João Almeida Viana, one of the last of the chief commandants in the territory told me when I visited.

Yet, when the dust eventually settled and moderate minds were able to look at all these issues dispassionately, one of the first conclusions reached was that as in the Rhodesian and South African wars – slowly gathering their own momentum once the Portuguese had returned to Europe – the bulk of the people of all those countries tended to side with their own.

In this respect, Colonel Lemos Pires, a Portuguese commander in Guinea made some pertinent observations, not only about the war in which his people were engaged, but about the nature of the guerrilla warfare in which he and his people were involved.

To be an insurgent today, it is fashionable to read the works of Mao and Ché Guevara, he declared. We, on the other side, as it were, also have to absorb these teachings. We have to try to understand what the enemy is thinking and possibly deduce what he may or may not do next.

But that hypothesis is historically inaccurate. It is also psychologically dangerous to think that Mao, Giap, Agostinho Neto and the rest of the contemporary bunch of revolutionaries invented the strategy and tactics that surround the present notion of guerrilla warfare.

Let us be clear and understand that insurgency was not the brainchild of the communists. Indeed, far from it. Nothing which the Soviets propagated at their prime was not known or put into operation in some earlier war.

Read Ptolemy and Caesar and you will see what I mean. Guevara knew nothing which the Arabist T.E. Lawrence did not record in his subsequent writings about his own experiences in the desert war, or what was practised by the Spanish guerrillas against Napoleon a hundred years before in the Peninsula Wars.

Similarly, Orde Wingate's campaign against the Japanese in World War II proved him a serious contender in this kind of struggle, using a tiny unconventional force to stymie the enemy at every turn.

As the African wars progressed, Lisbon conceded increasingly towards indigenous progress. Africans were increasingly brought into the administration of the territories and the changes that occurred at this point brought a new meaning to the concept of Africanisation. By the early 1970s this not only implied merely a growing percentage of locally recruited or black individuals incorporated in the regular forces fighting the nationalists, – in the same sense as the French *jeunissement* in Indochina – it now meant a process of creating and fostering combat units of Africans operating more or less irregularly and autonomously, and with high levels of operational efficiency.

As John Cann indicated in his work, by shifting the predominant burden of supplying manpower to run the wars from the *metrópole* to the *ultramar,* Portugal gained in four ways. First, it broadened the source of military manpower through an inclusion of the colonial population. Second, it reduced the cost of fielding troops through a reduction

After the Portuguese had pulled out, the FNLA mustered a huge force and marched to
do war with the MPLA. Despite superior numbers and good American backing in war
matériel, the Congo-based guerrillas were no match for government forces, by then solidly
bolstered by Cuban troops and Soviet advisors. This entire FNLA army, tens of thousands
strong, was routed on the road to Luanda and never recovered. (Author's collection)

in transportation and training costs. Third, it gained a large measure of almost indefinite
sustainability through the first two aspects. Last, it kept the conflict subdued and low-tempo
by moving a large portion of the conscription and casualties away from the *metrópole*.[2]

This change in attitude, which implied increased trust in the Africans, even if forced,
was not sudden, nor was it just due to theoretical considerations. In fact, in the second
half of the 1960s the military were facing serious problems related not only to a shortage
of troops but also to the question of what to do with the Africans demobilized from the
regular army.

Traditional fears that Africans that had left the regular force – combat veterans who
were capable of handling weaponry – might end up joining the nationalist guerrillas, lay
behind new efforts to create auxiliary troops where those men would be kept under the
control of military or civil authorities. Moreover, these troops were much cheaper than the
regular ones and their eventual casualties were much 'less repercussion-rich' than those of
metropolitan forces.

The Africanisation program was handled differently in the three African territories,
not just because of different local and regional contexts, but also owing to the different
attitudes and views of the respective commanders.

The results likewise varied. In Guinea General de Spínola planned and fought for
the creation of a regular, entirely coherent African army mirroring the metropolitan
one, possibly having in mind a future federation of Portuguese-speaking states. In
Angola, African irregular units were much more informal and diverse in nature. In turn,
Mozambique somehow combined aspects of the two.

The first unit entirely consisting of Africans was probably the *Tropas Especiais* (Special

Travelling on roads in the Tete region, we would often come upon mounted units, such as this one on the road to Beira. (Author's photo)

Troops, commonly known by the acronym TEs), which emerged in 1966 in Cabinda, when Alexandre Taty, a former UPA/FNLA cadre, deserted to the Portuguese side with 1,200 men.

Organised and controlled by PIDE, the Portuguese political police, they started to be used in action against the MPLA, which after having initiated operations in the Dembos, in Northern Angola, had spread its guerrilla activities to Cabinda in late 1964. The TEs operated in Cabinda, their home area, as well as in Zaire and Uíge, in Northern Angola.

Seminal to Portugal's entire war effort in Africa, and its eventual outcome, no military leader played a more significant role than General António Sebastião Ribeiro de Spínola

Wikipedia tells us that de Spínola entered the *Colégio Militar* in 1920, beginning what would be a very successful military career. By 1928, he was at Portugal's Military Academy, where he stood out as a rather promising young cavalry officer.

In 1939, he became adjunct-de-camp of the Republican National Guard and in 1941 de Spínola, then a young infantry officer, travelled to the German-Russian Front as an observer, to monitor *Wehrmacht* movements during the encirclement of Leningrad (Portuguese volunteers had been incorporated into Hitler's Blue Division).

In 1961, guided by António de Oliveira Salazar, he offered himself for voluntary service in Portuguese colonies of West Africa and between 1961 and 1963, he held the command of the 345th Cavalry Battalion in Angola, distinguishing himself and his unit. At the end of that tenure, he was appointed Military Governor of Portuguese Guinea from 1968, and again in 1972: throughout, his administration favoured a policy of respect for ethnic Guineans and the traditional authorities. At the same time, he continued to practice a range of initiatives in the war, from clandestine meetings (he met secretly with the President of Senegal, Léopold Sédar Senghor, at one point) to armed incursions to neighbouring states (such as Operation Green Sea, which saw the assault by Portuguese Army Commandos into neighbouring Guinea (Conakry).

In November 1973, shortly before the military putsch that overthrew Portugal's civilian government, General de Spínola – at the invitation of Salazar's successor, Marcello Caetano – returned to the *metrópole* to head the overseas portfolio. But he refused the nomination, due to his government's intransigence on the Portuguese colonies.

A month later, on 17 January 1974, he was asked to be the Vice-Chief of the Defence Council of the Armed Forces, on the advice of Francisco da Costa Gomes, a post from which he would be removed two months later. Shortly afterwards he published his famous political tract *Portugal e o Futuro* (*Portugal and the Future*), where he expressed the idea that the only solution to the Colonial Wars was the discontinuation of the conflict.

On 25 April 1974, as a representative in the MFA – *Movimento das Forças Armadas* – General de Spínola received from President Marcello Caetano the rendition of the Government (which, at the time, was in refuge in one of the military barracks in the city). Caetano insisted he would only surrender power to Spínola and this, ironically, allowed him to assume an important public place as a leader of the revolution, although that was not what the MFA originally intended. The formation of the National Salvation Junta, formed in the days following the 'Carnation Revolution', allowed Spínola to take on the role of President of the Republic.

Spínola lasted only four months as the country's first post-Revolution President, to be substituted by General Francisco da Costa Gomes. His resignation was due largely to what he regarded as the profound move of Portuguese politics towards the left and the effects this had on the military as well as the largely unresolved independence of the Portuguese colonies. There should have been a succession of national elections in Angola, Mozambique and Guinea , but by the time that Lisbon had delegated authority to the newly-emerged countries, all three had embraced hardline Marxist principles.

In 1981 de Spínola was promoted to the highest rank in the Army: Field Marshal. His prestige would be rehabilitated officially in February 1987, by President Mário Soares, who bestowed on him the honour of the *Grã-Cruz da Ordem Militar da Torre e Espada* for...his 'heroic military and civic service and for being a symbol of the April Revolution and first President of the Republic after the dictatorship...'

General António de Spínola died on August 13, 1996 at the age of 86, a victim of a pulmonary embolism.

While covering the war in Portuguese Guinea in the early 1970s, I discovered in General de Spínola a man who could echo sentiments that were both liberal and conservative. He was no radical, but neither did he espouse some of the Fascist concepts that had become ingrained among Lisbon's top echelons.

His role, he would declare, was a civilising one. At the same time he was determined to crush the enemy and was well on his way to doing so by 1971. De Spínola – after the Shulz debacle – had actually succeeded in reversing the course of the war and there was an air of

Events in Lisbon in 1974 resulted in a dramatic change of direction in the African territories and the settlers did not like it. Much violence from those who opposed ending the war resulted, particularly in Beira –as well as Lourenco Marques which was soon to become Maputo. (Courtesy The South African Argus Group of Newspapers)

optimism among the senior functionaries whom I met in Bissau. I reflected as much in my book. But that was before SAM-7s had been given to the PAIGC[3] and knocked at least one Portuguese Air Force Fiat G-91 fighter jet out of the sky.

Porch maintains in his book *The Portuguese Armed Forces and the Revolution,* that although de Spínola's book, *Portugal and the Future* was published in 1974, it was already written by 1971, which means that he was probably working on the manuscript or had just finished it while I was around.

It was interesting that, face-to-face, he hardly seemed the man who was later to say that war was at the root of the country's problems, or that 'the future of Portugal depends on an appropriate solution to the problems raised by the war which, by consuming lives, resources and talent, increasingly compromises the rhythm of development which we must have in order to catch up with other countries'.

I could not have met a more determined or articulate exponent of hard-line tactics. He was as uncompromising about the PAIGC as he was when we discussed the difficult terrain in which his men had to fight.

I quote from one of my interviews: 'You ask whether a military victory is possible for the Portuguese in this province? I say to you that we are already achieving victory with our forces in that we are guaranteeing and underwriting the security of the Guinean people.'

He accused the PAIGC of kidnapping young people to feed their war machine, of a meddlesome Soviet Union trying to implicate others in the struggle, and a conflict that already involved East and West for the domination ... of parts of the south Atlantic and West Africa as a whole. Going by what he believed in at the time, the man could easily have been a spokesman for the American State Department of the day.

The book authored by General de Spínola was ultimately read by everybody that mattered in Portugal at the time. One and all, they devoured it because nobody had been left unaffected by the conflicts in Africa: there was hardly a family that didn't have somebody in uniform serving abroad. Banned in the overseas provinces, it was an immensely popular work, but even in Africa it was circulated as a samizdat and the various guerrilla groups took note.

To the MFA, the armed forces movement behind the coup, *Portugal and the Future* was a godsend. It provided the revolutionary movement with clear political guidelines for the future. Indeed, there are many people who cite General de Spínola's book as catalyst for the revolution.

That was later contested by Otelo Saraiva de Carvalho, on the grounds that de Spínola was not radical enough. Curiously, de Carvalho was my escort officer while I covered the war in Portuguese Guinea and I found him an affable, quiet-spoken individual, in marked contrast to the anarchist he was to become. As a consequence of his radical actions, he was eventually jailed.

Prior to the coup, the MFA was regarded as 'Spínolist' both in doctrine and in leadership. Having been embraced by the young officers of the MFA to achieve their ends, they ditched the general as quickly as they embraced him. Within a year de Spínola was forced to flee into exile in Brazil. In the Portugal of the day, he ended up being regarded as a traitor, even though he was one of the most resourceful and competent leaders that the country had produced in modern times.

He never disguised his contempt for what he termed the 'Hermits in Power' in Lisbon. At the time, the young MFA officers had need of a general to lend prestige to their movement and initially they had tried to coerce General Kaúlza de Arriaga into joining them. But when it seemed that this staunch rightist – while accepting that change was necessary – was likely to end up using them instead of the reverse, they opted instead for de Spínola and there is no question: it was his book that did it.

One of the interesting sidelights of this publication was the attitude of the then Prime Minister, Caetano, who was notorious for spotting the sinister hand of international Marxism behind every door. General Costa Gomes, one of the brains behind the revolution and the dismantling of the African empire, sent Caetano a copy of the book.

In *O Depoimento* (later published in Rio de Janeiro after Caetano had himself sought sanctuary in Brazil) he wrote:

On the 18th, I received a copy of *Portugal and the Future* with the friendly dedication of the author. I could not read it that day, nor the following one, which was taken up

FRELIMO guerrillas cross the Rovuma River from Tanzania. The
weapon is a Chinese-made RPG-2. (Camerapix, Nairobi)

by the council of ministers. Only on the 20th after a tiring day, did I pick up the book
after 11 o'clock at night. I did not stop reading until I reached the last page. And when
I closed the covers, I understood that a military coup d'état, which for some months I
sensed had been brewing, was now inevitable.

The next day Caetano called both de Spínola and General Costa Gomes, then Chief
of the General Staff of the Portuguese Armed Forces to his office 'for the most serious and
disagreeable conversation of my life.'

The book, he said, 'contained a critical opening section which could not fail to influence
the desire of the armed forces to continue to defend the overseas provinces, and to weigh on
public opinion, affecting international affairs and reducing the already narrow margin of
manoeuvre open to the government in its foreign policy ... '

Written by the vice-chief of the general staff and approved by his superior...it opened a
breach between the Prime Minister and the highest chiefs of the armed forces.

'It would be impossible to continue to govern with an insubordinate officer corps and
discordant military chiefs,' was Prime Minister Marcello Caetano's view.

Once the revolutionary dust has settled in Lisbon and the country returned to democratic normality, General de Spínola again found favour with his former colleagues and if not exactly feted, he was treated with the kind of honour that had so far eluded him. General de Spínola slotted very neatly into the role of highly-respected elder statesman.

Veneration resuscitated, this quiet, unassuming retired officer was elevated to the rank of Field Marshal and provided with a permanent office, together with an attendant adjutant at Defence Headquarters in Lisbon.

Appendix A

African Troops in the Portuguese Colonial Army 1961-1974: Angola, Guiné-Bissau and Mozambique

João Paulo Borges Coelho of the Eduardo Mondlane University, Maputo, Mozambique[1]

Abstract: The colonial powers systematically included Africans in the wars waged to preserve their order. Portugal was not an exception in this respect. Since 1961, with the beginning of the liberation wars in her colonies, Portugal incorporated Africans in her war effort in Angola, Guinea-Bissau and Mozambique through a process enveloped in an ideological discourse based on 'multi-racialism' and on the preservation of the empire. African engagement varied from marginal roles as servants and informers to more important ones as highly operational combat units.

By the end of the Portuguese colonial war, in 1974, African participation had become crucial, representing about half of all operational colonial troops. This paper explores in a comparative framework the three cases of Angola, Portuguese Guinea (today Guiné-Bissau) and Mozambique, seeking the rationale behind the process and the shapes it took.

The abrupt end of the colonial war, triggered by a military coup in Portugal, paved the way for the independence of the colonies, but left a legacy difficult to manage by the newly independent countries. Shedding some light on the destiny of the former African collaborators during this period, the paper suggests that they played a role in the post-independence civil conflicts in Angola and Mozambique.

On 25 April 1974, a military coup in Lisbon paved the way to an abrupt end of the long Portuguese colonial adventure and, more narrowly, of ten harsh years during which colonial authority had been challenged by nationalist wars in Angola, Guinea-Bissau and Mozambique. These three wars left profound marks on the shape of the economies and societies of the three countries.

One of these marks was a legacy of thousands of Africans with a past of fighting side by side with the Portuguese defence forces against independence. This study seeks to discuss the historical rationale for such participation, as well as to shed some light on the post-independence impacts it produced, which are still far from fully understood.

It is almost a truism to say that the colonisation of the African continent would have been impossible without local collaboration. The stereotyped picture of immensely superior European forces defeating small, fragile and unarticulated African resistances rarely corresponds to the historical truth. Much closer to reality is the picture of European officials able to foster and manage internal contradictions, attracting African forces into their orbit to make them fight other African forces in order to install and preserve the colonial order.

One of the more interesting comments provided by the author of this dissertation was published almost a century before and came from Joaquim Mouzinho de Albuquerque. In a document titled *A reorganização dos exércitos ultramarinos*, he declared '... if it isn't to be a poor character with little utility, the European soldier will cost us too much. It is therefore natural that to the African, more adapted to the climate and much cheaper, the role will be reserved of chair à canon ...'[2]

In the two world wars of the last century, African troops fought in defence of the colonial powers' interests both in the African theatre and elsewhere. Particularly after the 1950s, when nationalist movements began to fight for their independence throughout the African continent, African participation in the struggle to preserve the old colonial order acquired considerable importance.

In the face of the decreasing resistance of locals to military service, the 1914 regulation prescribed the creation of a military reserve, which permitted the engagement of 25,000 Africans, or 44 percent of the total force, in the struggle against the German invasion of Northern Mozambique during the First World War.

Indeed, former US Navy Captain John P. Cann makes the point that the German experience with locally recruited forces, particularly the *Askaris*, was considered in Mozambique as highly positive. In 1915, he tells us, the German force in Tanganyika was composed of 2,200 European troops, 11,100 regular African troops and 3,200 irregulars, in 24 companies, each one roughly with a dozen Europeans and 300 Africans.[3]

From this point on, service in the armed forces began to be perceived as an important way of 'nationalising' the African population of the colonies. The regulation of June 1933 stipulated distinct service branches for 'common blacks' and for 'non indigenous blacks,' the latter being enrolled in the same service branches as Europeans born in the colonies. Africans were to be registered in the ranks under a Portuguese Christian name, and it was expected that military service would act as a powerful 'civilising' mechanism or, in the words of General Norton de Matos, as 'one of the most effective mechanisms for opening a breach in the tenebrous primitive civilisations.'

Local collaboration was fundamental to guaranteeing the colonial project. Portugal was not an exception in this respect, and often resorted to the recruitment of Africans in her war effort, namely since the so-called 'Pacification Campaigns' of the late 19th Century.

The present study looks at this collaboration in the context of the wars for independence in the former Portuguese colonies—a collaboration that has to be perceived at various levels, since its nature, importance and intensity varied throughout the period in which the wars were fought. Wars tend evidently to involve everybody within the area they cover. Here it will be useful, however, to narrow the focus and look at the involvement which directly derived from the colonial strategy—the 'African involvement as strategy' or, as it was called in those days, the *Africanisation* of the war effort.

This approach requires an historical perspective. Participation by African troops was indeed uneven throughout the 13 years of the Portuguese Colonial military campaigns. It began on the margins, limited to secondary roles or, at the war fronts, to population control, intelligence gathering and reconnaissance by informers and scouts. African troops became increasingly important, however, and on the eve of the military coup of 25 April 1974

Africans accounted for more than 50 percent of the contingent fighting the war.

What follows is an attempt to discuss this Africanisation and the impact it had on ending the war. We shall also examine briefly the profound traces the process left as a heritage passed on to the newly independent African countries.

Africans in the Colonial Defence Forces at the War of Independence

After the Second World War the Portuguese army, as part of the entire colonial system, began to be forced to change as a result of international pressures and as the nationalist wars were anticipated and approaching.

The *Estado Novo* was forced to repeal the *Estatuto dos Indígenas* which had assured for so long that the vast majority of the population remained without access to the status of citizens, and this required the army to deal with a new and unexpected problem: that of having a growing African contingent in its ranks. Until then the infantry recognised the categories of commissioned soldiers (white soldiers born in Portugal or in her overseas provinces), overseas soldiers (African *assimilados*), and native soldiers (Africans under the *indigenato* regime).

Forced to change this system, the regime, through the decree 43.267 of 24 October 1960, introduced the new categories of 1st, 2nd and 3rd class soldier, in practice corresponding to the previous ones. A little later, this too had to be changed, and although the colour of the soldiers' skin ceased to be a criterion, two classes were established on the basis of formal education and, in particular, of the ability to speak Portuguese correctly.

In practical terms this again meant a perpetuation of the old distinctions. Even so, however, the door was opening ever so slightly for the Africans.

Faced with the threat represented by the Africanisation of its army, a certain segment of the regime's establishment had every motive to resist. Firstly, ideological reasons played a role—paradigmatic in this respect is the strong position taken by Kaúlza de Arriaga, who in 1960, as Sub-secretary of State for Aeronautics, wrote to Salazar that 'a defence concept based on black troops is impossible, independently of the kind of white control ... It is therefore necessary to reduce the strength and size of our black troops.'

This view, undoubtedly common among the upper echelons, is very well conveyed by Felgas, who commenting on the consequences of a weak metropolitan contribution to the army wrote that 'it is not difficult to foresee that disorder would prevail, as well as insecurity, as happened in the first months of independence of the ex-Belgian Congo. Of course, we could adopt the same solution for Angola, to promote soldiers to colonels and corporals to generals. But the results would be identical: an army deprived of strength, cohesion, prestige and discipline.'

Associated with this view was one that, despite all the integrationist propaganda of the Nation in Arms, considered the Africans as little less than potential terrorists, in the international context of the Cold War. This led the Chief-of-Staff to write, as late as 1962, that engaging the native masses in a military effort posed great risks, since they were all heavily exposed to the 'propaganda of the enemy.'

As a result, and despite the strong effort to prepare the army for the African campaigns, undertaken from the late 1950s onward, the old 'philosophy' that had informed the defence and security system in the colonial territories remained basically unchanged, with 'expeditionary forces' from Portugal coming to fight the colonial wars and the locally recruited ones playing a limited and secondary role as second-line troops.

That this was indeed so is clear from the constant increase in metropolitan contingents as the wars started, first in Angola in March 1961, and then in Guinea in January 1963 and in Mozambique in June 1964.

Table 1 documents a 100% increase in the total metropolitan contingent during the first half of the period of conflict (until 1967). Figures in Table 2 show a correspondent modest increase in the numbers of locally recruited forces during the same period (from 18% in 1961 to 25% in 1967).

Table 1: Metropolitan Troops In the African War Theatres

Date	Angola	Mozambique	Guinea	Total
1961	28,477	8,209	3,736	40,422
1962	33,760	8,852	4,070	46,682
1963	34,530	9,243	8,336	52,109
1964	37,418	10,132	12,874	60,424
1965	41,625	13,155	14,640	69,420
1966	38,519	19,550	18,868	76,937
1967	43,051	23,164	18,421	84,636
1968	37,547	22,717	19,559	78,823
1969	36,911	23,286	22,866	83,063
1970	36,174	22,633	22,487	81,294
1971	36,127	21,795	23,402	81,324
1972	34,676	22,657	24,036	81,369
1973	37,773	23,891	25,610	87,274

Source: *Estado-Maior do Exército, 1988 I: 260.*

Table 2: Locally Recruited Troops In the African War Theatres (With percentage of Total Troops)

Date	Angola	Mozambique	Guinea	Total
1961	5,000 (14.9)	3,000 (26.8)	1,000 (21.1)	9,000 (18.2)
1962	11,165 (24.9)	3,000 (25.3)	1,000 (19.7)	15,165 (24.5)
1963	12,870 (27.2)	5,003 (35.1)	1,314 (13.6)	19,187 (26.9)
1964	15,075 (28.7)	7,917 (43.9)	2,321 (15.3)	25,313 (29.5)
1965	15,448 (27.1)	9,701 (42.4)	2,612 (15.1)	27,761 (28.5)
1966	17,297 (31.0)	11,038 (36.1)	1,933 (9.3)	30,268 (28.2)
1967	14,369 (25.0)	11,557 (33.3)	3,229 (14.9)	29,155 (25.6)
1968	20,683 (35.5)	13,898 (38.0)	3,280 (14.4)	37,861 (32.7)
1969	18,663 (33.6)	15,810 (40.4)	3,715 (14.4)	38,188 (31.4)
1970	19,059 (34.5)	16,079 (41.5)	4,268 (16.0)	39,406 (32.6)
1971	25,933 (41.8)	22,710 (51.0)	5,808 (19.9)	54,451 (40.1)
1972	25,461 (42.2)	24,066 (51.5)	5,921 (19.8)	55,448 (40.5)
1973	27,819 (42.4)	27,572 (53.6)	6,425 (20.1)	61,816 (41.4)

Source: *Estado-Maior do Exército, 1988 I: 261.*

Table 1 also reveals more modest increases in metropolitan troops during the second half of the war, while Table 2 shows correspondingly a much more pronounced increase in locally recruited troops, whose number reached nearly half of the total contingent in 1973.

Around 1968 there clearly occurred a certain break in the balance between metropolitan and local forces, with more marked increases in the latter.

This raises the question why, despite all the entrenched resistance discussed above, did the *Estado Novo* and its military apparatus change their attitude so dramatically?

Obviously, the fact that this change occurred when Marcello Caetano replaced Salazar as President of the Cabinet was not purely coincidental.

However, there are many other factors that also help to explain it.

The main argument for this Africanisation of the Portuguese colonial army has been based on Portugal's recruiting problems. In the late 1960s, according to Henriksen, Portugal, after Israel, had the highest percentage of people in arms in the world, with an annual increase of 11 percent between the 49,422 documented in 1961, and the 149,090 documented in 1973. In parallel, the percentage of deserters also doubled, from 11.6 to 20.9, for reasons linked both with avoidance of military service and with the fact that Portugal was a chronic provider of migrant labour to Europe and the Americas, through a process that gradually drained a population of potential recruits already small from the start.

To these quantitative difficulties, qualitative ones also have to be added, in the sense that the expeditionary contingents had serious problems of adaptation to the African war theatres and that, as the years passed, the Portuguese army faced an acute shortage of commanding officers, with obvious consequences for its military efficiency.

The number of officers graduating from the military academy rose sharply from 68 in 1962 to 146 in 1967, but from then on started to suffer an abrupt decline to only 40 in 1973, as a result of lack of volunteers. In consequence, the military authorities were forced to mobilise conscripts to fill the huge gaps in the professional cadres.[4]

Besides the issue of sheer human numbers, the financial difficulties that Portugal experienced in coping with the three wars also shed some explanation on Africanisation. According to this argument, the burden became so unbearable that the progressive sharing of the war effort with the colonies, through increasing local recruitment and financial participation, was a way to minimise the weight. Moreover, this would seem to be quite well in line with the old Salazar principle of involving each colony in the resolution of its own problems.

Notwithstanding these valid explanations, the shortage of metropolitan men and the high costs of war were not the only reasons behind the Africanisation process. Despite such difficulties and the fact that they were almost insurmountable, Portugal was indeed capable of sustaining some level of increase in the numbers of her metropolitan troops, and the costs involved were basically covered, even if at the price of going to the brink of economic and financial exhaustion.

Further factors have then to be brought in to explain the process of Africanisation. The first, which reveals one of the several internal contradictions of the *Estado Novo*, is of a historical and ideological nature. It was based on the appeal of the integrationist ideology of the Empire and its principle of race miscegenation, which translated into the revival of white settlement plans and into the 'promotion' of the African populations, particularly under the short but decisive mandate of Adriano Moreira as overseas minister.

In a sense, it bore elements of continuity with the early days of Salazar's regime, when important steps were made to include an African layer at the foundation of the colonial state and administration, with the involvement of local African authorities in population censuses, tax collection, and labour recruitment in their areas of jurisdiction.

As mentioned above, this 'attitude' also had led to the establishment of defence forces based on the inclusion of local troops in secondary roles. The overwhelming majority of these local troops were Africans, who served mostly as auxiliaries, servants in the barracks, and, given their knowledge of the terrain, as informers and scouts.

However, the nationalist wars also introduced a new phenomenon in the sense that a much broader African involvement became required, well beyond such targeted recruitment: early on in the process the colonial authorities understood that the war was also about conquering the population. The 'philosophy' of the Estado Novo, mixed with the first counter-insurgency techniques to 'win' the population, provided the core of a colonial psycho-social doctrine based on the two fundamental concepts of *comandamento* (command) and *accionamento* (driving, setting in motion).[5]

These served as a framework for the creation, in the early 1960s, of local militias of several kinds in the rural areas of the three colonies, as second-line troops under the authority of the civil administration and based on the principle of self-defence against subversive attacks. In 1961, Adriano Moreira, as Overseas Minister, issued legislative diplomas, which created the Militia Corps as second-line forces in the African colonies.

The militia took a wide range of organisational shapes, from very informal schemes of village forces acting under the authority of village chiefs, as happened in Angola, to more institutionally militarised groups assuring the defence of the *aldeamentos*, the protected villages formed along the lines of what the British had practiced in their counter-insurgency war in Malaya, or the North- Americans in Vietnam.[6]

As the war situation aggravated, and with the corresponding difficulties experienced by the armed forces, the militia contingents were brought into more active roles exceeding the traditional defensive ones.

Paradigmatic in this respect was the case of Guinea, where, besides the normal militias, special ones were created for offensive operations in their home areas. This new concept, which led to the emergence of very efficient troops, mixed the old colonial tradition with new counter-insurgency theories. General Carlos Fabião, the so-called 'father' of these new militias, would say with respect to their creation: 'I studied, I read ancient documents about the pacification campaigns of the end of last century [19th], and concluded that past wars in Africa had been fought more or less with the locals, particularly in Guinea'.

These theories, to which the Portuguese high military commanders were systematically exposed from the second half of the 1950s onward, had as one of their core concepts the so-called 'same element theory,' according to which the guerrillas could be fought more efficiently by troops mirroring their organisation, weaponry, knowledge of the terrain, and even race—i.e. by African combat units.

These theories became more extensively absorbed at a time when the need to adapt and to reinforce the Portuguese troops became more pressing.

The changes that started to occur at this point brought a new meaning to the concept of Africanisation. From now on this would not imply merely a growing percentage of locally recruited or black individuals incorporated in the regular forces fighting the nationalists, in the same sense as the French *jeunissement* in Indochina, for example.

More than that, it now meant a process of creating and fostering combat units of Africans operating more or less irregularly and autonomously, and with high levels of operational efficiency. It must be said that this change in attitude, which implied increased trust in the Africans, even if forced, was not sudden, nor was it just due to theoretical considerations.

In fact, in the second half of the 1960s the military were facing serious problems related not only to a shortage of troops but also to the question of what to do with the Africans demobilised from the regular army. Old suspicions that Africans demobilised from the regular force, already capable of handling weaponry, might simply join the nationalist guerrillas, lay behind new efforts to create auxiliary troops where those men would be kept under the control of military or civil authorities.

Moreover, these troops were much cheaper than the regular ones and their eventual casualties were much 'less repercussion-rich' than those of metropolitan forces.

This Africanisation was carried out differently in the three territories of Angola, Guinea and Mozambique, not just because of different local and regional contexts, but also owing to the different attitudes and views of the respective commanders.

The period when Marcello Caetano was in power roughly corresponds to an important decentralization in the conduct of the wars. If formerly these were conducted in a relatively centralized manner from Lisbon, now three generals with strong views were appointed to run them from the provinces. Spínola took charge of Guinea as Governor and Commander-in-Chief in May 1968; Kaúlza de Arriaga went to Mozambique as Commander-in-Chief in March 1970; and Costa Gomes was appointed as Commander-in-Chief of Angola in April 1970. In July 1969 the military operations in each theatre were centralised under each commander-in-chief.

The results likewise varied: while in Guinea General Spínola planned and fought for the creation of a regular, entirely coherent African army mirroring the metropolitan one, having perhaps in mind a future federation of Portuguese-speaking states, in Angola the African irregular units were much more informal and diverse in nature. Mozambique somehow combined aspects of the two.

The first unit entirely consisting of Africans was probably the *Tropas Especiais* (Special Troops, commonly known by the acronym TEs), which emerged in 1966 in Cabinda, when Alexandre Taty, a former UPA/FNLA cadre, deserted to the Portuguese side with 1,200 men. Organised and controlled by PIDE, the Portuguese political police, they started to be used in action against the MPLA, which after having initiated operations in the Dembos in Northern Angola, had spread its guerrilla activities to Cabinda in late 1964. The TEs operated in Cabinda, their home area, as well as in Zaire and Uíge, in Northern Angola.

Also in 1966, the war epicentre in Angola moved to the east, with the start of UNITA activities in that area and with the opening of MPLA's Eastern Front, which became a threat to the Moxico and Cuando Cubango areas in the south-east. Besides dispatching a TE unit to the area, PIDE also began to create what would become its private ethnic army.

The first experiment was conducted by Inspector Oscar Cardoso, who worked in Cuando Cubango with Bushmen (San) groups serving as scouts and information gatherers, and soon as true combat units, exploiting the cultural distance between these small men of San origin and the Bantu populations of the remaining areas.

Cardoso's subsequent comments on the *Flechas* are interesting: He mentioned, in particular: 'they didn't need logistical support. Gatherers since kids, they could live [on] nothing, with special ability to find food and water. We really had good operational results with them. We never had a desertion from the *Flechas*' ranks.' The experiment was so successful in operational terms that the concept soon spread to other areas, particularly Luso (Luena) and Luanda-Caxito, where the *Flechas* unit was almost entirely composed of ex-MPLA guerrillas. Towards the end of the war almost all PIDE sub-delegations in Angola's war zones had their own private units of *Flechas*.

A little later, in 1968, the military also favoured the creation of their own irregular troops, the *Grupos Especiais* (or GEs, Special Groups), formed of local volunteers who were submitted to the same training as the regular military forces.

Organised in combat groups of about 30 men each, they were controlled by the military, usually one Portuguese battalion having one or two of these groups nearby. Beside the fact that they were cheaper than the regular troops, one of the advantages gained from the creation of this force, which operated in the north, east and south of Angola, was their knowledge of local languages, culture, and terrain.

The sharp increase in the number of GE groups also had to do, however, with problems in furnishing replacements for regular troops that had concluded their operational commission.

Meantime, the infiltration in South West Africa by SWAPO and MPLA guerrillas [to the South] very much concerned the South Africans, who were ready to meet the costs of Portuguese reinforcements at battalion level in the area. However, the Portuguese could do little more than reinforce the area with some extra GE groups. Significantly, Lisbon was already getting some support in South Angola from SAAF Alouette helicopter gunships.

Also in the Eastern area of Angola, groups of Katangese gendarmes formerly supporting Moise Tshombe crossed the border into Angola during the second semester of 1967, and were received as political refugees by the Portuguese authorities.

In February 1969 they formed the Front for National Liberation of Congo, with the objective of overthrowing the Mobutu regime. At this time, facing an acute shortage of forces in the Eastern part of the territory, the Portuguese authorities launched the project *Fidelidade* (Fidelity), based on the promise to support the 'liberation' of Zaire in exchange for the participation of this force in counter-insurgency operations in Angola, particularly against the MPLA.

Code-named *Fiéis*, they received military supplies and training from the Portuguese armed forces, as well as political supervision from the PIDE.

This became one of the most effective forces in counter-insurgency operations, despite chronic problems with discipline that translated into frequent riots and desertions that stemmed from complaints about low pay and from the fact that these men did not feel they were receiving enough support from the Portuguese government in their struggle against Mobutu's Zaire.

At the same time and a little further to the south, a similar project, codenamed 'Operation Colt,' was implemented by the Portuguese to receive a smaller group of Zambian ANC dissidents who arrived in Angola in 1967. It says a lot that both the Rhodesians and South-Africans expressed their reservations towards Operation Colt mounted by the Portuguese, on the grounds that they did not believe the Zambian ANC had enough credibility to destabilise Zambia at the time.

In 1968, PIDE organised them into a combat group of 45 elements code-named *Leais*, under the same kind of agreement as the one established with the *Fiéis*, namely to fight against the Angolan liberation movements in exchange for support in their struggle to overthrow Kenneth Kaunda's Zambian regime.

The wide, flexible, and diverse utilisation of African irregular troops that was practiced in Angola did not have any parallel in the other war theatres. It was the result of several specific factors. The first one was, of course, the vast area to be covered in counter-insurgency activities, together with the great difficulties the Portuguese had in replacing, let alone increasing, the number of their troops, and together with the inevitable financial aspects.

The second factor was the competition among the three nationalist movements, which gave rise to desertions by trained guerrillas who went to join counter-insurgency operations.

Thirdly and very importantly, it is necessary to take into account the attitude of General Costa Gomes, who managed to establish a good relationship between the military and PIDE, one that undoubtedly allowed the spread of this kind of irregular war, so that unlike many of his fellow generals he was able to shift a significant operational burden onto the autonomous activity of the African units.

Interviewed in 2001, General Costa Gomes said that 'the reason why I got along with PIDE was the following: When I arrived in Angola already as Commander-in-Chief, I heard from the Department of Operations of a conflict which had occurred involving PIDE's *Flechas* and a Commando company of the army that resulted in casualties. I asked myself, how could PIDE be waging a war without the Commander-in-Chief knowing about it? I asked the Governor to convene a meeting with the people that mattered and told them: PIDE can do whatever wars but not on behalf of the Governor or PIDE itself. It has to be on my behalf'.

Interviewed by the *Washington Post* a decade before, in March 1971, he'd made the point that 'the African troops combating against subversion are increasing in number. Their training and experience rendered them outstanding professionals.' And in another interview with *Época* magazine, on 21 December 197, he declared: 'TEs are a very cohesive group (...) GEs are growing from year to year. (...) As do the *Flechas*. All the irregular troops have proven their merit. That is why we will make efforts to increase their numbers.'

Finally, besides the already discussed advantages inherent in the employment of foreign irregular troops, the colonial authorities in Angola also had in mind interfering at a broader regional level, keeping Zaire and Zambia in particular under pressure.

In Guinea developments were quite different in this regard. When the war started, locally recruited militia groups were created to assure the 'self-defence' of the populations, freeing the expeditionary army for offensive operations.

By 1966, Guinea already had 18 militia companies, and the authorities were requesting funds to create more, although still acknowledging the risks involved in having to deal with a 'considerable volume of people armed, equipped and trained'.

The substitution of General Schulz, a quite conventional and conservative commander, by General António Spínola brought profound changes. Through selective recruitment among normal militias, he fostered the creation of Special Militias organised in combat groups and operating fairly autonomously.

Spínola structured these militias along the structural lines of the Portuguese army, in companies subdivided into platoons. He faced a tough battle with the upper echelons to end the distinction between metropolitan and locally recruited soldiers, arguing that discrimination against the latter involved serious risks for the Portuguese African campaign, and threatening that its perpetuation 'would force us to redefine our counter-insurgency policy based on African forces.'

This conflict continued when Spínola pressed to increase the number of special militias. Of the five requested in 1968 only two had been authorized by 1970. Lisbon's resistance clearly had to do with financial constraints, and also with fears that 'the informality brought on by the Africanisation of the war is spreading to an informality of procedures.'

It was perhaps because of this, and in an attempt to counteract the tendency of provincial commanders to keep creating new African forces that, at the end of 1971, the Minister of Defence ordered the centralisation in Lisbon of all expenses relating to the irregular troops.

In 1970, Spínola again engaged in a struggle with the upper echelons in order to create – using elite African combatants from the militias and the organizational pattern of the Portuguese army – companies of African Commandos. These were structured very much like normal commando companies that had been created in the other theatres, but were manned entirely by Africans and carried out very special combat operations both within Guinea and in Guinea-Conakry and Senegal. The discussion of the project took two years, an inordinately long time, but not unusual for the Portuguese command structure. Only in 1972 did they become operational, which was not long before Lisbon's military putsch.

The Centres for Commando Instruction (CICs) were created in Guinea in 1964, Angola in 1965, and Mozambique in 1969, for training these elite troops. Many of the Guinea African commando combatants were trained in Angola.

In Mozambique, this process occurred a little later and, in a manner that combined features of the other two cases, as well as some that were specific to the area.

The first stages of the war unfolded under the command of General Augusto dos Santos, an admirer of the new counter-insurgency theories. It says a lot that this commander took it upon himself to translate Sir Robert Thompson's seminal book on unconventional warfare, *Defeating Communist Insurgency.*

In the mid-1960s, with Costa Gomes as second-in-command, dos Santos sponsored important 'experiments' involving local militias. One of these led to successful collaboration with the Rhodesian authorities to form units of African scouts, something Al Venter deals with, in collaboration with his old friend Colonel Ron Reid-Daly in his own work *War Stories by Al Venter and Friends.*[7]

However, by 1969 Kaúlza de Arriaga had replaced General Dos Santos. The new Commander-in-Chief had an entirely different way of conducting the war. For a long time the operational involvement of Africans was limited to local recruitment in the regular army or in commando companies, irregular African units being entirely out of the picture, with the exception of limited paramilitary experiments.

In Mozambique, the first four commando companies were created in Montepuez in 1969, and experienced limited growth, despite their relative operational success, to five in 1970, and eight by the end of the war in 1974. There was also the creation of paramilitary groups linked to PIDE, acting as hunters of wild game and, in fact, gathering intelligence on nationalist guerrilla movements and contacts.

Only in 1973 were the first solutions involving African units implemented on the ground, with the creation of Special Groups of Parachutists and other Special Groups, formed in the central regions of the country on an ethnic basis, recruiting volunteers, and operating in particular in their home areas, in coordination with and under the control of the military.

In contrast with the Angolan case, Kaúlza's reservations with regard to African forces operating outside the military's sphere of control, as well as his conflicts with PIDE, probably help to explain why the implementation of a Flecha-type project took so long in Mozambique.

The introduction of *Flechas* was being discussed between PIDE and the Rhodesian authorities since 1972. The latter were very much interested in the unfolding events in Mozambique and favoured 'lighter' and more local alternatives to the way the war was being conducted by Kaúlza de Arriaga.

It is therefore probable that discrete and low profile 'experiments' with *Flechas* under the aegis of PIDE were in fact taking place since 1972, despite the difficulties. As late as July 1973, the army refused to supply automatic weapons to the *Flechas*, on grounds that all the lots were already consigned. PIDE approached the South-Africans who expressed a willingness to finance the supply. Only in 1974, when Kaúlza de Arriaga had been already dismissed by Marcello Caetano, and on the eve of the military coup that ended the war, did they start to operate on the ground.

The comparative analysis of how Africans were used as soldiers by the Portuguese on all three fronts of the colonial wars, shows that, beyond very broad strategic guidelines, the factors that mattered were local context and local commanders. Costa Gomes, perhaps the most successful general, sought good relations with the civilians and employed African units within the framework of a counter-insurgency technique.

Spínola, by contrast, appealed for a more political and psycho-social use of African soldiers. Kaúlza, in contrast, the most conservative of the three (and the most ineffectual) feared African forces beyond his strict and immediate control. He never seemed to have progressed beyond his initial racist perception of Africans as inferior beings and terrorists.

Whatever the approaches and their degree of success in terms of furthering colonial interests, the fact is that on the eve of the war's end Africanisation had been accepted as the only way of maintaining the colonial project, in circles as high as that of the Portuguese Chief-of-Staff.

According to him, African troops were more efficient, more cost-effective, cheaper and susceptible of delivering better results not only in military terms, but also politically. Moreover, if properly organised in militarised villages, 'they could fight forever'.

In 1974 he therefore proposed a substantial reduction in the number of metropolitan troops and a decentralisation of the financial resources thus spared, so that the local commands could create further African units. Clearly, the plan was to promote preconditions for civil war in the African territories, if not politically, at least militarily.

Appendix B

The SAAF in Support of Portugal

Southern African military personnel were involved in Angola and Mozambique while the Portuguese were fighting rear-guard actions to save their African possessions. Rhodesian Special Forces were active in both countries. That followed the deployment of South African helicopter gunships to assist Portuguese troops in Angola. Former SAAF Brigadier Peter 'Monster' Wilkins was among the first to be tasked and this is his recollection of events.

After Operation Blouwildebees – the South African Police assault on Ongulumbashe in 1966 – South African Air Force elements were substantially involved in Southern Angola. Essentially, they went in to help the Portuguese Air Force and the clandestine arrangement survived until 1973, roughly a year before Lisbon pulled out of Africa, bags and baggage.

These operations were given various names. They included Op Bombay (1969 – 1970), Op Mexa (1971), followed by Op Atilla and Op Resgate in 1973. Two more operations have been mentioned in this context, but details are vague, except that it is believed that a pair of gunships was lost.

Initially, the main areas of operation involving gunships included northern Namibia, southern Angola and what was then Rhodesia, where SAAF pilots fought alongside their Rhodesian counterparts. The primary 'war-horse' for what had earlier been dubbed The Chopper Boys was the venerable Alouette III, or, in air force lingo, the 'Alo' – a relatively slow, seemingly frail, but nonetheless a remarkably resilient French-built helicopter which, despite being able to take innumerable hits, usually hauled their crews back to base and safety. If a round pierced the helicopter's hydraulics or removed a rotor blade, which occasionally happened, it was another story.

Among these survivors was Dave Atkinson (known as to his buddies as 'Double Dave' or 'Size Twelves', due to his boot size). He once emerged from a significant contact with enemy guerrillas after his chopper had taken more than three dozen AK hits in and around the fuselage.

Later, as the war escalated and Lisbon had withdrawn its forces from Africa, hostilities moved up several notches during onslaughts such as Operations Savannah and Protea and, in the course of events, a lot more of Angola was covered. In fact, some of the British-built maritime Westland Wasp helicopters operating from South African navy frigates deployed as back-up measures off the Angolan coast were also involved.

Once initial deliveries of the Aerospatiale Pumas started coming through, some of these larger transport helicopters were sent to forward operational postings in Sector 10; it was in Ovamboland that the air war entered a new and more versatile phase. Pumas deployed in combat conditions were used to good effect for moving troops into forward positions or perhaps bringing up reserves of ammunition and returning the wounded to hospital at Oshakati.

After a while their numbers were supplemented by even larger Super Frelons, which, though bulky and not suited to the hot and arid conditions of the northern reaches of South West Africa or southern Angola, those machines, despite some criticism, were an asset to the war effort. As Brigadier Wilkins put it, the Super Frelon had an increased lifting capacity and a greater range than the Puma, and, by chopper standards, 'it was also the most comfortable of SAAF helicopters'.

Affectionately known as 'Putco', after the public utility bus company active in Johannesburg, the Super Frelon was also involved in several military strikes into south-western Zambia. At that stage, these machines temporarily operated from Katima Mulilo in the Caprivi. It wasn't long before they were pulled back, in part because the machines were inordinately thirsty and their lifting capacity not proportionately much more than the average Puma.

In later years Puma helicopters were to join their Alouette counterparts in Rhodesian operations and both chopper types saw cross-border service into Mozambique.

Brigadier Wilkins continues:

Before the acquisition of Pumas by the SAAF, all military trooping was handled by the Alouette, which meant limited mobility in all departments. At best, these small choppers could take four, depending on the amount of kit, weapons and ammunition the troopies carried. The Portuguese would sometimes up that to five, six even, but then you had a good chance of stripping the gears.

Initially, all SAAF helicopters were based at the South African Air Force base at Ondangua. They were later deployed to positions further afield and that included Rundu (on the southern bank of the Okavango River which bordered on Angola) as well as to Katima Mulilo (at the eastern end of the Caprivi Strip, where the frontiers of Botswana, Zimbabwe and Zambia conjoined on the Zambezi River). Operations consisted mainly of stealthy day-time flights into Angola in support of Portuguese ground forces.

Lisbon had its own Alouette IIIs in these areas, but having to cope with three major wars in regions that stretched all the way across Africa – and were themselves half the size of Western Europe – their numbers were severely limited. Consequently, the Portuguese Air Force was hard-pressed to meet all military needs and it was axiomatic that the South Africans would be asked to help.

The fact was, the guerrilla armies then active in South Angola were our enemy too, and at the time they were giving good support to SWAPO cadres intent on infiltrating southwards into the country that was eventually to become Namibia. It was more or less taken for granted that the request would elicit a positive response from Pretoria, if only to provide the still-developing helicopters wing with combat experience. There was a cachet to the deal, though: SAAF operations inside Angola were to remain secret and the media was never to be privy to these developments.

The most active anti-Portuguese insurgent movement in the region at the time was UNITA, led by a mercurial, Swiss-educated Maoist by the name of Dr Jonas Savimbi. Based largely in the south-eastern Cuando Cubango province – which lay north of Caprivi – it made good sense to help the Portuguese, and that was where we came in.

Because the first Pumas had not yet arrived from France, we were equipped only with our modest little troopers, almost all of them unarmed Alouette IIIs and it remained that way from 1966 to 1969. The Portuguese, in contrast, fielded full-blown gunships – the same Alouette helicopters – but with 20mm cannon facing out the left rear door: we were only to receive our first gunship in the Caprivi in the third quarter of 1969.

I was operating out of Rundu at the time and I clearly remember the strict set of rules with which we were issued on arrival at the base. The thrust of it was that the restrictions imposed severely limited the versatility of the machines we operated in wartime conditions. But, as in most conflicts, the chopper crews had their own way of doing things and we soon figured out ways to get the most out of the choppers.

Bluntly put, South African air crews were not allowed 'to take the war to the guerrillas'. Instead, we were expected to account for every single round of HE (high explosive) fired by us. The word from Pretoria was that we were only to 'protect our own' and SAAF helicopters were not allowed to engage in 'seek and destroy' engagement. In short, we were never to be the aggressors, which, in wartime, was hogwash.

Of course, there were ways of circumventing the nonsense, that was probably the brainchild of some heavily- braided functionary who had never heard a shot fired in anger. The business ends of our HE rounds were painted green. Portuguese ones, in contrast, were orange and yellow, which made them easily distinguishable from each other. But we soon became aware that Portuguese aircrews had a singular weakness, which was the need for good South African wines, of which we had a lot. It wasn't long before we established a primitive barter system that involved trading a good bottle of wine for so many rounds of Portuguese HE: thank you very much!

That done, our gunners would insert scrounged Portuguese high explosive rounds into their ammo belts and leave a distinctive gap before inserting our own rounds, which ensured that the weapon stopped firing before our own rounds came into play. In a really hot contact, a quick pull by the gunners to reload their heavy machine-gun was a formality and the firefight would continue. We ended up using a lot less of our own ammunition to achieve the same result.

At the same time, ball or solid 20mm rounds were also studiously hoarded. Because we were officially allowed to use them for target practice, they were more freely available that HE rounds, so we jealously guarded our supplies of ball, and for good reason.

We had long ago been made aware of the fact that in heavily wooded country, such as we encountered in areas where the Portuguese forces were active, HE would explode on contact with the tree branches, often well short of the intended target sheltering below. Obviously this didn't achieve many results. But by inserting ball rounds into the ammo belts, we had excellent penetration. Though not spectacular, ball ammo was very effective against an enemy using heavy foliage and forest cover to secrete themselves.

Interestingly, this was a lesson we used in later years, when 20mm ball ammunition would easily penetrate the hulls of armoured vehicles like Soviet BRDMs and BTRs whenever they were deployed by the Soviets against South African forces.

Our choppers were also used to torch guerrilla camps by using our Very pistols. Every Alouette had at least one of these signal guns, ostensibly for rescue purposes.

My first border trip was scheduled for an operation that was launched in September 1966, but I had a problem with my ears and was grounded for the duration. The result was that I only experienced my first operational 'bush tour' after I'd returned to Ondangua in May 1967. It lasted more than two months and was the first of many.

Over a three year period, I completed more than two dozen postings to the Operational Area, some as long as three months and others, mostly on Pumas, for perhaps a week. Over a thousand of my operational hours were on Alouettes, with about 300 on Pumas. As the saying goes, it was many hours of boredom, interspersed by a few hairy moments of terror when we came under fire.

The first really 'hot' operations to which I was subjected came in 1968, when we were supposed to act solely in a supportive role for the Portuguese Air Force. While the troopers were initially not armed, they were later fitted with light machine-guns for self-protection. Additionally, the flight engineer carried an automatic rifle, whereas the pilots would take a 9mm pistol as well as a hand machine carbine (HMC), or perhaps an Israeli Uzzi on board with us.

We would load up a couple of eager-for-combat Angolan soldiers – usually commandos or Airborne Forces – termed *Grupos Especiais Pára-Quedistas* in local lingo – and they would lead us in the general direction of what they would claim were 'known' insurgent camps. It was all very much a hit-or-miss affair. Once arrived, in theory, we were required to circle overhead while the Portuguese gunships would go straight in. Frankly, this wasn't our idea of fighting a war and the SAAF crews wouldn't waste much time before getting involved.

The upshot of it all was that there was a good deal of illegal firing from our choppers, which often included the pilots who would sometimes join in the fray. Most quickly mastered the art of keeping the cyclic stick between their knees steady and firing at the enemy from their little side windows with their hand machine carbines.

That said, these were still early days in the bush war and the guerrillas rarely looked too threatening, which meant that we usually had things our own way: this was no Vietnam. When they did fire back, it was invariably inaccurate and usually 'blind', firing their guns over their shoulder or on the run. Their first mistake was actually to display their weapons, so we knew exactly which individuals running about on the ground below us needed to be picked off ...

On these cross-border operations into South Angola, we usually set out of Rundu with a squadron of six Alouettes.

Five of the troopers would form into a 'V' or 'Vic' formation, though this was usually quite loose, individual choppers being a kilometre or more apart throughout the flight. The lone gunship would slot in behind this formation, riding shotgun and keeping all the troopers in view. Because of the weapon and the amount of ammunition on board, this helicopter was much heavier than the others and also the slowest. It was left to its pilot to call a power setting for the leader to use.

Progress once across the Okavango River and northwards into the vast and almost featureless Angolan landscape was sometimes very slow, especially when the choppers were still heavy with fuel. Returning to base half-empty, in contrast, was a breeze. In-between, we billeted at established Portuguese bases in the interior.

The weight problem was a consistent problem, as the ops were usually three weeks long and we had to take with us just about everything we might need. Another problem was the shortage – in some areas, the non-existence – of drinking water and most times we had to take our own. For weight reasons, this was usually limited to a five-gallon canister per crew member.

With the crew, their clothes and water for three weeks, as well as the 20mm cannon and up to 480 rounds of ammunition weight was a perennial problem. Maximum fuel to keep the gunship within limits was usually 600 pounds (60 percent) for ops. But due to the shortage of infrastructure in Angola, one needed at least that much for the heavy ferry flights too, so flying out of Rundu we were always overweight. The legs between refuelling points were each about 1½ hours flying, so it was the gunship that set the pace and from the rear.

Most of our ops in Angola were pre-planned between the Portuguese army officers and our SAAF Air Liaison Officer or ALO, usually a major who was based in Angola with the Portuguese at Cuito Cuanavale.

The usual scenario was to fly troops into specific areas, close, but not too close, to known guerrilla camps. If the choppers ventured too close and were heard approaching by the enemy the operation could be compromised, in which case the guerrilla camp would be found deserted. Or, the troops could disembark into an ambush. Most of our initial trooping consequently was not into heavily contested combat zones: that came with later Rhodesian ops and when the Angolan war escalated.

Nonetheless, occasional shots were fired at us and the odd bullet-hole punched into an Alouette, even in those early days.

I was only hit once and didn't know about it until after we'd touched down back at base, when a bullet-hole was discovered in the panel behind the fuel tank: nothing vital was struck. In fact, we hadn't even seen any guerrillas during that sortie!

One pilot, Geoff Clark, was shot in the thumb, but none of our Alouettes were downed by guerrilla fire in the early days.

However, we were required to operate in an environment of 'ever-present danger', with the gunship pulling ahead prior to the landing, to seek out a safe-looking landing zone or LZ. If an enemy presence was detected, it would be its job to flush them out.

Because weight was always a critical factor, wind direction was important, which meant that when the troopers were on a long approach, the gunship would drop a smoke grenade into the intended area, give the lead trooper his LZ and his wind and allow him to make the necessary adjustments.

Drops were usually done beyond the tree line, as the choppers were usually too heavy for hover landings. Open ground between the trees and the many rivers in south-east Angola, was usually suitable for getting five troopers into a landing. They were taken in reasonably close proximity to one another, largely to ensure that troops were not too spread out.

The technique for landing, especially when heavy and while dropping troops, was to use whatever help was available.

Smoke grenades were an accurate indication of the wind, but the actual landings needed to be well timed: each chopper took advantage of the previous chopper's down-wash, essentially to conserve fuel. As a chopper landed, its down-wash would sometimes become a bit of an up-wash and add impetus to the wind factor; if the chopper behind had its timing right, wind factor would be increased, and that made for an easier landing and used less fuel.

The guys with whom we were operating were solid professionals: pilots like Hobart Houghton, Johan Ströh, Glen Williams, Gary Barron and Fritz Pieksma. They would get their timing spot-on and an entire drop would go off so smoothly and quickly that the gunship needed a single circuit and in very little time there were 20 soldiers deposited safely onto firm ground – literally 30 seconds or so.

There were a few difficult moments, of course. Sometimes, on arrival over the LZ, one or two choppers would find that there were obstructions in the grass, like tree stumps or anthills. For the troops this would necessitate a deplaning in the hover.

Because speed was of the essence and there was often a chopper right behind you, also wanting to get airborne immediately, we practised for this. Our flight engineers – who doubled as our gunners- taught the troops to slide the side doors open on final approach. This was done by way of hand signals, essentially showing both thumbs in a repeated reverse movement. The next signal was similar, but with thumbs pointed outwards – in other words, 'get the hell out'.

The regular Portuguese soldier, a youthful conscript, and many of them still in their teens, were really all that stood between Lisbon winning or losing everything in Africa.

Prior to being sent out to serve their two-year terms of military service, which, in the remote African context could be pretty demanding and rigorous, the majority had hardly been aware that the 'Dark Continent' even existed. Never mind that their country dominated two very substantial chunks of it that, cumulatively, were dozens of times the size of their home country. Unlike Angola – and Mozambique with a coastline that stretched more than 3,000 kilometres up the East African littoral – Portuguese Guinea (Guiné-Bissau today) was small fry, but conditions there – in a terrain composed mainly of low-lying mangrove swamps and semi-habitable jungle – were among the harshest of all the postings. Also, the enemy, Amilcar Cabral's PAIGC, was way ahead the most determined.

It was clear to us that apart from the odd exception, these youngsters weren't interested in what was clearly a colonial conflict, with Lisbon seeking to dominate huge swathes of the African continent, as it had done for the past five centuries.

These fellows were certainly not looking for a fight and some were so inexperienced in bush craft that they could quite easily misread the map and trek away from the targeted guerrilla camp after being put down by the choppers, instead of towards it. That meant that pick-ups after the supposed firefight required dollops of patience and, often enough, extra fuel, so that the necessary search could be conducted to find the troops who were nowhere near the designated LZ where we were supposed to fetch them. Those were the boys from the *metrópole*, as it was customarily phrased: and meant, of course, the Metropolis, or Europe.

Troops from Angola itself, in contrast were very different. These soldiers, black and white, had a stake in the country for which they were fighting. They knew Africa and were aware that if they didn't counter subversion, they'd be out of it, very much like the South African troops who followed in their wake not long afterwards in South West Africa.

'Home grown' Angolan troops were usually either Commandos – sometimes *Comandos Africanos* – or Airborne and they meant business. We could immediately see that they were a pretty handy bunch of fighters who enjoyed getting into a scrap when the occasion arose. As with Portuguese chopper pilots with whom we operated, they simply relished their bits of combat, especially since they always had a gunship or two hovering nearby to add something to the outcome.

Also, their basic intelligence was invariably more reliable than the kind of information provided by regular Portuguese army officers with whom we came into contact. Like the conscripts under them, their only interest was in staying alive: if they could avoid confrontation with the guerrillas, they would take the gap.

Many of the contacts that resulted with the elite Portuguese units were sporadic.

Some would last only minutes, others perhaps half an hour. No matter how long, there were usually a number of dead or wounded enemy soldiers left on the ground after their compadres had fled. So, with the pick-up effected we'd head back to base with our satisfied 'customers', together with a variety of booty acquired by them, usually firearms.

This practice was almost always frowned upon by the Portuguese army officers back at base because it wasn't part of their 'plan'. But the ebullient Portuguese chopper pilots would be quite adept at calming things down and eventually singing everyone's praises for what happened during this 'sudden and unexpected' occurrence of 'discovering' a guerrilla camp 'somewhere out there in the bush'.

Our main base of operations in the Cuando Cubango region of Angola was the town of Cuito Cuanavale, not long afterwards to become a major staging post for FAPLA, the military wing of the Marxist MPLA. That came after the country had been handed over as a one-party state to the newly-formed Luanda government without elections or a referendum by the departing Portuguese.

The Portuguese Air Force fielded some great pilots, real characters who were brave and totally dedicated to their cause. One example was a fellow by the name of Vidal, who seemed to have the inordinate ability to find enemy camps in the kind of bush country that seemed to go on uninterrupted from one horizon to the other.

We were operating from Cangamba and when he got up from the breakfast table and moments later all but fell over. We knew he'd had a touch of malaria but weren't aware that it was quite so serious. The man could barely stand unaided. Still, this didn't deter him from heading out to the airstrip, getting into his Alouette and heading into the bush. The operation that day was a marked success, in large part due to Vidal's efforts at egging on his own pilots: there were dozens of guerrillas killed and lots of captures.

Vidal was a remarkable character, always ready for a scrap. Our Cessna had flown me in to Cangombe before an operation to assist in the planning, which was when we made contact for the first time. Some operations would last a week or two and then the Portuguese squadron from Luso, the Saltimbancos, would take over from us for another few weeks, or vice versa.

The Portuguese officers were busy with the operation when I popped in, but everything seemed to be pretty quiet. The day had turned into a proverbial 'Lemon'.

Meantime, Vidal and another pilot by the name of 'Jailbird' – he was called that by his colleagues because, with his head shaved clean, his mates thought he resembled an Alcatraz inmate – were convinced that the planners, all of them 'full time jam stealers' from Portugal, were not really interested in 'mixing' it with the enemy. It was actually not difficult to sense the reticence of these backroom boys: they were very much more were interested in getting back to the mess for the day and the grog.

Undeterred, Vidal offered to take me up in his Alouette gunship, for what he termed would be 'an armed recce'!

In a discreet briefing after the planning session, he said that he had a bit of surprise for me, because he'd had info about a large insurgent camp not far into the interior and he was eager that he and Jailbird hit it with their two gunships before dark. The troopers would follow afterwards. Initially, he said, there would be only the two of us, plus Jailbird and his gunner, who was part of the plan. Those flying the trooping choppers believed that they were heading out on a routine reconnaissance mission. As the Portuguese gunships always ranged far ahead of the troopers, Vidal felt confident that nothing would appear amiss.

Once in the air, Vidal suggested that I fly his gunship, while he took up a position behind the gun. At least, that is what he told his colonel. So we got airborne and were on our way to the DZ for the 'dead' drop, when Vidal steered me off to the left, away from the troopers. About 20 minutes later we arrived over the camp.

This was no ordinary insurgent base, I soon discovered. It was, from what I could see from where we were perched, actually a very large and well laid out army base under the trees. There were even some rather untypical benches – probably for 'lectures' which was a feature of all insurgent bases, only this facility suggested that there were an awful lot of 'students'. Once the target had been confirmed, the turkey shoot began.

We were much lower than the usual 800 feet (on Vidal's insistence) and yes, as he'd enthusiastically declared earlier, it was a lot easier to pick up and knock off targets from lower down! But that wasn't the problem: finding targets was, as very few, if any of the guerrillas, fired back and we couldn't clearly make out much of value on the ground from where we hovered. Still, it was a job that needed to be done.

One of the guerrillas, obviously a good deal braver than the rest, actually did shoot at us, but from the cover provided by one of the larger forest trees. So Vidal called in Jailbird, who took out the recalcitrant from the other side. Otherwise Jailbird did his own thing – there was more than enough room to do so, while Vidal and I went after a few other options including stragglers heading for thick bush.

The idea was that at some stage I would take my turn behind the gun, but by now Vidal seemed that he'd forgotten. Then I took the helicopters into a clearing and landed and he quickly got the message. But by then it was almost over: we were out of ammunition and the troopers had been called in to land the troops whose job it was to clean up the camp. A stack of documents and weapons were uncovered and loaded on board. They also took back several prisoners.

The operation that day was certainly far more successful than any of the other 'official' operations I witnessed while I spent time with the Portuguese. But, of course, I was not 'officially' involved and I'm certain that Vidal and Jailbird got a massive rocket for their enterprise from their commander.

Looking back, it was obvious that the entire effort was make-shift and the planning, consequently, poor. For the rest of the 10 days that our six Alouettes worked with the Portuguese, we plucked only lemons. Clearly, at the behest of Vidal and 'Jailbird', they'd got the message and moved further into the bush.

One of the fixed-winged aircraft fielded by the Portuguese Air Force in Angola and its other African military theatres was the Lockheed PV Ventura – known as the 'Pee-Vee' in Angola. It had a reputation of good power in reserve and versatility, which one might expect from the Americans, who gave the machines to Lisbon in the first place. But, said one of the Portuguese pilots, 'beware the high wing loading if you have an engine cut.'

We were at Cuito once, when a PV was doing engine run-ups prior to going on a bombing raid. Initially, whenever the throttle was opened up, the starboard engine kept backfiring. Then the technicians would shut it down, work on it some more and fire it up again.

This rigmarole was repeated several times and went on until the pilot arrived, resplendent in a magnificent blood-red silk scarf and flying overalls that were so well pressed that he might have been heading out for a night on the town.

A few more adjustments followed, now with him at the controls, and then the other PV started up as well. That meant that we all congregated at the edge of the runway for what was certain to be an occasion. We watched with great interest as the bomb-laden PVs rolled away for an uphill – into the wind – take-off.

The 'good' plane dutifully waited for the ailing 'aircraft' to go first, which it did, after a perfunctory final engine run-up before rolling. Then, to nobody's surprise, the first backfire sounded, just as the tail came up. There was a little wiggle at the far end of the runway, the plane went tail down again and finally its engines opened up with a roar! After three more backfires the pilot got airborne, followed soon afterwards by his wing man. Then, in echelon, they turned into the sun and headed for their raid. They were obviously aware that we were all watching.

Everything must have gone off as expected, because they were back at the base within an hour, gun-ports whistling.

The PVs carried an impressive array of weapons, not all of them standard. There might be a mixture of anything from .303 and .50 Browning to 7.62mm NATO and 12,7mm guns – all in the nose of the plane. Several times I did a count and found that there could be anything from six to a dozen guns per PV, depending on availability. These were taped before departure, but once used, would whistle gaily to herald the standard beat-up after a raid. When the pilot of this large, noisy airframe swaggered up to his audience afterwards, we asked him whether the thought or the possibility of an engine cut on take-off, uphill, with a sick, backfiring motor didn't worry him.

'Oh no!' he said in fractured English. 'Long runway and if I 'ave an 'undred knots, it is no problem!'

Appendix C

Offshore Operations In Portuguese Guinea

Extract, without maps, from Chapter 8 of the book *The Brown Waters of Africa* by Captain John Cann, US Navy (Rtd)

On 22 November 1970, the imprisoned Portuguese aviator António Lobato received his passport to freedom. In the early hours of the morning he became aware of sporadic gunfire nearing his prison, *La Montaigne* in Conakry, and thought initially that there was a coup d'état in progress against the autocratic president of the Republic of Guinea, Ahmed Sékou Touré. It soon became apparent that shots were being exchanged with the prison guards. After several resounding explosions and over the continued crackle of small arms fire, a voice suddenly shouted, "Lobato! It is us."[1]

The door of the cell swung open minutes later, and Portuguese troops guided him to freedom. By 0430 hours that morning he was delivered on board the Portuguese patrol boat LFG *Dragão* (P 374) in Conakry harbour.

He shifted to the task force flagship LFG *Orion* (P 362) shortly thereafter, and received a warm welcome from the operational commander, *Comandante* Alpoim Calvão. The task force got underway at 0900 on a northerly course and arrived the next afternoon at the island of Soga in the Bijagós Islets of Portuguese Guinea. Instead of sleeping that evening, Major Lobato partied all night in celebration of his first day of freedom in seven and a half years and his return to Portuguese soil.[2]

For Lobato and his twenty-five fellow prisoners, the strike on Conakry was an unqualified success. Unfortunately, not everyone was to agree.

Operation Nebulosa was conducted between 15 and 27 August 1969 and was intended to intercept and destroy the PAIGC boats and any other enemy craft and their crews in the waters of the Inxanche River, which marked the frontier with Guinea.

In preparation for this mission, Alpoim Calvão began to form an intelligence picture, and in doing so, sought the counsel of the PIDE/DGS representative in Bissau, Inspector Alberto Matos Rodrigues. The inspector was holding in detention an older sailor named Abou Camará, who had served on PAIGC vessels, including the *Patrice Lumumba*, of which we shall hear more in a minute.[3]

Following some encouragement and an offer of amnesty, the prisoner became cooperative and decided to collaborate completely. He revealed several helpful facts about PAIGC operations:

- PAIGC transit of the Inxanche was always conducted at high tide. This was done to avoid grounding vessels and leaving them stranded and vulnerable to discovery and destruction by the Portuguese.

- All of the boats in Kadigné worked for the PAIGC, so any boat exiting from the village would be an enemy one.
- All of the transiting enemy boats needed to use and violate Portuguese territorial waters for their work and would thus be fair game.[4]
- Given these facts, Alpoim Calvão developed the following concept of operations. He would:
- Lay an ambush using *fuzileiros* in rubber boats hidden along the Portuguese shore.
- Make the assault when the targeted enemy boat had clearly entered Portuguese territory and was fully committed to infiltrating Guinea, for if it were sunk during the operation, then its status could not be contested.
- Reduce the number of men employed on a mission to the absolute minimum required to overcome a vessel. This minimalist approach was designed to preserve operational security and to maintain as low a profile as possible so as not to alert enemy intelligence.
- Arrange communications support to overcome the poor signal propagation and thus command and control problems along the rivers in Guinea. This would be done through radio relay by an orbiting air force aircraft at an altitude high enough to avoid daylight visual detection. A second aircraft would remain on ground alert as a backup.

In the first days of August, the LFG *Sagitário* (P 1131), whose commanding officer would act as the overall commander of *Nebulosa*, conducted a night reconnaissance of the anticipated area of operations.[5]

He took *Sagitário* to the vicinity and launched a rubber boat from it to explore the Inxanche riverbank. The small force made good use of the darkness, low tide, and frequent rain showers as cover for its successful and undetected reconnaissance. The conclusion was that the small mangrove island of Calebe was the ideal ambush site. This is one of those islands created from a seedling mangrove that at some point floated into a shallow, where it took root and began growing.

In a year a mangrove can grow to a meter in height. In three years it will have produced prop roots, and in five a small mangrove island will be established, assuming no natural disasters. The prop roots produce an intricately woven and formidable web that continuously expands and becomes home to a plethora of crabs, snails, barnacles, mussels, and oysters. It is also the roosting and nesting site for heron, egrets, pelicans, and other waterfowl. It was within the shelter of this densely populated ecosystem that the *fuzileiros* would hide.

Nebulosa began on the morning of 15 August 1969 with the launching of a task group composed of the *Sagitário,* commanded by Lieutenant (*capitão tenente*) Camacho de Campos, and an assault force composed of the junior lieutenant (*segundo tenente*) Alberto Rebordão de Brito, two sergeants, and 10 *fuzileiros*, all led by Alpoim Calvão.[6] The force embarked on *Sagitário* and waited in secretive isolation at the island of João Vieira among the offshore Bijagós Islets for opportune sea conditions. On 20 August the *Sagitário* moved to the Samba buoy and attempted to disembark four rubber boats, but the sea was running at 1.5 to 2.0 meters and frustrated the attempts.

The LFG consequently returned to João Vieira to repair some damage suffered, give the crew a rest from the bad weather, and wait patiently for an opening.[7]

Finally, on 24 August at 2300 the mission began again with a return to the Samba buoy and the launching of the four rubber boats. These were guided by the LFG radar for the three miles to the mouth of the Inxanche on a flood tide, and with their motors running in "quiet," continued by compass bearing and avoided the areas where it was impossible to navigate in the darkness without grounding. The small force reached its destination of Calebe by 0300 on 25 August completely undetected.[8]

When the boats reached the island, which was covered with thick foliage and a confusing entanglement of mangrove trees and their tough prop roots, the *fuzileiros* used a saw and machete to cut an opening through them and gain access to a narrow canal that would be their home for more than 54 hours. After backing the boats into the canal with their bows out, the entrance was camouflaged and closed with mangrove branches. The canal was so shallow that at low tide the boats could be completely grounded, particularly if the sea height was below normal. This was not anticipated to be a problem, as intelligence indicated the large PAIGC vessels came into the river only at high tide.

As time passed, the strong rain showers peculiar to the area resolved the drinking water problem and served to cover the noise of the outboard motors, all of which were tested routinely. During the rain the motors had to be covered, as the high humidity tended to make them unreliable.

After the rain came the mosquitoes.[9] During the waiting period the *fuzileiros* observed an intense amount of canoe traffic between the two sides of the river, principally at night. Indeed, the ambush cover was often brushed by these transiting craft, and their occupants felt wholly at home and chatted freely, oblivious to any danger. During the long and boring wait on 26 August, the *fuzileiros* heard a motor boat from Kadigné pass very close in the dark but were not permitted to assault it amid great disappointment and much cursing.[10]

On 27 August towards 0930 as the sea was beginning to ebb, the *fuzileiros* heard the muffled noise of a motor to the left of their position. All prepared for action, and as soon as the vessel was identified as being manned by the PAIGC and being in Portuguese territorial waters, the motors on the rubber boats were started for an attempted ambush.

The interception began with a stern chase, as the long immobilization of the motors caused some to operate unevenly. Alpoim Calvão's boat took the lead and pulled even with the target, a vessel that sailed without a flag or other identification. When the *fuzileiros* signalled for it to stop, it increased speed and veered toward the entrance canal to Kadigné. Alpoim Calvão's boat accelerated and drew to within five meters of the target, at which point he called in French and ordered it to stop. The response was some light arms fire, which was returned with a fusillade from the *fuzileiros*.[11]

Alpoim Calvão's boat closed the gap, and the sailor Tristão flung himself at the vessel, scrambled aboard, and entered the lower deck, followed by his translator Abou Camará.[12] Meanwhile Alpoim Calvão boarded the upper deck and engaged in some hand-to-hand combat that was rapidly concluded with the arrival of the other three boats and their *fuzileiros*. In the midst of the fray, a canister of tear gas was loosed, the helmsman of the vessel became incapacitated, and it went out of control. With its throttle wide open, it ran aground in the heavy growth lining the south bank of the river, and three or four men were tossed into the water. Petty Officer (*sargento*) André gained control of the helm, and Petty Officer (*cabo*) Abrantes Pinto, an experienced motorman mechanic, had no trouble with the engine. Between these two they refloated the vessel and set a course for the mouth of the Inxanche, all the while weeping from the effects of the gas.[13]

The vessel was identified as the *Patrice Lumumba* and carried 24 persons, who were made prisoners. It was also carrying several tons of provisions and a supply of weapons, mainly light arms. Among the passengers were three PAIGC officials, one of whom was section secretary for Kafarande. Unfortunately, he had been killed in the skirmish.

The vessel proceeded with *fuzileiro* escort to a rendezvous with *Sagitário*, which attempted to take it in tow for a return to Bissau. Things did not go well, and despite the best efforts of the crew, the *Patrice Lumumba* was too damaged from its collision with the formidable mangroves and the exchange of fire to continue afloat. It sank in 12 meters of water while being towed across the mouth of the Cacine River.

It was some months before another such operation was mounted, as the PAIGC initially seemed to take a more cautious profile on the Inxanche following the loss of the *Patrice Lumumba*. Nevertheless, the insurgents soon recovered and moved again into the security vacuum left with the completion of *Nebulosa* and the lack of any continuous naval presence on the Inxanche to challenge them. The navy was to return on 6 March 1970, some seven months later with Operation *Gata Brava* (Wildcat).

In the meantime, enemy logistic operations expanded dangerously with adverse consequences for Spínola's "A Better Guinea."

In the first days of February 1970, Spínola's staff received information that a PAIGC launch, possibly the *Bandim*, would be bringing an enemy element from Boké to Kadigné on or about the 25th of the month. Alpoim Calvão was given responsibility for planning an interception of the vessel and the capture of its personnel. Accordingly, he established an ambush with a team of eight *fuzileiros* in two rubber boats at the entrance of the canal leading to Kadigné over the evening of the 24th and the dawn of the 25th.

Unfortunately, the target did not arrive, and a thick fog developed that would have frustrated any action. Alpoim Calvão returned to other duties and was conducting operations on the Cacheu River near the northern border with Senegal, when new information indicated that the target had been delayed and would now arrive on 7 March.

Alpoim Calvão had to move quickly to re-establish the operation. He met a handpicked and specially briefed team of *fuzileiros* at Bigene, an unimproved airfield 40 miles north of Bissau, on the 5th at 1500, and within four hours all had returned to Bissau, were on board the LFG *Lira* (P 361), and underway. *Lira* arrived at its station next to the Samba buoy on the 6th in the early hours of the morning. Two rubber boats were put into the water, and eight *fuzileiros* embarked. The first boat (Nº 1) was commanded by Alpoim Calvão, and the second (Nº 2) by the junior lieutenant (*segundo tenente*) Barbieri, and both departed *Lira* at 0300 for the mouth of the Inxanche. They were guided by its radar until contact was lost at a range of about 3,500 meters.

After that, they followed the same route as in *Nebulosa* and proceeded slowly with the motors muffled to avoid detection. Guided only by compass and helped by a flood tide, the force found Calebe once more and backed the boats into the mangrove opening that had been made in August and that had remained undetected by the enemy. Indeed, there remained two sacks of combat rations left behind from *Nebulosa*.

By 0800 the sea began to ebb, and at 0810 the *fuzileiros* contacted one of the two Aeritalia/Fiat G-91 *Gina* aircraft that were making a visual reconnaissance of the area and were informed that the *Bandim* was not in Kadigné. Alpoim Calvão resolved to wait until nightfall, and within two hours the tide had receded to the point that the two boats were grounded and immobilized. By 1600 the tide began to flood, to penetrate the channel, and to lift the boats, and by 1730 they were completely afloat.

Towards 1800, as twilight came, the boats eased to the opening to be ready for action. After an hour, voices and the splash of paddles guiding a canoe were heard nearby.

Minutes later at 1910, engine noise was heard coming from an upstream bearing of 070 degrees magnetic and increasing in intensity. Within twenty minutes, the unmistakable silhouette of the motor launch *Bandim* emerged from the dusk with only a dim, shielded wheelhouse light readily visible. Alpoim Calvão ordered the motors started and the boats readied to spring the ambush. When they rushed from their hiding place, boat Nº 1 took station astern of the target, and boat Nº 2, a position on its starboard amidships. Boat Nº 1 immediately fired a bazooka at about 150 meters range, but it hit short of the target in the anxiety of the moment.[14]

Meanwhile, the *fuzileiros* opened fire with their MG-42 machinegun. The *Bandim* responded with light automatic weapons fire and turned sharply for the sanctuary on the Guinea side of the river. The boats manoeuvred rapidly to maintain their attack positions, and on the third try the bazooka rocket made solid contact with the *Bandim*.[15]

The *fuzileiros* found themselves in the midst of a trigger-happy enemy. From a position east of the town of Kadigné, there was a near-constant fire from six antiaircraft batteries in the direction of the contact, but the aim was quite high. There were also about 20 rounds of either artillery or heavy mortar fire from the same area ranging either short or long and revealing considerable confusion in the enemy camp. Also from a PAIGC position on the Portuguese island of Canefaque a heavy machinegun fired wildly at the *fuzileiros*, and its tracers lit the water. A PPSh-41 machinegun was fired over the boats from the earlier identified canoe as it fled the battle scene.[16]

The vicious running firefight with the *Bandim* continued with another Bazooka hit that disabled its steering and reduced it to circling. It ultimately entered a narrow estuary opposite Calebe, disappeared from view, and ran hard aground. The *fuzileiros* pursued the *Bandim* into the firth, delivered another *Bazooka* hit, and when within 10 meters, unloosed a barrage of hand grenades. Enemy automatic weapons fire erupted from the mangroves and was returned with a blast of MG-42 fire by the *fuzileiros* who were approaching the target.[17]

On boarding the *Bandim*, the *fuzileiros* discovered six enemy dead. Of these, one was at the entrance to the engine room and another in the pilot house amid the destroyed engine telegraph. The *fuzileiros* attempted to refloat the vessel, but the engine could not be reversed. The gear lever was blocked with debris from the damage, and a broken fuel line gushed gasoline everywhere. The engine was then stopped, and the *fuzileiros* considered the idea of towing the prize back to the *Lira*. Theoretically, a line could be attached to the *Bandim* with the two rubber boats acting as tugs.

Unfortunately, events conspired against such a plan, as the tide would turn shortly at 2030 and leave the vessel hard aground before the *fuzileiros* could act.

Facing mounting obstacles to the preservation option, Alpoim Calvão decided to destroy the *Bandim*. Accordingly gasoline was liberally spread throughout the vessel and lit as the *fuzileiros* departed. It began burningly slowly, and it was only when the *fuzileiros* had reached the centre of the river that a muffled explosion was heard, and flames began to reach high into the night. When the *fuzileiros* reached the appointed rendezvous point for *Lira* at 2200, the burning *Bandim* remained clearly visible.

Disconcertingly, the *Lira* was nowhere to be found. The *fuzileiros* attempted radio contact for two hours without success and finally located the *Lira* anchored 12 miles southwest of the rendezvous with a broken engine. It was not until 0100 the next morning that recovery was made.[18] The destruction of the *Bandim* and the death of its six crewmen threw the enemy into confusion, as judged by its intercepted and deciphered radio traffic.

In the space of six months, two key PAIGC motor vessels had been destroyed, and its logistical capability on the frontier dealt a substantial blow. The reduced PAIGC ability to supply its operations in Guinea would perforce reduce its military activity. These missions had exposed a glaring PAIGC vulnerability. Its logistical sea lines of communication from Conakry to the frontier were open to aggressive interdiction, as traffic was not protected en route by either armed escort or air cover and simply relied on international law and crewmen with small arms to defend it.

This method was based on a naïve premise for parties at war and merited further examination. If interdiction operations had been successful in the frontier zone, might they not be extended to Conakry proper, as a raid there had the potential of destroying the entire PAIGC fleet. The *fuzileiros* had proven themselves capable of conducting local strikes successfully, and thus with some imaginative and thorough planning, a long-range strike on Conakry was a realistic possibility.

Following *Nebulosa*, Alpoim Calvão had conceived the idea of neutralizing the PAIGC sea operations by sinking its key vessels in Conakry harbour with limpet mines. If the *fuzileiros* were going to go to Conakry, then perhaps rescuing Lobato in the same stroke was also possible. The aviator's freedom had over the years become a personal commitment of Alpoim Calvão.

In principle Spínola approved the bold proposal, although it remained largely in the conceptual stage, as the details had yet to be resolved. Alpoim Calvão next sought the advice of Reboredo. He was in concert with the proposed plan and agreed to support it logistically. In this vein, he authorized Alpoim Calvão to undertake an exploratory trip to the Republic of South Africa in the first days of September 1969 to review the latest demolition techniques.[19] Here, he was given a number of limpet mines and instructed in their use, returning to Portugal on a TAP commercial flight from Jan Smuts Airport with two 30-kilo handbags full of explosives.[20] This trip, however, occurred over a year before the envisioned operation, and much preparation lay ahead.

The concept of the mission, which came to be codenamed *Mar Verde* (Green Sea), was to send a raiding party from Guinea by sea to Conakry under cover of darkness and to undertake such operations there that would shatter both the ability of the PAIGC to continue its assault on Guinea and the ability of Sékou Touré to support the PAIGC.

Its primary objectives were to free Lobato and twenty-five other prisoners, destroy the fast patrol boats of the PAIGC and Republic of Guinea in the port, and disable the six to eight Guinean MiG-15 and MiG-17 jet fighter aircraft at the airport. Secondary objectives would be addressed as opportunity allowed. Destruction of the fast patrol boats and the aircraft was necessary primarily as a defensive measure, because the Portuguese task force would be vulnerable returning to Guinea in daylight on the open ocean.

The Portuguese vessels were considerably slower than the enemy boats, were more lightly armed, and lacked effective anti-air defences against hostile aircraft. Portuguese air cover from its primary base of Bissau in Guinea did not extend to Conakry, and thus the returning vessels could not be protected during their exposed daylight leg. Consequently, to pre-empt enemy pursuit and a sure disaster, its offensive capability must be neutralized in the port and at the airfield of Conakry.

The entire operation relied on the shock of complete initial surprise to enable the relatively small and unprotected Portuguese force to gain the immediate initiative and realize these three vital objectives.

As planning proceeded, the scope of the raid increased. It was decided that as a plausible cover the mission would include some 147 ex-Guinean soldiers who would stage a coup and replace Sékou Touré. These men were recruited largely from the National Front for the Liberation of Guinea (*Front National de Libération de la Guinée* or FNLG), which was the external organization seeking to overthrow the Guinean dictator through insurgent activity.

Up to this time it had not been a success largely because of the tight security in Sékou Touré's repressive police state and his paranoid murdering of opponents and advocates alike.[21]

Most of these recruits were veterans of the old French colonial army and were gathered from Senegal, The Gambia, Sierra Leone, and Ivory Coast. They were to be trained and supported by the Portuguese troops, and once ashore in Conakry, aided in their objectives until the Portuguese withdrew. The key in this process was the capture of Sékou Touré and his neutralization, so that the coup could be successful. Hand in glove with Sékou Touré's seizure was that of Amílcar Cabral. Cabral would be forcefully returned to Guinea and incarcerated there, while Sékou Touré would be delivered to the ex-Guinean soldiers. If either resisted, they were to be shot.

The capture of both of these individuals would effectively disrupt PAIGC war fighting capabilities in Guinea and remove considerable pressure from the Portuguese war effort there. So in the words of Alpoim Calvão:

"The concept was not bad, but it was dangerous. Especially because the international community would not forgive us when it learned that we were behind an offensive intended to topple the regime by force of arms. On the other hand, the surprise attack that we proposed was not compatible with the guerrilla operation that FNLG pursued – inevitably prolonged. And it was a choice between two concepts – ours and theirs – which reinforced the idea, to be precise, of inventing a coup d'état in the Republic of Guinea as cover for the real strike that we envisioned."[22]

The Portuguese intelligence picture on the Republic of Guinea was inexact at best. Most tactical information was developed by monitoring PAIGC radio transmissions, and as the Portuguese had broken the PAIGC codes, all signals traffic was readily accessible.

While this information was helpful, a more precise and tailored picture needed to be developed. Indeed, there was not even a map of the port of Conakry available to the planners. Discrete inquires were initiated with the national and foreign merchant ships that called at Bissau, and eventually an out-of-date chart was located. In order to revise it, Alpoim Calvão received permission from Spínola to conduct a reconnaissance mission in Conakry and consequently proceeded to the strategically propitious and isolated island of João Vieira in the LFG *Cassiopeia* (P 373) to plan the mission under the appropriate security conditions. There the launch was disguised as a PAIGC vessel, complete with an enemy flag flying and African elements of the crew visible topside, and continued to Conakry, arriving in the first hour of 17 September without arousing suspicion.

This was considered remarkable, as the ship had encountered a number of Guinean fishermen during the daylight leg of the voyage, and all waved in greeting.[23] Indeed, Petty Officer (*cabo fuzileiro*) António Augusto da Silva-Touré, posing as a Guinean and wearing the kepi of a major, returned each greeting with an impeccable salute.[24]

Conditions were such that the lights of the city were clearly visible, and the ship manoeuvred in a large turn, reconnoitring the port in an approach from the south and entering the channel between the Islands of Los and the Conakry peninsula at two in the morning. The patrol boat reduced speed, and the radar made a detailed scan of the harbour to record the modifications to the port that were not reflected on the chart. These were primarily new cargo piers.

By three in the morning the work was completed, and as the patrol boat was exiting the channel, its generators failed. The anchor was dropped, and repairs made under nerve-wracking conditions.

On returning to Soga, intelligence work continued. The chart was revised, and details of the city completed as information was gathered. A model of the port area was constructed with reasonable exactness; however, other unknowns were legion. The national intelligence service had distressingly little information on the Republic of Guinea. The Ministry of Foreign Affairs did not permit national intelligence service representatives at embassies, so there was no opportunity to fill the void from this traditional source.

There was some political and some strategic intelligence available, but there was virtually nothing at the operational or tactical level.

Alpoim Calvão consequently established an *ad hoc* intelligence organization devoted to the mission and to the collection of every piece of information, including open sources in books, tourist brochures, and testimony from former PAIGC elements and exiled Guineans. Most data was over two years old and thus quite stale and inaccurate. In early October 1970, a most important break occurred when a former Portuguese cabin boy and deserter escaped from Conakry, crossed the border, and surrendered to the authorities. In exchange for his cooperation, he was spared punishment. Not only was his help invaluable in completing the intelligence gaps, but he was also to return to Conakry and lead the raiding party to the prisoners. This timely and valuable development enabled Alpoim Calvão to complete his intelligence on the city, which proved to be 95 percent accurate during the operation.[25]

The complexity of the *Mar Verde* is reflected in its planning. Originally Alpoim Calvão identified 52 objectives on his map of Conakry; however, this number was reduced to a more manageable 25, as the raid would be over a weekend when many public services were shut. In turn each of these objectives required certain specific equipment, armament, and training for a reasonable assurance of success. The sequencing of operations was matched with the required support and a complicated plan evolved.

Still there were many unresolved operational questions. For instance, the airfield was some 45 minutes march from the harbor. If the troops had to fight their way to the field, then destruction of the MiGs would be a difficult assignment, if not an impossible one. Failure to destroy the aircraft would obviously hazard the successful withdrawal of the force.

There were also political questions that may have gone unanswered. A review of the modified target list indicated that about half were critical civil infrastructure and not important military objectives. If indeed Portugal seriously intended to topple Sékou Touré and install a new government, then destroying key infrastructure would certainly generate unwanted problems for the incoming leaders. A city without electricity and an inconvenienced population, for instance, would hardly be an auspicious introduction.

Further, the international community, whose condemnation was so feared, would understand a surgical strike to rescue prisoners and destroy military capability far more easily than any vindictive or wanton havoc.

The task force to transport the troops by sea consisted of the LFGs *Orion* (P 362), *Cassiopeia* (P 373), *Dragão* (P 374), and *Hidra* (P 376), and the LDGs *Bombarda* and *Montante*. The maximum speed of the force was 17 knots, so the unknowns of sea state, wind, and tide could change the speed of advance and thus the length of the voyage. Surprise could thus be jeopardized by these simple natural forces and any mistiming caused by them.

The weekend of 22 November proved ideal, given the moon phase, predicted tide height, anticipated seasonal winds, and other local conditions. These circumstances would not again be propitious for some months.

For deceptive cover, radio traffic would be conducted in French, and the ships would disperse to appear as fishing vessels during a portion of their approach. The raiding force would be composed of approximately 400 men drawn from:

- DFE 21
- A Company of African Commandos
- Elements of FNLG
- Various personnel from *fuzileiro* units specifically chosen for this operation.

Certain FNLG troops would be integrated with the Portuguese as guides, for they knew the target city of Conakry well. The troops would be inserted ashore from the six vessels by rubber boats and wear a specially manufactured olive drab battle dress for mutual identification as well as subterfuge. It was distinctive from both the traditional Portuguese battle dress and the Republic of Guinea uniforms and bore a light green arm band in sympathy with the predominantly Muslim population.

For the purpose of deception, Soviet bloc weapons would be used rather than Western arms, and these had been purchased quietly on the international arms market.

Operational security for the mission was paramount and presented certain difficulties. In order to maintain the required low profile, the remote island of Soga was chosen for training the force and launching the raid. By early November there were almost two hundred men on Soga comprised largely of FNLG elements and their instructors. These men required considerable training and fieldwork to become a credible fighting unit.

Adding to this obstacle was the need to keep the ex-Guineans politically organized and comforted, as tribal rivalries among them were a continuing problem. The other troops scheduled to participate would not be brought to Soga until the final days and would not know of the mission or their assignments until then. This process was dictated by a number of factors. First, the troops could not be relieved from their current duties for a long run-up to *Mar Verde*, as Portugal had few men to spare.

Second, many of the African *fuzileiros* and commandos had relatives who were fighting for the PAIGC, and leaks through familial channels would jeopardize operational security. Their fears of reprisal would also work against troop preparation. So to reduce these risks to manageable levels, Alpoim Calvão made the conscious decision to rely on their known fighting capabilities rather than specific mission training. His intent was to minimize their pre-operation exposure and thus opportunity for compromise through outside contact.

At the beginning of November, when the concentration of forces began on Soga, a diversionary operation commenced on the island of Como. Four days prior to *Mar Verde*, the detachment of African *fuzileiros* and the company of African commandos were brought to the staging point along with some European elements of *fuzileiros*, who added leadership strength and experience to the operation. Between this time and their departure on the evening of 20 November, the troops would become familiar with the tactical plan and operational procedures necessary for the mission.

The force, designated Task Group 27.2 (TG 27.2), was generally divided into a northern, central, and southern approach, as shown in Map 8.2. The *Cassiopeia*, *Dragão*, and *Montante* would execute the northern approach from the point of dispersion and land their forces north of the city on the mainland, which is separated from Conakry by an isthmus. *Orion* would proceed on a central approach directly to the city, and *Hidra* and *Bombarda* would approach from the south, *Bombarda* landing its forces in the southern part of the city (Conakry I), and *Hidra*, on the mainland next to the airport (Conakry II).[26]

Cassiopeia and *Dragão* together carried DFE 21, which was comprised of African *fuzileiros* and divided into 12 squads of six men each. It was further organized into four assault groups. Group one had two of the 12 squads; group two, three squads; and groups three and four, the remaining seven squads. The four groups together were known as Team Zulu and were led by the junior lieutenant Raul Eugénio Dias da Cunha e Silva. Each team was designated with a letter from the NATO phonetic alphabet and given a specific assignment, as shown in Table 8.1.

Montante carried the principals of FLNG and the Company of African Commandos, a 150-man unit commanded by Captain João Bacar. These troops were divided into Teams India, Mike and Oscar.

Orion carried Team Victor, which was composed of 14 *fuzileiros* commanded by the now promoted Lieutenant (*capitão tenente*) Rebordão de Brito, whose route is depicted in Map 8.3. *Bombarda* carried almost 200 men of FLNG divided into Teams Alfa, Bravo, Charlie, Delta, Echo, Foxtrot, Golf, and Hotel, and Team Papa composed of African Commandos. Lastly *Hidra* carried Team Sierra composed of 44 African Commandos and led by Captain of Paratroops (*capitão pára-quedista*) Lopes Morais.

Each team was assigned a specific set of objectives in Conakry and began to familiarize itself with the special drills and equipment that would be required for its portion of the mission. The mission and thus the task force would be organized by vessel with each carrying one or more teams with specific assignments.

On 14 November, Alpoim Calvão flew to Lisbon with a draft plan of the operation to present to Dr. Marcello Caetano, the prime minister, on Spínola's behalf. This formal request for approval of *Mar Verde* from the highest levels of government was necessary because of the political sensitivity of the operation and the possible fallout from its execution.

Caetano received Alpoim Calvão on 17 November and immediately granted permission to proceed with the caveat that no Portuguese fingerprints must be left on the operation in Conakry, a naïve condition.[27] Alpoim Calvão recalls Caetano opining that the coup attempt was problematical but if the prisoners were recovered, then the mission would be a success.[28] Alpoim Calvão returned to Guinea on the 19th and that same day continued to the island of Soga to begin final preparations for the operation.

With approximately 400 men projected to be ashore in Conakry within the week, it was going to be difficult, if not impossible, to hide Portuguese complicity.

In light of the potential for diplomatic fallout, the scope of *Mar Verde* should have perhaps been reduced. Within the 25 objectives, as noted earlier, was the destruction of a great amount of Guinean infrastructure that was not critical to mission success. Also, if Sékou Touré, the head of state of a neighbouring country, were killed or overthrown and imprisoned, the diplomatic repercussions for Portugal would be substantial. Further, if Amílcar Cabral, one of the most respected and prestigious leaders of any of the African liberation movements, were captured and imprisoned in Lisbon or Bissau, it would likewise prove troublesome for the Portuguese.

There was also no hard intelligence on the whereabouts of either Sékou Touré or Cabral, a fact that made success problematical. Their anticipated movements were only assumed. Too much was left to luck in this area for a successful kidnapping or assassination to occur. Even Caetano felt that a favourable coup was an unrealistic expectation.

Despite the despotic and murderous nature of his regime and the opposition that it generated, Sékou Touré was well guarded and had his secret police routinely identify and dispatch any hint of opposition within Guinea. The intelligence on the necessary internal opposition to support a coup was missing. A successful coup would have to overcome the difficult obstacles of decapitating Sékou Touré, neutralizing the entire leadership, and successfully installing a new leader. Such a process requires thorough planning, steadfast commitment to its execution, and subsequent extended support of the new government. Alpoim Calvão could not linger in Conakry without jeopardizing his small force and with such modest strength could not ensure that these actions would be completed. Certainly he would show the Portuguese hand, something to be avoided. All of these weaknesses were clear, and yet the mission was encumbered with this project in the hope that a risky political solution would solve the military problems of Guinea.

Local control of the operation rested with Alpoim Calvão, who was rightfully optimistic, ambitious, and confident. *Fuzileiros* are not picked to be otherwise, or their difficult missions would never be successful. Caetano put its success in the hands of Spínola, who had supreme confidence in Alpoim Calvão.

Caetano, who was responsible ultimately for fielding the diplomatic consequences, was seemingly unaware of the possible international repercussions, and even today his assuming such risk is difficult to understand. The geopolitical implications were potentially wide-ranging, given the problems that Portugal was experiencing in international forums justifying its 'colonial wars.'

While Spínola must ultimately answer to Caetano, he indeed had a local problem and was seeking a solution within the context of his duties as Commander-in-Chief and Governor-General of Guinea. The fact that both he and Alpoim Calvão were aggressive, brave, no-nonsense leaders probably fed upon each other's propensity to take the initiative with a daring move, particularly following a period of military ambivalence under the previous commander. *Mar Verde* was just such an answer. Regardless of certain obvious weaknesses, boldness and surprise in an operation by skilled troops would overcome many of these obstacles. Certainly it would overcome enough of them to attain the primary goals of rescuing the prisoners and neutralizing the enemy sea and air capability.

Preliminary to the operation, a P2V-5 *Neptune* patrol aircraft made a reconnaissance sortie on 18 November and confirmed that the warships remained in Conakry and that the sea was calm. Under this favourable omen, the force of six assault vessels loaded with troops departed Soga at 1950 hours on 20 November 1970 bound for Conakry. It rendezvoused near the island of Canhambaque at 2200 and continued south until 2020 the next evening, when the force split to enter Conakry harbour, and each vessel assumed its predetermined station.[29]

Shortly after midnight on 22 November all vessels were in position, and only the lights of the city illuminated the night. The first objective was the fast patrol boats. These were to be destroyed by Team Victor from *Orion* positioned northwest of the breakwater protecting the port of Conakry. At high tide on a calm and windless sea Rebordão de Brito and 14 of his fellow *fuzileiros* were launched and discretely made for the breakwater *Dique Norte*. From here, the *fuzileiros* identified their objective and moved to attack.

Arriving at the naval pier, Abou Camará silently eliminated the sentry and was followed by his fellow *fuzileiros* and a guide in three rubber boats. The *fuzileiros* eliminated the crew on each enemy boat and placed the charges, and in a great blast and subsequent eruption of fire, seven fast patrol boats and a landing craft were destroyed. Portuguese control of the sea was secured by 0215, and the team returned to *Orion* with two lightly wounded and no loss of matériel.

Team Zulu, assigned to rescue the prisoners, neutralize PAIGC headquarters, and capture Sékou Touré, was launched from *Dragão* and *Cassiopeia* anchored in five meters of water in a small bay to the north of the Conakry peninsula next to the shoals of *La Prudente* and three miles from its landing site. The rubber boats, 10 in number, left the two ships and experienced some difficulty.

They were slightly late in landing, as the propellers on some of their outboard motors had become fouled by local fishing nets. The element led by Cunha e Silva went immediately to *La Montaigne*, a two story building surrounded by a wall about three meters high. The prison guards began firing light weapons about 0215, causing one soldier to be gravely wounded. Fire was returned with a bazooka to the upper floor, which began to burn furiously.

The momentum of the exchange shifted to the attackers, and this allowed them to move forward, breach the wall with another bazooka round, and enter the prison compound. As the team moved through the building freeing the 26 prisoners, eight enemy bodies were discovered on the upper floor with an assortment of Soviet bloc weapons.[30] The element led by the junior lieutenant (junior grade) (*segundo tenente*) José Carlos Freire Falcão Lucas, headed for PAIGC headquarters and on arriving neutralized a series of sentries, destroyed five party buildings and six vehicles, and eliminated various hostile personnel.

The final element, led by the junior lieutenant (*segundo tenente*) Benjamin Lopes de Abreu, attacked Villa Silly, the residence of Sékou Touré. His force of 22 men forced entry into the militia camp and overcame the 60 residence guards. The dictator was not to be found.[31] With the conclusion of their various missions, the elements of Team Zulu returned to the *Dragão* and *Cassiopeia* at about 0400 and acted as a reserve force for the remainder of the operation.

Lopes Morais, with his group of 40 Portuguese and five FNLG troops, came ashore at 0130 after some navigation difficulty and began his march to the airport. During this march, he became separated from the junior lieutenant (*segundo tenente*) Januário Lopes and 20 of his men. Januário Lopes, as it turned out, in an act of betrayal hid and surrendered himself and his 20 men to the Guinean authorities the next day.[32] By 0215, Lopes Morais and his remaining force had breached the perimeter fencing and discovered that there were no MiGs at the field, only six commercial aircraft, two Sud-Est Aviation SE-210 *Caravelles* belonging to Air Afrique and four Fokker F-27 *Friendships*.[33]

Apparently, there had been a ministerial reorganization, and the MiGs had been moved. The runway was blocked as both a defensive measure and a compromise solution, although Lobato later commented that the MiGs only flew very high, manoeuvred cautiously, and were mostly for show.[34] The air threat was thus minimal in light of the Guinean aviators' elementary flying skills and the obstacle of the blocked runway.

With the freeing of the prisoners and control of the sea and air established, Alpoim Calvão turned his attention to the coup and the PAIGC leadership. Sékou Touré was not to be found anywhere. He was not in his villa and not in the presidential palace. Cabral was not at home either. Later it was discovered that Sékou Touré had been with his mistress and had remained hidden in her home, while Cabral was out of the country visiting Bulgaria, both intelligence shortcomings. Nevertheless, 400 political prisoners were released, the Guinean Minister of Defence was captured and delivered to the FNLG force, and Sékou Touré's Republican Guard alone suffered over 200 casualties.

The population turned to "jello" in Alpoim Calvão's words and watched passively as his force ranged throughout Conakry destroying military vehicles and certain PAIGC and civil buildings, perhaps too much so.[35]

The coup was clearly in jeopardy with Sékou Touré still in hiding and the people unwilling to be galvanized into action. Despite a plan to seize the radio station and make other coordinated efforts, the FNLG plotters seemed irresolute and confounded by the total apathy of the citizenry.[36] Sixty of them remained after Calvão and the task force had departed and eventually surrendered to the authorities only to be executed. For three months afterward Sékou Touré engaged in a witch hunt. Throughout Guinea there were more than a hundred public executions, and scores of other suspects were permanently incarcerated.[37]

Having achieved the primary objectives, Alpoim Calvão decided to terminate the operation and recovered his forces on board the vessels by 0900. One of the weaknesses encountered during the raid was the realization that a large portion of the Portuguese African troops were familiar only with fighting in the bush and jungle and, because they had never been in a city the size of Conakry, had difficulty finding their way around it.

To compensate for this predicament in the closing hour of the raid, Alpoim Calvão commandeered a taxi on the waterfront and travelled around the city to make certain that none of his men were left behind.[38]

His losses were three dead and nine wounded. Conversely, Sékou Touré had lost over 500 troops and many civilians, and presided over a partially destroyed and disorganized city.[39] By 1030, Alpoim Calvão's task force had stood out of Conakry and made its turn north.

From the strictly military point of view, *Mar Verde* was a success. It was the first of its kind ever undertaken by Portugal, and it proved once again the capabilities and effectiveness of the sailor-*fuzileiro* team. They had stormed a bastion in a city relatively far from their base of operations and relied on surprise to achieve the success necessary for a safe withdrawal. It had been an ingenious plan that ably addressed the limited resources, the unique operational security requirements, and an incomplete intelligence picture.

Of the three primary military objectives, the recovery of the prisoners and the destruction of the fast patrol boats were successful. The MiGs were missed because of deficient intelligence. In this regard intelligence failures came from a poor national intelligence organization that lacked the capability to gather sufficiently detailed and current information on a target country. The movement of the MiGs and the political will of the opposition to Sékou Touré are the most obvious.

While Alpoim Calvão would describe later that "At nine in the morning I held the city in my hands," in fact with the military objectives secured for all practical purposes, he made the political decision to depart rather than further support the coup, something that he could have done.[40] The longer he stayed, the more irrefutable the evidence against Portugal would be, with the result of international condemnation and possibly isolation. This judgment was well founded.

Unfortunately, the autocratic Sékou Touré was unharmed and proceeded to interrogate the FNLG prisoners who had remained behind and surrendered. Some of them described the operation at length and identified its sponsors.[41]

Sékou Touré took this evidence to the UN Security Council and earned an automatic reproval of Portuguese actions. The *pro forma* mission of inquiry was dispatched to Conakry. Sékou Touré appealed both to the Soviet Union and the United States for military aid, playing the superpowers against each other. The United States had a growing commercial investment in the Guinean bauxite mines, and thus President Richard Nixon in a confidential letter to Sékou Touré deplored the incident. It remained confidential for a day. Great Britain joined the United States in confirming that any repetition of an operation similar to *Mar Verde* might seriously endanger Washington and London support for Lisbon in its African counterinsurgency. Both feared that such adventures would unsettle the equilibrium in East-West relations. Indeed, the Soviet Union viewed the incident as an excellent opportunity to increase its influence in West Africa and as a result established a naval and air presence in Conakry.

The naval presence became known as the "West African Patrol," and it made regular visits to the ports in the region and shadowed U.S. and NATO naval activity. Soviet Bear-D long-range reconnaissance aircraft were also deployed to Conakry to track U.S. naval transits to the Indian Ocean. In an attempt to gain favour with Sékou Touré and counter Soviet influence, Nixon authorized the token sum of $4.7 million as a contribution to the rebuilding of Conakry.[42] Not surprisingly, most of this gift found its way into the bank accounts of Sékou Touré and his henchmen.

These developments made Portugal a controversial member of NATO. Caetano confided that in the case of *Mar Verde* the Republic of Guinea had not represented a problem. The real difficulty came at the international level, and in going to Conakry, Lisbon had tended to forget the broader picture.[43] Spínola did not agree, and many years later he confirmed that in his opinion it was mostly overblown.[44] *Mar Verde* had in part distracted the Nixon and Kissinger effort at *détente* with the Soviet Union, and this disturbance was not welcomed. On the local military level, the Soviet Union and its surrogate Cuba began to provide increased support for the PAIGC. Sophisticated Soviet arms and Cuban instructors appeared in Conakry, and by 1973 the military struggle had increased in intensity.

New weapons were changing the military balance, and three Portuguese aircraft were downed with Soviet SA-7 *Grail* hand-held ground-to-air missiles in late March and early April 1973. *Mar Verde*, it seemed, had marked a deepening of the Portuguese military agony in Guinea.

Mar Verde, the bold, daring, and successful rescue of 26 prisoners of war and the destruction of PAIGC naval capability, thus became a catalyst for increased superpower friction. Unfortunately, the customary benefits of such a mission seemed to be largely lost in the negative diplomatic and geo-strategic fallout. Sékou Touré had rebuffed traditional efforts to negotiate the exchange of prisoners and thus left a rescue mission as the only viable alternative.

The operation was kept simple in its military objectives and hence its success in this field. Its political objectives, however, clouded the picture and allowed the simple tactical mission to be termed an "invasion" in international forums. The broader risk-reward relationship was not deeply explored at any level, although Alpoim Calvão was certainly sensitive to it. The fires of international condemnation were ably fanned by Sékou Touré. He no longer held any hostages, and Portugal had handed him the wherewithal to play the injured innocent and secure the protection of the Soviet Union against future aggression. The PAIGC now had an inviolate sanctuary and the military might and sophistication of the Soviet Union fully behind its cause. As we shall see, this could be a burden as well as a boon.

Following *Mar Verde,* there were a number of developments that made the strategic resolution of Guinea vital to the success of any Portuguese solution. First Spínola believed that Cabral was his own man and despite a Marxist structure and philosophy in the PAIGC, he wished to be free of Soviet influence in establishing a new regime in Guinea.[45] One route that held the answer to this desire was the offer of independence under some sort of Portuguese federation in which Guinea would be part of a Lusophone organization similar to the British Commonwealth of Nations. With this concept in mind, Spínola began a series of overtures to Cabral through Léopold Senghor, the president of Senegal, in an attempt to end the war honourably for Portugal and to obtain independence for Guinea in a prudent way.

From 1970 onward, Spínola's objective had been to drastically reduce the military capacity of the PAIGC, tilting the balance in Portuguese favour. As time passed, Spínola's plans proved successful in checking the progress of the PAIGC and in gaining its respect to such an extent that it began to make sense to open negotiations for some form of self-government with a Portuguese alignment. By 1972 conditions were ripe for negotiations, and at the end of April, Spínola had his initial conversations with a Senegalese minister to arrange a secret meeting with Senghor. This took place on 18 May at Cap Skiring in Senegal, and Senghor took the opportunity to express great sympathy for Portugal and praise its social programs in Guinea.[46] Spínola explained his concept of Guinean independence, and Senghor indicated that he thought Cabral would be receptive to the idea and that he would act as an intermediary. This prompted Spínola to suggest that Senghor meet with Caetano in Bissau or perhaps metropolitan Portugal.

Later on 26 May in Lisbon in a meeting with Silva Cunha, the Portuguese Foreign Minister, and Caetano, the proposal was rejected out of hand under the rationale that such a move could not be controlled and that it would have grave consequences for the other colonies. In Caetano's view, a military defeat was preferable. Spínola was shocked and aghast at such a warped position, and in his view a great opportunity was lost. This experience prompted him to write his book *País sem Rumo* (Country without Direction) in which he voices his frustrations.[47]

Contact with Cabral continued through his brother Luis Cabral until shortly before his assassination on 20 January 1973.[48] Alpoim Calvão and Spínola remain convinced that Sékou Touré had an active hand in fomenting much of the internal dissention in the PAIGC in order to weaken Cabral as a leader and a perceived competitor.[49] This activity led to Cabral's death and with it any hope of negotiating an honourable conclusion for Portugal and a prudent one for Guinea.

Operations continued throughout 1972 during the negotiations with one of the more prominent ones being Operation *Verga Latina* (Lateen Yard). It was conducted between July and December from Bolama in support of the population on the peninsula of the same name. The operation was designed to build confidence in the local population through a military presence and various civic action projects. It is difficult to gauge the success of the mission, as the PAIGC was able to lob mortar rounds into the naval encampment Tabanca Nova da Armada on an almost daily basis from varying and proximate positions.[50]

By 1972 with the exception of the more important urban centres, the entire country was threatened by insurgent action. Guinea was shaped geographically in such a way that no part of the country was more than 60 kilometres from a neighbouring country, a fact that made the entire territory a virtual frontier. From Senegal and Guinea, PAIGC insurgent units would enter the country, ambush and attack Portuguese forces, intimidate the population, and retire across the border to sanctuary. When Portuguese forces were not present in the rural areas, control passed into the hands of the PAIGC. The conflict seemed to have entered what might have been called an advanced phase of revolutionary war.

Indeed, after Caetano refused to authorize negotiations with Cabral, the campaign in Guinea entered a waiting period during which there seemed to be a general expectation that some event would end the conflict. Spínola had at this point gained enough credibility to bring Cabral to the negotiating table, a situation about as propitious as one could achieve in the besieged environment of Guinea. Any conflict resolution would now have to come from another direction, and the war laboured on until 24 April 1974, when middle-ranking Portuguese officers effected a coup and toppled the government in Lisbon.

Portugal ultimately granted Guinea its independence, and the PAIGC assumed control of the government in 1975. It promised amnesty to all Africans who had fought on the side of Portugal and invited them to stay as citizens of the new country. No fewer than 27,000 former Portuguese soldiers and natives of Guinea accepted the offer and remained.[51] The PAIGC leaders, however, had kept company far too long with Sékou Touré and had assumed his worst habits.

Almost immediately arrests of the former soldiers, sergeants, and officers of elite units began, and their fate was inevitably execution. When questioned about these deaths, the PAIGC leaders denied any knowledge. General Almeida Bruno, a member of the Portuguese delegation to transfer the government of Guinea to the PAIGC and a former commander of the Commando Battalion there, did not accept this denial, "But this is not what happened, and the PAIGC barbarically shot the majority of my African officers from the Commando Battalion."[52]

This assertion was only the beginning. Ultimately the newspaper *Nô Pintcha* published a partial list of names, and those who survived to escape estimate that at least a thousand faced firing squads, some at airfields, some at soccer fields, and many in front of the civilian population. Thus for those loyal and courageous soldiers who had participated in *Mar Verde, Nebulosa, Gata Brava*, and the other operations against the PAIGC, betrayal by their new government was a final and sad footnote.[53]

Select Bibliography

Abreu, Adelino Ribeiro de: *Lembranças de Moçambique quimarães*, Lisbon, 1996-97

Abreu, António Graca: *Diário da Guiné*, Lisbon, 2007

Abshire, David & Michael Samuels: *Portuguese Africa – A Handbook*: Pall Mall Press, London, 1969

Afonso, Aniceto & Gomes, Carlos de Matos (co-ord.): *Guerra colonial,* Lisbon, 1998(?)

Afonso, Aniceto & Gomes, Carlos de Matos (co-ord.): *Os Anos da guerra colonial*, Matosinhos, 2010

Antunes, António Lobo: *Os Cus de Judas*, Lisbon, 1986

Antunes, José Freire (ed): *A Guerra de África*, 1961-1974, 2 Vols, Lisbon 1995

Attwood, William: *The Reds and the Blacks*, Harper & Row, New York, 1967

Beckett, Ian & John Pimlott (eds.): *Armed Forces and Modern Counter Insurgency,* Croom Helm, London, 1985.

Bernardo, Manuel A: *Combater em Moçambique*, Lisbon, 2003

Brandão, José: *Cronologia da Guerra Colonial*, Lisbon, 2008

Burchett, Wilfred: *Southern Africa Stands Up*, Urzan Books, New York 1978

Cabrita, Felícia: *Massacres em África,* Lisbon, 2008

Caetano, Marcello: *Depoimento*, Distribuidora Record, Rio de Janeiro, 1974

The Cambridge History of Africa Volume 8 c.1940 – c.1995: Desmond J. Clark (ed.), J.D. Fage (ed.), Roland Anthony Oliver (ed.), Richard Gray (ed.), John Flint (ed.) and G.N Sanderson (ed.); Cambridge University Press 1986

Cann, John: *Counterinsurgency in Africa: The Portuguese Way of War 1961-1974,* Hailer Publishing, St Petersburg FL, 2005

Cann, John: *Brown Waters of Africa: Portuguese Riverine Warfare 1961-1974*, Hailer Publishing, St Petersburg FL, 2007

Cann, John P: *Counterinsurgency in Africa: The Portuguese Way of War (1961-1974),* Helion, Solihull, 2012

Cann, John: *Brown Waters of Africa: Portuguese Riverine Warfare 1961-1974*, Helion, Solihull, 2013

Silva Cardoso, António: *Angola: Anatomia de uma Tragédia*, Lisbon, Oficina de Livro, 2000

Carvalho, Nogueira e: *Era Tempo de Morrer em África*, Lisbon, 2004

Castilho, Rui de: *O capitão do fim,* Lisbon, 2002

Chilcote, Ronald: *Portuguese Africa*, Prentice-Hall, New Jersey, 1967

Chiwale, Samuel: *Cruzei-me com a História,* Lisbon, 2008

Cobanco, Jorge: *Onze Meses de Guerra em Angola,* s.l. 1970

Coelho, João Paulo Borges: *O início da luta armada em Tete,* Maputo, 1989

Coelho, João Paulo Borges: *African Troops in the Portuguese Colonial Army, 1961-1974: Angola, Guinea-Bissau and Mozambique;* Eduardo Mondlane University, Maputo.

Coelho, Joaquim: *O Despertar dos Combatentes,* Lisbon, 2005

Cornwall, Barbara; *The Bush Rebels*, Andre Deutsch, London 1973

Cunha, J. da Luz , et al, *África, a Vitória Traída*: Intervenção, Lisbon, 1977 [Background by pre-coup commanders in Angola, Mozambique and Portuguese Guinea]

Davidson, Basil: *The Liberation of Guiné*: Penguin African Library, Harmondsworth, 1969

Davidson, Basil: *In the Eye of the Storm*: Longmans, London, 1972

Dos Santos, Marcelino: *Moçambique: Frelimo*, LSM, Canada 1973

Duffy, James: *Portuguese Africa*, Harvard University Press, Cambridge MA, 1959

Ellert, Henrik, *The Rhodesian Front War*, Gweru, Zimbabwe, 1993

Estado-Maior do Exército. *Resenha Histórico-Militar das Campanhas de África, Vols. I–VI* [Historical Military Report of the African Campaigns, Vol. I–VI], Lisbon: Estado-Maior do Exército, 1989-2006

Felgas, Hélio: *Guerra em Angola*, Edição do Autor, Lisbon, 1968

Ferraz, Carlos Vale: *Nó ceg,* Amadore, 1983

Fraga, Luís Alves de: *A Força aérea na Guerra em África,* Lisbon, 2004

Garcia, Francisco Proença: *Análise global de uma Guerra,* Lisbon, 2003

Garcia, João Nogueira: *Quitexe-61,* Vila Nova do Ceira, 2003

George, Edward: *The Cuban Intervention in Angola, 1965-1991*, Routledge, London, 2005

Gibson, Richard: *African Liberation Movements,* Oxford University Press, London, 1972

Gleijeses, Piero: *Conflicting Missions: Havana, Washington, and Africa, 1959-1976*, University of North Carolina Press, Chapel Hill NC, 2002

Matos Gomes, Carlos de: *Moçambique 1970, Operação Nó Górdio.* [Mozambique 1970, Operation Gordian Knot], Lisbon, Prefácio, 2002

Gouveia, Daniel Alves: *Arcanjos e Bons Demónios*, Lisbon, 1996

Greene, T.N. Colonel: *The Guerrilla and How to Fight Him, Selections from the Marine Corps Gazette*; Praeger, New York, 1967

Grundy, Kenneth: *Guerrilla Struggle in Africa,* Grossman Publishers, New York, 1971

Guerra, João Paulo: *Memória das Guerras Coloniais*, Porto, 1994

Guerra, João Paulo: *Descolonização Portuguesa*, Lisbon, 1996

Henricksen, Thomas: *Revolution and Counterrevolution,* Praeger, Westport CT 1983

Jorge, Paulo: *MPLA – Angola*, LSM, Canada

Lortie, Michelyne & Martin, Diane & Paquette, Claude: *Tout près de l'oubli,* Chesterville, Quebec, 2006

MacQueen, Norrie: *The Decolonisation of Portuguese Africa*, Longman, London, 1997

Maier, Francis X: *A Luta Continua – Revolution and Terror in Mozambique,* The American African Affairs Association, Washington DC, 1973

Marcum, John A: *The Angolan Revolution Volume I: Anatomy of an Explosion (1950-1962)* and *Volume II: Exile Politics and Guerrilla Warfare (1962-1975),* MIT Press, Cambridge MA, 1969 and 1978

Marinho, António Luís: *Operacão Mar Verde*, Lisbon, 2005

Martins, Manuel Alfredo de Morais: *Angola*, Lisbon, 2008

Mateus, Dalila Cabrita: *A Luta pela Independência*, Mem Martins, 1999

Mateus, Dalila Cabrita: *A PIDE/DGS na Guerra Colonial,* Lisbon, 2004

Mateus, Dalila Cabrita: *Memórias do Colonialismo e da Guerra*, Lisbon, 2006

Mesquita, José Alberto: *O inferno verde de Moçambique;* Lisbon 2004

Minter, William: *Portuguese Africa and the West*, Penguin, Harmondsworth, 1972

Minter, William: (ed.): *Operation Timber: Pages from the Savimbi Dossier*; African World
    Press Inc., Trenton NJ, 1988

Mondlane, Eduardo: *The Struggle for Mozambique*, Penguin Books, Harmondsworth, 1969

Morris, Michael: *Armed Conflict in Southern Africa*, Citadel Press, Cape Town, 1974

Nguyen van Tien: *Notre Stratégie de la Guérilla,* Partisans, Paris, 1968

Nogueira, Inácio: *Cavaleiros do Maiombe*, Coimbra, 2004

Nunes, António Pires: *Angola 1966-74*, Lisbon, 2002

Nunes, António Pires: *Angola. 1961*, Lisbon, 2005

Paige, Jeffery M: *Agrarian Revolution*, Free Press, New York, 1978

Pacavira, Manuel Pedro: *O 4 de Fevereiro pelos Próprios*, Leiria, 2003

Pepetela: *Mayombe,* Lisbon,1982

Pimenta, Fernando Tavares: *Angola no Percurso de Um Nacionalista*, Porto, 2006

Porch, Douglas: *The Portuguese Armed Forces and the Revolution*; Croom Helm, London and
    Hoover Institution Press, Stanford CA, 1977

Paret, Peter, and John W. Shy: *Guerrillas in the 1960s*, Praeger, New York, 1962

Portuguese Ministry of Foreign Affairs; *Portuguese Africa – An Introduction*, Lisbon, 1973

Pélissier, René : *Les Guerres Grises: Resistance et Revoltes en Angola (1845-1941),* Editions
    Pélissier, Orgeval, 1977.

Pélissier, René : *La Colonie du Minotaure, Nationalismes et révoltes en Angola (1926-1961),*
    Editions Pélissier, Orgeval, 1978

Pélissier, René: *Angola – Guinées – Mozambique – Sahara – Timor, etc. Une bibliographic
    internationale critique (1990-2005),* Editions Pélissier, Orgeval, 1979

Pélissier, René: *Du Sahara à Timor, 700 livres analysés*, Editions Pélissier, Orgeval, 1979

Pélissier, René: *Explorar: Voyages en Angola et autres lieux incertains*, Editions Pélissier, France
    1979

Pélissier, René: *Le Naufrage des Caravelles. Études sur la fin de l'empire portugais (1961-1975),*
    Editions Pélissier, Orgeval, 1979

Pélissier, René: *Africana. Bibliographies sur l'Afrique luso-hisanophone (1800-1980)*, Editions
    Pélissier, Orgeval, 1981

Pélissier, René: *Naissance du Mozambique: Résistance et Révoltes Anticoloniales (1854–1918),*
    Editions Pélissier, Orgeval, 1984.

Pélissier, René: *Naissance de la Guiné, Portugais et Africains en Sénégambie (1841–1936),*
    Editions Pélissier, Orgeval, 1989.

Policarpo, Fernando: *Guerra de África. Guiné 1963-1974*, Matosinhos, 2006

Ribeiro, Jorge: *Marcas da guerra*, Porto, 1999

Reid-Daly, Colonel Ronald Francis: *Staying Alive: A Southern African Survival Handbook*,

Ashanti Publishing, Rivonia, 1990

Rocha, Nuno: *Guerra em Moçambique*, Lisbon, 1969

Shay, Reg and Chris Vermaak: *The Silent War*, Citadel Press, Salisbury, Rhodesia, 1971

Simões, Martinho: *Nas Três Frentes durante Três Meses*, Lisbon, 1966

Sitte, Fritz: *Flammenherd Angola*, Kremayr & Scheriau, Vienna, 1972

Spínola, General António de: *Portugal and the Future,* Lisbon, 1973

Steward Lloyd-Jones and Antonio Costa Pinto: The Last Empire: Thirty Years of Portuguese Decolonization, Intellect Books, Bristol/Portland, 2003

Stockwell, John: *In Search of Enemies: A CIA Story,* W.W. Norton, New York, 1984

Sykes, John: *Portugal and Africa,* Hutchinson, London, 1971

Taber, Robert: *War of the Flea*, Paladin, London, 1970

Teixeira, Bernardo: *The Fabric of Terror,* Devin Adair, Old Greenwich, USA, 1965

Thompson, Sir Robert: *Defeating Communist Insurgency*, Chatto & Windus,London, 1966

Trinquier, Roger: *Modern Warfare – a French View of Counterinsurgency,* Praeger, New York, 1962

Van der Waals, Brigadier-General Willem: *Portugal's War in Angola 1961-1974*, Ashanti Publishing, 1993/Protea Books, Pretoria, 2011

Vaz, Camilo Rebocho*: Norte de Angola 1961*, Coimbra, 1993

Venter, Al J: *The Terror Fighters*, Purnell, Cape Town, 1969

Venter, Al J: *Portugal's War in Guiné-Bissau*, Munger Africana Library, California Institute of Technology, Pasadena, 1973. Also published under the title *Portugal's Guerrilla War*, John Malherbe, Cape Town, 1973

Venter, Al J: *Africa at War,* Devin-Adair, Old Greenwich, 1974. Also published as *War in Africa* by Human and Rousseau in Cape Town

Venter, Al J: *The Zambezi Salient*, Timmins, Cape Town, 1974

Venter, Al J: *Challenge: South Africa in the African Revolutionary Context,* (ed.), Ashanti Publishing, 1988

Venter, Al J: *The Chopper Boys: Helicopter Warfare in Africa:* Stackpole Books, Mechanicsburg PA/Greenhill Books, London, 1993: New edition forthcoming from Helion and Company, Solihull 2015

Venter Al J: *War Stories by Al Venter and Friends*, Protea Books, 2011

Venter Al J: *Biafra – A Tribal Conflict in Nigeria That Left a Million Dead*, Helion, 2015

Venter, Al J: *African Stories by Al Venter and Friends*, Protea Books, 2013

Verdasca, José: *Memórias de um capitão*, Lisbon, 2004

Wheeler, Douglas L and René Pélissier: *Angola*, Pall Mall Press, London, 1971. An updated and much-enlarged edition has been translated and published by Edições Tinta-da-China, Lisbon, under the title *História de Angola*

Notes

Prologue

1   Minter, William (ed.), *Operation Timber: Pages from the Savimbi Dossier*, African World Press Inc., Trenton, New Jersey, 1988, p.2.

2   Van der Waals, Brigadier-General Willem S. (Kaas), *Portugal's War in Angola 1961-1974*, Protea Books, Pretoria, 2011.

3   Porch, Douglas, *The Portuguese Armed Forces and the Revolution*, Croom Helm, London, 1977.

4   Desmond Clark, J., J.D. Fage, Roland Oliver, Richard Gray, John Flint and G.N Sanderson (eds.), *The Cambridge History of Africa Volume 8 c.1940 – c.1995*, Cambridge University Press, Cambridge, 1986.

5   Cann, John P., *Counterinsurgency in Africa: The Portuguese Way of War 1961-1974*, Hailer Publishing, St Petersburg FL, 2005.

6   Several factors motivated the early navigators to explore beyond Europe's real or imagined frontiers. The first was the knowledge that somewhere beyond the horizon – towards the East especially - there were other great civilizations and cultures that were not only immensely enticing, but were prosperous, outward looking and had an awful lot to offer. Make contact and there are fortunes to be made, was the dictum. It was these early voyages of discovery that ultimately caused Lisbon to establish a series of 'replenishing posts' along the African coastline that became the basis of Portugal's colonial empire. Thus came into being countries that we recognise today as Angola, Mozambique and Guiné-Bissau.

7   Stiff, Peter, *Silent War: SA Recce Operations 1986-1994*, Galago Books, Alberton, 1994.

8   *Introduction to Staying Alive: A Southern African Survival Handbook*, by Ron Reid-Daly, Ashanti Publishing, Rivonia, 1990.

9   Personal communications with Captain John Cann US Navy (Rtd), March 2013.

Chapter 3

1   Venter, Al J., *The Terror Fighters*, Purnell, Cape Town, 1969.

2   Venter, Al J., *Portugal's War in Guiné-Bissau*, Munger Africana Library, California Institute of Technology, Pasadena, 1973. Also published under the titled Portugal's Guerrilla War by Malherbe, Cape Town, 1973.

Chapter 5

1   Even when aircraft and helicopters were acquired, usually from the French, there were enough radical movements back in the Metropolis to ensure that some of it was never deployed to Africa. A dozen Aerospatiale troop-carrying Puma helicopters – the same machines used by South Africa in its Border Wars - were sabotaged near Lisbon shortly before they were due to be shipped to Angola and Portuguese Guinea in the later stages of the war.

2   Chapman, F. Spencer, *The Jungle is Neutral: A Soldier's Two-Year Escape from the Japanese Army*, The Lyons Press, 2003.

Chapter 6

1   The mercenary-led war against Savimbi's rebel forces – involving Executive Outcomes - is dealt with in some detail in the author's *War Dog: Fighting Other People's Wars*, Casemate Publishers, Philadelphia, 2007, Chapters 15 to 18, pp.340-444.

2   During the final phase of the Portuguese Army's withdrawal from Angola, the author travelled from Luanda to Nova Lisboa (since renamed Huambo) to join Daniel Chipenda's Chipa Esquadrao as a mercenary, largely in order to get the story he was after (see photo). The relationship did not last long. South African Army units had meantime invaded northwards from South West Africa (Namibia today) and had made inroads almost as far north as Luanda. Obviously, his presence as a South African journalist impeded progress since the entire operation was supposed to be covert.

3   Marcum, John A., *The Angolan Revolution, Volume II: Exile Politics and Guerrilla Warfare (1962-1976)*, MIT Press, Cambridge MA, 1978.

Chapter 7

1   Military jargon for Situation Reports.

2   Several hundred RPG-7s were used, almost like artillery barrages to bring the US Army Black Hawks down in the Mogadishu contact that crippled two helicopters and eventually left 18 American servicemen dead.

3   African beer made from fermented maize or sorghum, to which anything can be added to make it potent, including drain cleaner.

Chapter 9

1   *In the Eye of the Storm*: Longmans, London, 1972 and before that The Liberation of Guiné, Penguin African Library, 1969, both by Basil Davidson.

Chapter 11

1   Clark, Desmond J., Roland Anthony Oliver, J. D. Fage, A. D. Roberts (eds.), *The Cambridge History of Africa*, Cambridge University Press, Cambridge, 1986.

2   *Umkhonto We Sizwe* (Spear of the Nation) was founded partly in response to the Sharpeville Massacre of March 1960. Its leader, Nelson Mandela, was arrested shortly after its manifesto was published and sentenced to life in prison. He was released in 1990, with the end of apartheid.

3   Cann, John P., *Counterinsurgency in Africa: The Portuguese Way of War 1961-1974*, Hailer Publishing, St Petersburg FL, 2005.

4   Israel, like Egypt, still receives a bountiful $2 billion a year from the United States, originally agreed under the Camp David Accords, the framework for peace in the Middle East negotiated in 1978.

5   Van der Waals, W.S (Kaas), *Portugal's War in Angola 1961-1974*, Protea Books, Pretoria, 2011.

Chapter 12

1   Porch, Douglas, *The Portuguese Armed Forces and the Revolution*; Croom Helm, London, 1973.

2   Venter, Al J., *Report on Portugal's War in Guiné-Bissau*, Munger Africana Library, California Institute of Technology, Pasadena. Also published in South Africa under the title *Portugal's Guerrilla War*, Malherbe,

Cape Town, both in 1973.

Chapter 13

1 Cann, Captain John, US Navy (Rtd).
2 Venter, Al J., *Portugal's Guerrilla War: The Campaign for Africa,* Malherbe, Cape Town, 1973 and later published as a monograph by the Munger Africana Library, California Institute of Technology, Pasadena.
3 Cann, Captain John, US Navy (Rtd).
4 Castanheira, José Pedro, "Memórias da Guerra e da Paz: Spínola" [Memories of War and Peace: Spínola], *Expresso Revista* (30 April 1994), p.26.

Chapter 14

1 Guilherme Almor de Alpoim Calvão, correspondence with J.P. Cann, 9 May 2005, Cascais.
2 Afonso, Aniceto and Carlos de Matos Gomes, *Guerra Colonial* [Colonial War] (Lisbon: Notícias, 2000), p.79.
3 Carvalheira, José Alberto Lopes, "Acção da Marinha em Águas Interiores (Guiné)," 7 Telo, p.585.
4 Ibid.
5 Ibid., 6.
6 Afonso and Matos Gomes, p.81.
7 João Bernardo "Nino" Vieira, correspondence with Rui Demba Djassi and Domingos Ramos, 3 March 1964, undisclosed PAIGC base in southern Guiné, typewritten transcript furnished by Guilherme Almor de Alpoim Calvão in correspondence with the author, 9 May 2005, Cascais.
8 Afonso and Matos Gomes, p.81.
9 Ibid., p.80.
10 Guilherme Almor de Alpoim Calvão, correspondence with the author, 22 June 2005, Cascais.
11 Guilherme Almor de Alpoim Calvão, correspondence with the author, 9 May 2005, Cascais.
12 Afonso and Matos Gomes, p.81.
13 The *tache d'huile* technique was perfected by Louis-Hubert Lyautey during his Moroccan campaigns of the early Twentieth Century in which he progressively reoccupied hostile territory by offering Arab tribes French protection and access to commerce and social help. His expansion on a broad social-military front with the notion of building an Arab nation succeeded where his predecessors had relied on subjugation by the military column.
14 Indeed, an FAP Neptune landed at the remote N'Riquinha airstrip in south-eastern Angola while this author was briefly embedded at the base, then under the command of Captain (later Major) Vitor Alves, who was to become a prominent player in the army putsch of April 1974.

Chapter 16

1 Ration Pack.

Chapter 19

1 Venter, Al J., *Portugal's War in Guiné-Bissau,* Munger Africana Library, California Institute of Technology, Pasadena, 1973.

Chapter 20

1 Air Combat Information Group (ACIG): Guiné (Portuguese Guinea) by Tom Cooper and Pedro Alvin, November 13, 2003.

2 COIN: The Portuguese in Africa 1959-75, Robert Craig Johnson, worldatwar/chandelle/v3/ v3n2portcoin.html.

3 Venter, Al J: *The Chopper Boys*, Stackpole Books (US), Greenhill Books (UK) and Southern Publishing (South Africa) 1993

Chapter 22

1 Though Stockwell only arrived in the Congo after the Portuguese wars had ended, his outspoken observations do provide a significant insight into the machinations that went on during that period: a fascinating read in all departments. Stockwell was extremely critical of what the CIA was trying to achieve in Africa: he finally left the agency in disgust and went on to become one of its most outspoken critics.

2 Venter, Al J., *War Stories by Al J. Venter and Friends* (Protea Books, Pretoria, 2011) and The Chopper Boys, Stackpole Books, US and Greenhill Books, London, to be reissued as a new edition by Helion and Company in the UK in 2014.

3 *Quimbo* or *Kimbo* – An African village in south-east Angola.

Chapter 23

1 Cann, John P., *Counterinsurgency in Africa: The Portuguese Way of War 1961-1974*, Hailer Publishing, St Petersburg FL, 2005.

2 For insurance purposes, essentially, the conflict in Malaya, though it lasted years, was never declared to be a full-blown war. It remained an 'emergency' throughout.

3 John P. Cann, Ibid.

4 Beckett, Ian and Pimlott, John (eds.), *Armed Forces and Modern Counter Insurgency*, Croom Helm, London, 1985.

5 Porch, Douglas, *The Portuguese Armed Forces and the Revolution*, Croom Helm, London, 1977.

Chapter 24

1 Personal interview with Lt Colonel Ron Reid-Dale, founder –commander of the Selous Scouts at his False Bay, Cape home in 2004.

Chapter 25

1 Greene, T.N., *The Guerrilla and How to Fight Him: Selections from the Marine Corps Gazette*, Praeger, New York, 1967.

2 Cann, John P., *Counterinsurgency in Africa: The Portuguese Way of War 1961-1974*, Hailer Publishing, St Petersburg FL, 2005

3 Venter, Al J., *Portugal's Guerrilla War: The Campaign for Africa*, Cape Town, 1974, also published by the Munger Africana Library, Pasadena, California as Report on Portugal's War in Guiné-Bissau: California Institute of Technology.

Appendix A

1 Paper presented at the Portuguese/African Encounters: An Interdisciplinary Congress, Brown University, Providence MA, April 2002. An earlier version that focused on the Mozambican case was presented at the Second Congress of African Studies in the Iberian World, held in Madrid, Spain, in September 1999 and published as *João Paulo Borges Coelho, "Tropas negras na Guerra colonial: O caso de Moçambique,'* in José Ramón Trujillo, ed., *Africa hacia el siglo XXI* (Madrid: Sial Ediciones, Colección Casa de África 12, 2001). Permission to use this material in this volume granted personally to Al J. Venter during his visit to Maputo in March 2012.

2 *Revista Militar* 41 (7) (15 April 1989).

3 Cann, John P., *Contra-insurreição em África, 1961-1974. O modo português de fazer a guerra.* Estoril: Edições Atena, Portugal 1998.

4 See David Martelo, *Pessoal e orçamentos. Esforço de guerra,* in Afonso and Gomes, *Guerra colonial,* pp.519-20.

5 According to Ferraz de Freitas, *Conquista da adesão das populações* (Lourenço Marques: SCCIM, 1965), p.6, ordering is based exclusively on physical power and provokes the repulsion of culturally different populations, and for this reason its efficiency tends to decrease in proportion to the decline of the physical power of the one who exerts it. On the contrary, commanding requires knowledge and ability to handle the 'social forces,' is based on participation, and promotes adhesion of the commanded. As to *accionamento,* it was defined as 'the set of moves one needs to take to make sure that the population works with us and becomes prejudiced towards the propaganda of the enemy (...). [Through *accionamento*] we attract the populations into our orbit, integrate them in our environment, in our culture, in our civilisation and nationality (...). This would be one of our purposes. The other is to make them work actively with us in detecting and combating subversion (...)' (GDT/*Serviços Distritais de Administração Civil, 1966:45, Arquivo Histórico de Moçambique, Secção Especial,* nº 237). For the psycho-social work with local communities in central Mozambique, namely in organising popular operations conducted by traditional authorities to detect guerrilla movements, see João Paulo Borges Coelho, "A 'Primeira Frente' de Tete e o Malawi", *Arquivo* (15) (1994) 72.

6 João Paulo Borges Coelho, 'Protected Villages and Communal Villages in the Mozambican Province of Tete (1968-1982): A History of State Resettlement Policies, Development and War' (PhD.Dissertation: Department of Social and Economic Studies, University of Bradford, 1993), p.165 and *passim.*

7 Venter, Al J., *War Stories by Al J. Venter and Friends,* Protea Books, Pretoria, 2011, Chapter 10: Ron Reid-Daly: 'A Tribute to the Man and his Scouts', pp.178-206.

Appendix C

1 António Lobato, *Liberdade ou Evasão* [Freedom or Evasion] (Amadora: Erasmos Editora, 1996), 172.

2 Ibid., 172–177.

3 Alpoim Calvão, 57.

4 Ibid., 57–58.

5 LFG *Sagitário* (P 1131) was one of the final two vessels of the *Argos* class launches and was completed in September 1965 at the Arsenal do Alfeite, Lisbon. The other was LFG *Centauro* (P 1130).

6 Alpoim Calvão, 58.

7   Ibid.

8   Ibid., 59.

9   José Freire Antunes, *A Guerra de África 1961–1974* [The African War 1961–1974] (Lisbon: Temas e Debates, 1996), 513.

10   Alpoim Calvão, 59.

11   Ibid.

12   Abou Camará, an ex-PAIGC sailor, was enlisted in the *fuzileiros* as part of the Portuguese policy of rehabilitating former insurgents. He was later assigned to DFE 21, a *Destacamento de Fuzileiros Especiais Africanos* (Detachment of African Special *Fuzileiros*), which was established in February 1970. He was to participate in *Mar Verde* and be awarded the Cruz de Guerra for his heroism.

13   Alpoim Calvão, 60.

14   The M20 *Bazooka* is a World War II-vintage 88.9mm rocket-propelled grenade launcher with a maximum range of 800 meters and a recommended moving target acquisition range of 185 meters.

15   Alpoim Calvão, 62.

16   The PPSh-41 (*Pistolet-Pulemet Shpagina*, from the Russian, and *41* from the 1941 date of manufacture) was the result of two national catastrophes for the Soviet Union. The first was the Winter War with Finland in 1939–1940 when the Finns used submachine guns with devastating effect during close combat in the forests, and the second was the German invasion of 1941 when the Soviets lost in the retreats both huge quantities of small arms and much of their engineering capability. There then arose an urgent demand for a light and simple weapon capable of a high volume of fire, and the answer to this was the PPSh-41, designed by Georgii Shpagin. It was much cheaper and quicker to make than the preceding models and was finished roughly. The barrel was still chromed, however, and there was never any doubt about its effectiveness. About five million PPSh guns had been made by 1945, and the Soviets adapted their infantry tactics to take full advantage of such huge numbers. In the Soviet Union, the PPSh went out of service in the late 1950s, but it has been supplied in enormous quantities to the satellite and pro-communist countries, so that it will be seen for many years.

17   Alpoim Calvão, 63.

18   Ibid., 64.

19   Ibid., 64–65.

20   José Manuel Saraiva, "Asslto a Conakry" [Assault on Conakry], *Revista do Expresso* (23 November 1996): 97–98.

21   Jean-Paul Alata, *Prison D'Afrique* (Paris: Éditions du Seuil, 1976); Lobato, 97.

22   Saraiva, 96.

23   Saturnino Monteiro, 198.

24   Alpoim Calvão, 65.

25   Ibid., 71.

26   António Luís Marinho, *Operação Mar Verde* [Operation Green Sea] (Lisbon: Temas e Debates, 2006), 108.

27   Alpoim Calvão, 72

28   Guilherme Almor de Alpoim Calvão, interview by the author, 14 March 1997, Lisbon.

29   Alpoim Calvão, 76.

30   Raúl Eugénio Dias da Cunha e Silva, "21st Detachment of Special Marines, Operation 'Green Sea,' Relating to the Period from 170300 to 252000 November 1970," after action report written at the headquarters of DFE 21, Buba, Guiné, 30 November 1970, TMs [photocopy], 2.

31   Alpoim Calvão, 76–77.

32   Aniceto Afonso and Carlos de Matos Gomes, *Guerra Colonial* [Colonial War] (Lisbon: Notícias, 1998), 503. Januário Lopes and his men were ordered shot by Sékou Touré shortly after the UN investigative team had interviewed them.

33   Alpoim Calvão, 81.

34   Lobato, 175.

35   Guilherme Almor de Alpoim Calvão, interview and correspondence with the author, 3 February 1998, Lisbon. The force destroyed quite a number of military vehicles and damaged some official buildings and civil infrastructure. As the force carried only small demolition charges and not the explosives needed for heavy blasting, the damage was initially light. The PAIGC buildings were very insubstantial structures, and five of them were severely damaged during the exchange of fire when looking for Amílcar Cabral. The fighting, however, continued for three or four days after the Portuguese force departed, and further damage occurred during that period.

36   Alata, 51.

37   Ibid., 89.

38   Guilherme Almor de Alpoim Calvão, correspondence with the author, 29 January 1998, Lisbon. Alpoim Calvão in his correspondence describes the adventure of one of his men, Francisco Nhanque, who arrived late at the departure rendezvous in Conakry because he had been celebrating Sékou Touré's impending fall with some bystanders. On seeing that the force had departed, he did not hesitate to leap into the sea and begin to swim westwards after the distant ships. Eventually, as he progressed about three miles out to sea, he was rescued by a passing Dutch freighter bound for Monrovia, Liberia. On arrival there, he requested and received political asylum. He located a job at a bar owned by a Brazilian, with whom he had established a rapport as a fellow Portuguese speaker. There was no Portuguese embassy or consulate in Liberia at the time. After several years, he had saved enough money to purchase an airline ticket, and he flew to the Canary Islands. He worked a further year to save for the fare to Lisbon, and when he arrived there, the airport authorities, on hearing his story, telephoned Alpoim Calvão for confirmation. Alpoim Calvão rushed to the airport to greet this fine soldier who had been reported missing in action in a war long since concluded.

39   Saraiva, 104.

40   José Freire Antunes, "Calvão evoca Conakry: «Às 9 da manhã eu tinha a cidade nas mãos»⊠ [Calvão remembers Conakry: "At 9 in the morning I held the city in my hands."], *Semanário* (10 December 1988): 16.

41   Ahmed Sékou Touré, *L'Agression Portugaise contra la Republic de Guiné* (Conakry: Livre Blanc, 1970).

42   José Freire Antunes, "Invasão de Conakry, Novembro de 1970: A 'Baía dos Porcos' do General Spínola" [Invasion of Conakry, November of 1970: The "Bay of Pigs" of General Spínola], *Semanário* (29 October 1988): 21.

43   Ibid.

44   Castanheira, 28–30.

45   Castanheira, 28.

46   There are many reports of Senegalese crossing the border into Guiné to take advantage of the medical care administered to the local population there. Senghor undoubtedly knew of this generosity.

47   Castanheira, 30–31; António de Spínola, *País sem Rumo* [Country without Direction] (Lisbon: Editorial SCIRE, 1978), 25–28.

48   Alpoim Calvão, 88–96.

49   Castanheira, 31; Alpoim Calvão, 89.

50   J.C. Moura da Fonseca, *Viagens e Históras da Marinha* [Voyages and Stories of the Navy] (Lisbon: Edições Culturais da Marinha, 1995), 120–121.

51   Eduardo Dâmaso and Adelino Gomes, "Falecidos por Fuzilamento" [Death by Shooting], *Pública* (30 June 1996): 48.

52   Ibid.

53   Ibid., 47.

Index

Related titles published by Helion & Company

*Counterinsurgency in Africa. The Portuguese
Way of War 1961-74*
John P. Cann
216pp Paperback ISBN 978-1-907677-73-1

*Brown Waters of Africa. Portuguese Riverine
Warfare 1961-1974*
John P. Cann
280pp Paperback ISBN 978-1-908916-56-3

Africa@War series, all 72pp Paperback

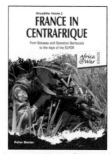

1: *Operation Dingo. Rhodesian
Raid on Chimoio and Tembué 1977*
(Dr J.R.T. Wood)
ISBN 978-1-907677-36-6

2: *France in Centrafrique – from
Bokassa and Operation Barracude
to the days of EUFOR* (Peter
Baxter) ISBN 978-1-907677-37-3

3: *Battle for Cassinga – South Africa's
controversial cross-border raid,
Angola 1978* (Mike McWilliams)
ISBN 978-1-907677-39-7

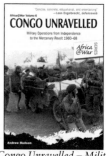

4: Selous Scouts – Rhodesian
Counter-Insurgency Specialists
(Peter Baxter)
ISBN 978-1-907677-38-0

5: *Zambezi Valley Insurgency
– Early Rhodesian War Bush
Operations* (Dr J.R.T. Wood)
ISBN 978-1-907677-62-5

6: *Congo Unravelled – Military
operations from independence
to the Mercenary Revolt 1960-68*
(Andrew Hudson)
ISBN 978-1-907677-63-2

7: *Mau Mau – The Kenyan
Emergency 1952-60* (Peter Baxter)
ISBN 978-1-908916-22-8

8: *SAAF's Border War. The South
African Air Force in Combat
1966-89* (Peter Baxter) ISBN 978-1-
908916-23-5

11. *The Flechas. Insurgent Hunting
in Eastern Angola, 1965-174*
(John P Cann)
ISBN 978-1-909384-63-7